Rethinking Social Movements

People, Passions, and Power
Social Movements, Interest Organizations, and the Political Process
John C. Green, Series Editor

After the Boom: The Politics of Generation X edited by Stephen C. Craig and Stephen Earl Bennett

American Labor Unions in the Electoral Arena by Herbert B. Asher, Eric S. Heberlig, Randall B. Ripley, and Karen Snyder

Citizen Democracy: Political Activists in a Cynical Age by Stephen E. Frantzich

Cyberpolitics: Citizen Activism in the Age of the Internet by Kevin A. Hill and John E. Hughes

Democracy's Moment: Reforming the American Political System for the 21st Century edited by Ron Hayduk and Kevin Mattson

Gaia's Wager: Environmental Movements and the Challenge of Sustainability by Gary C. Bryner

Multiparty Politics in America edited by Paul S. Herrnson and John C. Green

Multiparty Politics in America, 2nd ed., edited by Paul S. Herrnson and John C. Green

Rage on the Right: The American Militia Movement from Ruby Ridge to Homeland Security by Lane Crothers

Rethinking Social Movements: Structure, Meaning, and Emotion edited by Jeff Goodwin and James M. Jasper

Social Movements and American Political Institutions edited by Anne N. Costain and Andrew S. McFarland

Teamsters and Turtles? U.S. Progressive Political Movements in the 21st Century edited by John C. Berg

The Social Movement Society: Contentions Politics for a New Century edited by David S. Meyer and Sidney Tarrow

The State of the Parties: The Changing Role of Contemporary American Parties, 3rd ed., edited by John C. Green and Daniel M. Shea

The State of the Parties, 4th ed., edited by John C. Green and Rick D. Farmer

Waves of Protest: Social Movements since the Sixties edited by Jo Freeman and Victoria Johnson

Forthcoming

Chimes of Freedom: Student Protest and the American University by Christine Kelly

Citizen Democracy: Political Activists in a Cynical Age, 2nd ed., by Stephen E. Frantzich

Coalitions Across Borders: Transnational Protest and the Neo-Liberal Order edited by Joe Bandy and Jackie Smith

Ralph Nader, the Greens, and the Crisis of American Politics by John C. Berg

The Art and Craft of Lobbying: Political Engagement in American Politics by Ronald G. Shaiko

The Gay and Lesbian Rights Movement: Changing Policies! Changing Minds? by Steven H. Haeberle

The U.S. Women's Movement in Global Perspective edited by Lee Ann Banaszak

Rethinking Social Movements

Structure, Meaning, and Emotion

Edited by
Jeff Goodwin and James M. Jasper

ROWMAN & LITTLEFIELD PUBLISHERS, INC.
Lanham • Boulder • New York • Toronto • Oxford

ROWMAN & LITTLEFIELD PUBLISHERS, INC.

Published in the United States of America
by Rowman & Littlefield Publishers, Inc.
A wholly owned subsidiary of The Rowman & Littlefield Publishing Group, Inc.
4501 Forbes Boulevard, Suite 200, Lanham, Maryland 20706
www.rowmanlittlefield.com

P.O. Box 317, Oxford OX2 9RU, United Kingdom

British Library Cataloguing in Publication Information Available

Library of Congress Cataloging-in-Publication Data
Rethinking social movements : structure, meaning, and emotion / edited
by Jeff Goodwin & James M. Jasper.
    p.   cm. - (People, passions, and power)
    Includes bibliographical references and index.
    ISBN 0-7425-2595-3 (Cloth : alk. paper) — ISBN 0-7425-2596-1 (Paper :
alk. paper)
    1. Social movements.   2. Social structure.   3. Emotions.   4. Political
science.   I. Goodwin, Jeff.   II. Jasper, James M., 1957–   III. Series.
HM881.R48   2003
303.48′4-dc21   2003008629

Printed in the United States of America

Contents

Introduction

JEFF GOODWIN AND JAMES M. JASPER

The circumstances create the need, and the need, when it is great
enough, creates the circumstances.

—José Saramago

There is currently a good deal of theoretical turmoil among analysts of
social movements. For some time the field has been roughly divided
between a dominant, structural approach that emphasizes economic
resources, political structures, formal organizations, and social networks
and a cultural or constructionist tradition, drawn partly from symbolic
interactionism, which focuses on frames, identities, meanings, and emotions. The gaps and misunderstandings between the two sides—as well
as the efforts to bridge these perspectives—closely parallel those in the
discipline of sociology at large, with such approaches as Marxism or systems theory on the one hand and micro-sociological, constructionist
approaches such as interactionism, pragmatism, and ethnomethodology
on the other. This book aims to further the dialogue between the two
approaches to social movements, but we think it has broader implications
for social science as a whole as it struggles with issues such as culture,
emotions, and agency.

The more structural school (dominant now for thirty years) is trying
hard to synthesize existing knowledge about social movements—or to
insist that such a synthesis has emerged by itself out of empirical
research, despite conflicting theoretical frameworks. The structuralists,
more often (but we think misleadingly) known as "political process" theorists, sometimes boast that their paradigm is simply the leading con-
tender by virtue of its empirical findings, but others claim that we have
passed into a post-paradigm phase in which there is considerable agreement on basic findings so that we need only to refine our models. To make

good on this claim, they must find a place for culture in their structural models and metaphors—usually as distinct variables or mechanisms.

The constructionist school, on the other hand, has been more content to develop useful concepts that anyone could use than with self-conscious comparisons or syntheses of different traditions. Its practitioners are more likely to see culture as permeating, indeed defining, all aspects of protest and its environment, including the "structures" emphasized by political process theorists. But, unwilling to present themselves as an alternative paradigm, cultural approaches have often been subsumed under the supposed political process consensus, especially in the form of "frames" and "identities."

Claims to post-paradigm normal science suggest that this is just the time when skepticism is most needed, the moment to pause and assess the major concepts, theories, and findings that we use to understand social movements. We hope that the debates in this volume will help the reader assess the claims of synthesis at a theoretical level. Adequate empirical tests, which we feel have been missing, are being conducted separately (e.g., Goodwin, forthcoming).

Paradoxically, we know both too much and too little about the favorite topics of political process theory. For example, its focus on the state as the main player with which social movements interact may have a quality of misplaced concreteness to it. There is a tendency to see the state, that is, as a unified actor—a "structure"—rather than as a complex web of agencies and authorities, thoroughly saturated with culture, emotions, and strategic interactions (see, e.g., Jasper, 1990; Steinmetz, 1999). Beyond the state, too, there are many additional audiences for the words and actions of social movement activists; indeed, sometimes they are more important than the state. Much of the work of the process paradigm has been theoretical, with less empirical testing than practitioners of the paradigm tend to admit (Jasper and Young, 2002).

At the same time, there are aspects of social movements about which we know almost nothing. There is still a lot to learn about culture, as several of the contributions in part II of this volume demonstrate. But we know even less about the emotions of social movements (the subject of chapter 11; see also Goodwin, Jasper, and Polletta, 2001) and about the way in which strategic choices are made (chapter 12). Psychology and social psychology also have insights not yet incorporated into the study of social movements. And issues of agency—the term structuralists use when they throw up their hands and recognize the limits of their explanations—have yet to be addressed squarely.

Process theorists disagree whether their paradigm merely needs refinement and elaboration or we need a more fundamental rethinking of collective action. David Meyer (in chapter 4, and in Meyer, Whittier, and

Robnett, 2002) offers a list of emendations to what he considers a basically sound program. Yet the founding fathers of that same program have taken our criticisms more to heart, distancing themselves enormously from their own previous work. McAdam, Tarrow, and Tilly (2001:84) are ready to "abandon efforts to repair the boxes and arrows of the classic social movement agenda by adding variables, reinterpreting its elements, or specifying new connections among them." Although we find that their structural training still shows through, they are at least trying to avoid invariant models; to introduce dynamic, interactive elements into their explanations; and to recognize that opportunities and mobilizing structures must be interpreted as such and that they can be created if they do not already exist. They have even admitted the importance of emotions (Aminzade and McAdam, 2001).

Some of the questions this volume addresses are: Can the structural approach absorb the insights of cultural constructionism without a major rethinking of its own concepts? How can cultural approaches integrate the insights of structuralists? Does cultural interpretation mediate between political structures and action, or does it help create both of them? Do we have a suitable vocabulary for answering the basic questions that interest scholars of social movements? Is the political process approach still a progressive research program, or has it begun instead to constrain intellectual discovery? Where are the frontiers of theory and research in this vital area of sociology?

This book started small but quickly snowballed. We set out to write a review essay on Doug McAdam, John McCarthy, and Mayer Zald's edited volume, *Comparative Perspectives on Social Movements: Political Opportunities, Mobilizing Structures, and Cultural Framings* (1996). This book suggested that there existed a basic intellectual framework or paradigm for explaining social movements—its three main components listed in the book's subtitle—around which there was a growing consensus among social scientists. However, we had strong misgivings about this political process framework, and the very idea of a dominant paradigm made us suspicious.

The more we thought and talked about political process theory, the more our critique grew, eventually becoming the paper published as chapter 1 of this volume. As a sweeping commentary on the dominant paradigm for social movement analysis, it naturally aroused a lot of attention, especially from the paradigm's defenders (chapters 2 through 5). We expected that political process theorists would not agree with all or even much of what we had to say, but we were surprised by the ardor of some of the responses. (An interesting observation, which may tell us something about the intellectual styles of structuralists and constructionists, is that virtually all the leading political process scholars are men, whereas many of the voices concerned with culture and emotions belong to women.)

After this material was published in *Sociological Forum* in 1999, we learned of others eager to weigh in on the debate, hence chapters 8 through 12. (Chapter 7 is an expanded version of Polletta's contribution to the original symposium.) While some mediate between the positions, others point in new directions altogether. Finally, two of the original architects of the dominant paradigm recently published essays on the state of social movement research today; they appear as chapters 13 and 14. Of special note is Doug McAdam's attempt (in chapter 13) to recast political process theory in a more constructionist vein. While we continue to find McAdam's model conceptually too narrow, it demonstrates how theoretical debates can contribute to new and better understandings of social movements.

We hope that the debates and reflections in this volume raise more questions than they answer, bringing theoretical reflection back to a field that has had too little of it in recent decades.

NOTE

For her painstaking editorial assistance with this book, we would like to thank Julie Stewart of New York University.

Part I

POLITICAL PROCESS THEORY: OPPORTUNITY OR CONSTRAINT?

1

Caught in a Winding, Snarling Vine: The Structural Bias of Political Process Theory

JEFF GOODWIN AND JAMES M. JASPER

The employment of invariant models . . . assumes a political world in which whole structures and sequences repeat themselves time after time in essentially the same form. That would be a convenient world for theorists, but it does not exist.

—Charles Tilly (1995a:1596)

The symbols of social order—the police, the bugle calls in the barracks, military parades and waving flags—are at once and the same time inhibitory and stimulating: for they do not convey the message "Don't dare to budge"; they cry out "Get ready to attack."

—Frantz Fanon (1986:45)

One of the exciting developments in recent research on social movements has been extensive conceptualization of the political environments that movements face, which has largely taken the form of "political opportunity" or "political process" approaches. Thanks to the prolific efforts of senior scholars such as Bert Klandermans, Hanspeter Kriesi, Doug McAdam, John McCarthy, Sidney Tarrow, Charles Tilly, and Mayer Zald, political process theory (hereafter, PPT) is currently the hegemonic paradigm among social movement analysts.[1] A younger generation of scholars—including Edwin Amenta, Elisabeth Clemens, Marco Giugni, Ruud Koopmans, David Meyer, Cathy Schneider, Christian Smith, and Suzanne Staggenborg, to name a few—has now taken up aspects of PPT, the most telling sign of a "hot" paradigm. Although not all scholars deploy its concepts, PPT dominates the field of social movement research by powerfully shaping its conceptual landscape, theoretical discourse, and research agenda. Scholars from other theoretical camps cannot help but sit up and take notice. PPT may be criticized, but it cannot be ignored.

The weaknesses that we see in PPT derive from the same sources as its popularity, especially a strong bias in favor of metaphors of "structure." Despite its vast influence, moreover, PPT remains conceptually muddled insofar as political process theorists have been unable to reach agreement about the definitions of its basic concepts. This imprecision has allowed PPT to be applied in diverse settings, but it has hindered the testing and refinement of theoretical propositions. It sometimes seems as if there were as many political process approaches as theorists. The apparent rigor of labeling something a political opportunity "structure" may help to explain why so many causal variables and mechanisms have been analyzed under this rubric.

We also argue that two of the most influential strands of PPT—what we call the political opportunity thesis and the political process model—are (depending on how they are understood) tautological, trivial, inadequate, or just plain wrong. At best, PPT in its current form provides a helpful, albeit limited, set of "sensitizing concepts" for social movement research. It does *not* provide what it frequently, often implicitly, promises: a causally adequate, universal theory or "model" of social movements. Such an invariant, transhistorical theory is simply not possible and should therefore not be the goal of research (see Tilly, 1994, 1995a). But PPT's language of causal structures encourages such ambitions.

The bias lurking beneath these problems is that "structural" factors (i.e., factors that are relatively stable over time and outside the control of movement actors) are seen and emphasized more readily than others— and non-structural factors are often analyzed as though they were structural factors. We shall identify the results of this bias in several places. Although the original term "political opportunity structure" (a.k.a. POS) has generally given way to apparently more fluid concepts such as "process" and "opportunities," these are still usually interpreted in unnecessarily structural ways.

A number of factors have been added to political opportunities in recognition of the influence of non-structural variables—but without being accurately theorized as non-structural. These include strategy and agency, which have to do with the active choices and efforts of movement actors as well as of their opponents and other players in the conflict, and cultural factors that deal with the moral visions, cognitive understandings, and emotions that exist prior to a movement but that are also transformed by it. Process theorists tend to wash the meaning and fluidity out of strategy, agency, and culture so that they will look more like structures. The two main categories that process theorists have added to political opportunities are "mobilizing structures," which contain much that is not structural, and "framing," which is their effort to include culture but actually leaves out most of culture. This bias is especially clear in a recent volume, *Comparative Perspectives on Social Movements* (McAdam, McCarthy, and Zald, 1996a), a programmatic statement intended to establish some conceptual consensus among those following this approach.

We write as sympathetic critics of PPT, impressed by the quantity and quality of empirical research that has been carried out in its name. We have used kindred concepts in our own work (Jasper, 1990; Goodwin, 1999). Because we do not believe that an invariant model of social movements is possible, we do not pretend to offer another, "better" model than those proposed by political process theorists, but rather a more expansive set of concepts and distinctions for the analysis of social movements. Most of our critical remarks about PPT, finally, can be found in the work of political process theorists themselves, especially McAdam and Tilly. But these criticisms have not had the radical impact on PPT that they require. They have not resulted, above all, either in the abandonment of the chimerical quest for an invariant general theory or model of social movements or in the eradication of PPT's structural bias.

Not all political process theorists view general theory as their goal; instead, some explore how the organizational forms, repertoires, and consequences of social movements are contingently shaped by historically shifting constellations of political processes (see, e.g., Kriesi et al., 1995; Kriesi, 1996; Rucht, 1996). But many, especially when discussing the emergence of social movements (as opposed to their forms, strategies, and impact), remain enamored of sweeping, transhistorical formulas and invariant models. Others imply such a goal in their language of necessary and sufficient causation.

THE POLITICAL OPPORTUNITY THESIS

The narrow political opportunity thesis claims that *social movements emerge as a result of "expanding" political opportunities*. As Tarrow writes in *Power in Movement* (1994:17–18; also 81, 150): "The main argument of this study is that people join in social movements in response to political opportunities and then, through collective action, create new ones. As a result, the 'when' of social movement mobilization—when political opportunities are opening up—goes a long way towards explaining its 'why.' . . . [E]ven groups with mild grievances and few internal resources may appear in movement, while those with deep grievances and dense resources—but lacking opportunities—may not." Tarrow here loosens the narrow thesis by emphasizing that social movements, once they have emerged, can themselves further expand the political opportunities that allegedly gave rise to mobilization in the first place (see also Meyer and Staggenborg, 1996). The passage nonetheless suggests that neither intense grievances nor extensive resources are sufficient *or even necessary* for movement mobilization to occur. Collective-behavior and resource-mobilization theories, in other words, are barking up the wrong trees. What *is* necessary and, it would seem, virtually sufficient for social movement mobilization to occur—since "groups with mild grievances and few internal resources" can probably be found in any society, at any time—is *the "opening up" of political opportunities.*[2]

Whether this thesis make sense depends, of course, on what is meant by "political opportunities." The broadest definition makes the thesis tautological: Movements cannot emerge where people are unable, for whatever reason, to associate with one another for political purposes. (Imagine the fictive society described by George Orwell in *1984*.) But Tarrow *defines* movements as a form of association, as *"collective challenges by people with common purposes and solidarity in sustained interaction with elites, opponents and authorities"*—challenges that employ "disruptive direct action against elites, authorities, other groups or cultural codes," usually in public places (1994:3–4, emphasis in original). A social movement does not simply presuppose, but is *itself* an expression of the associated activities of some group or field of actors. So if "political opportunities" means something like "the chance for people to act together," then it is certainly true that social movement mobilization requires political opportunities. Understood in this way, however, the thesis is tautological: political opportunity is built into the definition of a social movement.

Recognizing this, most political opportunity analysts have attempted carefully to disaggregate and operationalize various types of political opportunities or, more usually, a range of variables that cause political opportunities to "expand" or "contract." Specified in this way, the political opportunity thesis becomes falsifiable, in principle. At just this point, however, political opportunity analysts find themselves on the horns of a definitional dilemma: The more broadly one defines political opportunities, the more trivial (and, ultimately, tautological) the political opportunity thesis becomes; conversely, the more narrowly one defines political opportunities, the more inadequate or implausible the political opportunity thesis becomes as an explanation for the rise of any particular social movement. This definitional dilemma may be a reason for the lack of consensus as to the precise meaning of "political opportunities."

On one horn of this dilemma, political opportunities can be specified as *all* those factors or processes that in one way or another affect "the chance to act together"—including processes that we would not normally think of as "political" at all. In this case, however, the political opportunity thesis again approaches tautology or, at best, triviality; any statement that X leads to Y (in our case, expanding political opportunities give rise to social movement mobilization) is not very illuminating when X includes, as it were, everything under the sun. Gamson and Meyer recognize this danger:

> The concept of political opportunity is in trouble, in danger of becoming a sponge that soaks up virtually every aspect of the social movement environment—political institutions and culture, crises of various sorts, political alliances, and policy shifts. . . . It threatens to become an all-encompassing fudge factor for all the conditions and circumstances that form the context for collective action. Used to explain so much, it may ultimately explain nothing at all. (Gamson and Meyer, 1996:275)[3]

Defined this broadly, "political opportunities" explain social movements with the same precision that "social structure," say, explains criminal behavior. Ironically, Gamson and Meyer themselves define political opportunities in a way that includes political institutions and culture, crises of various sorts, political alliances, and policy shifts, among still other factors (Gamson and Meyer, 1996:281, Figure 12.1). As McAdam notes, "Gamson and Meyer could well be accused of contributing to the very problem they seek to remedy" (1996a:25).

McAdam's own definition of political opportunities, however, demonstrates the difficulties of the other horn of the dilemma, when the specification of political opportunities is restricted to a short list of "narrowly political factors" (McAdam, 1996a:26). McAdam proposes what he calls a "highly consensual list of dimensions of political opportunity":

1. The relative openness or closure of the institutionalized political system
2. The stability or instability of that broad set of elite alignments that typically undergird a polity
3. The presence or absence of elite allies
4. The state's capacity and propensity for repression (McAdam, 1996a:27).

However, the other contributors to the same volume in which McAdam's proposal is made (including Gamson and Meyer) do not restrict themselves to this "consensual" list; they find it necessary to employ additional—and sometimes historically and situationally specific—political opportunity variables to explain the movements that interest them. McAdam's four variables cannot by themselves explain the rise of these movements—nor could any *other* specification of political opportunity that is this narrow.

In his analysis of the 1989 revolts in Eastern Europe, for example, Oberschall adds the legitimacy of the state, the international environment, and a number of "short-term events" in that region (including failed reforms from above) as dimensions of political opportunity (1996:94–95). In his analysis of new social movements in Western Europe, Kriesi suggests that a political system's "informal procedures and prevailing strategies with regard to challengers" must be seen as an important dimension of political opportunity (1996:160; see also Kriesi et al., 1995). Rucht includes the "policy implementation capacity" of the state as yet another dimension of political opportunity in his cross-national study of movement structures (1996:190).

Other recent studies suggest additional dimensions to the political opportunity concept. Costain conceptualizes "independent state action" by "subgroups within government" as a crucial dimension of political opportunity (1992:24). In his study of the U.S. Central America peace movement, Smith (1996:88–108) views as political opportunities such factors as President Reagan's "preoccupation" with Central America, the "Vietnam Syndrome" (i.e., popular opposition to U.S. intervention in Third World conflicts), and a series of White House "policy blunders." In this extreme case, political opportunities seem to include even the grievances—Reagan's policies—that inspired the movement's formation. Thus, analysts of political opportunities conspicuously fail to agree on just what factors to include, with no short list sufficient to explain the actual cases that interest them.

WHAT IS A POLITICAL OPPORTUNITY?

Disagreement over what counts as a political opportunity allows a structural bias to operate subtly and usually inadvertently. For example, McAdam insists that political opportunity variables should only include "structural" factors and *not* cultural processes: "The kinds of structural changes and power shifts that are most defensibly conceived of as *political* opportunities should not be confused with the collective processes by which these changes are interpreted and framed" (1996a:25–26, emphasis in original).

McAdam's distinction between political opportunities and people's perceptions of those opportunities is a case of misplaced concreteness: Culture is recognized but excluded from what really counts (although he elsewhere analyzes "cultural opportunities" [McAdam, 1994:39]). Opportunities may be there even if no one perceives them. McAdam insists that distinguishing culture from political opportunities will allow us to understand interesting cases where political opportunities do not lead to collective action, and those where collective action arises in the absence of favorable opportunities. From a cultural constructionist perspective, however, *both* of these cases depend on cultural interpretation, regardless of "objective" opportunities. There may be no such thing as objective political opportunities before or beneath interpretation—or at least none that matter; they are all interpreted through cultural filters. Tarrow implicitly recognizes this by defining political opportunities as those "dimensions of the political environment that provide *incentives* for people to undertake collective action by affecting their *expectations* for success or failure" (1994:85, emphasis added). Incentives and expectations necessarily involve interpretation.

In the volume edited by McAdam, McCarthy, and Zald (1996a), Gamson and Meyer present an alternative to the editors' framework, one that recognizes how completely culture penetrates institutions and political processes. The distinction between the two becomes analytic, not concrete. Although this cultural constructionism has been adopted by increasing numbers of social movement scholars, especially Gamson, the editors of this volume do not treat it seriously. Furthermore, the idea of political opportunities as "structural changes and power shifts" suggests that structures are not so fixed as the word normally implies. How often do they change, and under what conditions? Can movements affect them? As with past formulations, McAdam's has a structural bias, confounding relatively fixed aspects of a polity (constitutions, electoral systems) with constantly (or potentially) shifting strategic alliances and choices. McAdam wants to deal with the latter but treats them as though they were the former. For example, McAdam's fourth dimension of political opportunity collapses the actual use of repression, which is a strategic choice, into structural capacities for repression, which are more a matter of physical and human resources. The conflation of physical capacities and their use reveals the same structural bias as that between willingness and opportunity: people's intentions, choices, and discretion disappear in a mechanical play of structures (Jasper, 1997). Analysts do not ask why some people become inclined to protest, or why some states use their repressive capacities. The United States federal government certainly has far more repressive capacity now than one hundred years ago, but it is actually less likely to send troops to massacre striking trade unionists.

A structural sensibility pervades not only what is seen as a political opportunity and how it is analyzed but also the choice of movements to be studied. Most process theorists have tested their theories on movements pursuing political participation or rights, notably the labor and civil rights movements—what Jasper (1997) calls "citizenship movements." McAdam (1982:25, emphasis added) even *defines* social movements as "those organized efforts, *on the part of excluded groups*, to promote or resist changes in the structure of society that involve recourse to noninstitutional forms of political participation." Assuming he means legal or political exclusion, this definition focuses attention on protesters' interactions with the state, and on those movements or activities that challenge existing laws, state policies, or states as such. Ignored are movements populated by the middle class, especially those that challenge extant "cultural codes." Not only cultural movements, but any movements that do not target the state as their main opponent, are poorly served by political process models. Jasper and Poulsen (1993) showed that only state-oriented movements, especially movements of oppressed groups, face the regular, automatic repression that process models assume. Movements of those with full citizenship rights, especially many of the so-called new social movements, do not; they do not have to wait for "expanding political opportunities" in the form of reduced repression.

Prominent process theorists admit that challenging cultural codes is a central goal of certain social movements, even many that are substantially or primarily oriented toward the state or polity (e.g., women's movements, ecology movements, and gay and lesbian movements).[4] Yet the cases they study—including those in recent volumes edited by process theorists (e.g., Traugott, 1995; McAdam, McCarthy, and Zald, 1996a)— include few countercultural movements or movement activities. Process theorists have mostly ignored literary, musical, and other artistic movements that challenge dominant beliefs and symbols, influence collective identities, and even penetrate more state-oriented movements—efforts such as the folk revival of the 1950s and 1960s (Cantwell, 1995), the contemporary "hip hop" movement (Rose, 1994), or the steelband movement in Trinidad and Tobago (Stuempfle, 1995).

Moral or "prefigurative" movements that put unorthodox values or norms into practice—including religious movements, utopian communities, and self-help movements—receive scarcely more attention (cf. Smith, 1991). Like artistic movements, these movements challenge dominant cultural beliefs and ideologies without directly confronting, and in some cases intentionally avoiding, the state or polity members. Of course, such movements are never hermetically sealed off from broader political forces, but neither do they look to exploit—or even care much about— specific political opportunities. Other things being equal, we would expect the political opportunity variables proposed by McAdam to tell us less about these types of movements than about more state-oriented ones.

One might object that the political opportunity thesis was never meant to explain countercultural movements like these. Perhaps it only works, or works best, for citizenship movements such as labor and civil rights. But if so, why? Must the state be target, audience, and ultimately judge for a movement's demands? In this case, the collective identity in whose name a movement speaks has already been legally defined; it requires less cultural construction (Morris, 1992).[5] And if the repression is obvious and constant, as for Southern blacks in the 1950s, then grievances and the will to protest are likely to be there already. In such cases, repression can be assumed, with its removal leading to collective activity. Only by sorting political opportunities into a variety of component variables can we begin to see which are relevant to what movements.

A bias exists not only in the kinds of movements studied but also in the activities observed and explained in those movements. Countercultural and prefigurative practices of movements, even of movements that *are* more directly oriented toward states and polities, tend (again, with a few exceptions) to be slighted. When these practices *are* examined, furthermore, they are explained not by political opportunities but by "framing processes" (see below). Whether they intend to or not, then, process theorists tend to ignore precisely those types of movements *and* movement activities for which "narrowly political" opportunities are least relevant, focusing on those movements and activities that best "prove" the usefulness of political opportunity variables.

HOW DO OPPORTUNITIES WORK?

We have argued that the conceptual looseness of "political opportunities," combined with an appealing aura of rigor and structure, has encouraged their broad application to social movements. Political opportunities have become a kind of theoretical Rorschach blot that researchers can apply, in a variety of ways, to the movements that interest them. Political opportunities, in sum, have suffered the fate that "resources" often did within resource-mobilization theory: virtually anything that, in retrospect, can be seen as having helped a movement mobilize or attain its goals becomes labeled a political opportunity. Yet if one attempts to avoid the triviality or tautology of an expansive definition of political opportunities, they explain a correspondingly smaller and smaller part of movement emergence. For an extraordinarily large number of processes and events, political and otherwise, potentially influence movement mobilization, and they do so in historically complex combinations and sequences.

The misapplication of structural metaphors makes it difficult to specify *how* political opportunities affect movement actions. As Gamson and Meyer (1996:282, emphasis added) note, "for many of the political opportunity variables . . . there is no consensus on exactly *how* they affect opportunity. Some seem to open and close political space simultaneously." If Gamson and Meyer are right, there is logically no way to specify the political opportunity thesis in a way that would render it unambiguously (and non-tautologically) true.

When political opportunities are visualized as stable structures, it should be obvious how they constrain action. But most theorists insist that they change over time—often a very short time—in ways that "open" opportunities for movements.[6] In that case, political opportunities are metaphorically seen as "windows" that open and close (Kingdon, 1995). They are either there or not there. Instead, we might think of them as institutional avenues that channel protest in certain ways rather than others, only rarely closing it off altogether. Most frequently, political action is invited to go down legal rather than illegal routes, electoral rather than disruptive channels, into hierarchical rather than egalitarian organizational forms. Only at the extreme is it blocked altogether, ultimately through military or police force. Even then it may take other forms, such as complaining, jokes, or gossip (Scott, 1985, 1990). Political structures and opportunities normally open up certain routes even while they discourage others.

This is a simple point about structures. Giddens (1984) insists that structures enable action as well as constrain it—although he too often reifies structure into a thing of its own (Sewell, 1992). As Foucault often showed, power and institutions *produce* actions, sensibilities, and ideas—they do not merely constrain them. Process theorists seem to see power as a purely negative constraint, preventing people from doing what they want. So when they find an opening, they break loose and protest. The term "opportunity" implies a preexisting desire waiting for a chance at fulfillment. If instead we think of a shifting playing field, with various institutions, cultural constructions, and strategic players, we can see that political action (and the impulses, grievances, and interests that go into it) is both channeled and created in a variety of ways without having to lapse into "window" metaphors. Institutions inspire and demand action as well as constrain it.

Gamson and Meyer, for example, discuss how elections shape social movement mobilization. Because competitive elections are an element of a relatively open political system in McAdam's terms, they would seem to indicate that political opportunities do in fact exist for movement mobilization. As Gamson and Meyer point out, however, things are not quite so simple:

> Do elections . . . open opportunity for a debate and resolution of central societal conflicts? Or do they close it by suppressing debate on these conflicts and diverting attention to the personalities and characters of candidates

rather than their differences on public policy? There is some evidence for both, but the precise mix of opportunity and constraint that elections provide remains an open question. (Gamson and Meyer, 1996:282)

The question remains "open," in fact, because the precise effect of elections—or of any other political opportunity—on movement mobilization is not invariant, but historically and situationally contingent. Their effects depend on structural factors such as electoral systems, strategic ones such as shifting alliances, and cultural ones such as resonant slogans and images. These factors channel political action toward certain paths, away from others.

Two other factors generally cited as political opportunities—the availability of elite allies and access to political authorities—are equally ambiguous in their effects, as Kriesi suggests in his discussion of new social movements:

> Support from a powerful ally is ambivalent from the point of view of the development of an SMO [i.e., a social movement organization]: On the one hand, such an ally may provide important resources; on the other hand, it may also reduce the autonomy of the SMO and threaten its stability in the long run. Similarly, the establishment of a working relationship with the authorities also has ambivalent implications for the development of the SMO: On the one hand, public recognition, access to decision-making procedures and public subsidies may provide crucial resources and represent important successes for the SMO; on the other hand, the integration into established systems of interest intermediation may impose limits on the mobilization capacity of the SMO and alienate important parts of its constituency, with the consequence of weakening it in the long run. (Kriesi, 1996:155–156)

Kenneth Roberts, reviewing a number of recent studies of social movements in Latin America, has similarly noted how in some cases democratization "may provide social actors with new channels of access to political institutions, but it can also remove authoritarian rulers against which opposition forces unified and mobilized, inject divisive forms of partisan competition into social organizations, and resurrect political parties and electoral activities that can siphon off energy from social networks" (1997:139).

Finally, consider the impact of state violence on mobilization. McAdam seems to imply that the absence or "lifting" of repression is an opportunity for mobilization, but many have argued the opposite. The effect of state violence on movement mobilization depends on many additional circumstances, mostly cultural and strategic. Sometimes the relationship is not inverse, but curvilinear. Brockett's recent study of protest in Central

America shows how indiscriminate state violence initially resulted in the *expansion* of popular mobilization, including the overthrow of the Somoza dictatorship in Nicaragua:

> Although . . . violence became increasingly widespread, brutal, and arbitrary, initially it did not deter popular mobilization but provoked even greater mass opposition. Opponents who were already active redoubled their efforts, and some turned to violence. Increasing numbers of nonelites gave their support to the growing revolutionary armies, many becoming participants themselves. Previously passive regime opponents were activated, and new opponents were created as the indiscriminate violence delegitimized regimes, on the one hand, and created incentives for opposition, such as protection, revenge, and justice, on the other. (Brockett, 1995:132)

Brockett's observations suggest, finally, that the political opportunity thesis is not simply tautological, trivial, insufficient, or ambiguous; it is, as an invariant causal hypothesis, just plain wrong. There are innumerable instances of social movement mobilization in contexts where political opportunities can only be described as *contracting*. Indeed, mobilization is often a defensive *response* to contracting political opportunities. "For some challengers," note Meyer and Staggenborg, "increased political openness enhances the prospects for mobilization, while other movements seem to respond more to threat than opportunity" (1996:1634). By itself, the political opportunity concept does not allow one to predict which of these dynamics (if either) will actually occur.

McAdam's analysis of the emergence of the gay rights movement in the months following the Stonewall riot of June 1969 is a case in point. "It is hard to account for the rise of this movement," he suggests, "on the basis of expanding political opportunities" (1995:225). There were no particular changes in existing political institutions, McAdam notes, that suddenly advantaged gays at this time, nor did the movement benefit from a major political realignment:

> In fact, the movement was preceded by a highly significant electoral realignment that can only be seen as disadvantageous to gays. I am referring, of course, to Richard Nixon's ascension to the White House in [1969], marking the end of a long period of liberal Democratic dominance in presidential politics. If anything, then, it would appear that the movement arose in a context of *contracting* political opportunities. (McAdam, 1995:225, emphasis in original; see also McAdam, 1996a:32)

McAdam argues, more generally, that political opportunities "would appear to be largely irrelevant in the rise of spin-off movements"—that is, movements that are inspired to varying degrees by earlier "initiator" movements. He suggests that "one would be hard-pressed to document a significant expansion in political opportunities in the case of all—or even most—spin-off movements" (1995:224). But if most movements arise in the wake of "initiator" movements, as components of larger "cycles of protest" (Tarrow, 1994:chap. 9), and if most of these "spin-off" movements are not the result of expanding political opportunities, then it follows that *many if not most social movements are not the result of expanding political opportunities.*

None of this is to deny the obvious—that any number of political processes may powerfully influence movement mobilization. But mobilization does not necessarily depend on expanding opportunities (except in the tautological sense), and such opportunities, when they *are* important, do not result from some invariant menu of factors, but from situationally specific combinations and sequences of political processes—none of which, in the abstract, has determinate consequences.

Table 1.1 is both an effort to distinguish different kinds of political opportunities and a demonstration of the structural bias that we have discussed. It sorts factors by two important dimensions: how stable or impermanent the factor is, and the extent to which movements themselves can affect it. "Structures," as the term is usually used, should be relatively stable and unaffected by movement strategies—the top part of the left column. In table 1.1, neither boundary is absolute. New laws and court decisions may be influenced by movement lobbying, but once

TABLE 1.1
The Political Environment of Social Movements

| Timescale | *Can movement actors affect it?* | |
	Usually not, or marginally	*More often, or more powerfully*
Longer-term factors	Political structures, e.g., electoral systems, implementation powers, administrative structures	Laws
		Court decisions
	Constitutions	Administrative procedures
	State's physical capacity for repression	
Shorter-term factors	External events, e.g., accidents	Actions of opponents, state
	Information revealed, e.g., scandals	Media coverage of protest
	Shifts in elite alliances	State repression

enacted they become part of the longer-term structural context. Likewise the distinction between shorter- and longer-term factors is a continuum, so that for example a nuclear accident like Chernobyl can have long-lasting reverberations. This is especially true because, while the antinuclear movement did not cause the accident, it guaranteed it a life in public memory. Which brings us to another point about the table: With the partial exception of the structures in the top part of the left column, *all* these factors are affected by conscious strategies, decisions, and (ultimately) actions of protesters, their opponents, and state actors. These factors tend to get treated as though they were stable structures rather than the outcomes of actions informed by strategic calculations. A common example, we saw, is that actual state repression is collapsed into the state's capacity for repression, as though it were automatic (Jasper and Poulsen, 1993). Like culture, strategic action pervades this typology.

Most of these opportunities are better analyzed as strategic than as structural—although both kinds of opportunity exist. Proper conceptualization of strategic thinking would entail an attention to timing, the choice of tactics from *within* repertoires, the psychology of expectations and surprise, and sources of credibility and trust. We would need to examine, as game theorists suggest, the mutual expectations of different strategic players, and not just those of the state and protesters but of bystanders, the news media, potential allies, and non-state targets. Because strategy is necessarily open-ended, it has been especially poorly studied under structural predispositions. Of the several questions one could ask about strategy—where do the available repertoires of tactics come from, how do activists choose from among them, how do they apply the ones they choose, what effects do different choices have—only the first and last, the most structural issues, have been well addressed (see Tilly, 1978; and Gamson, 1975, respectively). The actual choice of actions from within the repertoire—not to mention issues of timing and style in their application—have been almost completely ignored (see Jasper, 1997:chaps. 10, 13).

Political opportunities were once called political opportunity structures—an oxymoron that collapsed fleeting strategic opportunities into stable structures. Presumably "political opportunities" were meant to avoid this trap, but they continue to be treated as structures, even when they are seen as changing or changeable. Structures and strategies, despite their different logics, get conflated. What are structures if not something fixed, stable, and outside our control? We must work within structures, taking their shapes into account. But if they change frequently or easily, especially as a result of strategic choices, then they should not be labeled structures. Certain aspects of the political environment are difficult to change, and others change frequently—which should probably be the starting point for any effort to categorize political opportunities. But the utility of restricting the definition of political opportunities depends, in the end, on what other factors are then added to the mix.

THE POLITICAL PROCESS MODEL

The political process model addresses some of the difficulties with the narrow political opportunity thesis, adding social/organizational and cultural factors to the latter's political ones. McAdam, for example, while extensively employing the political opportunity concept, has complained about "mechanistic" theories that "depict social movements as the inevitable by-products of expanding political opportunities" (1996b:339, 354). No less than the political opportunity thesis, however, the broader process model frequently aims at a chimerical general theory of social movements and relies on overly structural conceptualizations. For instance, "mobilizing structures" (primarily social networks and formal organizations) are supposed to be a recognition of the dynamic element in movement emergence, but analysts tend to view them as *preexisting* structures, not as creations of movement organizers. Networks are seen as almost physical structures, rather than the information, ideas, and emotions that "flow" through them (Emirbayer and Goodwin, 1994; Jasper and Poulsen, 1995).

The political process model claims that *social movements result when expanding political opportunities are seized by people who are formally or informally organized, aggrieved, and optimistic that they can successfully redress their concerns.* As McAdam, McCarthy, and Zald put it (1996b:8):

> Most political movements and revolutions are set in motion by social changes that render the established political order more vulnerable or receptive to challenge. But these 'political opportunities' are but a necessary prerequisite to action. In the absence of sufficient organization—whether formal or informal—such opportunities are not likely to be seized. Finally, mediating between the structural requirements of opportunity and organization are the emergent meanings and definitions—or frames—shared by the adherents of the burgeoning movement.

Social movements emerge, then, not just when political opportunities are expanding but also when would-be "insurgents have available to them 'mobilizing structures' of sufficient strength to get the movement off the ground" *and* "feel both aggrieved about some aspect of their lives and optimistic that, acting collectively, they can redress the problem" (McAdam, McCarthy, and Zald, 1996b:5, 13).[7] But if McAdam, McCarthy, and Zald really mean that "most" movements arise in this way, which ones are the exceptions? And how can political opportunities be "necessary" prerequisites if they aren't always necessary? For practical purposes, these authors seem to believe that they *are* always necessary; "most" is a qualifier that receives no theoretical attention. We have here, then, what seems like an invariant recipe for social movements, the necessary and sufficient ingredients of which consist of political opportunities (which come first, either logically or chronologically), mobilizing structures, and ("mediating" between them) cultural framings. The political process model also tells us why movements—*all* movements—decline or disappear: Political opportunities contract, mobilizing structures weaken or disintegrate, *or* cultural frames come to delegitimate or practically discourage protest.

The model proposed by McAdam, McCarthy, and Zald and by Tarrow is basically an updated version of that first presented by McAdam in 1982 (see figure 1.1). Where McAdam once spoke of "indigenous organizational strength," political process theorists now speak of "mobilizing structures" or "social networks"; where McAdam spoke of "cognitive liberation" (or "insurgent consciousness"), political process theorists now speak of "cultural framings." Otherwise, these models appear the same. As we have suggested, a diagram of this scope is either a way of categorizing a vast array of causal mechanisms—in which case it says little about what actually causes any particular social movement—or (if it is meant as a causal diagram) an unrealistically simple, invariant model.

Does the political process model remedy the narrowness of the opportunity thesis? Does it explain mobilization? If, as we argued, expanding political opportunities are *not* in fact necessary, let alone sufficient, for movement mobilization, then the process model may be indefensible for

FIGURE 1.1
McAdam's Political Process Model of Movement Emergence

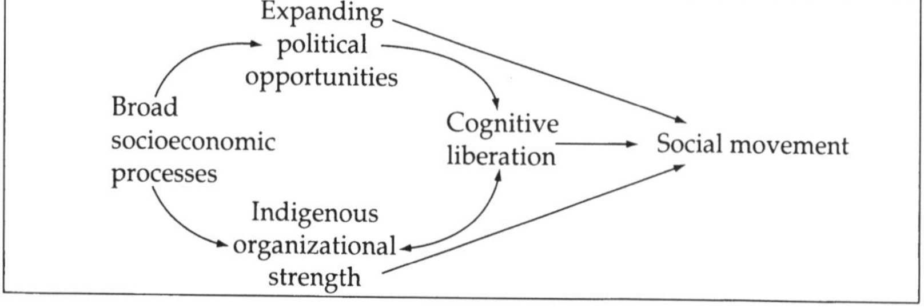

Source: McAdam, 1982:51.

this reason alone. Nonetheless, for the sake of argument, let us assume that expanding political opportunities, however defined, *are* necessary for social movement mobilization. The question then becomes: When such opportunities exist, do certain "mobilizing structures" and "cultural framings" explain the emergence of social movements? The answer again depends on what these concepts mean, and again there is considerable conceptual slippage due to PPT's structural bias.

Certainly, social movements cannot emerge where people are unable, for whatever reason, to form the minimal solidarity necessary for mounting and sustaining a challenge to authorities or cultural codes. Nor can movements emerge among a population with no shared beliefs. According to the earlier definitions, a social movement does not simply presuppose, but is *itself* an organized and self-conscious field of actors with grievances and common purposes, however shifting and negotiable. So if "mobilizing structures" means something like "organizations and advocacy networks" (Gamson and Meyer, 1996:283) and "cultural framings" means something like collective identities, grievances, and shared goals, then they are certainly prerequisites to social movement emergence. Understood in this way, however, the political process model is simply circular, with mobilizing structures and cultural framings built into the definition of a social movement.

Process theorists exhibit somewhat more consensus in specifying "mobilizing structures" and "cultural framings" than they do with "political opportunities." Unfortunately, structural biases have led "mobilizing structures" to be specified so *broadly* that the political process model becomes trivial, if not (once again) tautological, while "cultural framing" has been specified so *narrowly* that it fails to capture some of the most important ways that culture matters for social movements. Mobilizing structures, in fact, have been called on to do much of the explanatory work of culture. Let us examine each of these problems in turn.

Political process theorists do not agree on a single, consistent definition of mobilizing structures, but they clearly conceptualize such structures very broadly. McCarthy, for example, defines them as:

> those agreed upon ways of engaging in collective action which include particular "tactical repertoires," particular "social movement organizational" forms, and "modular social movement repertoires." I also mean to include the range of everyday life micromobilization structural social locations that are not aimed primarily at movement mobilization, but where mobilization may be generated: these include family units, friendship networks, voluntary associations, work units, and elements of the state structure itself. (McCarthy, 1996:141)

McAdam, McCarthy, and Zald offer a somewhat different but equally broad definition: "By mobilizing structures we mean *those collective vehicles, informal as well as formal, through which people mobilize and engage in collective action.*" These "collective vehicles" are said to include "meso-level groups, organizations, and informal networks," "various grassroots settings—work and neighborhood, in particular," "churches and colleges," and "informal friendship networks" (1996b:3–4, emphasis in original).

There are two problems with these and kindred specifications of mobilizing structures. The first is that the concept is so broadly defined that no analyst could possibly *fail* to uncover one or another mobilizing structure "behind" or "within" a social movement. The concrete specification replaces tautology with triviality. Indeed, one would obviously have a difficult time finding any person on the face of the earth—within or without social movements—who was not "aboard," so to speak, one or another (and probably several) such "collective vehicles." Anyone alive inhabits such structures (Piven and Cloward, 1992). The concept thus begs the question of how and when certain of these "structures," but not others, actually facilitate collective protest.

Second, these "collective vehicles"—indeed, social relations as such—can just as easily drive people away from social movements as hitch the two together. Affectual relationships, for example, can solidify social movements, but they are also a potential threat to group solidarities (see, e.g., Kanter, 1972; Goodwin, 1997). For example, as Philip Slater suggested, "an intimate dyadic relationship always threatens to short-circuit the libidinal network of the community and drain off its source of sustenance" (1963:348). Indeed, most of the "mobilizing structures" noted by McAdam, McCarthy, and Zald are probably, most of the time, *demobilizing* structures. "In point of fact," McAdam and Paulsen point out:

> Social ties may constrain as well as encourage activism. Our failure to acknowledge the variable impact of social ties is due, in turn, to our failure to take account of the "multiple embeddings" that characterize people's lives. . . . [I]ndividuals are invariably embedded in many organizational or association networks or individual relationships that may expose the individual to conflicting behavioral pressures. (McAdam and Paulsen, 1993:645, 641)

Social movement organizations themselves, ironically, can potentially discourage movement mobilization because "the formation of formal organizations renders the movement increasingly vulnerable to oligarchization, co-optation, and the dissolution of indigenous support," especially if "insurgents increasingly seek to cultivate ties to *outside* groups," including "elite allies" (McAdam, 1982:55–56, emphasis added). In the absence of clear thinking about *how* mobilizing structures operate, their various specifications—like those of "political opportunities"—have ambiguous and contradictory effects on movement mobilization, making it impossible to specify the political process model in an unambiguous (and non-tautological) way.

Finally, what kind of mobilizing "structures" are necessary for movement recruitment? Can a small number of organizers *create* their own mobilizing structures? If so, what is "structural" about them? Many dedicated activists were initially recruited into social movements—and many other people recruited into specific collective actions orchestrated by movements—despite the absence of social ties or organizational affiliations linking such people to those movements (or to one another). In her well-known study of the early pro-life movement in California, Luker found that two-thirds of the pro-life activists whom she interviewed were "self-recruits" to that movement: "That is, they encountered on their own information about the abortion situation that distressed them, and then they actively sought out an organized political group that shared their values" (Luker, 1984:147). Jasper and Poulsen (1995) found a large number of animal-rights activists who, at the time they were recruited, knew no one else in the movement. In other words, certain types of movement mobilization may not require "mobilizing structures" of the structural sort envisioned by process theorists. The use of leaflets and television advertising can, in some cases, replace personal and organizational ties.

When Snow et al. (1980), reviewing the literature on recruitment, found that personal ties to someone already in the movement were the best predictor of who would join, they already showed a structural bias. They concluded that "the probability of being recruited into a particular movement is largely a function of two conditions: (1) links to one or more movement members through a pre-existing or *emergent* interpersonal tie; and (2) the absence of countervailing networks" (798, emphasis added). Through the qualifier "largely," networks are asserted as more important than other factors. More significant is the (untheorized) idea of "emergent" ties, meaning that a recruit will meet people in the movement and develop personal bonds with them (Wallis and Bruce, 1982). This kind of tie, created by or within the movement itself, is crucial for the retention of members. It is not at all a pre-existing "structure," but the result of a movement's own activities, guided by strategic choices. Just as protesters can create their own political opportunities, they can create their own mobilizing structures.

That people can be recruited outside pre-existing networks suggests the independent importance of cultural persuasion as a factor explaining mobilization. Its influence, however, is often obscured by the structural concentration on networks. Networks and culture are often discussed as though one *or* the other could affect recruitment, but in fact networks amount to little without the ideas and affective bonds that keep them together. Mobilizing structures are thus credited with much of the explanatory power of culture (meanings and affects) and active strategizing (on the part of the activists who build networks and found organizations). We have here a classic instance of conceptual reification: Ongoing, strategic reasoning and actual collective action have been transformed into inert, impersonal "structures" and "vehicles."

Table 1.2, which categorizes elements of movements' social and organizational environments, is parallel to table 1.1. The "structural" items in the top left column are the factors most favored by process theorists; other factors, such as movement-created networks, are often discussed as though they belonged in this same analytic space. Cultural factors are again slighted, for they permeate all of the variables listed here, even the most structural ones. Strategy again tends to be ignored in favor of more structural factors.

TABLE 1.2
The Social Environment of Social Movements

| | Can movement actors affect it? | |
Timescale	Usually not, or marginally	More often, or more powerfully
Longer-term factors	Preexisting networks of potential recruits	Endowed movement organizations
	Communications and transportation infrastructure	Social networks developed by movement
	Residential or occupational density	"Free spaces"
	Formal organizations independent of movement: churches, professional associations, unions	Collective identities, boundaries
	Demographic shifts	
Shorter-term factors	Mobilization and activity of other movements	Short-lived movement organizations
		Protest events, arguments that attract attention
		Network ties activated by movement

FRAMING AND CULTURE

In one sense, the notion of cultural framings—like political opportunities and mobilizing structures—is overly broad, subsuming a variety of factors that are potentially contradictory in their effects and which need to be carefully disaggregated, including collective identities, grievances, goals, repertoires of contention, and the sense of efficacy or empowerment.[8] In another sense, however, political process theorists have defined cultural framings so narrowly that the concept is inadequate for grasping the many ways in which culture shapes social movements.[9]

In an example of misplaced concreteness, process theorists tend to reify culture—to conceptualize it as a distinct (and delimited) empirical social sphere or type of social action—instead of conceptualizing (and analyzing) culture as a ubiquitous and constitutive dimension of *all* social relations, structures, networks, and practices. The distinction between "cultural framings," on the one hand, and "political opportunities" and "mobilizing structures," on the other, is too often taken to mean that the latter two somehow stand outside of culture, which "mediates" between them (see Williams, 1977, for a critique of the "mediation" model of culture). To be sure, a number of process theorists clearly reject this implication—suggesting, for example, that political contexts and the organizational forms of movements are as much cultural as "structural" (see, respectively, Gamson and Meyer, 1996; and Clemens, 1996). Nonetheless, for most process theorists, "framing" and "culture" continue to be more or less equated with *the self-conscious activities of social movement participants, especially leading activists*. All non-structural factors get rolled into this tiny ball, but the reduction of culture to strategy does justice to neither.

McAdam, McCarthy, and Zald tell us that they intentionally want to "define framing rather narrowly" in just this way because "recent writings have tended to equate the concept with any and all cultural dimensions of social movements," a reduction, they add, which "threatens to rob the [framing] concept of its coherence" (1996b:6). This is reasonable. However, instead of opening up the political process model to new forms of cultural analysis that might help us understand "any and all cultural dimensions of social movements," McAdam, McCarthy, and Zald seem to call for cultural analysis based solely upon this "rather narrowly" defined notion of framing.

According to this definition, framing refers (or should refer) to "the *conscious, strategic efforts by groups of people to fashion shared understandings of the world and of themselves that legitimate and motivate collective action*" (McAdam, McCarthy, and Zald, 1996b:6, emphasis in original).[10] Such efforts are undoubtedly important, but culture—in such diverse forms as traditions, "common sense," material artifacts, idioms, rituals, news routines, know-how, identities, discourse, and speech genres—also constrains and enables collective action in ways that are not always or even usually intentional or instrumental (see, e.g., Geertz, 1983; Swidler, 1986; Bakhtin, 1986; Sewell, 1992; Steinberg, 1995).[11] Indeed, culture in this larger sense shapes framing processes themselves, typically in ways unrecognized by actors themselves. For example, what Steinberg calls "discursive repertoires" constrain the frames that actors may fashion: "They bound the set of meanings through which challengers can articulate claims and ideologically mediate the decision to act instrumentally" (1995:60). Identities, too, are logically prior to the strategic pursuit of interests; a group or individual must know who they are before they can know what interests they have (Ringmar, 1996). There is no logical or theoretical reason, in short, to privilege frame analysis as the preferred form, much less the only form, of cultural inquiry for the study of social movements.

The bias here is that frames are dichotomized as either successful or not, with organizers and recruiters trying a series of frames until they find those that work, which "fit" or "resonate" with the sensibilities of potential recruits. In this view, frames are like political opportunities—"windows" that are either open or closed. (The structural imagery is clear; even though "framing" is meant to connote process, it is still based on the structural metaphor of a frame.) But the statements and actions of organizers and protesters—actions send messages just as surely as words do—affect a variety of audiences in a variety of ways. Even when narrowed to recruitment, they affect potential recruits in diverse ways, perhaps changing people's sensibilities without, or before, recruiting them. What is lost is the broader culture within which *both* organizers and recruits operate.

An instrumental or structural perspective on culture distorts. McAdam, for example, argues that the Reverend Martin Luther King Jr., by employing Christian themes (among others) in his speeches, "brought an unusually compelling, yet accessible frame to the [civil rights] struggle" (1996b:347). For example, "the theme of Christian forgiveness that runs throughout King's thought," notes McAdam, "was deeply reassuring to a white America burdened (as it still is) by guilt and a near phobic fear of black anger and violence" (1996b:347). But does McAdam believe that King made a calculated decision to employ Christian themes in his speeches as part of a "strategic effort" to legitimate the civil rights movement? That is like saying King made a strategic choice to speak English, rather than seeing English as part of the culture shared by King and his audiences. McAdam's definition of framing seems to imply this kind of strategizing, yet he produces no evidence to support this claim. Nor does he mention the possibility that King employed Christian themes because, as a Baptist minister with a doctorate in theology, he actually believed that those "themes" were true or valuable for their own sake.

Finally, frame analysis suffers from an ideational or cognitive bias. Not only do the dramatically staged *actions* of social movements send symbolic messages as important as those in movement rhetoric (McAdam, 1996b), but the affectual and emotional dimensions of social movements are as important as the cognitive and moral. For example, collective identities and attributions of injustice ("injustice frames") are typically viewed by proponents of the process model as the outcomes or achievements of framing processes (see, e.g., Hunt, Benford, and Snow, 1994). In McAdam's early effort to add culture to process models, he argued that "objective" opportunities only lead to action when potential protesters undergo "cognitive liberation." As he described it, "the altered responses of members to a particular challenger serve to transform evolving political conditions into a set of 'cognitive cues' signifying to insurgents that the political system is becoming increasingly vulnerable to challenge" (McAdam, 1982:49). Although the term seems to imply a radical change in worldview, cognitive liberation appears to be a relatively instrumental reading of available information ("cues") about the state's willingness to repress dissent.

Yet collective identities and injustice frames—not to mention group solidarity and commitment (see, e.g., Kanter, 1972; Zablocki, 1980)—are usually more than simply cognitive or discursive framings; they often have powerful emotional and psychological—and not always fully conscious—dimensions (see, e.g., Hunt, 1992). Jasper (1997) shows that basic concepts such as cognitive liberation, collective identity, and frame analysis gain much of their causal force from the emotions involved—although at the theoretical level these are ignored by researchers. The same is true of the social networks and "mobilizing structures" concepts, which invoke social ties that are often affectual or libidinal (Goodwin, 1997) or otherwise saturated with emotions. Unfortunately, PPT and frame analysis in particular provide little conceptual or theoretical space for these issues within their research agendas. What Scheff (1994a:282) says about studies of nationalist movements applies to PPT more generally: "Descriptions of . . . movements note [their] passion, indeed the very pages crackle with it. But these descriptions do little to conceptualize, analyze, or interpret it." (Recall McAdam's passing allusion, quoted above, to "a white America burdened [as it still is] by guilt and a near phobic fear of black anger.")

Table 1.3 lays out some of the cultural and strategic factors important to social movement emergence and success. The boundaries continue to be permeable, because shorter-term developments can have long-term effects, and movements, if successful, can alter the broader cultural envi-

TABLE 1.3
Cultural and Strategic Factors

	Can movement actors affect it?	
Timescale	Usually not, or marginally	More often, or more powerfully
Longer-term factors	"Plausibility structures" Institutionalized news media routines Standard cultural repertoires of images, tropes, language, assumptions Tactical repertoires, "know-how" Master frames	Slogans, policy proposals Affective bonds within movement Movement identity, pride Skills of particular leaders, recruiters
Shorter-term factors	Fashions in media attention Opponents' efforts to affect public opinion, sensibilities, media Governmental efforts to influence opinion, sensibilities, media	Symbolic effects of protest events Arguments, rhetoric that attract attention Outrage, indignation over opponents' policies Credibility of opponents Frames Strategic choices about timing, style, application of tactics

ronment. We include strategic factors here because they are a form of knowledge and skill like other aspects of culture. The structural bias is often at work here, as it is in the concentration on explaining tactical repertoires of contention rather than choices about their actual employment (parallel to explaining capacities for repression rather than their use). Framing, absorbing as it must all of culture and much of strategy, cannot fall into the top left column but must fall into its diagonal opposite. Undue focus on the concept obscures the interaction between movement framings and the broader culture, as well as ignoring the many other dimensions of culture that appear in table 1.3. It should be obvious how many of these factors affect a movement's ability to create, interpret, and use mobilizing structures and political opportunities.

SOME MODEST PROPOSALS

Theoretical critiques are like sociopaths: Their aggressive drives are rarely balanced by constructive instincts. Instead of ending on a purely negative note, accordingly, here are several suggestions that we hope might improve social movement analysis:

1. *Abandon invariant models.* The search for universally valid propositions and models, at least for anything so complex as social movements, is bound to fail. As Tilly suggests, it would be nice if history had such a tidy causal structure, but it does not: "real history, carefully observed, does not fall into neat, recurrent chunks; it winds and snarls like a proliferating vine. What is more, in real history time and place make a difference to the way that ostensibly universal processes . . . unfold" (Tilly, 1994:59). If he is right, it makes little sense to search for that presumptive handful of necessary and sufficient causes that allegedly explain each and every social movement. Nor does it make sense to lump under one rubric all of the potentially important causal factors that empirical research has uncovered. Even when they do not intend to, process theorists appear to propose invariant models because of the structural models they deploy; greater attention to strategic choice, cultural meanings, and emotions would highlight the complex, open-ended quality of social conflict.

At the empirical level, we need to be sensitive to the historically shifting and situationally contingent combinations and sequences of processes and events that give rise to varying forms of social movements and collective action more generally. At the theoretical level, we need to recognize that a variety of concepts and theories may help us "hit" this moving target. Fidelity to, say, three big concepts is the last thing we need. Rather, the explanation of empirical variation will likely require considerable conceptual and theoretical variation as well. Some kinds of movements require political opportunities, while others do not; some recruit through pre-existing social networks, while others do not; some require powerful grievances or collective identities, while others do not. Parsimonious models are not very useful when they explain only a limited range of the empirical cases that they are meant to cover.

2. *Beware of conceptual stretching.* As we have seen, some process theorists have stretched the concept of "political opportunities" to be virtually synonymous with the larger "environment" in which social movements are embedded. The concept of "mobilizing structures," for its part, seems to have been coined in the first place so as to encompass a vast range of formal and informal organizations and networks as well as (for some) strategic and tactical repertoires. Even the concept of "cultural framings," which excludes many important forms of culture, subsumes such diverse factors as grievances, purposes, collective identities, repertoires of contention, and the sense of power or efficacy. Unfortunately, this type of "conceptual stretching" quickly becomes self-defeating (see Sartori, 1970; Collier and Mahon, 1993). To begin with, it tends to undermine the shared understanding of concepts that is a necessary foundation for any research

program or, indeed, for rational communication. When original definitions are subverted and new ones proliferate endlessly, an Alice-in-Wonderland pseudo-dialogue ensues: Everyone uses the same words but gives them different meanings. As concepts include more and more variables or specifications, the theoretical hypotheses built upon them tend to become trivial and, ultimately, tautological. Conceptual hyperinflation, like its economic analogue, destroys whatever explanatory value concepts once had. Conceptual stretching is especially problematic in a field where many scholars know well only one movement, or one type of movement, so that they lack a sound comparative base for assessing the plausibility of their models (Jasper, 1997).

3. *Recognize that cultural and strategic processes define and create the factors usually presented as "structural."* Culture permeates the political opportunities and mobilizing structures of process theorists. Perceptions are not only necessary for potential protesters to recognize opportunities, but in many cases perceptions can *create* opportunities. In addition to opportunities, meanings and emotions keep social networks alive, and do much of the work normally credited to network "structures." Formal organizations too depend on cultural expectations for much of their force (Powell and DiMaggio, 1991).

Other cultural dynamics are not captured by framing. We need a better appreciation of the symbolism of events and individuals, so that we can see how they discourage or encourage political action. We also need to understand the logic of emotions and of moral principles and intuitions. We should never assume a willingness, even eagerness to protest—if only the opportunities were there!—but must see how this is created.

Political opportunities and mobilizing structures are also heavily shaped by strategic considerations, by the choices movement leaders and activists make. As we have emphasized, activists can sometimes create their own opportunities and mobilizing structures. Strategic decisions depend heavily on interaction between movements and other players (especially, but not exclusively, their opponents and the state), and this interaction is strongly shaped by the expectations that each side has of the other. Each side tries to surprise, undermine, and discredit the other. Such strategies are themselves a form of cultural learning. They also depend heavily on psychology: Certain individuals are especially adept at knowing how to do what when, how to invent new tactics, how to time an action or response. Social movements can find themselves constrained by strategic stalemates (of the kind games theorists have described), not just by political structures or lack of resources. But few strategic situations leave no room for choice or maneuver. Serious attention to strategy would be an additional way to understand true process, rather than structures parading as process.

4. *Do some splitting to balance the lumping.* The concept of political opportunities is designed as a way of talking about the environments of social movements, but researchers have begun to discover the complexity of these environments. They contain far more actors than just the state, and even the state contains diverse agents and institutions. Lumping together legal courts with the general public with agents of physical repression seems misguided. Efforts should continue to distinguish different kinds of political opportunities, different kinds of mobilizing structures, and different kinds of culture. We should, for starters, distinguish stable political structures from shifting strategic opportunities, the state from other elite institutions, physical resources from their strategic use, and strategic from other aspects of culture.

Its very proliferation of definitions and applications demonstrates the utility of PPT, which has established the importance of the political environment to a social movement's creation, dynamics, and effects. It is possible to keep these insights while recognizing the open-ended nature of the conflict and change that these movements set in motion. The apparent rigor of structural images can lead us to see things that are not there and to overlook many things that are; foremost among the latter are culture and strategy. Process theorists simply need to live up to their name.

NOTES

Previously published in *Sociological Forum* 14, no. 1 (March 1999). Reprinted with permission.

1. The concept of "political process" was popularized by Doug McAdam's (1982) book on the black protest movement in the U.S., although, as McAdam notes (1982:36), he took the term from an article by Rule and Tilly (1975).

2. The concept of "political opportunities" is generally attributed to Peter Eisinger (1973). The more general concept of "opportunity structure" originates with Robert K. Merton (1968:229–232, 1996); ironically, Merton, who is never cited by political opportunity theorists, is a major figure in a theoretical tradition (structural-functionalism) anathema to most political opportunity theorists.

3. Tarrow (1996a:881) similarly complains that "if opportunity structure is allowed to become a catch-all term for any interaction between a group and the state, or if the concept is specified post hoc, then we will end up with ad hoc analyses that border on descriptions."

4. McAdam suggests that if social movements "are to become a force for social change," they must "ultimately shape public policy and state action" (1996b:339–340). But this may prejudge the ways in which social change occurs.

5. Although most process theorists would deny any kinship with rational-choice approaches to social movements, both tend to assume that group interests are well defined in advance of mobilization.

6. The more political opportunities are restricted to the most stable aspects of a political system, the more useful they become for explaining cross-national differences in mobilization and protest, and the less useful they become for explaining changes over short periods of time. European scholars seem to think more readily in cross-national terms, so that it is natural to describe political-structural "variables" that are usually quite stable over decades; they vary instead in comparative perspective. Many American scholars seem to insist that their "structural" variables must vary over time, usually to explain why a movement arises when it does. This pushes researchers like McAdam into the position of talking about how basic structures change, sometimes rapidly—which suggests that they may not be so "structural" after all.

7. Tarrow's formulation is similar: "Triggered by the incentives created by political opportunities, combining conventional and challenging forms of action and building on social networks and cultural frames is how movements overcome the obstacles to collective action and sustain their interactions with opponents and with the state" (Tarrow, 1994:1).

8. The following paragraphs draw on Emirbayer and Goodwin, 1996a, 1996b.

9. Frame analysis, first developed by Erving Goffman (1974), was imported into social movement theory by Gamson, Fireman, and Rytina (1982) and Snow et al. (1986). For critiques, see Jasper and Poulsen (1995), Emirbayer and Goodwin (1996a), Kane (1997), and Benford (1997).

10. A "frame" has been defined as an "interpretive scheme that simplifies and condenses the 'world out there'" (Snow and Benford, 1992:137).

11. McAdam, McCarthy, and Zald do recognize that "at the outset, participants [in social movements] may not even be fully aware that they are engaged in an interpretive process of any real significance" (1996b:16). But is the implication that we should ignore such processes because they are not "conscious" and "strategic"?

2

Wise Quacks

CHARLES TILLY

Before the late nineteenth century, all sorts of people had the right to provide health care in the United States. Midwives, pharmacists, herb sellers, wise women, and a colorful variety of physicians dispensed their services to the sick and infirm without benefit or restriction of governmental licensing. Then, in a rush, arrived:

- diffusion of bacteriological medicine and complex diagnostic devices such as X-rays
- establishment of major American medical schools on science-based European models
- suppression of private apprenticeship as a path to medical practice
- multiplication of hospitals as sites for medical training, practice, research, and health care
- proliferation of hospital-based nursing schools
- strengthening of the American Medical Association as a professional pressure group
- fortification of county medical societies in alliance with the AMA
- establishment of physicians' licensed monopoly over prescription or administration of many drugs and treatments

Those changes intertwined to define eclectic, homeopathic, osteopathic, chiropractic, faith-based, and herbal medicines—which had previously thrived—as forms of quackery deserving suppression or at least aggressive containment. Even wise quacks lost their right to a hearing.

At the same time, state-backed organizational changes in health care subordinated nurses, midwives, pharmacists, and other licensed medical practitioners to the authority of chartered physicians. With governmental assistance and collaboration of other licensed professionals, physicians greatly restricted the operating zones of their fellow health care specialists. Pharmacists lost their previously broad mandate to dispense medicines, advise the suffering, and treat minor ailments or injuries. Midwives almost vanished; they attended roughly half of all American births in 1900, far less than 1 percent in 1973. Except as modified by increasing capitalization of hospitals and massive movement of graduate nurses from private care to hospital employment, that physician-dominated establishment ruled American health care up to the recent past. But it only stabilized between 1875 and 1920 after immense sectarian struggles among advocates of different strains in medical thinking.

No one, thank goodness, licenses explanations of political contention. Yet James Jasper and Jeff Goodwin (hereafter Jaswin; see chapter 1) write about political process analyses with some of the contempt for rival views that animated late nineteenth-century medical practitioners. "Tautological, trivial, inadequate, or just plain wrong," they call existing treatments of political process and opportunity. The tone strikes a practiced ear as odd, since Goodwin and Jasper are well established analysts of political processes, and since—as the chapter's abundant quotations from ostensible offenders reveal—their complaints echo dissatisfactions other political process analysts have been voicing for some time.

Who then are the vile vine-vending quacks, and what constitutes their quackery? For Jaswin, all purveyors of political process models have committed some degree of fraud by treating prevailing conceptions of political opportunities, mobilizing structures, framing processes, and contention itself as an adequate set of concepts for social movement analyses. To that extent, political process practitioners qualify as quacks. As an aging practitioner of political process analyses who narrowly escapes the Jaswin excommunication and as a frequent collaborator of Doug McAdam and Sidney Tarrow (who bear the brunt of Jaswin fulminations), I fear for my license to practice.

Our good doctors' diagnosis and prescription therefore raise pressing questions:

- How accurate is their critique?
- On what reasoning does it rest?
- How does it explain the malady?
- What remedy does it propose?
- How likely is that remedy to cure the illness?
- What alternatives to their proposed treatment might we try?

My comments will address those six questions in order.

HOW ACCURATE IS THE JASWIN CRITIQUE?

Despite heroic recent synthesizing efforts by Mark Lichbach, Sidney Tarrow and others, analyses of contentious politics remain a zone of intense intellectual contention, right down to disputes over the relevant domain: contention, collective action, social movements, identity-formation, or something else? Jaswin pick up and knot together significant strands of the prevailing self-criticism and mutual recrimination among students of contentious politics. They capture, for example, the enduring conflict between views of political opportunities as 1) durable organizational differences among governments and 2) change in organizational environments of particular political actors. They accurately identify the tendency of social movement specialists to concentrate on movements that match their theoretical preconceptions—indeed, on the whole, their political and moral preferences. They rightly complain of the propensity to apply basic explanatory concepts flexibly after the fact, thus reducing or extinguishing those concepts' rigor. They properly identify the search for invariant models of political processes—one size fits all, or at least all members of a category—as a wild goose chase. All these weaknesses of recent work deserve castigation and, especially, correction.

Jaswin also declare that "The bias lurking beneath these problems is that 'structural' factors (i.e., factors that are relatively stable over time and outside the control of movement actors) are seen and emphasized more readily than others—and non-structural factors are often analyzed as though they were structural factors." This claim is either incorrect, tendentious, or so badly stated as to be misleading. It is incorrect if it means that analysts of contentious politics ignore fluctuations in actors' environments as incitements to collective action and likewise obscure the importance of interactions between actors and their environments, including other actors within those environments. It is tendentious if it means that factors Jaswin happen to regard as important have not received enough attention in previous work. It is misleading if by non-structural factors it does not actually mean (as the parenthetical definition implies) fluctuating elements that respond to movement actors' actions but (as later discussions suggest) contenders' cognitive and emotional states. In a spirit of reconciliation, I lean toward the verdict "badly stated."

Jaswin go on to indict analyses of political opportunity structure on dual grounds: a) different analysts propose contradictory definitions and components of political opportunities, and b) the same analysts believe that political opportunities supply the necessary and sufficient conditions for social movements. The first indictment is correct, but not very helpful, because it simply reiterates the conventional characterization of social movement theories (and theories of contentious politics as a whole);

reviewers and synthesizers usually describe political process thinking as a zone of flux and controversy. The second misrepresents the usual practice of political process analysts, who actually have the habit of intoning not a single slogan but a four-part litany: political opportunities (including, not so incidentally, threats), mobilizing structures, framing processes, and contentious interaction. That the four elements do not yet constitute a compelling causal theory, political process analysts are usually the first to remark. No active participant in the debate claims that political opportunities constitute the necessary and sufficient conditions of contention.

ON WHAT REASONING DOES THE CRITIQUE REST?

Despite an epigraph condemning invariant models of social processes, the chapter assumes that general explanations, when they exist at all, take the form of covering laws. Since no covering laws apply to contentious politics, Jaswin reason, analysts can only seek to describe and explain particular instances of contentious politics. Explanation becomes interpretation: empathetic reconstruction of an actor's orientations. Although in recent decades many social scientists have followed the same logical path, the path goes wrong at two different turnings:

- First, it fails to recognize that an alternative mode of explanation is readily available: the identification of wide-ranging, recurrent causal mechanisms that concatenate into different structures and sequences according to context; most scientific explanation actually invokes such mechanisms instead of invariant laws.
- Second, such an argument implicitly claims that the deep causes of social processes reside within individuals, in some interplay of emotion and consciousness, in what many psychologists and philosophers call propositional attitudes.

The basic Jaswin critique translates into something like these terms: the structural bias of political process theorists leads them to ignore or distort the mainsprings of human behavior, which are propositional attitudes. The confusion worsens when Jaswin identify propositional attitudes with culture, thus locating culture in individual minds and bodies rather than in social relations and interaction. Hence the unjustified charge that McAdam's distinction between political opportunities and people's perceptions of those opportunities commits the fallacy of "misplaced concreteness." If individual awareness is the only or fundamental reality, attribution of existence to other entities does, indeed, misplace concreteness. But what if it is *not* the only or fundamental reality?

HOW DO JASWIN EXPLAIN THE MALADY?

In truth, they don't try very hard. They blame the "prolific efforts of senior scholars" and the spuriously precise appeal of structural metaphors, but make no effort to analyze the changes through which various political process ideas (once no more than a gleam in the eyes of a few Marxist scholars) came to dominate North American social movement writing. Jaswin leave open two possibilities: a) that for unavowed (but indubitably nefarious) reasons the elders deliberately foisted an unsound doctrine on their juniors, b) that the elders remain too befuddled, or too enchanted with their own meager accomplishments, for recognition of their position's evident weaknesses. As one of the elders, I defy Jaswin to document either alternative.

WHAT REMEDY DO JASWIN PROPOSE?

They propose a four-step treatment: 1) Abandon invariant models, 2) Beware of conceptual stretching, 3) Recognize that cultural and strategic processes define and create the factors usually portrayed as "structural," 4) do some splitting to balance all the lumping. The first and the fourth, in the Jaswin rendition, amount to the same remedy: particularize, differentiate, forget about generalization. Although the second prescription—beware of conceptual stretching—also becomes identical to the first and fourth when taken to an extreme, short of an absolute version it wisely warns analysts to prefer slim models over fat ones.

As for recognition that cultural and strategic processes define and create the factors usually portrayed as structural, the admonition amounts to advocacy of phenomenological fundamentalism. It asserts that consciousness exists prior to interaction, forms independently of interaction, and to some degree causes interaction. To those of us who hold to other ontologies, such as relation realism, holism, or even methodological individualism, the remedy entails bitter medicine.

HOW LIKELY IS THAT REMEDY TO CURE THE ILLNESS?

Here we arrive at the deepest ground of disagreement. Phenomenological fundamentalism constitutes a very unlikely source of explanations for

social processes, and a very likely source of explanatory tautologies in
which people do things because they have propensities to do those things.
Any thoroughgoing phenomenologist who wants to explain observed
social processes, however, will have to rely much more heavily on cognitive science, neuroscience, linguistics, and/or evolutionary genetics than
social movement analysts, including Jaswin, have so far shown any incli-
nation to do. If you analyze mental events, you must create or adopt a
theory of mind. Jaswin offer us no program for explanation of phenome-
nology and its changes.

Let's get this straight. Good conceptualization delimits zones of causal
coherence and identifies analogous processes while minimizing fruitless
analogies. Good description establishes what is to be explained. Sympathetic reconstruction of actors' situations often—but not always!—helps
separate superior from inferior explanations. But the long-run object of
the enterprise is explanation, the tracing of connected causes and effects.
The Jaswin program does not take us far in that direction.

WHAT ALTERNATIVES TO THE PROPOSED
TREATMENT MIGHT WE TRY?

Without replaying all the relational music I have been broadcasting in
recent years, let me suggest several tacks that social movement analysts—
and students of contentious politics in general—might fruitfully take:

- Define the problem not as the explanation of social movements but
  as the explanation of contentious politics, including both a) differences in the operation of contrasting forms of contentious politics
  within the same regimes, and b) differences in the operation of contentious politics within contrasting regimes. Social movements, in
  such a perspective, become just one historically shaped form of collective, mutual claim making.
- Interrogate received categories concerning the phenomenon to be
  explained, with their implication that each one represents either a
  causally coherent phenomenon or a well defined location within a
  coherent causal space; ask whether social movements, rebellions,
  nationalism, guerrilla, and other conventionally differentiated forms
  of contention represent coherent units or sites for causal analysis.
- Search not for universal patterns at the level of whole structures or
  sequences but for a) analogous causal mechanisms such as coalition
  formation, cyclical effects on claim making, innovation in repertoires,
  and representation of identities, b) conditions governing the combination and sequencing of those mechanisms.

- Recognize that, at best, such a search will not yield total accounts of complex events, processes, or structures—social movements or otherwise—but reliable, transferable explanations of significant elements within complex events, processes, or structures.
- Integrate the explanation of changing phenomenologies, identities, and collective representations into the analysis of interaction instead of treating it as prior to or separate from contentious interaction.
- On pain of permanent exclusion from the pages of *Sociological Forum*, ban forever the whole class of criticisms that complain, essentially, "You're underestimating the importance of the variables I find interesting."

That is the program that Doug McAdam, Sidney Tarrow, and I have been pursuing in collaboration for some time.

These days theories of contentious politics remain, as Jaswin say, contested, inconsistent, and poorly integrated. We bedside doctors need all the help we can get, especially when it comes to prescribing effective treatment. In a time of great uncertainty about diagnoses and prescriptions, after all, the quacks may actually turn out to be wise guys.

NOTE

Previously published in *Sociological Forum* 14, no. 1 (March 1999). Reprinted with permission.

3

Paradigm Warriors: Regress and Progress in the Study of Contentious Politics

SIDNEY TARROW

RASHOMAN IN CHIAPAS

In 1994, the Mexican economy is overheating. The poor are getting poorer and the rich—though richer—are dissatisfied with the palpable corruption of their government. The dominant political party, the PRI, in the saddle for a half-century, is divided between *politicos* and *tecnicos*. Internally divided, the PRI oligarchs no longer dare to repress their opponents as they have done in the past. Opposition parties of left and right are gaining leverage in local and state politics. Sensing blood, they offer their support to insurgent challengers outside the polity.

This is the opportunity insurgents have been waiting for. Taking advantage of the structural determinants outlined above and of the resources offered by indigenous anger, movement entrepreneurs launch a rebellion in the state of Chiapas. The government's repressive efforts are feeble and uncertain, and the opposition parties seize the opportunity offered by the rebels to attack it. Facing pressure from the U.S. government, amid a collapsing economy and increasingly bold challenges, the government has no choice but to negotiate. The Chiapas social movement succeeds because—like all social movements everywhere—it is able to seize political opportunities.

It is again 1994. The local people of Chiapas are suffering deprivation caused not only by their material poverty but by their cultural isolation. Made up largely of indigenous campesinos, they speak a language unrelated to Spanish, have little sympathy for those who rule them from the capital, and fear the loss of their native culture to North American market forces and the government's neo-liberal policies. Over the years, they have constructed a worldview in which those who work the land possess virtue, while those who own it lack legitimacy. The local cacique, the grain merchant, the policeman: all are the linear descendants of the conquistadores who conquered their land and destroyed their ancient community.

The rebellion of Chiapas is a rebellion in the name of these suppressed indigenous identities. But insurgent identities are not inherited wholesale from the past; they are actively constructed through agency into mobilized ones by cultural leaders. In this process, the personal narratives of ordinary people are transformed into dynamic worldviews and arrayed as collective stories in a cognitive struggle with hegemonic elites. Symbols of the Mexican past, like Emiliano Zapata, inspire them, while leaders resembling the heroes of successful Latin American revolutions, like Subcomandante Marcos, assure them that the justice they struggle for is greater than their own grievances.

CARTOONS AND CARICATURES

The Rashomanic sketches above are, of course, cartoons. Though both are recognizable as foreshortened versions of the rebellion that was mounted in Chiapas in 1994, there are at least three things wrong with them:

First, each is inaccurate and misleading in crucial details. Both ignore the considerable importance of the international media and of North American e-mail networks in publicizing the claims of the insurgents (Bob, 1997). Both underspecify the cleavages within Chiapas and ignore the considerable suspicion in which Marcos and his comrades were held by other Mexican progressive groups (Van Cott, 1997). Both elide the complex strategic evolution of the EZLF—from guevarist *foco* to neo-populist movement in response to the diffidence of the peasantry.

Second, both are theoretically impoverished. Cartoon One frames the Chiapas rebellion as a mechanism practically without agency, wholly dependent on structural opportunities and producing mobilization through the clever calculation of movement entrepreneurs. The forms of contention used, the mobilizing structures built, the frames of resistance developed, and the actors' interaction with significant others are either derivative of structural constructs or are simply ignored.

Cartoon Two ignores opportunities, mobilizing structures, repertoires, and interactions, raising agency and identity to monocausal virtues and providing no clue as to why the rebellion occurred when it did. After all, cultural assault, market incursion, and indigenous collective identities are hardly new to rural Mexico in the 1990s!

But these are not the greatest disadvantages of these two cartoons. From the standpoint of building a cumulative social science of popular contention, each is based on a caricature of a paradigm. While Cartoon Two has the virtue of calling attention to the actors involved, it sees them but from the standpoint of the sympathetic observers' idea of how poor peasants ought to resist oppressive others. As a result, it underspecifies the political factors that produced the Chiapas rebellion when it occurred, the opportunities opened up to insurgents by the recent NAFTA agreement, and the factors in Mexican politics that led it along the path it took.

In recognizing the importance of domestic opportunities in the launching of the rebellion, Cartoon One does propose an answer to the "Why Now?" question. But it specifies opportunity so broadly that any political change can be inferred as an opportunity post hoc. In focusing on a single social movement organization, it ignores other local conflicts—for example, between small-holders and local landless peasants, members of different religious denominations, and followers of the PRI and its political opponents[1]—as well as the transnational dimensions of the rebellion. We do not get very far in understanding real-life contentious politics with cartoons, or with the caricatures of paradigms that produce them.

PARADIGM WARFARE IN
SOCIAL MOVEMENT RESEARCH

I have of course drawn these cartoons tongue-in-cheek, to illustrate the dangers of one-sided and simplistic renderings of social movements embedded in complex and shifting contentious realities. But my cartoons are not all that different from how the history of social movements has been written over the past thirty years. Rather than a search for more synthetic models that can account for these histories, or focusing different models on different parts of the mobilization process (Klandermans, 1997a), such canned histories are often written by paradigm warriors seeking to vanquish the last stage of research. Since the 1960s, each time a general model has been proposed, a new wave of paradigm warriors steps forward, swords in hand, ready to slay the dragon of hegemonic discourse. As Howard Aldrich writes in another context, "Some observers write about . . . paradigms as if the competition between theories takes place at the levels of ideas, with 'good ideas' battling with 'bad ideas' in some sort of ideational arena" (1988:19).

For example, in the 1960s and 1970s, a resource mobilization model was developed that was antagonistic to the inherited collective behavior approach. Its proponents made a major advance on its predecessor, but they did it an injustice in zeroing in on its most simplistic torch-bearers and ignoring the complexities in its more thoughtful members. Resource mobilization got its comeuppance: in the 1980s, two new paradigms appeared. One hearkened back to political scientists' work of the late 1960s and 1970s (Eisinger, 1973; Lipsky, 1968; Piven and Cloward, 1971; Tilly, 1978) and came to be called "political process theory"—although that term considerably condensed its proponents' concerns (McAdam, 1982; Tarrow, 1983). The second, "new" social movement theory, drew on European structuralism but went considerably beyond it in the direction of social construction and identity politics (Melucci, 1985, 1988, 1996; Offe, 1985). Both groups smote resource mobilization for its excesses of economism and its apparent indifference to the beliefs of the aggrieved, but—in their urge to reify the "new" (see the critique in Calhoun, 1995), they foreshortened its contributions and ignored how deeply it influenced subsequent social movement research. But both drew on and learned from this tradition and, in turn, helped to influence its proponents' later research (see, for example, McCarthy et al., 1991, 1995; Zald, 1996).

Now in the mid-1990s, drawing half-consciously on the first tradition, two new paradigm warriors, Jeff Goodwin and James M. Jasper, launch a phenomenological critique of the second. Like their predecessors in the sequence of paradigm warfare, they regard their target as "hegemonic." They are assisted in doing so by a considerable effort of compression (including within it some authors—like Bert Klandermans and Mayer Zald—who might be surprised to find themselves in such company) and of reduction and selectivity (they focus on the recent generation of work in this perspective, exempting from attack its most prominent inventor, Charles Tilly, and forgetting that its origins lie in political scientists' and social historians' work of the 1960s and 1970s). Although they do not miss the lack of unanimity in the tradition in specifying political variables, their narrow focus leads them to overlook one of its dangers—excessive syncretism (see the critique in Lichbach, 1997).

Indeed, in the best tradition of paradigm warfare, Goodwin and Jasper reduce their focus to one aspect of the approach they criticize—in this case, to the concept of political opportunity structure. They deal with the extensive work on mobilizing structures and framing in the tradition as if they were afterthoughts of a structuralist fixation, largely ignoring the concepts of repertoires and cycles that are central to the political process approach (Traugott, 1995). Most important, they elide the fundamental interest in the mutual interaction among challengers, opponents, and third parties that has been central to this tradition since Tilly's construction of a polity model in the late 1970s. Although practitioners can certainly be found who mechanically regard political opportunity structure as the be-all and end-all producing mobilization, in centering on that concept as a kind of Rosetta stone of political process theory, Goodwin and Jasper ignore the fact that most political process theorists try to explain movements as the outcome of a combination of both structural and cultural, long-term and contingent factors and of the interactive logics of the political struggle (Tilly, 1978).

Goodwin and Jasper quote *Power in Movement* to the effect that "people join in social movements in response to political opportunities and then, though collective action, create new ones" (see chapter 1; Tarrow, 1994:17–18). It is *de bonne guerre* in paradigm warfare to quote a snippet of an author's work to reduce it to inconsequence. But turning only eight pages back in the same book, they would have found the following:

> Movements do have a collective action problem but it is social: coordinating unorganized, autonomous, and dispersed populations into common and sustained action. They solve this problem by (1) responding to political opportunities through the use of (2) known, modular forms of collective action, by (3) mobilizing people within social networks, and (4) through shared cultural understandings. (Tarrow, 1994:9)[2]

This fixation on POS is unfortunate, for it allows Goodwin and Jasper to paint their opponents as advocates of invariant models, and to virtually ignore their emphasis on identity formation within collective action (Tarrow, 1994:chap. 7; Tilly, 1997a), their historical rootedness (Meyer, 1990; Piven and Cloward, 1971, 1977; McAdam, 1988a; Tarrow, 1989; Schneider, 1995; Tilly, 1978, 1986, 1995b); the nesting of social movements in broader historical cycles (Goldstone, 1980a; McAdam, 1995; Tarrow, 1989; Tilly, 1995b); and especially their bringing interaction with states, opponents, and significant others into the study of contention (Brockett, 1995; della Porta, 1995; Kriesi et al., 1995).

Paradigm warfare need not be reductionist. Consider the creative encounter between the advocates of European "new" social movement theory and their American positivist opponents in the 1980s, documented in a series of conference volumes (Klandermans and Tarrow, 1988; Morris and Mueller, 1992). It led, among other things, to new social movement theorist Hanspeter Kriesi and his collaborators' *New Social Movements in Western Europe* (1995). Or think of the sharpening of perspectives about the fuzzy concept of "globalization" and its implications for transnational contention in Margaret Keck and Katherine Sikkink's *Activists Beyond Borders* (1998) or the recent debate on global flows of labor and capital in *International Labor and Working Class History* (1995). In contrast with these debates, Goodwin and Jasper employ an ax to chop down a two-dimensional shrub of their own creation, in place of the scalpel that would be needed to dissect the many-sided synthetic plant that their subjects have been cultivating over three decades of work.

FROM SOCIAL MOVEMENT REDUCTIONISM TO CONTENTIOUS POLITICS

Let me illustrate the dangers of paradigm warfare with one example. Goodwin and Jasper argue that advocates of political process models promise "a causally adequate, universal theory or 'model' of social movements" (see chapter 1). Now social movements make a nice target; but in narrowing their scope to movements, Goodwin and Jasper ignore a major innovation of the political process approach over its predecessors: to embed the study of movements within a larger universe of contentious politics and thence to politics in general (McAdam, Tarrow, and Tilly, 1997; Oliver, 1989; Tarrow, 1994; Tilly, 1995b).

Political process theorists argue that the social movement is a historically specific subtype of contentious politics, and not its sole and universal expression (Tarrow, 1994; Tilly, 1995b). That argument cannot even be critically examined by critics who assume that "social movements" are the alpha and omega of the writers they criticize. Ignoring this point leads Goodwin and Jasper to elide some of the major contributions of political process theorists: their discoveries about the modularity and institutionalization of repertoires of contention (Tilly 1978, 1986, 1995b and the contributions to Traugott, 1995); their work on the complex and recursive reciprocity between movement challengers and members of the polity (Costain, 1992; Tarrow, 1989, 1994; Tilly, 1978, 1995b); how the structure of opportunities intersects with historical cleavage structures to produce substantially different patterns of contention from country to country or from region to region (Amenta et al., 1992; Kriesi et al., 1995; Tarrow, 1994:chap. 4); the impact of contentious experiences on participants' lives long after the movements in which they took part have disappeared (McAdam, 1988a); and how, in cycles of protest, movements both gain resources and contribute opportunities to other forms of contention and to more institutional actors (Tarrow, 1989, 1998b; Giugni, McAdam, and Tilly, 1999).

This author is not alone in his plea that polemical attacks on paradigms give way to more serious confrontations between data, variables, and models. From one theoretical perspective, John Lofland regrets that theory bashing has become common practice in movement literature (1993). From another, Bert Klandermans regrets excessive disciplinary fragmentation and surveys different attempts for synthesizing theoretical frameworks (1997b). From a third, Freidhelm Neidhart and Dieter Rucht elaborate a subtle and complex grid of variables for the study of contention (1993).

With my collaborators, Ron Aminzade, Jack Goldstone, Elizabeth Perry, Doug McAdam, William Sewell Jr., and Charles Tilly and our associates from a number of universities, and with the support of the Mellon Foundation and the Center for Advanced Study in the Behavioral Sciences, we have been attempting, from different theoretical perspectives, to broaden the compass of social movement theory to other areas of contention, and from the western democracies from which most of our current models derive to other parts of the world and to other types of systems. Our hope is to challenge our own political process models by confronting them with new and more demanding contexts and different theoretical traditions.

Paradigm warfare has a place in the annals of research. But to the degree that it is reductive, selective, and polemical, it produces caricatures instead of critiques and cartoons instead of research. Towards the end of their article, Goodwin and Jasper sketch the first outlines of a different research agenda. Rather than political process models, they call for a phenomenological individualism that will overcome the defects of what they see as an overwhelming emphasis on the political process. In future contributions, they will hopefully specify what this will mean in practice and how it will take us beyond a call for better description. Their readers await with interest their success in doing so.

NOTES

Previously published in *Sociological Forum* 14, no. 1 (March 1999). Reprinted with permission.

I am grateful to Ron Aminzade, Clifford Bob, Judy Hellman, Doug McAdam, and Charles Tilly for help in preparing this chapter.

1. I am grateful to conversations with Judy Hellman for this information. The simple "peasant-landlord" dichotomy that underlies much North American research on peasants is belied by the complexity of conflicts between different linguistic groups, religious denominations and those with different political affiliations.

2. Even reading page one of the same book would have told them that its author believes that: Triggered by the incentives created by political opportunities, combining conventional and challenging forms of action and building on social networks and cultural frames is how movements overcome the obstacles to collective action and sustain their interactions with opponents and with the state (Tarrow, 1994:1).

4

Tending the Vineyard: Cultivating Political Process Research

DAVID S. MEYER

Goodwin and Jasper's criticisms of various iterations of political process theory are incorrectly applied to the entire developing paradigm. Their indictment offers a rigid and narrow representation of the theory and rejects the social science enterprise of building theory altogether. At the same time, their criticisms raise important puzzles for scholars working on social movements, particularly about defining opportunities, and studying culture. I answer their criticisms of the theory, acknowledge useful questions and challenges that they offer, and conclude by suggesting an agenda for research on social movements in the future.

Consumer reporters on television news have learned that one way to garner ratings is to jury-rig some piece of machinery to explode. It's not so difficult: take a coffee machine, pull out any flame-resistant safety protections, fray the power cord, double the amount of electricity going to the machine, then wait. Eventually you'll get the flames that television producers know produce a bump in the ratings. The flaming machine makes for good pictures and momentary attention, and is a viable device for an ambitious reporter seeking exposure. Manufacturers' assertions that the reporters operated in reckless disregard of perfectly understandable directions garner less attention than the dramatic fire in the studio kitchen. Professors Goodwin and Jasper have treated political opportunity approaches like coffee machines, dismantling and distorting them, then complaining that they don't make very good rice or wine either.

If Goodwin and Jasper are indeed caught in a "winding, snarling vine," it is clearly their own doing. Still, if well-meaning and intelligent scholars can become so confused, perhaps their errors can lead us to recognize challenges for political opportunity approaches in the future. Because we

47

work, after all, in a *social* science, it's better to point out some of the twists
and kinks the critics have found in political process theories, perhaps to
help them disentangle themselves, or to suggest directions for work in the
future.

In responding to their criticisms, I will briefly review their charges, noting where they have gone astray. I will then sketch the development of
the political process approach, suggest a few places where Goodwin and
Jasper can lead us to do better work within it, and argue for concerted
efforts to answer some essential questions about the relationships
between mainstream politics and protest movements.

THE INDICTMENT

Goodwin and Jasper argue that the "political process" tradition (hereafter
PPT) has become an hegemonic straitjacket for the study of social movements, although it is "conceptually muddled," and that major strands
within it (e.g., political opportunity, "political process model") are
unduly vague, tautological, or just wrong. Overly biased toward "structural" factors, the political opportunity approach "promises" an "invariant model" of social movements that it cannot deliver, and mechanizes
the analysis of social protest and contention. PPT further mandates a limited and distorted means of studying culture, frame analysis. Structure is
overemphasized, culture is flattened, and the study of social movements
suffers as a result.

Goodwin and Jasper want to make a strong rhetorical case, and this
leads them to make if not fallacious, surely misleading, claims about the
target. Such rhetorical strategies are easily recognizable; they are the academic equivalent of the flaming coffee machine:

1. Inflating the claims of your chosen opponents (for example, the
   stress on the essentially nonexistent invariant models);
2. Selecting the opponents' exemplars with your goals of discrediting
   what they exemplify in mind (that is, the linking of political process
   and ideationally oriented frame analysis, a connection essential to
   PPT only in the writing of these critics);
3. Defining the opponents and allies without describing how. Thus,
   McAdam and Tarrow represent the bad political opportunity theorists, while collaborator Tilly is exempted from rhetorical fire. Some
   of my own writing, firmly within PPT, is cited as criticism of that
   tradition. The PPT boundaries are drawn in such a fashion that they
   can be redrawn momentarily to accommodate any given charge.
4. Emphasizing contradictory formulations by people within PPT, of

which there are more than a few. (Implicitly, of course, this belies the notion that political process has really become hegemonic, but why quibble.)

These are time-honored and sporadically effective rhetorical devices, and it would be ungracious to deny the critics their flourishes. Further, Goodwin and Jasper have identified some unresolved issues in the study of social movements that could provide coherent research agendas for those of us concerned with coming up with viable explanations and building more general theories of the emergence, development, and outcomes of social protest. At the same time, Goodwin and Jasper have understated the concerns and qualifications of PPT analysts, while overinflating their claims, in such a way that these critics have undermined their own case and neglected important developments on the horizon in our field. We need to start by addressing the history of social movement studies, tempered with a little recognition of the way social science works, then figure out where we need to go from here.

THE DEVELOPMENT OF POLITICAL
PROCESS THEORY

The political process approach arose in response to both empirical and theoretical inadequacies in existing studies of social protest movements. More comprehensive literature reviews are available elsewhere (e.g., recent reviews are included in Gamson and Meyer, 1996; Meyer and Staggenborg, 1996), but a brief one follows: After World War II studies of social movements emphasized the irrational elements of protest, such that "collective behavior" was used to describe large groups of people gone crazy—like Nazis in interwar Germany. The basic tenets of collective behavior approaches (that is, irrational activity by atomized individuals lacking other means of pursuing their claims) didn't stand empirical examination in explaining any cases, much less the politics of protest in America in the 1960s.

In looking at the protest movements of the 1960s, "resource mobilization" (e.g., Lipsky, 1970; McCarthy and Zald, 1977) provided something of a corrective to collective behavior, emphasizing the intentionality and rationality of protesters, but treatments often neglected the political factors that provided grievances, resources, and openings to challengers. Even at this point, however (see Perrow, 1979 for a distinction among resource mobilization approaches), some scholars were very attentive to the broader social processes and political circumstances that affected the ability for challengers to lodge claims effectively (e.g., Piven and Cloward, 1977; Lipsky, 1970; Tilly, 1978; Gamson, 1990).

The essential emphasis of the PPT approach, as it developed in the 1970s and 1980s, is that activists don't choose goals, strategies, and tactics in a vacuum. Rather, the political context, conceptualized fairly broadly, sets the grievances around which activists mobilize, advantaging some claims and disadvantaging others. Further, the organization of the polity, and the positioning of various actors within it, makes some strategies of influence more attractive, and potentially efficacious, than others. The wisdom, creativity, and outcomes of activists' choices, briefly their agency, can only be understood and evaluated by looking at the political context and the rules of the games in which those choices are made (structure). Thoughtful explanations of particular movements, and even broader theories of politics and change (e.g., Lipset, 1963; Huntington, 1968) recognized this, but explicit theorizing about how context affects choices about claims and tactics developed more slowly.

If we want to understand the choices that activists make, we need to assess not only the resources available to groups of challengers, but also the available avenues for making claims. In order for organizers to mobilize protest, potential activists need to be convinced that this tactic is both necessary and potentially effective in getting them what they want from government. If government appears likely to respond to less disruptive means of participation, it will generally be hard to convince many people to take on the risks and difficulties of protesting. And, if government makes protest even less attractive, perhaps by harshly repressing protesters or by offering no prospects of responding to dissent, protest mobilization is less likely. This all makes sense, as does the recognition that governments can make protest less likely by *either* offering less costly, often more institutional, means of participation or by repressing protest more aggressively. Thus, greater openness or less openness can shut down the prospects for a social movement to emerge, and the opportunities for protest are essentially *curvilinear* (see Eisinger, 1973; Tilly, 1978). Obviously, some constituencies are more likely to respond to greater openness, which enables them to express political grievances through collective action. Others are more likely to resort to protest when the prospects for meaningful access through more conventional political participation are foreclosed; provocation and exclusion are more significant opportunities in such cases.

Openings were most important for providing meaningful opportunities for political protest to African Americans in the United States during the heyday of the civil rights movement. Building upon the recognition of context in some resource mobilization work, McAdam (1982) offered a fully elaborated and theoretically grounded case study in the political process tradition, one that emphasized the connections between this social movement and the world around it. His work offered a good analysis of why African Americans mobilized in different ways at different times by looking at the political context. He offered a model for refinement and testing based on this theory, a model that has in fact been opened rather than more narrowly specified. In subsequent political opportunity work, most analysts have been content to add to, rather than contest, particular aspects of political opportunity (Meyer and Minkoff, 1997).

An Invariant Model?

Some of the particulars, as Goodwin and Jasper contend, don't generalize as well as McAdam's earlier writing would lead us to hope—although the figure they reproduce from the 1982 book has not, to my knowledge, appeared anywhere else in the intervening fifteen years. In other words, no one ever offered the McAdam figure as an "invariant model." It is hardly surprising to any serious scholar, least of all McAdam, that the factors affecting the political prospects of African Americans would be different than those affecting, say, environmental activists. Specifically, African Americans, excluded from meaningful institutional participation in the South, needed openings, that is, more political space, in order to generate a significant political movement. In contrast, environmental groups, comprised primarily of educated middle- and upper-middle class people, who normally enjoy access to conventional politics and potential influence on policy through conventional mechanisms like voting and lobbying, are more likely to respond with protest when institutions close their doors (see Schlozman and Tierney, 1986).

Given McAdam's (1982) topic, it is understandable that he focused on openings, and it is also completely understandable that the pattern defined by African-American mobilization in the United States doesn't apply to every other social movement. Goodwin and Jasper have taken McAdam's general framework, turned it into a template, offered it as a cookie-cutter model for all sorts of claimants, then reacted with feigned alarm when it doesn't always work.

Because McAdam's civil rights model doesn't explain all social movements, Goodwin and Jasper seem to contend, we should abandon altogether the project of developing a more general model of protest politics. Such desperate resignation seems to me to be contrary to the very spirit of social science. Goodwin and Jasper's call to abandon invariant theories reads like a cry of despair. Rather than throw up our hands in the face of complexity and variation, it seems to make more sense to work to examine and test particular propositions across cases, and to work to develop more complex and variegated models for understanding protest politics. If we want to develop a broader understanding of the processes that give rise to social protest, Goodwin and Jasper have pointed to exactly the challenges we face in doing so: the definitions of political opportunity employed, and the relationship of political opportunity variables to social mobilization.

Affixing Frames?

Most PPT analyses focus on the world outside the social movement and observable phenomena that allow social protest to emerge. But opportunities do not *cause* protest; once we acknowledge this, our attention rightly turns to the factors that contribute to successful mobilization when opportunities are available. Because a potential activist needs to believe that protest is both necessary and potentially effective, it is entirely appropriate to examine the sources of those cognitions. Some work within PPT explicitly examines the development of the belief that protest is an appropriate strategy, as organizers project and mediate news of external events to encourage political mobilization (e.g., McAdam, 1982; Meyer, 1990, 1993; Gamson and Meyer, 1996; Kurzman, 1996). Surely the connection between political affairs and citizens' perceptions of those affairs and their own efficacy is an important area for empirical research and theorizing in the study of social protest. Frame analysis is one approach to conducting such studies.

Some political process analysts, however, make no mention of frames in their work, while other scholars who work with frames pay little attention to political opportunities (e.g., Benford and Hunt, 1992; Snow and Benford, 1992). Because, however, one important edited volume (McAdam, McCarthy, and Zald, 1996a) devotes a section explicitly to framing, Goodwin and Jasper propose that framing is an essential part of political process theory, and the only method that the PPT offers for studying culture. Having asserted a necessary relationship between frame analysis and PPT, Goodwin and Jasper then lodge substantial charges, some deserved, against some research using frames, and by implication, damn PPT.

The critics' unfortunate use of a polemical broad brush should not prevent us from seeing some merits in their charges. Goodwin and Jasper contend that frame analysis offers only a partial window on culture, which it tends to flatten and reify, that it suffers from an ideational bias, and that it provides an overly instrumental or rationalist perspective on both culture and dissident culture. The rapid spread of frame metaphors to all sorts of research in the social science means that it is quite easy to find published work that exhibits all of the unfortunate tendencies that

Goodwin and Jasper identify—as well as others that contradict their charges. Each overly rationalist frame treatment is counterbalanced by another one that is unduly ideational or postmodernist. Ultimately, the charges and defenses of frame analysis may merit a debate and symposium of their own. In the meantime, however, let us turn to productive ways that this work can be used in the study of social movements.

First, although some work on frames suffers from an ideational bias that flattens culture, such that culture comes to mean the self-conscious activities of organizers, much work explicitly does not (e.g., Clemens, 1996; Gamson and Meyer, 1996). Indeed, analysts with an interest in helping activists make claims argue persuasively that activists are insufficiently strategic in crafting analyses and claims, and advise them how to do better (see Ryan, 1991). A promising area of research, following McAdam (1996b), is to look at the material bases of framing, and the ways in which dissident analyses can be projected (see also Meyer, 1995).

Second, effective organizers, like Martin Luther King, *are* strategic in making choices about language, claims, and opponents, but they are constrained in what they can say and do, not only by their own experiences, but also by the experiences of the people they are trying to mobilize (see Tarrow, 1994). Swidler's (1986) "tool kit" metaphor is helpful here, as dissidents make choices about presentation of self and claims, but not in circumstances of their own design.

Third, Goodwin and Jasper are absolutely right that we need additional and more productive ways to study culture and social movements. Fortunately, a small cohort of scholars are developing productive ways to look at culture within movements. Most promising, I think, is the attention to "cultural practices" or "identity practices," that is, what people do, as a means of observing and understanding culture. Scholars use the tools of long-form interviews, participant-observation, and other elements of the ethnographer's craft (see Kurtz, 2002; Lichterman 1996; Whittier, 1995). This is promising work, and leads, much to the surprise of some of these scholars, back to political process, that is, the external context that movements draw from and seek to change.

The development of more work on the connections between cultural practices, social movements, and political dissent will help us understand the degree to which PPT, which explicitly addresses only movements that make explicit political claims, can explain other sorts of movements, including apolitical or cultural movements.[1]

THEORY AND SOCIAL SCIENCE

Goodwin and Jasper's criticisms are strangely negligent about the way social science research takes place. Although they are right to recognize

that PPT is becoming the dominant paradigm in the study of social protest movements, this is hardly a cause for despair. They complain at once
that all adherents to PPT do not agree on all the details and hypotheses
they work with, and simultaneously that advocates of PPT offer a rigid
and inflexible approach to understanding social protest. The contradictions that so annoy Goodwin and Jasper may stem from their fundamental misunderstanding of paradigms in the social sciences. The dominance
of a paradigm doesn't imply that all of the essential questions are settled,
or even that there is an essential consensus on research agendas and
methods.[2] Rather, a paradigm organizes the gathering of research, and
the ordering of observed facts, as well as setting the critical questions for
subsequent research (Kuhn, 1970), and PPT offers the most promising
way of working to settle many of the outstanding questions we now confront.

PPT correctly turns analysts' attention to the world outside social
movements, but not to exclusion of strategy and tactics. Indeed, if we are
to develop a good understanding of the process by which activists make
choices about strategies and tactics, and the wisdom of those choices, we
need to understand the weight that external factors play in those calculations. Meaningful understanding of agency can only come with attention
to structure. Political process emphasizes the connections between challengers and those they challenge, particularly in more conventional politics and political institutions, in order to understand what they do and
what impact they have (e.g., Soule, 1997). This approach has been winning the day within serious studies of movements, progressively gaining
more adherents and informing more empirical and theoretical treatments
of cases, because it explains cases and organizes research better than the
approaches it is supplanting. Even scholars who do not employ the terminology of opportunities pay more attention to context and the inside of
the political arena. This is all to the good, but it does create some of the
problems that Goodwin and Jasper point to about nomenclature, specificity, predictive values, and overgeneralization. As a result, there is a
great deal of work to be done in working out details of a more comprehensive political process model, and in resolving apparently contradictory propositions within the theory.

Much of this will occur naturally through the scholarly process, encouraged through peer review. Authors of journal articles soon learn the
importance of "qualifying" the universe of cases that they mean to
explain, as well as calling for exactly the kind of further research that will
determine the boundaries of qualified cases. Collegial criticism, such as
Goodwin and Jasper's critique, is also a part of this process. Alas, rather
than trying to help sort out some of the key issues in building PPT, Goodwin and Jasper ask us to back away from larger theoretical concerns and

ambitions and simply explain particular cases. It's but a half-step from here down the slide to a dreary postmodern abyss. We must do better.

WHAT IS TO BE DONE

While some of the key proponents of political process approaches are out to cultivate new areas in political sociology and political science (see McAdam, Tarrow, and Tilly, 1996, 1997), there remains a great deal of work to be done within the paradigm, examining, refining and testing hypotheses, and confronting paradoxes, and building a broader understanding of the way in which social protest works. Goodwin and Jasper's critique fortunately affords us an opportunity to pose some of the most salient puzzles and problems that merit coherent efforts at empirical research and theoretical development.

1. *Separating Opportunities, Mobilization, and Influence.* Goodwin and Jasper contend that PPT explains so much that it explains nothing at all. These critics are right that analysts who do this work are generally interested in movements, so they look for movements and then read back to find expanding political opportunities. This approach risks conflating opportunities with mobilization, which can be a problem, but it is one of method more than theory. Goodwin and Jasper suggest that analysts make no effort to separate the two, implicitly producing the causal argument that they seek to hang on PPT adherents. This is both unfair and untrue. At least one political process analyst wrote in 1990:

> Movements . . . are the product of more than opportunity; they represent the efforts of groups and individuals not only to take advantage of opportunity but also to alter the subsequent opportunity structure. . . . A breakdown in the functioning of the state or society increases the political space available for dissident social movements. *It does not, however, create these movements, nor does it ensure their success. . . . A movement's success in mobilizing or achieving policy goals is a function of how well it and its competitors . . . respond to that limited opportunity and the extent to which they fill or expand the available political space.* (Meyer 1990:8, emphasis added)

It's possible that Goodwin and Jasper missed my work, or perhaps forgot to acknowledge representations of political opportunity that defy their critique. At the same time, it's harder to think that they would ignore the explicit warnings of their explicit targets. As example, McAdam (1982:40) is clear that opportunities are chances for excluded groups, who under normal circumstances face large obstacles in advancing their interests, to act collectively and effectively, and Tarrow (1998b) opens his book with this same qualification. Similarly, Tilly (1978:100) writes about opportunities as factors that raise or lower the costs of collective action, thus making some strategies more attractive than others. Nowhere do any of them suggest that opportunities force the decisions about choices and claims, so much as frame those decisions.

Another problem is implicitly identified here. PPT analysts look at opportunities to act collectively (e.g., McAdam, 1982; Tilly, 1978) and opportunities to act effectively, that is, to influence policy (e.g., Piven and Cloward, 1979), although there is no necessary relationship between these two sorts of opportunities. Indeed, for groups that mobilize in the face of increased exclusion, we would expect opportunity to mobilize extra-institutionally to be inversely related to the opportunity to exercise meaningful influence on policy. Too rarely have analysts separated these issues analytically (but see McAdam, 1996a; Meyer and Minkoff, 1997), and Goodwin and Jasper are right to press us to do so.

2. *The Good News/Bad News Paradox.* Goodwin and Jasper are right that McAdam's "expanding opportunities" (expressed as enhanced openings) model is either applicable only to a limited set (albeit perhaps extensive) of social movements, or unduly vague. McAdam's (1982) work on the civil rights movement suggests that openings in government, represented by favorable decisions on matters of policy, rhetorical concessions from political leaders, and the increased number of substantial allies in government, all aid mobilization. In this formulation, good news on matters of policy is also good news for mobilization. Costain (1992) finds a similar pattern for women mobilizing in the second wave of the women's movement. But in my own work on movements against nuclear weapons (Meyer, 1990, 1993), the opposite seems to be the case. Antinuclear movements in the United States have emerged in the face of unfavorable decisions on policy and when their established allies were excluded from the inner councils of policymaking. When they got favorable changes in rhetoric, policy, and political inclusion, extra-institutional mobilization faded. Smith (1996) identifies a similar pattern for activists against the United States' intervention in Central America. Similarly, in matters of abortion policy in the United States, one side mobilizes in response to envisaged threats from government. Thus, we are treated to the sight of both sides eagerly claiming defeat in the wake of ambiguous or vague Supreme Court decisions (Meyer and Staggenborg, 1996).

One answer, that offered by Goodwin and Jasper, is to stop trying to make sense of this apparent puzzle. But if the test of a good theory is its ability to generate useful, and presumably solvable, puzzles (Kuhn, 1977:276), PPT has indeed been fruitful. We should certainly be mindful of the sorts of cases particular sequences of causes apply to, but we should not hesitate to try to build broader theories and larger generalizations. Rather, we should be working to figure out the circumstances under which different sorts of constituencies mobilize. We should be able to identify what sorts of movements respond to what sorts of opportunities, specifically, why some claimants protest in response to favorable policy from the state, and others to unfavorable policies. My hunch is that the curvilinear nature of political opportunity is critical here, that some claimants need to be enabled to make protest claims, whereas others will only do so when disabled from using more conventional strategies effectively. Empirical research, of course, can resolve this issue.

3. *Missed Opportunities.* If, as I have suggested above, movements are efforts to take advantage of opportunities, and are not always successful at doing so, then we should begin identifying elements of favorable opportunity when strong extrainstitutional movements don't take place. In this regard, periods of apparent quiescence can be as interesting as periods of mobilization (see Gaventa, 1980). Understanding the whys and wherefores of such *missed opportunities* may give us heretofore unseen analytical insight into the importance of strategic and tactical choices made by activists. It may also produce something on the order of an activist social science that could be of use to people who want to make, and not just study, social change.

4. *Movement-Movement Influences.* With a few notable exceptions (e.g., Gamson, 1990; Tarrow, 1989; Kriesi et al., 1995; Tilly, 1995b), most studies of movements concern the trajectory (or some smaller piece) of one movement in one country. This sort of work can answer important questions, but does less to refine the model of political opportunity than could otherwise be the case. What's more, people usually study movements they like—although the study itself may change initial feelings of affection. This means that certain kinds of cases don't get studied, and this is problematic for the development of theory, and indeed, for the comprehensiveness of knowledge produced by the academy. Goodwin and Jasper make much of McAdam's (1995) provocative and untested proposition that political opportunities are less important to so-called "spin-off" movements than to "initiator" movements. Subsequent research that details the web of relationships among movements over time may show that grouping movements in one of these categories is neither so easy nor so useful. We need to know how movements alter the opportunities for both allies (Meyer and Whittier, 1994; Minkoff, 1997) and for opponents (Meyer and Staggenborg, 1996).

5. *Political Processes in Different Settings.* The PPT approach that Goodwin and Jasper criticize is forged almost exclusively in the context of advanced industrial democracies (but see Brockett, 1995; Boudreau, 1996; Hochstetler, 1994; Schneider, 1995; Schock, 1996). The degree to which these theories are applicable to the rest of the world is not known. Comparative work in less developed countries, and work that addresses the

effects that other nations and supranational bodies have on opportunities for dissent within them, will inform and broaden political process explanations for social protest. Such work will necessarily consider both structural factors (e.g., the multinational economic boycott of apartheid South Africa) and cognitive factors (e.g., the support and encouragement Vaclav Havel claimed to take from peace campaigners in the United States and Western Europe).

6. *Opportunities Within Particular Venues.* Within any state, claims-making takes place in different venues, and challengers' choices of venues are dependent upon the nature of rules, institutions, norms, procedures, and alliances well below the broad level of the state. We would benefit from work explicitly addressing the ways states can channel conflict or dissent into particular political institutions, and how movement conduct changes over time as result. In a liberal polity, we would expect the openness of the courts to challenges on rights, for example, to influence the strategic choices that dissidents concerned with rights make, perhaps focusing on the courts to the exclusion of other venues (e.g., Meyer and Staggenborg, 1998). It will be important to understand why movements choose to make their demands in particular institutions at particular times, and the role that states have in conditioning these choices.

7. *Tactical Innovation.* Political process approaches should give us considerable latitude in understanding the choice of tactics, and not just from a social control point of view (channeling and learning). The issue of tactics at once raises two critical issues: how activists choose the tactics they do; and, the differential effects of tactical choice, that is, when does nonviolent protest, for example, produce the outcomes activists desire? Alas, little work explicitly considers particular tactics or tactical evolution, although McAdam (1983) and Tilly (1995b) offer promising models for subsequent research.

8. *Public Policy.* Public policy is both a dependent variable, as a measure of movement success, and a component in political opportunity that movements address. Yet, at least partly a function of the odd division of labor between political science and sociology, few scholars of movements explicitly consider changes in policy. The language used by policy analysts (e.g., Kingdon, 1984; Baumgartner and Jones, 1993) is strikingly similar to that of PPT analysts, but the literatures generally speak past each other. Changes in policy can be the achievements (e.g., Piven and Cloward, 1979; Amenta, Dunleavy, and Bernstein, 1994; Burstein, Bricher, and Einwohner, 1995) of social movements, as well as the grievances for subsequent movements (e.g., Meyer, 1993; Smith, 1996). We need to develop a better understanding of how policy and movements affect one another.

9. *Hard Cases.* When scholars began to see movements as continuous

with more conventional politics, they studied phenomena that made sense within this framework. We need work on more marginal groups, as well as more established ones, seeing the sorts of signals to which they respond. I think that the marginalized groups are also related to the political process, and this is something that needs more explicit empirical work. The political process approach has encouraged researchers to pay more attention to more rational challengers. In moving away from earlier mass society approaches we've risked neglecting that crazy people also engage in social protest, as anti-abortion evangelist and murderer John Salvi's tragic life and death reminds us. Current work within political process tells us little about this. Journalistic accounts of movements on the marginal right (e.g., Finnegan, 1997) suggest the promise of analytical opportunity treatments in understanding these problems.

10. *Nomenclature.* As Goodwin and Jasper point out, people use the same phrase to describe different things, and alas, there is no easy way to resolve this, save for the long-term process of continued publication, review, and careful reading. In the natural and technical sciences, where patents or lawsuits may follow the nomenclature, well-established investigators can negotiate binding settlements about naming, as Drs. Montagner and Gallo did over the AIDS virus. It doesn't work that way, alas, in social science, and persuasively argued cases and terms may ultimately win out, but not necessarily quickly or easily. After all, people who work in this field still argue about the operational definition and the qualifying cases of both social movements and revolutions—as Goodwin well knows.

There is then a great deal to be done in developing the political process approach and we should be grateful to Goodwin and Jasper for raising challenges for the community of scholars engaged in research on social protest. It is, however, no time to step away from the larger challenge of building theory. Rather, we should put on a pot of coffee and get to work.

NOTES

Previously published in *Sociological Forum* 14, no. 1 (March 1999). Reprinted with permission.

1. I have no interest in refuting the charge that political process accounts don't explain movements that don't make political claims; political process analysts have never claimed to explain movements that are not explicitly political, like "hip-hop." It will be interesting, however, to see the degree to which external political circumstances affect the development of non-political movements.

2. As Kuhn notes (1970:17) "To be accepted as a paradigm, a theory must seem better than its competitors, but it need not, and in fact never does, explain all the facts with which it can be confronted."

5

Political. Opportunity. Structure. Some Splitting to Balance the Lumping

RUUD KOOPMANS

THE CRITIQUE

A question: what is a "ubiquitous and constitutive dimension of all social relations, structures, networks, and practices" that "permeates all variables, even the most structural ones"? The Holy Lord? An unholy alliance between the CIA, the Mafia, and Saddam Hussein? Or maybe that structurally biased, conceptually overstretched, invariant, vile vine called political opportunity structure that suffocates social movement research? No, it is none of these. It is Culture, long-time and unrivaled world champion in the Hall of Fame of winding, snarling, and concept stretching.

The proposal to drive out the devilish sins of political opportunity structure by the Beelzebub of culture written large is one of a number of contradictions in Goodwin and Jasper's critique of the political opportunity model.[1] Although there is much reason to criticize this model—and Goodwin and Jasper adequately identify many of these flaws—the authors do not really seem interested in curing it from its ills. No matter which version of the model they inspect, the verdict is always guilty: if not of tautology, than of triviality or inadequacy; if not of invariant modeling, than of too much variety. The only thing that never changes is the solution: culture. Let us briefly discuss Goodwin and Jasper's arguments.

Is Political Opportunity Structure an Invariant Model or a Variety of Models?

It is both. If we may believe Goodwin and Jasper, one of the political opportunity model's most serious sins is its tendency toward invariant modeling in a search for universal covering laws. This claim remains an assertion, since no examples of such disrespect for history and context are actually presented. On the contrary, the authors point out that most analyses employ the concept in ways that are geared to specific movements and research questions and, as they grudgingly have to admit, "employ . . . sometimes historically and situationally specific . . . variables." Does this make Goodwin and Jasper happy? Of course not. They simply turn their argument around and criticize such analyses for failing to agree on one invariant model.

Is Political Opportunity Structure Too Broad or Too Narrow?

Again, it is both. Some versions of the political opportunity model are rightly criticized for their overstretching of the concept and for including many things that are not political, not opportunity, not structural, or none of these three. Verdict: trivial and ultimately tautological. Goodwin and Jasper's critique is hardly original here, as many authors have emphasized that political opportunity structure should stick to its turf. But Goodwin and Jasper are hard to please. While the broad versions commit the crime of wanting to explain everything and thereby ultimately explain nothing at all, the more modest, narrow operationalizations receive the verdict "inadequate or implausible" because they do not explain everything.

The Solution: Anything Goes (As Long As It Contains a Healthy Dose of Culture)

To argue for context sensitive theory is one thing; to embrace all-out theoretical eclecticism is quite another. Too much parsimony may not be what we need, no parsimony at all is hardly an attractive alternative. No doubt a bombardment with "a variety of concepts and theories may help us 'hit' this moving target" (i.e., collective action and social movements). If one theory or concept does not work, then another will: "Some movements require political opportunities, while others do not; some recruit through preexisting social networks while others do not; some require powerful grievances or collective identities, while others do not." If this is the answer, could someone please repeat the question?

WHAT IS REALLY WRONG WITH POLITICAL OPPORTUNITY STRUCTURE?

Even though their alternative is unconvincing and their critique is sometimes inconsistent, Goodwin and Jasper do point at some major deficiencies in the way in which political opportunity structure has been theoretically conceptualized and empirically employed. Even staunch adherents must acknowledge that the political opportunity perspective in its present state has done everything to deserve the kind of beating it receives from Goodwin and Jasper. A tendency to overstretch the concept is apparent, the notion of structure is often vague, and the lack of agreement on even the most basic common denominator indeed blocks theoretical advancement. As Goodwin and Jasper point out, one of the signs of vagueness and confusion is the alternate use of "political opportunity structure" and "political opportunities" as if they were the same. In fact, the situation is worse still. Draw a random text from the political opportunity literature and there is a fair chance that you will encounter not only these two labels but also "opportunity structure" and plain "opportunities," all used as synonyms or convenient shorthand. The problem is that they do not mean the same thing and are often used to refer to different things without this being acknowledged. Read "opportunity structure" and be aware of the introduction of explanatory factors that are not political; read "political opportunities" and watch for factors that are not structural in any sense; read "opportunities" and witness the inclusion of "context" or "environment" in a general sense, structural or not, political or otherwise. Because such additional explanatory factors are implicitly subsumed under the umbrella of "political opportunity structure," the model is indeed often guilty of structural imperialism, political imperialism, or a combination of both.

Opportunity

The notion of political opportunity structure in fact contains three logically independent claims about the origins of social movement emergence and development that need to be distinguished and have to be evaluated separately:

(1) variations in opportunity are the most important determinant of variations in collective action;
(2) relevant variations in opportunity result primarily from the interaction of social movements with political actors and institutions; and
(3) variations in such opportunities are not random or a mere product of strategic interaction, but are to an important extent structurally shaped.

The core idea uniting the approach is that opportunities are the most important determinant of variations in levels and forms of protest behavior among social groups, spatial units, and historical periods, and not grievances (motivations), resources (capacities), or something else. "Opportunity" is seldom defined, but generally refers to constraints, possibilities and threats that originate outside the mobilizing group, but affect its chances of mobilizing and/or of realizing its collective interests. Structural characteristics of political systems, the behavior of allies, adversaries and the public, societal "moods," economic structures and developments, cultural myths and narratives all of these can be sources of mobilization opportunities.

But if opportunity can be so much, would Goodwin and Jasper say, is it anything at all? The crucial point here is the qualifier "sources of." Almost anything, as long as it is outside the movement, can affect opportunities, but none of these things is an opportunity in and by itself. Is this a problem? Not necessarily. Almost anything can be a source of discontent, almost anything can affect collective identities, almost anything can be used as a resource, and just about everything can be framed. Does this make discontent, identity, resources, and frames hollow concepts?

But if opportunity is none of these things, what is it? Here, unfortunately, silence reigns in the political opportunity literature. Implicitly, however, two related but different meanings are attached to the concept, which can also be found in the popular usage of the term. First, opportunity refers to options for action, which may be either available or not. In nondemocratic systems, for instance, the option "vote for a different party in the next election" is not available, as is the option "appeal to the Constitutional Court" in countries that do not have such an institution. Obviously, the set of options available at any particular time and place affects the strategic repertoire that social movements have at their disposition. This is not to say that such repertoires are constrained and enabled by the political context only. Repertoires, as we all know, also depend on the cultural environment, which facilitates options that are known and acceptable, and excludes those that are unknown or unacceptable.

Opportunity also contains a notion of uncertain outcomes. The second meaning of opportunity therefore refers to the chance that certain options will bring about desired outcomes and the risk that they will have undesired outcomes. If the option "vote for a different party" entails the choice between political parties that are all hostile to a movement's aims or if like-minded parties are marginal and systematically excluded from the decision-making process, then this option is not likely to be chosen and neither is an option that is likely to be met with heavy repression. Again, chances and risks are not necessarily politically determined. The same form of action may have a higher probability of success in one culture than in another, for instance, because it refers to shared cultural myths or historical examples.

By combining the two meanings we may define opportunities as options for collective action, with chances and risks attached to them, which depend on factors outside the mobilizing group. The opportunity thesis then amounts to the claim that people choose those options for collective action that are (a) available and (b) are expected to result in a favorable outcome.

Is this a theory, or is it stating the tautologically obvious? The opportunity thesis would be trivial if it would just say that opportunities are necessary for collective action. It would be a theory, but an obviously inadequate one, if it would say that opportunities are a sufficient condition for mobilization. Opportunities alone can never explain collective action, which at least also requires motivations, capacities to act, and a sense of collective identity. The opportunity thesis becomes truly relevant as a theory when it says that variations in levels and forms of collective action depend primarily on variations in opportunities. This implies the claim that variations in other obviously necessary preconditions for collective action are either unimportant (e.g., the common claim that grievances or resources are ubiquitous), inconsequential in the absence of favorable opportunities, or dependent on variations in opportunity. This is still a rather general, but nonetheless empirically falsifiable theory, which excludes—as good theories should—a range of alternative explanations. It may not be true, or it may not always be equally true, but that is a matter for empirical investigation.

Political Opportunity

Since opportunities in this view are neither necessarily political nor structural and leave ample room for cultural factors and agency ("making opportunities"), Goodwin and Jasper would perhaps not object to this most general formulation of the opportunity thesis. The second claim, however, that the most relevant opportunities for collective action are derived from the interaction of social movements with political actors and institutions, is certainly a greater source of disagreement. Goodwin and Jasper do not stand alone when they criticize the inherent assumption in the political opportunity model that social movements should primarily be seen as political phenomena. Many scholars on both sides of the Atlantic, working within the framing perspective or the so-called "new social movements approach," have criticized the political opportunity literature for missing the essence of (contemporary) social movements, which they see as challengers of cultural codes and promoters of new lifestyles and collective identities, rather than as a special form of interest politics.

Goodwin and Jasper have a point when they note that the political opportunity literature has a tendency to concentrate on the latter type of challengers—which they call "citizenship movements"—to which its political explanations most plausibly apply. On the other hand, this point can only be upheld if we acknowledge that this category of movements is much more inclusive than adherents of the cultural perspective would have it. Ethnicity and ethnic movements are favorite examples of allegedly "cultural" phenomena, but political opportunity explanations of the black civil rights movement in the United States have actually done a reasonably good job in explaining the rise and fall of this movement. I am not aware at least of any rival explanations from a cultural perspective that presents a better account of the movement's development. The same is true for European new social movements. Whatever we may learn from them about the "meaning" of new social movements, scholars like Melucci and Touraine have failed to address, let alone explain, these movements' historical careers or the important cross-national differences in their levels and forms of collective action.

Nevertheless, it would be unwise to overstate the point. Obviously, not all movements are political to the same extent. Not all movements are primarily motivated by collective aims that require the provision of collective goods or the removal of collective bads by external authorities. For some movements, which one may call subcultural or countercultural, the expression of collective identities through collective action is the primary concern. Since such movements produce their own collective benefits, they will have a greater degree of autonomy from their political environment and thus be less adequately explained by political opportunities. The same is true for movements or movement groups that are externally oriented but seek to change social and cultural norms, practices and consciousness rather than political rights or policy changes. The women's movement, or at least part of it, is an obvious and important example and it is probably no coincidence that this movement has received less attention from political opportunity scholars than it deserves.

Political Opportunity Structure

Disagreement mounts further when we introduce the third claim: the opportunities relevant for explaining variations in collective action are to an important extent structurally shaped. The question, of course, is what structural refers to in this context. Goodwin and Jasper define structure in an unnecessarily narrow way as both fixed and stable, and outside the control of a social movement. Not surprisingly, therefore, they find a lot of "non-structural" factors that political opportunity scholars include among "structures." At least some of this "structural bias" is easily repaired by a more appropriate definition of structure in this particular context. If opportunities are configurations of options, chances, and risks originating outside the mobilizing group, then, from the point of view of the movement, any such opportunities appear as structurally given that cannot be influenced, at least not in the foreseeable future, by collective action. Such opportunities may be relatively stable and fixed, for example, the chances that are provided by the electoral system, but they may also change from one day to another. Consider elections and a subsequent change in government. The composition of parliament and government may not be a structural variable from a social systems point of view because it changes every four years or so; from the point of view of most movements at most times and places such variables appear as important, but immutable conditions that have simply to be taken as a given in considerations of whether and how to mobilize.

Of course, even such variables can sometimes be influenced by social movements. Intense protest campaigns occasionally bring governments down and contribute to constitutional changes or even to the overthrow of entire political systems. We may call such outcomes of mobilization "structural impacts" (Kitschelt, 1986). An example is the electoral breakthrough of green parties in several European countries. The mobilization of the German peace and environmental movements certainly contributed to the election victory of the Greens in 1983, which for the first time brought them into the national parliament, in which they have been represented ever since. However, this change can be interpreted as a shift from one structural situation to another. Before 1983, German new social movements faced a situation in which they had no reliable and influential ally in the national political arena. Since 1983, they have such an ally, or even several allies, because as a result of the competitive pressure from the Greens the traditional parties have become more open to new social movement demands, too.

Theoretically it is possible that in the period immediately before the 1983 elections, some social movement organizations took a possible election victory of the Greens into account in their strategic calculations and did things they would not have done in the absence of such a perspective. Such reasoning is of course more common in revolutionary situations, in which everything seems possible and revolutionary groups often shun short-term gains in order not to lose momentum for the anticipated ultimate and total victory. Structural change has become part of strategic considerations in such situations and therefore we cannot speak any longer of political opportunity structure in the strict sense. Political opportunity structure may still be helpful in explaining how revolutionary situations come about, but it is much less suited to explain the further development of revolutionary situations, let alone revolutionary outcomes. To a lesser extent the same may be true for intense (non-revolutionary) protest cycles in which not the whole political opportunity structure, but significant parts of it, may be in a state of flux.

Thus, political opportunity structure alone can and will never fully account for the development of many, if not most, social movements. If this is what Goodwin and Jasper wanted to make clear, then they have a point, albeit a superfluous one. I at least would be hard-pressed to mention even one author who has made such an extreme claim. The idea of political opportunity structure involves not more (and not less) than the claim that not all of the variation in levels and forms of collective action is due to the strategic wit, courage, imagination, or plain luck (or the lack of those) of the different actors involved in conflict situations, but that an important part of it is shaped by structural characteristics of the political context in which social movements, willingly or unwillingly, have to act. The relative extent to which structure and agency contribute to the explanation of such variation will undoubtedly vary from case to case and is, again, a matter for empirical investigation.

What seems clear is that political opportunity structure will generally provide more powerful explanations for cross-national comparison than for longitudinal, single-country studies. Cross-national differences in political opportunity structures often concern the most stable and deeply rooted aspects of political systems, and are thus structures beyond reasonable doubt. In within-country analyses these most structural aspects of political opportunity structure will be constants and therefore generally less helpful in explaining variations over time.[2] This is not to say that structural changes may not be important in explaining temporal variations within countries, but these will often concern variables that are, at least potentially, not as fully independent from mobilization as most cross-country differences.

SOME SUGGESTIONS FOR
CONCEPTUAL CLARIFICATION

At present, the theoretical development and empirical persuasiveness of the opportunity model, whether in its broad or in its more specific political and/or structural versions, are hampered by conceptual unclarity and the coexistence of dozens of different operationalizations. One step toward clarification would be to distinguish more clearly and explicitly among the different concepts and theoretical claims outlined above. Opportunity is not always political opportunity, and political opportunity is not always structural.

Structural opportunities, moreover, do not have to be political in origin. In spite of the ritualistic opposition between structure and culture that pervades so much of social science (including Goodwin and Jasper's critique), culture has a structural face too. Much of the cultural context in which social movements act is beyond their sphere of immediate influence and may thus be characterized as a cultural or discursive opportunity structure (Koopmans and Statham, 1999). To acknowledge this may contribute to a better integration of the political opportunity perspective with cultural approaches such as frame analysis. So far, frame analysts have had difficulty to account systematically for the obvious fact that some frames are successful, while others, no matter how internally consistent and elaborate they are, fail. The notion of a discursive opportunity structure could help to analyze this intriguing question more systematically. In their efforts to frame the presence of foreign migrants as a problem, extreme right and xenophobic movements in France and Germany, for instance, are confronted with widely divergent notions of national identity and definitions of what constitutes a citizen (Koopmans and Kriesi, 1997). Some of these differences have materialized in constitutions and citizenship legislation, and may thus be considered part of these countries' political opportunity structures. But obviously national identity has deep cultural roots, too, which may be as consequential for the mobilization of xenophobic movements as formal legislation.

Further, the relation between opportunities and structures has to be made clearer. Opportunities are not structures, though they may be derived from structures. And structures as such are not opportunities, though they may affect them. This does not mean that Goodwin and Jasper are right when they claim that the concept of opportunity structure is an oxymoron. After all, when we say "social structure," we do not imply that social life is a structure, either. When we say "opportunity structure" we just say that not all of opportunity is agency, but that some of it is structured.

The distinction between opportunity and opportunity structure also leads us to ask if the search for conceptual unity has thus far perhaps concentrated on the wrong level of analysis. Given the enormous variety among social movements as well as among political systems, and the range of questions we may ask about their relation to each other, the search for one single conceptualization of political opportunity structure that adequately explains and answers them all may well be chimerical. Aspects of political opportunity structure that are central in cross-national research on social movements may be irrelevant or of marginal importance in longitudinal, single-country designs, and vice versa. For peace movements the structural location of a country in the system of international relations will be an important variable and the relative autonomy of local governments will be of marginal importance; for neighborhood and community groups the reverse will be true. And finally, a conceptualization of political opportunity structure that fits democracies as well as communist dictatorships, France today, as well as in the eighteenth century, will have to be—if possible at all—so general that it will be useless for meaningful empirical analysis. This does not mean that generalizations are altogether impossible (e.g., "divided elites generally imply favorable conditions for challenger mobilization"), but it does imply that the present disagreement surrounding concise lists of the type "political opportunity structure consists of A, B, C, and D" can and will not vanish. Such operationalizations will inevitably be challenged or disregarded by empirical researchers, who will find that these lists miss things that are important for the cases they study, and perhaps include things that are unimportant.

If taken seriously, then, (political) opportunity structure is a context-sensitive analytical tool par excellence. That should please Goodwin and Jasper. However, they would probably—and justifiably—still insist on the necessity of at least some common ground to which all these context-sensitive analyses refer. I would suggest that such a common point of reference is more likely to be found on the level of political opportunities than in the structures that shape them. Although the sources of opportunity may differ widely among political systems and have to be specified for each movement individually, the types of opportunity that result can be systematized in a general, but relatively simple way. This requires two assumptions, though: (1) social movements have aims and use collective action to further them; and (2) in doing so they weigh the relative advantages and disadvantages of the options open to them.

Following the first assumption, we may distinguish opportunities that affect the realization of aims from opportunities that affect collective action itself.[3] Regarding both, positive or negative reactions from the political environment to a particular option for action (i.e., chances and risks of that option) may be anticipated by a social movement actor. With regard to aims, authorities may be expected to respond favorably, that is, to change their policies in the direction of the movement's aim—we may call this reform—or unfavorably, that is, to change policies in the opposite direction—we may call this threat. Of course, there is also the possibility of some mix of reform and threat or of no response at all. With regard to collective action, authorities may either be expected to apply sanctions that increase the costs of collective action—repression—or to reward collective action, for instance by providing resources or moral support facilitation. Again, the anticipated response may also be a mix of repression and facilitation, or no response at all.

In considering such opportunities, social movements always have the choice among several options for action. On the most concrete level, it does not seem possible here to generalize. Available action repertoires differ widely from one historical or spatial setting to another and from one movement to another. However, at least two dimensions of choice seem to have broad relevance. The first and most basic is the choice between collective action, whatever its form, and no collective action. Taking these two options systematically into account solves many of the apparent contradictions the political opportunity model has run into. Take a situation where a government that promises reforms in accordance with a social movement's demands ascends to power. Now consider two possible variations on this situation. In situation A the government holds a large and undivided majority in Parliament and has a strong capacity to act. In situation B the government rests on a narrow and unstable majority and is restricted in its capacity to act by strong opposition from entrenched societal opponents of reform. In the general sense of "favorable" or "unfavorable" political opportunity structures, situation B would seem to offer bleaker prospects for collective action than situation A. However, considering mobilization decisions as a choice among options leads to the conclusion that collective action may actually be more likely in situation B. In situation A there is little need to mobilize since collective benefits are expected even in the absence of collective action. Collective action may even be seen as potentially counterproductive because it may destabilize the government or provoke the mobilization of groups that are opposed to reforms. In situation B, on the contrary, the likelihood that the government will be able to implement reforms on its own is not very great. From the perspective of reform-oriented social movements, then, mobilization in support of the government's reform platform becomes an attractive option that may help push the balance of power more firmly to the side of the proponents of reform. Thus, it is not the general "favorableness" of a political situation, but the relative attractiveness of collective action compared to the alternative of not acting that counts in explaining mobilization decisions.

A second distinction we may make is the choice within the collective action alternative between protest and other more conventional forms of collective action such as lobbying, participation of social movement organization in consultative bodies, or electoral mobilization through a political party. Again, considering these alternatives may lead to conclusions that are obscured by the usual phrasing of opportunities as "expanding" or "contracting," "closed" or "open." Consider a result from the cross-national comparison of social movements in France, Germany, the Netherlands, and Switzerland (see Kriesi et al., 1995:44ff.). An analysis of these countries' political systems reveals that the range of channels of access to decision making available to social movements increases in the order in which the countries are mentioned, from hyper-centralized France to the fragmented, consensus-oriented Swiss state with its direct-democratic institutions. Conclusion: Switzerland has a more "open" opportunity structure than France, and therefore more collective action? It depends on our focus. If we include the participation of the Swiss in signature campaigns for referenda and popular initiatives and their membership in social movement organizations, then yes. But if we look at protest in the sense of strikes, demonstrations, and collective violence, then the answer is no, for this form of participation is most frequent in "closed" France. Exit political opportunity structures? Not really, at least not if we see them as affecting different options for collective action differently. Swiss movements have an important option their French counterparts do not have (direct democracy). Moreover, conventional collective action is generally more attractive because of the multiple points of access to the political system at the local, regional, and national levels and because of the consensus-oriented strategies that (usually) prevail among the Swiss political elite. By contrast, French politics, which are traditionally hostile toward associations that intervene between the state and the citizenry, offer few opportunities for conventional, organizational mobilization, which is not facilitated and not likely to be listened to. No wonder then that professional social movement organizations in France are much weaker than in the other three countries and that the protest alternative is a more popular way of striving for change.

Operationalized along these lines, political opportunities provide a link between structure and action. On the one hand, they refer to concrete options, chances, and risks that directly inform mobilization decisions by social movement actors. On the other hand, they can easily be linked to political structures. In analyzing the effects of elite divisions, for instance, we would have to spell out how they affect experiences and expectations of reform, threat, facilitation, and repression and thus the relative attractiveness of different options for collective action.

Opening the "black box" between political opportunity structures and movement action in this way will certainly not make our tasks easier. Instead of the convenient, but unrealistic, shortcircuiting of structure and action we will have to consider unique mixes of options, chances, and risks that are affected by structural factors and agency simultaneously. We will also have to theorize the precise effects of opportunities. If we just consider the literature on the effects of repression on mobilization, it becomes clear that we cannot expect simple one-to-one causal relationships of the type "repression works" (Tilly, 1978:114) here. Depending, for instance, on the type of repression and its consistency, on whether it hits a rising movement or one already in decline, on whether the aims of the movement in question are reformist or revolutionary, instrumental or identity-oriented, repression may sometimes succeed in intimidating protesters while at other times it may activate them. In addition, the effects of one aspect of opportunity may well be conditional on the presence or absence of other types of opportunity. For instance, repression by law-

and-order factions of the political elite is perhaps less effective when other parts of the political elite simultaneously facilitate mobilization.

If this perhaps provides an answer to Goodwin and Jasper's critique of the opportunity model's "structural bias" and "invariant modeling," it still is very much a political approach to collective action. It would be a challenge but one that clearly transcends the limits of this chapter: to develop similar, parallel concepts for the systematic analysis of discursive opportunities. Embedding the ideas developed by David Snow and his colleagues (1986) on the dimensions of frame resonance ("empirical credibility," "narrative fidelity," etc.) in a more structural framework might be a fruitful starting point here.

NOTES

Previously published in *Sociological Forum* 14, no. 1 (March 1999). Reprinted with permission.

1. I will concentrate here on Goodwin and Jasper's critique of the political opportunity thesis. The "political process model" is basically a combination of at least three explanatory models: the political opportunity model in the strict sense, as well as elements of the resource mobilization and framing approaches. Goodwin and Jasper's critique of the political process model primarily concerns its selective incorporation of the two other models and the fact that political opportunity structure remains the core explanatory factor. Thus, most of what they find fault with in the political process model parallels their criticism of the political opportunity thesis in the narrow sense.

2. The qualifier "generally" is appropriate here. The often-repeated, common-sense assertion that "constants cannot explain change" is not always true. Regime intransigence sometimes breeds mobilization, and, conversely, elite reforms (i.e., change) sometimes prevent mobilization (i.e., explain a constant).

3. I elaborate here on ideas presented by Charles Tilly in his *From Mobilization to Revolution* (1978) and by myself in *Democracy from Below* (1995).

6

Trouble in Paradigms

JEFF GOODWIN AND JAMES M. JASPER

> Movements are supposed to do what politicians can't do, which is to imagine a different future.
>
> —Pam Solo (quoted in Meyer, 1990:263)

> The truth of the matter is that the decision about when to rise up didn't take national politics into account. That's not so important to the comrades, not so much as not being able to stomach things any longer, regardless of the national or international conditions.
>
> —Subcomandante Marcos (quoted in Collier, 1994:87)

We are gratified by the thoughtful attention such gifted scholars have given to our article, even when we disagree with their conclusions. Their responses are as varied as the applications of political process theory (PPT), with each defending a somewhat different version. Sidney Tarrow and David Meyer defend PPT at its most grandiose, as a scientific paradigm. Ruud Koopmans and Charles Tilly seem more comfortable defending PPT as a tool kit of concepts and causal mechanisms (see also Kriesi et al., 1995; Amenta and Zylan, 1991), although Tilly apparently believes that the best defense is a good offense! A third possibility, more or less explicit in some of our critics' remarks, is that PPT is nothing more than a sensitivity to the contexts that social movements face, or perhaps a sensitivity to structural contexts or to changes in structure. Francesca Polletta (see chapter 7) makes a more positive contribution, trying to figure out what both sides mean when they talk about culture.

MECHANISMS AND THEORIES

We ourselves favor causal explanations based on small-scale mechanisms and middle-range theories over those with pretensions to universality.

Jon Elster (1989) defends this "explanation by mechanism," distinguishing it both from general covering-law explanations (which look for necessary or invariant connections, try to make predictions, and often confuse correlation with causation) and from storytelling (which Meyer apparently sees as the only alternative to covering-law approaches). By referring to and even discovering mechanisms that appear in more than one case, and often in many, this approach avoids the mere description of individual stories. Tarrow's description of us as "paradigm warriors" is thus fundamentally misleading; we obviously see serious problems with PPT, which we believe merit careful and honest scrutiny, but we are not (and will never be) advocates of any alternative paradigm, as that concept is generally understood. Tilly and Meyer, for their part, are wrong in arguing that we envision nothing but descriptive case studies as the goal of social-movement research, as though this were the only alternative to invariant theories.

Although Tarrow and Meyer defend both forms of PPT, they reveal the difference between mechanisms and general theories. They mention a number of important mechanisms at work in political struggle, such as the channeling of protest into calmer legal means, or the way in which movement success may increase (or decrease) further mobilization. But as a general theory, PPT seems only to require attending to "the external context that movements draw from and seek to change" (Meyer) or to "the mutual interaction among challengers, opponents and third parties" (Tarrow), based on the supposed insight that movements do not exist in a vacuum. Surely this makes the paradigm trivial. No alternative view exists or ever has existed, except in straw-man form.

As implied by his use of the word "model," Meyer favors concentrating on a small number of factors by specifying more finely their range of applicability. This would lead to a healthy concentration on causal mechanisms, except that so few mechanisms are recognized by PPT. Far too many factors lie outside PPT for theoretical "refinement" to be a reasonable strategy. We prefer a more open-ended approach to theory where the goal is to increase the number of tools in our conceptual repertory and to develop a keener sense of when and how they are applicable, in order to have greater flexibility and range in understanding empirical cases.

This approach to theory does not make us foes of parsimony, as Koopmans fears. Like most social scientists, we want the simplest adequate answers to our questions; we just don't believe that the conceptual framework of PPT can provide those answers. (Indeed, some of the questions that interest us can't be posed in the first place within the conceptual framework of PPT.) Simple explanations are not necessarily adequate explanations. Nor does our approach preclude investigations about when certain dynamics are more likely to be at work; but the goal is not to expand some general theory. Meyer's goal of specifying ever finer conditions of applicability can only mean, ultimately, that he hopes to approach a general, invariant theory.

Tilly graciously acknowledges the importance of our criticisms of invariant modeling. And well he might, since we took these criticisms from his own recent writings. Tarrow, Koopmans, and Meyer, by contrast, don't see any problem. As far as they can tell, no process theorist has ever proposed invariant models, nor do we provide evidence of such. But what do they make of McAdam's (1982) model, which we reproduce, and its attendant claims? Isn't the point of that model that social movements—all social movements—have the same three proximate causes? We also quote McAdam, McCarthy, and Zald's more recent statement that political opportunities are "necessary prerequisites" for social movements and revolutions. Doesn't "necessary" mean "always," and doesn't "always" suggest an invariant relationship? Finally, Tarrow's recent book, *Power in Movement* (1994), is chock-full of statements suggesting that political opportunities are invariably necessary for social movements (see, for example, 1, 17–18, 78, 81, 99, 150). (We quoted, albeit it in a footnote, Tarrow's summary statement on the first page of his book about the alleged "triggering" of social movements by political opportunities.) Does anyone who has read Tarrow's book (or his response to our article) think that he is referring to just a few social movements, or even a bare majority of movements?

Koopmans and Meyer claim that process theorists can't possibly be accused of invariant modeling because they invoke all sorts and types of political opportunities to help explain social movements (which we view as problematic, of course, not something to be celebrated!). Tarrow adds that process theorists have indeed been sensitive to the "historical rootedness" of collective action. But these points have no bearing whatsoever on our critique of invariant modeling. The a priori assumption remains that some sort of political opportunity, or "expanding" political opportunity, must help explain whatever movement is at hand. This assumption disables our capacity to imagine how things might be otherwise—a key skill for social-movement scholars as well as activists. With invariant theories, as with implicit paradigms, one "knows" the answers to one's questions in advance; research is about filling in the particulars.

Consider Tarrow's discussion of Chiapas. Tarrow sees a kernel of truth in both of the "cartoon" versions of the Zapatista rebellion which he presents. Despite its limitations, Tarrow seems to like the first "cartoon" for at least "recognizing the importance of domestic opportunities in the launching of the rebellion." But this may say as much about Tarrow's theoretical assumptions as about the Zapatista uprising. After all, most informed observers attribute this rebellion to the repeated failure of independently organized peasants to secure benefits through legal channels or peaceful protest; to the Mexican government's reform of the constitution, which effectively eliminated the opportunity for peasants to acquire land legally; and to the escalation of repression in Chiapas by "the state's judicial police and military or at the hands of private ranchers' hired gunmen and thugs, who are tolerated and sometimes even abetted by the state" (Collier, 1994:78; see also Harvey, 1995). These are presumably not the "opportunities" to which Tarrow is referring! The decision to launch the uprising on January 1, 1994, furthermore, seems to have been motivated primarily by the rebels' own organizational concerns and growing impatience with "politics as usual," not by any specific change or event in the external political context (see the statement by Subcomandante Marcos which we have used as an epigraph). The inauguration of the North American Free Trade Agreement (NAFTA) on January 1, 1994, we now know, was simply a convenient pretext for launching the rebellion (Collier, 1994:86). Of course, if one simply assumes the necessity of political opportunities for collective action, one will undoubtedly discover some such opportunities (especially if opportunities are very broadly defined); the danger is that one will also overlook those aspects of political contexts that do not fit so neatly into the "opportunities" category.

Take another example: the Christian fundamentalist dogma that AIDS is a result of immoral, un-Christian behavior. This is an invariant explanation in our view, although "immoral, un-Christian behavior" may be specified in a number of ways (e.g., homosexuality, having sex with prostitutes, intravenous drug use). The fact that AIDS might have nothing whatsoever to do with "immoral, un-Christian behavior" is literally unthinkable to many fundamentalists. Similarly, the fact that social movements—even movements that seek to change public policy or overthrow the state—might rise and fall for reasons having little or nothing to do with political opportunities is literally unthinkable to many process theorists.

When a paradigm works well, alternatives to its main assumptions cannot even be imagined. Is this why some of our critics think that the main point of our article was to question the idea that political opportunities are sufficient to explain social movements? We thought it obvious that the putative necessity of political opportunities for movements was the more important target of our critique. Indeed, perhaps no other idea is more closely associated with process theory. Our critics, however, not only fail to defend this idea, but don't even seem to sense that it's being questioned. In this regard, neither the passage from his 1994 book that Tarrow quotes nor the passage from his 1990 book which Meyer quotes "defies" our critique. On the contrary, these passages exemplify precisely what's wrong with PPT: the a priori assumption that political opportunities are always necessary for social movements and other forms of collective action.

To be sure, many of the causal nuts and bolts of process theory seem important for understanding social movements. But this is hard to say since no one presents PPT at this level, and none of our critics (including the mechanism-mindful Tilly) seems to have listed the important mechanisms at work in PPT. Nonetheless, specific mechanisms invoked by process theorists could be tested easily enough. For example, when does an increase in repression, or the use of certain types of repression, lead to greater mobilization, and when to less? What kinds of elites form what kinds of alliances and with what effects? When do elite allies provide legitimacy for protesters, when material aid? And when are elite allies burdens for social movements? Normal science like this would generate better understanding of repression and elite alliances in their various forms.

In truth, the few mechanisms emphasized by process theorists are not actually new. Theorists as diverse as Trotsky and Smelser have emphasized the importance of repression. Divided elites and the elite allies of movements were a specialty of resource-mobilization theorists. Nor do we think that these mechanisms stand or fall together in some kind of all-or-nothing package. They are compatible with the general spirit of the PPT paradigm, but there has been little theorizing about how they fit together or apply to different kinds of movements.

Several responses to our article deal with the issue of how widely the process model is applicable. Most process theorists begin with McAdam's application to the civil rights movement (Meyer finds the concept of openings "most important" for this movement, less so for others), then perhaps add the labor movement, and work out from there. We think PPT seriously distorts these two movements and is even less applicable to others. The real problem is that the model is now widely proclaimed to have been demonstrated, without having undergone much rigorous testing on a variety of movements. A project is now afoot to systematically do just this (Goodwin, forthcoming). But in the meantime we should recall just what kind of testing has occurred. Each process theorist's list of important political opportunities is usually derived from the case she or he knows best.[1] In some instances the lists do not have any overlap at all (compare McAdam, 1996a, with Smith, 1996, for instance). So little is really being tested across cases in a systematic way, except a vague metaphor. (The main exception here is Kriesi et al.'s [1995] four-country study, although the authors' definition of political opportunities is typically idiosyncratic.) What is being shown is that sensitivity to context is useful, or that some events and actors external to movements affect some movement actions. Is this news to anyone?

We also suggested that citizenship movements and "post-citizenship" movements (composed of people already integrated into a polity as citizens) face different kinds of constraints, so that a different set of causal mechanisms may be relevant to each (Jasper, 1997). Koopmans similarly suggests that "political" movements differ from other, especially "countercultural," movements (although surely movements that challenge dominant culture beliefs are also, for that very reason, "political"). Yet in overstretching to show its worth, process theorists tend to treat all movements the same. Traditionally, much of the nuance of theories of social movements has come from typologies of a wide variety of movements, a kind of theorizing that could link the broad and the narrow parts of PPT. Tarrow reminds us that process theorists view social movements as a subtype of contentious politics, yet few process theorists have attempted to typologize social movements themselves. Koopmans' work along these lines represents a step in the right direction, although he may exaggerate the importance of political opportunities even for narrowly "political" movements (see Koopmans, 1995; Kriesi et al., 1995:83–87).

Koopmans' distinction between "political" and "countercultural" movements, furthermore, raises an important question: Just what is the "political" of "political process" all about? This is a question that has received curiously little attention from process theorists. Koopmans implies that politics is about "the provision of collective goods or the removal of collective bads by external authorities." But we find this definition unnecessarily circumscribed, especially if "external authorities" are understood to be state officials alone. Meyer similarly distinguishes movements that are "explicitly political"—by which he means movements that "make political claims," presumably against the state—from those that are not (including, he suggests, the "hip-hop" movement). Meyer claims that "political process analysts have never claimed to explain movements that are not explicitly political" in this narrow sense—quite an admission, in our view! But in truth, even though process theorists have not attempted to explain such movements, their definitions of "social movements" typically encompass them. Meyer himself has written that "A social movement is a sustained and self-conscious challenge to authorities *or cultural codes* by a field of actors" (Gamson and Meyer, 1996:283, emphasis added). If process theorists are now suggesting that they cannot explain movements that primarily challenge cultural codes, then our article will have served a useful purpose for that reason alone. For we sense that a lot of people are under a very different impression.

It also seems odd to us to describe any movement, and "hip hop" in particular, as nonpolitical for the sole reason that it does not make claims on the state or routinely contend with political authorities. Much rap music—indeed, hip-hop cultural practices more generally—certainly seems "explicitly political" to us, with lyrics decrying racism, police abuse, and (at least when Queen Latifah's at the mike) misogyny. In 1989, certain FBI officials were so incensed by a song by the rap group NWA (Niggas with Attitude) that FBI assistant director Milt Ahlerich sent an unprecedented official letter to the group, complaining that "recordings such as the one from NWA are both discouraging and degrading to . . . brave, dedicated [police] officers" (quoted in Rose, 1994:128). Ahlerich's letter apparently activated an informal fax network among police agencies, which were urged to cancel NWA's concerts. So while the hip-hop movement has not primarily targeted the state, the state has certainly targeted hip hop.

And what about other movements that do not target the state? How do we understand movements that make claims on universities, research centers, corporations, retail outlets, trade unions, or professional associations? What about religious movements (see Bainbridge, 1997)? What about self-help or mutual-aid movements, or movements to save souls? Are all these movements also nonpolitical by definition? Is PPT therefore inapplicable to these movements as well? (Our guess would be that PPT would not often shed a great deal of light on such movements.) Whatever the answers to these questions, surely we should be attuned, as Verta Taylor urges, to forms of organized protest beyond the streets, in "the arenas of medicine, mental health, law, religion, and education," among others—arenas in which "peculiarly modern forms of power operate, reinforcing fundamental social inequalities" (1996:17–18). To be sure, process theorists have usefully emphasized that social movements are situated within a larger field of "contentious politics," yet they have not (yet) gone far enough in this regard. Their definition of politics, contentious or otherwise, remains quite narrow and conventionally state-centered. This conception of power and politics has its uses, but we should recognize its limitations as well.

Tarrow thinks that our critique of PPT somehow carries less weight precisely because social movements are just one type of the "contentious politics" that process theorists study. But this simply begs the questions and avoids the issues raised by our critique. Indeed, if process theorists cannot adequately explain social movements—or, more accurately, the specific type of "political" movements which they've chosen to examine—why should we believe that they can explain other types of "contentious politics" any more adequately? Christian fundamentalists have explanations for all sorts of maladies besides AIDS, but that doesn't mean that their explanation for AIDS must therefore be correct! So whether or not social movements are the "alpha and omega" of PPT has no bearing on our critique: either PPT offers an adequate explanation of social movements, or it doesn't.

Considerable work also remains to be done on the causal mechanisms that make up PPT. For instance, we are baffled by Meyer's insistence that "opportunities do not cause protest," since every other process theorist seems to see them as a necessary condition. Perhaps he means that opportunities alone do not cause protest, that they are not a sufficient condition. Who could disagree with this? Still, we would ask, what kinds of opportunities, and what kinds of movements?

Koopmans makes an interesting move in defining opportunities as options available to movement organizers. In so doing he builds considerable choice and awareness into the concept, since he means perceived options. This is close to our idea that action is channeled in certain ways, both negatively and positively. It pushes structural factors into the world of strategic calculation and choice. Koopmans avoids the problematic distinction between "objective" and perceived opportunities, but by bringing the environment into the movement he may lose the ability to look at the relationship between the external environment and movement choices, often thought to be at the heart of PPT. As he admits, "political opportunity structure in the strict sense" disappears. Good riddance, except that we may need to come up with new concepts to get at those abiding aspects of political structure that used to be sheltered under the generous umbrella of political opportunities!

Meyer emphasizes how scholars might improve PPT, but in so doing he demonstrates again what we think is wrong with it. He admits that PPT has concentrated on certain kinds of political protesters, but then seems to lump everyone else together as "crazy people." PPT works best with pre-defined populations facing legal barriers that make the state their target and works less well with movements of those who are already full citizens or who are not targeting the state. It has no place at all for lone individuals or small cliques who protest, not just "crazy people" but effective whistleblowers and others. Meyer admits that factors other than "structural" ones should be added to PPT models, but his vision seems restricted to "cognitive factors." Emotions, rituals, moral intuitions, psychology, personality, and individual idiosyncrasies have no place, perhaps because they would undermine the core of the PPT paradigm.

This is not the place to tally the evidence for and against various process mechanisms. Our suspicion is that none has the range of applicability that process theorists believe. But the real problem is that scholars—presumably encouraged by their belief in the paradigm's power—tend to accept them as fact and finding without much systematic testing. (Perhaps this is why Meyer implies that we critics of PPT can only be ambitious hucksters seeking exposure. Indeed, some of our critics treat us like religious heretics who have abandoned some unassailable faith!) We also believe that explaining why certain mechanisms are important in some cases but not others will require attention to a range of other mechanisms that are alien to the process paradigm—unless that paradigm turns out to be able to include any and every kind of factor! But in the latter case, there is no point in defending the idea that PPT represents a distinctive paradigm. We could all simply go back to searching for the many causal mechanisms that—in historically specific concatenations, as Tilly would say—help drive collective action. Not a bad idea, come to think of it.

PARADIGMS

Paradigms cannot be observed and tested across a range of cases in the way that causal mechanisms can. The language, assumptions, and methods that make up part of a paradigm, along with the more explicit theories and propositions, are the stuff one would use to test it, but of course using them implies acceptance of the paradigm. As evidence for the utility of the process paradigm, Meyer seems to include any study that uses its language, even those that turn up evidence against its specific propositions. Thus, Kurzman (1996) showed that the Pahlevi regime in Iran showed no signs of weakness, no "opportunities" that might have "cued" potential revolutionaries that their moment had come. Yet Meyer cites this work as evidence of the flexibility of process theory. Flexibility indeed! More recently, Kurzman has flatly stated that "expanding political opportunities ought not, based on the current state of research, be granted significant explanatory power in the case of the Iranian Revolution" (Kurzman, forthcoming). With "friends" like this, PPT hardly need critics like us.

Meyer also cites his own recent work with Minkoff (1997) on the civil rights movement. This interesting and important study proposes a variety of measures of Tarrow's four-fold specification of political opportunities (Tarrow, 1994:85–89). Like other process theorists, Tarrow suggests that these four types of opportunity encourage or facilitate popular mobilization (although not all nor any one of these factors necessarily helps to explain any particular social movement). Meyer and Minkoff's study, however, has a surprising result, although it's not one that the authors themselves seem to notice: Most of the statistically significant correlations between their measures of political opportunity and civil rights mobilization turn out to be *negative*. Tarrow's "opportunities," in other words, usually suppressed mobilization for civil rights. (Of course, in the Alice-in-Wonderland world of PPT, even threats, legal obstacles, countermovements, and repression are often conceptualized as "opportunities.")

These findings contradict the widespread assumption, based largely on McAdam's (1982) work, that political opportunities for black protest were clearly expanding until about 1965. Again, it seems strange to cite such a study as evidence for the PPT paradigm. But this is part of a more general tendency among process theorists to cite all sorts of incommensurable and even contradictory findings as evidence for the explanatory power of political opportunities—a logical result, alas, of what Koopmans terms "conceptual unclarity and the co-existence of dozens of different operationalizations."

Of our critics, only Tarrow and Meyer explicitly defend the idea of PPT as a paradigm, although others do so implicitly. Not even Tarrow and Meyer, however, attempt to defend the unwieldy concept of "mobilizing structures," nor does any critic address our misgivings with frame analysis. This silence is fairly remarkable, and it reinforces our sense (pace Tarrow) that the concept of "political opportunities" remains, warts and all, the core theoretical contribution of process theory.

Meyer misrepresents us in implying that we are interested in repairing the PPT paradigm; we wish, rather, to restrict the pretensions of PPT to being a paradigm, returning it to a more useful life as one set of important causal mechanisms among others. If we are "paradigm warriors," as Tarrow says, we are making war on the idea of paradigms, not attacking one in favor of another. (Tilly correctly senses our animus, but not our ultimate goal.) The whole problem with PPT is this inflation of a few important factors and concepts into an entire approach or paradigm (with its own name). Paradigms focus attention by excluding a lot of things; they also distort reality to fit their own metaphors. Anyone who wanted to explore Meyer's list of "what is to be done" would get further, we think, by backing away from the idea of "refining" PPT, and instead rethinking cultural and psychological dynamics such as the construction of meanings, the importance of individuals, strategic decision making, and emotions. In sum, we should try to extend understanding, not paradigms.

PPT's rise to paradigmatic status began with McAdam's (1982) well known study. In trying to proclaim the importance of his "new" approach, he sharply contrasted process theory with collective-behavior and resource-mobilization approaches, necessarily transforming the latter two into straw men and requiring that one of the three theories (guess which?) be declared the hands-down winner. We agree with Tarrow that this disparages the contributions of earlier approaches and obscures their deep influence on subsequent research. Indeed, when intellectual life is made into this kind of zero-sum competition among simplified models, intellectual progress is the real loser. PPT's ability to "beat" other theories may be the source of many process theorists' false feeling that we already have the conceptual language that we need and that—the main issues of social-movement theory having been answered—a little more theoretical "refinement" is all that's now required.

In Koopmans' sensible version of process theory, he still uses language describing political opportunities as the "most important" determinants of movements, a strong statement that seems sure to be disproven in many cases and that is likely to bias researchers as they take it as an assumption rather than an open empirical question. At one point, even Koopmans attempts to save the idea that PPT is a distinctive paradigm rather than a handful of causal mechanisms, when he proclaims PPT as superior to "rival explanations," returning us to the idea that intellectual life is a zero-sum competition among distinct competing theories.

PPT is best known for two claims, both of which have become "known truth" based on evidence from a distressingly small number of movements. One is that movements emerge when political opportunities open. The other is that personal networks are the main way that individuals are recruited to social movements (cf. Jasper and Poulsen, 1995; Jasper, 1997; Emirbayer and Goodwin, 1994). Both claims gain extra (and undue) force from the (untested) presupposition that political and social structures— blanched of cultural meanings—must be the most important causal factors at work in any situation.

One of the core assumptions of the process paradigm is that there are certain groups of people who are systematically "excluded" from the polity. The usual image is of legal exclusion: Southern blacks or European workers in the nineteenth century who could not vote, for instance. Some groups may indeed be ready and waiting for an opportunity, already aware of their interests and solidarity. But other protesters are relatively full economic and political participants, with the right to vote, who contribute money to favorite causes and candidates, hold well-paying jobs, and so on. They are excluded only in the sense that their policy preferences are not being followed, typically because other "interests" have more influence on policymakers or politicians. For them, creating a movement entails creating an identity, grievances, and interests. To speak of a movement like that against nuclear weapons as needing a political window of opportunity to open is like saying that my heart attack gives an ambulance driver an opportunity to come to my house, as though she had been circling my block just waiting for her chance. For many movements, there is simply not a preexisting group of people with interests that are being thwarted; their grievances need to be constructed in the process of building the movement.

The obverse of the problem of exclusion is another issue: opportunities to do what? The opportunity to vote without danger, to pursue any job or career, to build networks, to form organizations, to organize protest, to talk to state officials, to gain media attention, and so on are rather different opportunities, corresponding to different forms of "exclusion." If the concept of exclusion were cleared up and differentiated, that of opportunity would be too.

Tarrow and Meyer believe that we were selective in the concepts and scholarly works that we chose to represent PPT. Of course, in one sense such selectivity is unavoidable within the parameters of a single journal article, and we certainly plead guilty to Tarrow's complaint that we have focused mainly on "the recent generation of work" by process theorists. (Note that Meyer, by contrast, finds our examples dated.) Tarrow also complains that we are "fixated" on political opportunities and that we treated mobilizing structures and framing as "afterthoughts." But we paid considerable attention to the latter concepts (too much, according to Meyer), our criticisms of which Tarrow completely ignores. And if we devoted disproportionate attention to political opportunities, that is because this is clearly the privileged concept in PPT, as Koopmans points out, including Tarrow's own work. One commentator even describes the work of McAdam, Tarrow, and Tilly as "synthetic political opportunity theory" or "SPOT" (Lichbach, 1997). Informed readers can judge for themselves whether our lengthy discussion of the political opportunities concept paints a "cartoon" version of PPT, as Tarrow claims, or realistically conveys the principal concerns of most process theorists, as suggested by the responses by Meyer and Koopmans to our article, which also focus on the political opportunities question.

As if our article hadn't bitten off enough, Tarrow would also like us to have discussed the concepts of repertoires and cycles, which he claims are "central" to PPT. But the scholarly literature on mobilizing structures (a.k.a. indigenous organization and social networks) and framing processes—not to mention political opportunities—is simply much more developed than that on repertoires and cycles (see, e.g., Crist and McCarthy, 1996), so we focused on the former. As Tilly has recently noted, "I cannot say that the notion of contentious repertoires has been a roaring success. . . . If Tarrow had not spread the word, indeed, he and I might be the only researchers trying to implement the study of repertoires" (Tilly, 1995c:38). The study of cycles of protest, so far as we can tell, remains even less well developed.[2] In Tarrow's own work, furthermore, cycles of protest are portrayed as largely derivative of "the opening, diffusion and the closure of political opportunities" (Tarrow, 1994:155). This is a debatable proposition—yet another claim that would benefit from rigorous testing—but it too suggests that our focus on the political opportunities question was not at all misplaced. The purpose of our article, in any event, was clearly not to offer a comprehensive review of every concept that process theorists have utilized!

Meyer, for his part, finds us fixated on the work of McAdam and Tarrow. Yet we think that McAdam and Tarrow are the exemplars most cited by process theorists themselves, especially since each of them presents his approach self-consciously as PPT (see the references, e.g., in Foweraker, 1995; Kriesi et al., 1995; and Schneider, 1995). Meyer does not think that McAdam's original formulation generalizes well (and we concur), but it still seems to be the main model of the paradigm (see the references, e.g., in Smith 1991, 1996; and Costain, 1992). McAdam's causal diagram of 1982 has not been widely reproduced, then, because it does not need to be. No process theorist has rejected it or fundamentally altered it, only refined and extended it; so far as we know, McAdam still defends it.

As alternatives to McAdam and Tarrow, Meyer mentions his own book on the nuclear freeze movement and Christian Smith's (1996) work on the U.S. movement for peace in Central America. We are well aware of these works, since one of us has reviewed both of them for the *American Journal of Sociology*. They are similar in that both insist on the centrality of PPT in introductions and (in Smith's case) the conclusion, but tend to ignore it in between. Both rely considerably on a range of dynamics (moral and religious principles; moral shocks, fear, and other emotions; rhetoric and ideas; individual creativity) that have no clear or obvious place in PPT and may well be at odds with it. Well researched, illuminating, and rich as case studies, both are uneven exemplars of the process paradigm. Of course, no rich empirical case study is ever fully reducible to its theoretical frame—but that should hardly be taken as proof of the theory's flexibility.

Tarrow and Meyer also wonder, rather ironically, why we do not criticize Tilly more. Meyer suggests, in a vaguely sinister tone, that we go easy on Tilly because he is a collaborator. Well, we do know Tilly, but it just so happens that we also know all of the major process theorists whom we cite. For the record, though, we have not collaborated in research or writing with any of them. But all of this is quite beside the point. We have tried not to do what Meyer (and Tilly) do, namely, personalize the debate. We have never labeled any process theorist "confused" or "befuddled" (quite the contrary). Nor have we impugned their motives by implying that they are all just a bunch of "ambitious" professors "seeking exposure" and attempting to "garner ratings." And we certainly never claim, pace Tilly, that process theorists nefariously and "deliberately foisted an unsound doctrine on their juniors." Why would we possibly claim such a thing? And how does this red herring contribute to the debate?

Just because Meyer has written within the process tradition, furthermore, does not mean that he (or McAdam or Tilly) cannot also criticize that tradition (as all three have) or write in a way that seems to contradict the main thrust of the tradition (as Smith has; see Jasper, forthcoming). If we criticize Tilly less often than other process theorists, it is because he tends to talk about causal mechanisms, not theoretical approaches or paradigms. We criticize him less, in short, because he makes fewer of the mistakes that we are criticizing.

In answer to Koopmans, yes, we do think that PPT is both too broad and too narrow. It is too broad when it claims to be a paradigm, to have vanquished other paradigms, or to have been "proven" in a broad range of empirical settings. It is too narrow when it suggests ad hoc (or post hoc) lists of political opportunities for each movement under study and then claims that the approach is confirmed whenever such a list can be derived. Of course, we prefer narrow as opposed to broad specifications of political opportunities, as for other concepts (e.g., "resources" and "mobilizing structures"). But process theorists can't have their cake and eat it too: If they're going to propose narrow and falsifiable claims about opportunities, as opposed to broad and tautological ones, then they have to accept that their claims will not always be supported by evidence from particular movements. And this means giving up any notion of the supposed "necessity" of political opportunities for social movements and revolutions (Goodwin, forthcoming).

There are, in sum, few connections between the broad and the narrow in PPT, such as a sense of the limits of its own applicability, of why certain factors are relevant for some movements but not others, of what other causal factors there might be that are not part of the paradigm, and of what different kinds of movements there are. In other words, PPT needs to be more self-reflexive about why it fits diverse movements so differently, if at all. This middle-range theorizing, we think, will lead us far beyond the political process paradigm.

CULTURE AND STRUCTURE

The main blind spot we see among process theorists is a failure to recognize or incorporate the insights of the cultural constructionism of the last twenty years. Tilly oddly attributes to us several positions that no serious scholar of culture holds today: that propositional attitudes are the mainsprings of human behavior, that culture exists only in individual minds, that explanation should consist of interpretation—in a phrase (Tilly's phrase), "phenomenological fundamentalism." We would be skeptical of cultural approaches too, if we thought they were similar to Tilly's or Koopmans' characterizations.

Some of our respondents seem exercised over our very mention of culture, making us more sure than ever that this is a real gap in their approach. Tilly has recently admitted as much, noting that he and his fellow process theorists "will have to analyze many more . . . cultural elements" before they can claim to have an adequate perspective on contentious politics. "We never claimed to be there now," Tilly adds (1997a:111). Some of our critics apparently assumed that, by waving the word "culture," we were proposing a full-blown alternative paradigm to process theory. But even if we were interested in doing this—which we aren't, for reasons that should be clear by now—it hardly seems fair to expect us to build an alternative approach (as an aside?) in an article that is primarily a critique. After all, it has taken process theorists thirty years and hundreds of publications to build up what they consider a paradigm.

Tilly's misreading of our constructionist standpoint leads him to characterize (and trivialize) our position as "You're underestimating the importance of variables [we] find interesting." While that is certainly true, we also think that process theory systematically discourages investigation of those variables. Even more importantly, we think that inattention to those factors distorts and limits process theorists' understanding of the very political and social structural factors that they themselves favor. As Polletta points out, what they call structures already contain a heavy dose of culture. These structures are, as the saying goes, "always already" cultural. This debate is not about adding or subtracting a few "variables," but about the dangers of reifying and thereby misunderstanding much of political and social life (see also Alvarez, Dagnino, and Escobar, 1998). Our purpose in introducing the idea of culture was to get at some of what was missing from the very core of the PPT tradition. Even a quick glance at our table 1.3, furthermore, should dispel Koopmans' (and Tilly's) fear that we're proposing an undifferentiated view of culture, or a view of culture as purely attitudinal or completely unstructured.

Contrary to the impression we seem to have given Meyer, we do not think that frame analysis is an essential part of PPT. Rather, it is the principal way in which process theorists have tried to take serious account of cultural meanings, when they have tried at all, and we find it inadequate. McAdam, McCarthy, and Zald's (1996a) volume, incidentally, is hardly the only effort to fuse frame analysis onto process theory, as Meyer suggests. Similar efforts have been made by Tarrow (1994:chap. 7), Noonan (1995), Diani (1996), and Klandermans (1997a), among many others. In fact, Meyer himself has made such an effort in an chapter coauthored with Gamson and Meyer (1996). In any event, we believe that fuller attention to other dimensions of culture (and psychology) besides framing would force process theorists to rethink what they mean by opportunities and process. Attention to strategic choice, cultural meanings, and social and individual psychology would ease the structural bias of PPT. This would take us far beyond the bounds of frame analysis. (On the limits of frame analysis as the main way to deal with culture and meaning, see Kane [1997] and Benford's [1997] "insider's critique.")

Despite his humorous medical simile, Tilly never quite gets around to defending political process models. He spends much of his time questioning our own approach, reducing it (from what little evidence there is) to a few simplistic labels. Neither of us would argue that interpretation is the only proper explanatory strategy, or that individual attitudes and culture are co-extensive. Some factors are of course usefully analyzed as structural. We agree wholeheartedly with Polletta and Koopmans that culture itself is often usefully analyzed as structural (see, e.g., Goodwin, 1994; Emirbayer and Goodwin, 1996b; Jasper, 1990). We ourselves believe in the importance of political and social-structural factors, yet we think that they are better understood when there are cultural factors with which they can be compared, and when the cultural character and specificity of such "structures" themselves are explicitly recognized.

In much of sociology, not just in the field of social movements, structural aspects of social life are overemphasized, often unwittingly. But this distortion is especially problematic in the study of politics and protest, which contain a great deal of intention and will, strategy and choice, desire and fantasy (or imagination, as Meyer's interviewee put it in the quote we chose as an epigraph). Real human actors are eclipsed most completely in narratives about long-term processes such as urbanization, industrialization, and state formation, but they also tend to disappear in the shorter-term accounts of movements by process theorists (cf. McAdam, 1988a). Good sociology, if it is to get a solid purchase on explaining social life, must balance agency and structure, conscious intentions and unintended consequences, individuals and the constraints they face. Here, we are in complete accord with Koopmans.

These are abiding tensions, dilemmas of the craft of sociology which will not disappear by waving around simplistic slogans such as "phenomenological fundamentalism" or "phenomenological individualism"—slogans, we fear, intended to dismiss a whole range of phenomena having to do with meanings, intentions, and strategies, and the way these lodge in individuals. In the end, most process theorists seem to have no place for individuals. They thereby miss much of social life. As C. Wright Mills famously wrote, "The sociological imagination enables us to grasp history and biography and the relations between the two within society. That is its task and its promise" (1959:6). Moving beyond structures is not simply a value call; it is necessary for full (and, yes, parsimonious) explanations: "Neither the life of an individual nor the history of a society can be understood without understanding both" (Mills, 1959:3).

To get to this sad point, two reasonable insights have been conflated in PPT. One is that politics is an ongoing process, full of opportunities, responses, mistakes, and triumphs. The other is that there are structured arenas within which all this strategizing occurs. Process, however, gets reduced to structure again and again. One reason is the structural bias we discussed in our article. Another may be that a very narrow group of researchers has usurped the term "game theory" for what they study (or assume), and their work has little to interest most students of protest. But strategic games abound, and it is perhaps time to pay attention to them, recapturing the game metaphor for a more realistic approach to politics.

The mistake is to treat the world as mere "context" for movements. States, parties, corporations, news media, and individuals, with their meanings and practices and emotions and strategic choices, get reduced to passively shifting structures when they are theorized as "context." To be fair, Meyer's own 1990 book avoids this reduction. In addition, one of us has written a book about the states and other actors faced by the anti-nuclear movements of several countries, showing that these "contexts" were not simply structures but complex arrays of groups and individuals maneuvering strategically with a variety of cultural perspectives and individual psychologies. The constraints facing the movements shifted rapidly and strategically, and it took their opponents years to establish anything approaching a stable "structure" that worked against these movements (Jasper, 1990).

Tarrow and Meyer fall into the same contrast between structure and agency or structure and culture that we are trying to overcome. But Francesca Polletta has done such a good job of explaining how thoroughly imbued with culture all structures are that we need not repeat her analysis (see chapter 7; Polletta, 1997; Berezin, 1997). We think that the analysis of both strategic choice and cultural meanings are paths for opening up the blind spots of PPT. Scholars of social movements and contentious politics have a lot to learn from recent efforts in social theory which take culture, agency, and creativity into account without losing sight of social systems (e.g., Giddens, 1984; Castoriadis, 1987; Touraine, 1995; Joas, 1996; Emirbayer and Mische, 1998).

CONCLUSION: FUTURE RESEARCH

Meyer and Koopmans have laid out some interesting refinements to process theory, and we hope that future researchers will explore them. We are just as sure that most of these questions can be better answered by incorporating factors outside of (and, we think, alien to) the process approach than by "refining" PPT. Will we ever understand the diverse effects of state repression, for example, without grasping subtle psychological and emotional dynamics—fear, inspiration, intimidation, revenge? Can we understand the possibilities for group solidarity or for alliance-building if we ignore these same dynamics? There is a whole world of similar mechanisms poorly accommodated within PPT. Indeed, because process theory lacks, in our view, adequate microfoundations, it frequently turns to assumptions borrowed (inadvertently) from rational-choice theorists, an unnecessary weakness given all the efforts at integrating levels of analysis in sociology today.

Tarrow suggests that we now go forth and put into practice the type of research that we have called for (which he misrepresents, echoing Tilly, as "phenomenological individualism"). But there's no need to wait. Plenty of important research has already been conducted—by many others, not just by ourselves—which explores the cultural, strategic, psychological, and emotional mechanisms that fit poorly within any coherent definition of the process paradigm, even when the findings of this research are distorted until they look as though they are compatible. We would include among this research not only the work of such well known European scholars as Touraine (1981); Laclau and Mouffe (1985); and Melucci (1996); but also the work of Zablocki (1980); Luker (1984); Mazón (1984); Kimeldorf (1988); Fantasia (1988); Hirsch (1989); Aho (1990); Epstein (1996); Marx (1992); Hunt (1992); Jenness (1993); Scheff (1994b); Calhoun (1994); Jamison and Eyerman (1994); Whittier (1995); Kurzman (1996); Lichterman (1996); Bainbridge (1997); Groves (1997); Kane (1997); Teske (1997); and Beisel (1997). None of this research is framed, so to speak, in the conceptual language of PPT, yet it has greatly enriched our understanding of social movements—sometimes in ways that directly contradict certain propositions of process theory—and it has greatly expanded our conceptual repertory.

Most process theorists are not quite willing to recognize the full extent of the constructionist revolution of recent decades, which to us makes it unreasonable to view political (or "mobilizing") structures as standing outside of meaning and interpretation. If process theorists prove flexible enough to absorb new insights about individual and social psychology, emotions, cultural meanings and actions, and strategic decision making, then their paradigm will no longer have any clear boundaries and will dissolve into its component causal mechanisms. But if process theorists continue to insist on remaining a distinct paradigm, resisting these trends, we expect that they will simply be displaced, with their important insights and mechanisms absorbed into a broader vision of social and political life.

NOTES

Previously published in *Sociological Forum* 14, no. 1 (March 1999). Reprinted with permission.

1. See Crist and McCarthy (1996) on the prevalence of the case-study approach in social movement research. This is also a problem in the framing literature (see Benford, 1997).

2. A Sociofile search reveals a total of 17 citations for "cycles of protest" from 1974 through 1997, compared to 509 citations for "framing" during the same period. The Sociofile database contains article and dissertation abstracts from 1,900 journals of sociology and related disciplines published worldwide, including all abstracts from *Sociological Abstracts* (after 1974) and from *Dissertation Abstracts* (after 1986). Our thanks to Chris Bonastia for this information.

Part II

BEYOND DOMINANT PARADIGMS

7

Culture Is Not Just in Your Head

FRANCESCA POLLETTA

Political process theorists have increasingly recognized the limitations of strict political opportunity models, in which the existence of political opportunities is the necessary and sufficient cause of mobilization. In particular, they have argued that identifying objective shifts in political alignments without probing how people make sense of those shifts is simply inadequate to understanding how and when mobilization occurs. Instead, they have argued for paying more attention to the cultural frameworks through which people evaluate political structures, perceive opportunities, and come to believe in their collective capacity to take advantage of those opportunities (see, inter alia, McAdam, 1994; Johnston and Klandermans, 1995a).

However, efforts to theorize the role of culture in mobilization have been hampered by a tendency to view (political) structures as noncultural. Like Goodwin and Jasper, I believe that we can usefully adopt a less anemic conception of culture than some political process analyses have done without making actors, interests, strategies, and resources simply figments of a culturalist imagination. Goodwin and Jasper's solution to what they call the "structuralist bias" of current approaches is to recognize activists' strategic abilities to recognize and create opportunities. Culture and strategy, they argue, matter more than structure. My solution is different. Structures are cultural (though not only cultural), I argue. The task is not to abandon an emphasis on "objective" political structures in favor of analysis of potential insurgents' "subjective" perceptions of political structure but to probe the (objective) resources and constraints generated by the cultural dimensions of political structures. To develop this argument, I critique formulations of the culture/structure relationship by leading political process theorists. I note that each author who figures in my criticisms has also contributed to the analytical alternatives I endorse. This suggests that the problem lies less with particular people or approaches than with widely held but constricting understandings of culture. In the second part of the chapter I present several lines of investigation based on what I believe is a more fruitful approach.

CULTURE VERSUS STRUCTURE

Consider Doug McAdam's (1994) critique of political process theory, notable given his central role in developing that theory.[1] "The dominance, within the United States, of the 'resource mobilization' and 'political process' perspectives has privileged the political, organizational, and network/structural aspects of social movements while giving the more cultural or ideational dimensions of collective action short shrift" (36), McAdam argues. By implication, then, the "political, organizational, and network/structural aspects of social movements" are not cultural. McAdam goes on:

> It is extremely hard to separate these objective shifts in political opportunities from the subjective processes of social construction and collective attribution that render them meaningful. . . . Given this linkage, the movement analyst has two tasks: accounting for the structural factors that have objectively strengthened the challenger's hand, and analyzing the processes by which the meaning and attributed significance of shifting political conditions is assessed. (1994:39)

McAdam distinguishes "objective" "structural" opportunities from the "subjective, cultural" framing of those opportunities. Culture mediates between objective political opportunities and objective mobilization, in this view; it does not create those opportunities (see also McAdam, McCarthy, and Zald, 1996b:8; McAdam, Tarrow, and Tilly, 1997:158).

This formulation, in which culture is located in insurgents' framing efforts, seems to make sense. But it reflects a deeper opposition between structure and culture that has proven unhelpful in sociological analysis generally (Sewell, 1992; Hays, 1994), and in social movement analysis in particular. In scholarship on movements, the opposition takes the following form. Political opportunities are seen as structural, not cultural; activists' capacity to take advantage of those opportunities is cultural (though only in part cultural, because it depends also on the prior structural networks that make people available to participate). The contrasts underpinning this conception of culture's role in mobilization are listed in table 7.1.

TABLE 7.1
Conceptions of Culture and Structure in
Recent Political Process Analyses

Culture	*Political Structure*
1. subjective	1. objective
2. malleable	2. durable
3. enables protest	3. constrains protest
4. mobilized by the powerless to challenge structure	4. monopolized by the powerful to maintain power

So, cultural processes shape potential challengers' perceptions of objective opportunities (contrast no. 1); culture is malleable whereas structure, by definition, refers to relations that are beyond the control of individual actors (no. 2); political structures and processes make possible the expression of preexisting grievances and identities, they do not constitute them (no. 3); and cultural processes shape the actions of insurgents, not those of institutional political actors (no. 4).

Two confusions lie behind these claims, neither specific to the authors I have named and neither restricted to the analysis of social movements. First, since "structure" is counterposed both to "agency" and to "culture," the latter two are often implicitly aligned (see also Hays, 1994, on the point). Culture becomes agency. The result is that culture is made overly subjectivist and voluntarist; the ways in which culture constrains are obscured. This is evident in McAdam's argument that "expanding political opportunities . . . offer insurgents a certain objective 'structural potential' for collective action. Mediating between opportunity and action are people and the subjective meanings they attach to their situations" (1982:48; see also McAdam, 1994, 1996; McAdam, McCarthy, and Zald, 1996b). In other words, structural opportunities are "given," are beyond actors' control; actors' strategic cultural construction of those opportunities turn them into an impetus to action. So culture constrains action only insofar as it impedes actors' capacity to perceive the system's objective vulnerability.[2] The second confusion is between culture as a sphere of activity and target of protest and culture as a dimension of all structures and practices, including political ones. Political process theorists—and sympathetic critics—have tended to miss the latter. So, William Gamson and David S. Meyer argue, "Opportunity has a strong cultural component and we miss something important when we limit our attention to variance in political institutions and the relationships among political actors" (1996:279), implying that these are noncultural. Gamson and Meyer's typology of factors generating political opportunities relies on a "cultural (society)—institutional (state)" axis, again suggesting that state institutions are noncultural. So "cultural factors or processes" are contrasted both with structure, which is given, not interpreted, and with political institutions and developments, which are noncultural.[3]

We can conceptualize culture differently. Think of it as the symbolic dimension of all structures, institutions, and practices (political, economic, educational, etc.). Symbols are signs that have meaning and significance through their interrelations; the pattern of those relations is culture. Culture is thus patterned and patterning; it is enabling as well as constraining; and it is observable in linguistic practices, institutional rules, and social rituals rather than existing only in people's heads. This conception of culture puts us in a better position to grasp conceptually and empirically the generation of cultural but "objective" opportunities— objective in the sense of prior to insurgents' interpretative activities (in contrast to claims 1 and 4); to grasp culture's durable character (in contrast to claim 2); and to identify political institutions' and processes' role in constituting grievances, identities, and goals (in contrast to claim 3). Let me develop these points.

CULTURE AND OPPORTUNITY

Culture plays an important role in creating political opportunities, and not just in the subjective perceptions of insurgents. As Gamson and Meyer (1996) point out, differing political opportunity structures reflect not just different political systems, for example limits on the executive branch and a system of checks and balances, but also different public conceptions of the proper scope and role of the state. "State policies are not only technical solutions to material problems of control or resource extraction," Roger Friedland and Robert Alford argue in the same vein. "They are rooted in changing conceptions of what the state is, what it can and should do" (1991:238). Such conceptions extend to state-makers and managers who, like challengers, are suspended in webs of meaning (Goodwin, 1994). In explaining the rise of the civil rights movement, John Skrentny (1998) shows that the American government's post-war sensitivity to charges of racism before a world audience was a function of the prior institutionalization of a transnational culture of human rights. The structural opportunity for activists was the superpowers' Cold War competition for influence in the developing nations, but that competition was shaped by nations' obligation, new since World War II, to adhere to human rights standards to claim status as a world leader.

Another example of the cultural dimensions of structural opportunities: Elections are often represented as key components of the political opportunity structure, but whether elections "open" or "close" political opportunities surely has to do with whether elections have historically been catalysts to collective action, and whether there is an institutional "collective memory" of state-targeted protest. Something as ostensibly noncultural as a state's repressive capacity reflects not only numbers of soldiers and guns but the strength of constitutional provisions for their use and traditions of military allegiance. In her discussion of protest policing, Donatella della Porta observes that while the West German police force viewed itself as a part of a normative order that accepted the rule of the law, the Italian police "since the creation of the Italian state had been accustomed to seeing itself as the longa manus of the executive power, and thus put preservation of law and order before the control of crime" (1996:83). These views in turn shaped the opportunities for different forms of protest. Charles Brockett likewise draws attention to the role that collective memories of state repression played in Salvadoran and Guatemalan elites' calculation of the costs and benefits of repression:

> Guatemalan elites considering violence only needed to refer to 1966–72 when over 10,000 innocents were murdered or to the 22-year reign of terror of Manuel Estrada Cabrera early in the century. Going further back in time, elites in both countries evaluating violence as an instrument of control could recall the coercion employed in converting peasant food-crop land to elite-owned coffee land beginning in the latter third of the nineteenth century, or they could go all the way back to the massive violence of the Conquest itself and the consequent coercion utilized to maintain colonial society. (1995:129–130)

Brockett quotes Ted Gurr approvingly: "Historical traditions of state terror . . . probably encourage elites to use terror irrespective of . . . structural factors" (130).

Note that these traditions, principles, codes, and arrangements cannot easily be "thought away" by insurgents. They are supra-individual and constrain individual action. But they are also symbolic; they are ways of ordering reality. By limiting the operation of culture to insurgents' "subjective awareness," their "perceptual" capacities (McAdam, McCarthy, and Zald, 1996b:8), political process theorists have obscured these potentially important and observable features of political systems. Note also that some of the above, for example, state officials' ideological assumptions, may exercise only transient and/or weak influence on political opportunities. Others, such as state legitimacy (Oberschall, 1996), may have stronger effects and be less malleable, and still others, like conventions of political commemoration (Olick and Levy, 1997), may be somewhere in between. The durability/malleability of culture is variable rather than definable a priori. Finally, all of these factors operate in the sphere of institutional politics. To take culture into account does not detract from a focus on political processes in generating opportunities. Rather, it simply recognizes the cultural dimensions of those processes. Curiously, cultural elements have often been included, though not labeled cultural, in political process theorists' enumeration of "objective" "structural" opportunities. For example, McAdam characterizes the early political process model—anticulturalist, by his own account—as attributing the timing of movements to the "shifting institutional structure and ideological disposition of those in power" (1996a:23).

In that last phrase, McAdam gets at some of what I am talking about. So why even bother distinguishing culture? How does a focus on the cultural dimensions of political structures contribute to our understanding of movement emergence? Structures, in Sewell's (1992) persuasive definition, are cultural schemas invested with and sustaining resources, in other words, schemas that reflect and reproduce unevenly distributed power (note that schemas and resources are equally important to the definition).[4] This helps to explain structures' durability and their transformation. It is not that structures bring about their own mutation, not that they have agency, but that they are invested with meanings that provide resources for insurgents challenging those structures. People can "transpose schemas" from one setting to another, can turn the worker solidarity fostered by capitalist production, for example, into a force for radical action. Sewell's scheme also reveals, contrarily, overlooked cultural obstacles to protest. Activists' vocabularies of protest, the "master frames" (Snow and Benford, 1988) they have at their disposal, are shaped and limited by ostensibly noncultural political, economic, and legal structures.

Let me be more specific about what this kind of conceptualization, of structure as cultural (though not only cultural), does for our understanding of movement emergence. First, it suggests more careful attention to the cultural traditions, ideological principles, institutional memories, and political taboos that structure the behavior both of political elites and challengers. To study the comparative role of elections in facilitating insurgency, we should establish whether a well-known history of election-centered protest exists, memorialized in popular narratives, holidays, and other political rituals. In comparing levels of repressive capacity, we should note not only the number of guns and soldiers available to the government but also constitutional provisions and precedents (and prevailing interpretations of those provisions and precedents) for its use of force. The changing legitimacy rules for world leadership provide activists with differential opportunities to embarrass national governments into a more receptive or proactive stance. Again, all of these are features of institutional politics; all are cultural; none exists just in insurgents' heads.

Second, whereas political process models, like their resource mobilization forebears, take collective actors as given, albeit unmobilized, this approach directs our attention to the state's role in their mobilization and, indeed, in their very constitution. For example, sudden and draconian state policies may supply the "moral shock" (Jasper, 1997) that compels people to participate who before didn't see themselves as having much stake in the issue in question. The Supreme Court's 1986 *Bowers v. Hardwick* decision upholding a Georgia antisodomy statute, in the context of government unresponsiveness to the AIDS crisis, led to militant and oppositional AIDS activism (Gould, 2001). Or, quite the opposite, state actors may deliberately encourage protest. The National Organization for Women was formed after a meeting of state-appointed members of Commissions on the Status of Women. They were encouraged also by federal officials from the Equal Opportunity Commission (Skrentny, forthcoming; Costain, 1992). Finally, state policies may help to create new social categories that later become the basis for mobilization. The identity of "Hispanic" did not exist in the United States before President Nixon proclaimed a National Hispanic Heritage Week in 1969 and a variety of government agencies began to use the term for classification purposes; since then, people of Latin American descent living in the United States have mobilized around it (Oboler, 1995). In his study of nineteenth-century British contention, Charles Tilly (1998b) attributes the eclipse of local identities like spinner, neighbor, or tenant of a particular landlord by broader ones such as "citizen" and "worker" to the increasing salience of the national state in people's lives. Rather than appeal to a powerful patron or unleash their rage directly on the object of their dissatisfaction, claims makers increasingly made public demonstrations of their numbers and commitment to bid for participation in a national polity. Contrary to the assumption that only weakened states supply opportunities for insurgency, these cases suggest that strong states may do so, and indeed, may help to create collective actors. Rather than seeing political structures, states, and actors as separate from the insurgents who confront them, this perspective sees mobilization potential in their linkages (for a similar perspective, see McAdam, Tarrow, and Tilly, 2001).

Studying the cultural dimensions of political structures can improve explanations for the emergence of protest in a third way, by helping to account for the resonance of particular collective action frames. For example, to understand the currency of an "individual rights" frame versus a "human rights" frame, or versus a class-based frame, one would have to understand the legal and political traditions, systems, and rules through which those terms have become meaningful. When Sidney Tarrow

(1996b:50) observes that "the French labor movement embraced an associational 'vocabulary' that reflected the loi le Chapelier, while American movements developed a vocabulary of 'rights' that reflected the importance of the law in American institutions and practice," he points to that kind of inquiry. In a similar vein, Anthony Marx (1998) shows that whereas in the United States and South Africa the legal institutionalization of racial privilege generated severe and pervasive inequality and provided the basis for black mobilization and rights claims, in Brazil the absence of legalized racial categories, agencies, and statistics impeded black mobilization. The point is that separating the spheres of "politics" and "culture" and treating only the latter as the source of mobilizing meanings obscures those meanings' relations to, and in some cases sources in, political structures, institutions, processes, and macrohistorical changes. But this is precisely what we need to get at: how the "master frames" that shape and constrain movement idioms themselves emerge and are transformed through contention inside and outside institutional politics.

Of course, movements invent new ideas and popularize conceptions—of gender, work, politics, speech, etc. How do they do that? In the case of novel rights formulations, legal scholars have argued that rights' polyvalence—their containment of multiple and subversive meanings— allows people to claim and mobilize around rights that have yet to be recognized or enforced by legal authorities (Minow, 1990; Hunt, 1990; McCann, 1994; Schneider, 1986; Villmoore, 1985). But if novel rights formulations are always possible, then under what circumstances are they likely to be advanced by challengers and to resonate with a broader public (whether or not such claims are authorized by legal authorities)? The culturalist accounts that predominate have focused on cultural impediments to novel rights claims, for example, the "public/private" dichotomy that marginalizes a variety of claims, and the opposition of sexual difference to sexual equality (Scott, 1988). We should also be asking about the political and organizational circumstances in which rights innovation is likely to occur. In my research on the Southern civil rights movement (Polletta, 2000), I identified three such circumstances: in settings where social institutions (legal, religious, familial, economic) enjoy relative autonomy; where organizers are at some remove from state and movement centers of power; and during periods of interorganizational movement competition.

With respect to the first situation, one of the ways in which activists may develop resonant rights claims is by combining rights discourse with other normative languages, say religion or the obligations of family life. Such transposition is probably especially useful in countering the individualist and state-dependent biases of conventional rights discourse. It is more likely where institutional spheres—religion, politics, the family—enjoy some autonomy. By contrast, in a society characterized by a high level of "mimetic" or "coercive isomorphism" (DiMaggio and Powell, 1991b), where organizations adapt their structures and mandates to those of other organizations, it is more difficult for people to challenge one institution by adopting standards or warrants from another. Activists who are distant from national centers of state and movement power are better able to do that work of transposition, to combine standard rights formulations with locally resonant justificatory rhetorics. Numerous scholars have argued that decentralized movement structures encourage tactical and ideological experimentation as activists adapt agendas to the needs, aspirations, and skills of local people (Gerlach and Hine, 1970; Flacks, 1988:chap. 5; Robnett, 1997). Indeed, organizers' dispersal in indifferent or hostile political terrains often forces them to be ecumenical in their appeals. For example, the debates about anticommunism and fellow-traveling that galvanized the early national leaders of Students for a Democratic Society (SDS) had little meaning for new left activists in Austin, Texas (Rossinow, 1998). However, SDS chapters' autonomy allowed Austin activists to draw on ideological currents that were foreign or unappealing to new leftists in New York, Chicago, or Ann Arbor, chiefly a populist-inflected liberalism and a social gospel tradition. In the Southern civil rights movement, organizers from the Student Nonviolent Coordinating Committee (SNCC) found that those most willing to court certain repression by attempting to register to vote were not middle-class residents but sharecroppers and domestic workers. They were often illiterate and were officially deemed "unqualified" for political participation. SNCC workers began to call for rights for "the unqualified," a formulation that proved powerfully mobilizing and spurred a broader challenge to conventional criteria of political representation (Polletta, 2000).

In addition to the relative autonomy of institutional arenas and organizers' distance from national centers of state and movement power, a third condition may facilitate ideological innovation generally and novel rights claims specifically: interorganizational competition. Movement groups' jockeying for money, allies, members, public attention, and legitimacy may lead them to concentrate on distinctive goals, tactics (Zald and McCarthy, 1980), frames (Benford, 1993), or constituencies. Organizations may carve new movement niches by claiming to speak for people who have not yet been spoken for, and because Americans tend to formulate identity claims in terms of rights, this process may generate novel rights formulations. Consider the movement group advocating for bisexual or transgendered people in relation to the gay and lesbian rights or women's movements. By asserting the "rights" of this until-now unrecognized group, activists invoke a nonradical liberal discourse; they are only asking that transgendered and bisexual people be treated like everyone else. At the same time, by drawing attention to the fact that this group's needs palpably cannot be met by the rights claims being advanced by mainstream movement organizations, they are challenging rights' alleged universalism.[5] "Deaf" activists (who distinguish themselves from mainstream deaf activists by the capital "D") demand rights but refuse the label of "disabled." Likening deafness instead to ethnicity, they call for reforms that would accommodate the needs of deaf people rather than forcing them to conform to hearing society. Such demands are radical in their implications—challenging the line between "difference" and "disability"—if conventional in their formulation. When SNCC workers asserted the rights of the unqualified, they were demanding that the rights of citizenship be extended to those who had been disqualified by a system that denied them basic education and were questioning more broadly what counted as political expertise. In each of these cases, conventional rights claims were expanded to encompass the needs of people as yet unrecognized by those claims—and unrepresented by existing movement organizations. For activists representing a marginalized subgroup, it makes little sense to forward claims in an altogether new lexicon or to operate entirely independently of the mainstream movement, which has resources and political clout that it does not. Deaf activists, for example, have been unwilling to "cut [themselves] off from the larger, savvier, wealthier disability lobby" (Dolnick, 1993:43). Instead they have forwarded rights claims that are radical simply because they expose the normative assumptions built into ostensibly universalistic rights.

   None of these conditions for ideological innovation can be described as noncultural. For example, the institutional autonomy that gives activists the resources for integrating normative discourses is a result of broad cultural understandings. Mosques played a crucial role in Kuwaiti opposition to Iraqi occupation because of their long-standing and "morally unassailable" authority to challenge the state (Tetreault, 1993:278; see also Polletta, 1999a). What is important in the approach I am advocating, rather, is that it concentrates on the conditions in which the dynamic in question is likely to operate, whether the dynamic is individual participation, the generation of resonant frames, or insurgents' perception of opportunities.

CULTURE AND STRUCTURE IN ONGOING MOVEMENTS

Such an approach should help us to understand more than movement emergence. We still do not know much about how activists select among strategic options, allocate resources, and set agendas, for example. A classically rationalist formulation, in which movement leaders adjudicate among competing options by rationally assessing their potential to further such instrumental tasks as winning allies, avoiding repression, and sustaining rank and file enthusiasm (Barkan, 1979; Kitschelt, 1986; McAdam, 1983; McAdam, McCarthy, and Zald, 1988; McCarthy and Zald, 1977), has been unappealing to scholars who point to activists' normative commitments. Strategies, tactics, and organizational forms are not only means to other ends but are also ends in themselves, ways of communicating something important about those who use or participate in them (Jasper, 1997). Gary Downey (1986) writes that the antinuclear Clamshell Alliance saw itself not only as the atomic-industrial establishment's opponent, dedicated to stopping nuclear power, but also as its "opposite," seeking to eradicate domination within its own operation. Activists accordingly sought to balance an ideological "egalitarian" commitment with an "instrumental" one.

But this perspective errs in restricting culture or ideology to the self-conscious normative statements of activists. Bureaucratic forms of organization symbolize just as much as collectivist ones do. All organizations, like all strategies and tactics, have symbolic associations. Elisabeth Clemens (1997) points out that certain associational forms are seen as "appropriate" for women, or appropriate for working-class people, or appropriate for explicitly political claims making. Activists are not entirely constrained by such repertoires; on the contrary, they can combine forms creatively. Thus Clemens shows how women activists barred from formal politics in the late nineteenth and early twentieth centuries drew on alternative associational forms—the club, parlor meeting, and charitable society—to become a major force for social reform. But Clemens's account also suggests that we examine the conditions under which the normative assessments of particular organizational forms or tactics change and the consequences for activists' strategic choices. Along those lines, Rebecca Bordt (1997) has examined the process by which collectivist organizations became normative among radical feminist activists in the 1970s. While the pressures exerted by funders, professional agencies, and government to adopt conventional hierarchical and bureaucratic structures continued strong during this period, feminists setting up collectives also operated in an "alternative environment" of feminist bookstores, therapists, health centers, schools, food coops, foundations, and media—all providing support for collectivist ideals. The result was that collectives took on "a rule-like status" (Bordt, 1997:146); collectivism became feminism. By pointing out that organizations operate in multiple environments, some of which may support and, indeed, require nonconventional forms, Bordt gets at one of the conditions for the institutionalization of new organizational forms.

Based on research on the Southern civil rights movement, I have argued that even earlier, the collectivist forms described by Bordt had shifted from being seen as "black" to being seen as "white" by radical black activists (Polletta, 1997, 2002). As a result, and at a time when their counterparts in the new left were eagerly abolishing national offices and insisting on consensus-based decision making, black activists implemented more centralized and bureaucratic procedures. Procedures that had previously been seen as instrumental were now viewed as ideological, self-indulgent, and white. Each of these studies probes the cultural templates that structure strategic decision making but also inquires into the processes by which such templates come into being and the conditions responsible for their influence and change. They help us to better understand the variable character of what is strategic.[6]

CONCLUSION

I have argued for taking fuller account of the cultural dimensions of political structures in explaining movement emergence. Doing so requires more than recognizing insurgents' creative capacities for interpreting political conditions in new ways. A tendency to conflate culture with agency has made it difficult for sociologists to grasp objective (rather than only subjective), enduring (rather than transient), and constraining (rather than only enabling) aspects of culture and made it difficult for them to see culture operating within political institutions as well as outside them.

Political actors, processes, and institutions are important in accounting for the emergence of protest, previous research suggests. And we can assume that insurgents are on the lookout for opportunities to have political impact. My view is similar to political opportunity theorists' in these two respects. But I would add, first, that the list of possible political opportunities should be expanded to include constitutional provisions for the use of political power, collective memories, and other cultural norms. Second, political actors, institutions, and processes not only provide opportunities for already-constituted collective actors but in some cases help to bring them into being. Third, political institutions shape the mobilizing frames available to activists. If the first point suggests that activists have more resources at their disposal than conventional accounts would allow them, the third suggests that they are more constrained.

Although I have taken structuralists to task for missing the cultural dimensions of politics, I have also urged proponents of a culturalist approach to specify the conditions in which people are likely to see themselves as members of an aggrieved group, in which activists are likely to perceive new opportunities for insurgency, and in which they are able to develop novel yet resonant formulations. Probing insurgents' subjective assessments of objective structures wouldn't get us very far in that task. Luckily, our analyses of culture need not be so limited.

NOTES

Acknowledgments. For valuable comments on previous versions of this chapter, thanks to Jeff Goodwin, James M. Jasper, Kelly Moore, Jeffrey Olick, John Skrentny, Marc Steinberg, and Charles Tilly.

1. Political process theorists have used the term "structure" in two ways: to describe a configuration of political opportunities ("political opportunity structure") and to describe those political institutions, arrangements, and processes that distinguish one political context from another (in comparative studies of movement emergence) or that change in some crucial fashion (in longitudinal studies of movement emergence). My objections are to the latter use of the term "structure." With respect to the former, political process theorists now more commonly refer to "process" and "opportunities" than to a "political opportunity *structure*" (see, e.g., Tarrow, 1998b:77).

2. In recent work, McAdam, Tarrow, and Tilly talk not about opportunities but about "opportunity spirals," which involve the "perception of significant environmental uncertainty on the part of state and non-state elites and challengers alike" (2001:97). The question remains, however, when such perceptions are likely. On the other hand, by showing how the collective identities that operate in routine political contention shape bids for recognition on the part of challenging groups, the authors effectively theorize the cultural continuities between institutional politics and protest. In their recent work, McAdam, Tarrow, and Tilly also advance an understanding of culture that is neither purely subjectivist nor limited to the perceptions of challengers. See also Tilly (1995b).

3. Elsewhere, McAdam (1994) outlines a set of "cultural opportunities"—sudden disasters like Three Mile Island—that spur public opposition to a broader condition, or events, like the *Brown v. Board of Education* decision, that demonstrate system vulnerability. But his distinction between structural and cultural opportunities is not accompanied by any discussion of their relationship, leaving the impression that there is none and that structural opportunities are noncultural.

4. John Hall proposes a model of *"cultural structuralism,* in which social 'structural' arrangements of power and of practices are infused with cultural bases, if culture is understood, not as necessarily holistic, but as diverse configurations of institutionalized meanings, recipes, and material objects that may be differently drawn on by various actors within the same social arena or society" (1992:278).

5. On transgendered activists' rights claims making, see the websites of the following organizations: It's Time, America (www.tgender.net/ita/), Transgender

Francesca Polletta

Menace (www.apocalypse.org/pub/tsmenace/), and The International Conference on Transgender Law and Employment Policy, Inc. (www.abmall.com /ictlep/). See especially, Jessica Xavier, "TS Feminism and TG Politicization" (www.tgender.net/ita/library/); and Sarah DePalma, "1995 Editorial on HRCF and ENDA" (www.tgender.net/ita/library/). On bisexual activism, see Tucker (1995); and BiNet U.S.A. (www.binetusa.org).

6. For good recommendations on how to integrate structuralist and culturalist perspectives in the study of formal movement organizations, see Minkoff (2001).

8

The Poststructuralist Consensus in Social Movement Theory

CHARLES KURZMAN

I ask you to overlook the barbs and outrage of part I of this volume. I urge you to ignore both sides' claims of victimization: the "hegemonic" grip of the "winding, snarling vine" of structuralism (Goodwin and Jasper, hereafter "Jaswin," chapter 1), or the AMA-like monopolistic tendencies of the antistructuralists (Tilly, chapter 2). I propose that the debate boils down to this:

Jaswin decry the structuralist bias in social movement theory; leading figures deny that there is a structuralist bias in social movement theory. For example, Jaswin quote Tarrow (1994:17) sounding structuralist: "The main argument of this study is that people join in social movements in response to political opportunities." Tarrow's response (chapter 3) denies that this "snippet" represents the "main argument" of the book and offers a counter-quotation that downplays political opportunity structures. Jaswin identify Tilly as one of the perpetrators of structuralism; Tilly responds that he is not now, nor has he ever been, a structuralist—at least by Jaswin's definition—nor is any "active participant in the debate" (chapter 2). Jaswin quote Gamson and Meyer's (1996) critique of political opportunity structures, reproaching leading figures for "not treat[ing] it seriously." Meyer's response reiterates and elaborates the critique but quotes leading figures as agreeing with him (chapter 4).

Will nobody defend structuralism? Koopmans offers a backhanded defense, arguing that structures may play a role—sometimes, in cross-national comparisons, if movements choose to obey (chapter 5). Only Polletta (chapter 7) comes out to defend structuralism, at least a cultural structuralism.

In my view, then, the disagreements hide a near-consensus: structuralism is on the outs in social movement theory. But practices, I would argue, have not caught up with the poststructuralist norms.

THE DECLINE OF STRUCTURALISM

When did structuralism cease to motivate social movement theory, and why wasn't I informed? A decade ago, when I was beginning my doctoral research, I thought I was clever and iconoclastic to criticize structuralism in social movement theory. I entitled my dissertation "Structure and Agency in the Iranian Revolution of 1979" to highlight my contribution to the literature, and I organized a large part of the theory chapter as a critique of what I took to be the reigning state-structuralist orthodoxy in the study of social movements and revolutions. I quoted examples of analytical statements that privileged state structure:

"The dramatic turnabout in the political environment originated in economic trends and political realignments that took place quite independent of any 'push' from insurgents." (Jenkins and Perrow, 1977:266)

"In the first place, an adequate understanding of social revolutions requires that the analyst take a nonvoluntarist, structural perspective on their causes and processes." (Skocpol, 1979:14)

"[C]ontinued pressure from the international system, conjoined with certain structural characteristics, precipitates revolution." (Goldstone, 1980b:449)

"The opportunities for a challenger to engage in successful collective action do vary greatly over time. And it is these variations that are held to be related to the ebb and flow of movement activity." (McAdam, 1982:40–41)

"Considerable evidence now exists suggesting the crucial importance of changes in the 'structure of political opportunities' (Eisinger 1973) for the ebb and flow of movement activity." (McAdam, 1988b:128)

"These findings suggest that it may be primarily the conditions of national politics and not factors internal to social movements which determine their 'careers.'" (Klandermans and Tarrow, 1988:17)

Who knew that I was merely a puppet of the zeitgeist? It turns out that my concerns about structuralism were commonplace, and that structuralists were abandoning the donkey even as I was trying to pin the tail on it. No statement like any of the above appears in part I of this volume, and I would be surprised if these stark statements have many supporters these days.

Today, statements about state structure are generally hedged and modified, and causal factors accumulate like Occam's stubble. John Foran (1993) has called this "conjunctural modeling": states matter, culture matters, social structure matters, accidents of history matter—everything matters! This is the same credo that emerges from the defendants in part I: "political process analysts . . . actually have the habit of intoning not a single slogan but a four-part litany: political opportunities . . . , mobilizing structures, framing processes, and contentious interaction" (Tilly, chapter 2); "most political process theorists . . . try to explain movements as the outcome of a combination of structural and cultural as well as long-term and contingent factors and of the interactive logics of the political struggle" (Tarrow, chapter 3).

These laundry-list formulations reduce opportunity, particularly the structure of political opportunity, to one of a number of causal factors that may or may not be operative in any particular case. Gone is the confident logic of the Millian method of difference that animated structuralist analyses: where political opportunities are absent, protest does not occur (or does not succeed); where political opportunities are present, protest occurs (and succeeds). In its place is a cautious logic of multivariate probabilism: political opportunity is one of a number of factors that may increase the likelihood of the emergence or success of some protest movements. Political opportunity has shrunk from a structure to a variable; as noted by Koopmans (chapter 5), the word "structure" is now often dropped from the phrase "political opportunity structure."

The abandonment of structuralism is starkly evident in the two editions of Sidney Tarrow's *Power in Movement* (1994 and 1998b). Perhaps others have also noticed how the conclusion changes? The first edition concludes that "the main incentives for movement creation and diffusion are found in the structure of political opportunities. Increasing access to power, realignments in the political system, conflicts among elites and the availability of allies give early challengers the incentives to assault the power structure and create opportunities for others" (Tarrow, 1994:189). In other words, conducive structural conditions allow protest to emerge (although, Tarrow adds, protesters may not have enough solidarity and collective identity to take advantage of the opportunity). The second edition concludes:

Enough has been said about changes in political opportunities and constraints in this study to make it necessary only to repeat that, while they do not on their own "explain" social movements, they play the strongest role in triggering general episodes of contention. . . . If we were to elevate political opportunity structure into a general covering law, we would always find movements it cannot "explain" and those that arise as opportunities are closing. But that has not been the claim of this study. Instead, I have tried to show how movements develop as specific interactions within general phases of contention, depending on the forms of mobilization they employ, their meanings and identities, and the social networks and connective structures on which they build. (Tarrow, 1998b:200)

The prose has turned self-referential, and the claims made by the analysis are now made modest. Conducive political opportunities (not structures) no longer allow, but simply play a leading role in triggering, protest, along with other factors. Instead of the structuralist sequencing of factors in the first edition, Tarrow's second edition constructs a probabilistic multivariate model (see figure 8.1).

IMPLICATIONS OF THE IRANIAN CASE

I am proud that part of my work on the Iranian Revolution of 1979 (Kurzman, 1996) is cited by both sides in part I (Meyer, chapter 4; Jaswin, chap-

FIGURE 8.1
Tarrow on Political Contention

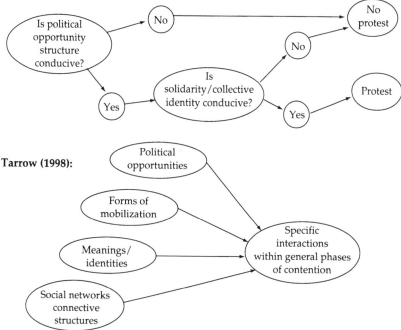

ter 6), and not just because I want to be liked by everyone. Meyer cites me among other scholars within political process theory who take protesters' beliefs seriously, and who regard opportunity as mediated by belief; Jaswin cite me as concluding that the Iranian Revolution emerged and succeeded despite a lack of political opportunity. I am comfortable with both of these statements, and, if I may be allowed a moment of special pleading, I would like to extend these implications of the Iranian case for two of the methodological points I've just tried to make.

First is taking protesters' beliefs seriously. In the case of the Iranian Revolution, taking protesters' beliefs seriously means recognizing that the leaders of the revolutionary movement were highly skeptical of any liberalizing move on the part of the government (Kurzman, forthcoming). They did not adapt their protests to take advantage of opportunities offered by the Iranian monarchy—when private oppositional meetings were allowed, they held public meetings; when free elections were promised, they refused to participate—and they were scornful of the moderate oppositionists who played by the rules of the game. At the same time, the revolutionaries explicitly rejected the fatalistic implications of other opportunity structures as well: the Islamic opposition's lack of institutional resources (Kurzman, 1994:56–60); the quiescent ideology that dominated Islamic thinking in Iran at the time (Kurzman, 1994:60–63); and socioeconomic conditions from which bazaaris, construction workers, and other clerical supporters were profiting (Kurzman, 2003). All of this suggests either that opportunities cannot be held responsible for the emergence of the revolutionary movement, or that opportunities had an effect that operated behind the backs of the protesters, outside of their consciousness, and despite their best intentions—that is, structurally. There is no middle position—non-structuralist opportunity—in this case.

If protesters' beliefs indicate that the revolutionary movement emerged without opportunity, or even against opportunity, what accounts for the disconnect? Why did the opportunity variable fail? In a separate paper (Kurzman, 2003), I approach this issue by comparing Iran in 1975 with Iran in 1978. "Objective" opportunity was similar in both years, I argue, yet a seminary student protest repressed with casualties in 1975 had virtually no public echo, while a similar event in 1978 quickly became a rallying point for widespread revolutionary protests. What changed in the meantime, I argue, was the revolutionary clerical leaders' perception of the "readiness" of the Iranian people. In 1975, these leaders foresaw a long preparatory period before revolutionary protest would be effective; in late 1977, small protests led these leaders to change their minds and declare Iranians "awakened." With this judgment, they mobilized their cadres and launched numerous, though still small, demonstrations. To abstract from this detail, it seems to me that the movement began because the revolutionary opposition conceived of opportunities differently than sociologists do, combining judgments of state power, popular ideologies, and risk assessment. Even if sociologists were to agree on how to define opportunity, their definition(s) would not be as important in understanding this case as the protesters' definitions of opportunity; it was the protesters' definition, not ours, that motivated them to mobilize. The concept of opportunity thus dissolves into perceptions of opportunity.

The second point is success without opportunity. If opportunity is a characteristic of actors' environment, and perceived opportunity is a characteristic of actors, the Iranian Revolution appears to be a case where the latter trumps the former. That is, the revolutionary movement arose, gained momentum, and succeeded even in the absence of a conducive environment, as indicated by state breakdown, say, or international constraints on state repression. Not all revolutionary insurrections succeed, even those that are confident of success, so it would be absurd to argue that perceptions always prevail over the environment. One can convince oneself that a brick wall doesn't exist, but running into it will still be painful. The significance of the Iranian Revolution, then, is that—at least once in the recent past—revolutionaries were able to will away the brick wall. That is, their perceptions were self-fulfilling; they were able to generate a movement so strong that the lack of political opportunity didn't matter.

If a movement once trumped an unconducive environment, then we can no longer explain the failure of other movements simply by documenting the presence of unconducive environments. We need to ask how unconducive environments are able to stymie movements. The Iranian Revolution, though it is only a single case, rules out some hypotheses. We know that states cannot subdue revolutions simply by threat of force, since the Iranian monarchy issued many such threats, to no avail. We know that states cannot subdue revolutions simply by arresting and shooting demonstrators, since the shah's government tried that too. Bloodshed spurred protest rather than cowing it. (Perhaps greater or lesser force or different means or targets would have had the opposite effect? How would we know?)

The closer we inspect the brick wall of unconduciveness, the more it looks like trial and error. The state tries threats, or violence, or co-optation, and waits to see what works. What "works" is entirely the product of the protesters' response. Opening fire on a thousand unarmed protesters sitting peacefully in a public square, as the Iranian monarchy did on September 8, 1978 ("Black Friday")—does this cause the survivors and their compatriots to cease and desist protesting, or to redouble their efforts? This is the "double-edged sword" of repression. The back edge— the edge facing the state—can take two forms. If protesters are willing to face prison, torture, and death, or even welcome such fates, then repression will not faze them. If protesters do not wish to face such a fate but know that many of their compatriots are outraged and expect them to join in protest, then they may decide there is safety in numbers and join as well. I am fond of a metaphor provided by Talcott Parsons (1967:chap. 9), of all people: State coercion is like the reserves of a bank. It is not intended to be drawn on by everyone at once, and if too many people make demands, it will soon run out.

The brick wall of unconduciveness, then, is in a meaningful sense a figment of protesters' imaginations. Its effects lie in protesters' responses to it. How, then, do revolutionary movements ever fail? Clearly, confidence does not always carry the day. The answer lies in the distribution of responses in the population. Revolutionary leaders may be optimistic or ready for martyrdom, but the rest of the country may not be. The distribution of optimism or masochism must be great enough to reach a rolling critical mass for the less optimistic and the more cost-wary to decide to join in. Unfortunately for those who would like to predict the outcome of protest movements, this distribution can probably never be known in advance. What sort of scenario would we present to survey respondents? Could we expect their cost-benefit calculations to be the same in the cool of the moment?

STRUCTURALISM IS DEAD! LONG LIVE—WHAT?

The "post" prefix makes an awkward label, except perhaps on cereal. Poststructuralism is no exception. It tells us what has gone before, but surely there is a better label for the current consensus in social movement theory. "Conjuncturalism" captures the multivariate tendency, but I prefer "constructionism." It announces the view that people construct their own history—not under circumstances chosen by themselves, certainly, but under circumstances they have the power to change. Opportunity, ultimately, is what people make of it.

Yet if social movement theory has adopted constructionist norms, in that few scholars are willing to defend structuralism any more, the field has not yet fully adopted constructionist methods. Studies of opportunity, in particular political opportunity, still frequently treat it as a structure, not a variable. I propose that three tasks remain before practices catch up with norms.

The first task is establishing probabilistic effect. If opportunity affects social movements only sometimes, as poststructuralist norms insist, then how do we know that it is worth continuing to study? The modal sociological response to such issues is multivariate regression, in which a variable is deemed important if has a statistically significant coefficient, net of other variables. I am not suggesting that the study of social movements must abandon case studies for regression analysis, but some approach ought to be developed to deal with the issue of multivariate probabilistic effects. Jeff Goodwin's Boolean analysis of opportunity's effect on protest in his forthcoming volume on "opportunistic protest" is an example of this sort of approach.

Constructionist norms about the importance of process imply that the outcome of movements cannot be foreseen in advance. Yet construction-ism need not involve a postmodern abdication of causal reasoning, as structuralists sometimes suggest. There's a fair bit of this bogey waved by the defendants in part I, and I think it's misplaced. First, constructionism does not necessarily mean the rejection of causality. One can still order one's analysis analytically and inquire about the relationship of concepts in a causal space. Second, constructionism does not necessarily involve a reduction of the unit of analysis from groups (or groups of cases) to indi-viduals (or individual cases). One can still generalize across a group, so long as the generalization is held to be heuristic. Third, constructionism does not necessarily dissolve patterns into chaos. One can still seek pat-terns in social life, so long as the patterns are recognized as social con-structions. What constructionism changes, then, is the epistemological status of causes and patterns. Let us speak of these as heuristic inventions, not discoveries.

The second task is focusing on mechanisms of effect. In structuralist analysis, one needs only to show correlation between the outcome and conducive structural characteristics. Poststructuralism, by contrast, prob-lematizes the mechanisms of causal effect. Opportunity can no longer be expected to operate automatically, so the question arises: How does it operate? But few studies of social movements address this question. In particular, evidence of "objective" opportunity is too often presented without evidence that protesters were aware of, or motivated by, that opportunity.

Since this chapter was first drafted, a major book by McAdam, Tarrow, and Tilly (2001) has been published emphasizing this point. The authors acknowledge that they "come from a structuralist tradition" (22), but—as in their contributions to this volume—they repudiate this tradition as static and mechanistic. Opportunity, they say, cannot "invite mobilization unless it is a) visible to potential challengers and b) perceived as an opportunity" (43). They propose to focus on "mechanisms" too, defining mechanisms as "events that alter relations among specified sets of ele-ments in identical or closely similar ways over a variety of situations" (24). This definition, however, leads in a somewhat different direction from the approach that I am trying to propose. It emphasizes patterns across cases—which is fine—but de-emphasizes the subjective perceptions that allow causes to have effects. "Mechanism," in the construction-ist approach, is an actor's or group's response to a given shift in the environment. There is still a residue of structuralism in McAdam, Tarrow, and Tilly's emphasis on shifts rather than responses to shifts.

Does this mean that social movement studies must "take every epoch at its word and believe that everything it says and imagines about itself is true," a position that Karl Marx mocked: "While in ordinary life every shopkeeper is very well able to distinguish between what somebody pro-fesses to be and what he really is, our historians have not yet won even this trivial insight" (Marx, 1978 [1845–1846]:175). A constructionist analy-sis may well privilege the words of the subjects, at the risk of appearing naive to hard-nosed materialists who claim to know a priori what moti-vates people. But the study of popular perceptions need not stop with the recording of subjects' self-impressions. For example, the way people talk about opportunity may not fit with their consciously expressed self-image—I have interviewed demonstrators who talk about running away from the police, then describe themselves as not afraid to sacrifice for the cause. Such a disjuncture between accounts of actions and accounts of motivation is itself an interesting finding that only comes from focusing on mechanisms of effect.

This does not mean that opportunity is meaningless. I could hardly hold that position, having participated in extensions of the concept of political opportunity in recent work to organizations (Kurzman, 1998) and to the international polity (Barrett and Kurzman, n.d.). What I pro-pose is that opportunity should be operationalized primarily as perceived opportunity, as a characteristic that protesters impute to their environ-ment. Opportunity references protesters' relation with external actors, in the same way that "network" references their relations with one another, and "frame" references their relations to broader cultural contexts. Con-structionism turns each of these "structural" factors into distributions of perceptions: perceptions of the political environment and what can feasi-bly be accomplished, of social ties and what can be expected of them, of cultural norms and their application to a given movement.

The third task is exploring deviant cases. If the effect of opportunity is probabilistic, then there must be—and are, as Tarrow (1998:200) noted in the block quote above—cases in which opportunity exists but no protest occurs (or succeeds), and cases where no opportunity exists but protest occurs (or succeeds) anyway. These cases appear to be far less frequently studied than cases where opportunities and outcomes run hand in hand, but—regardless of the frequency of such cases, which is unknown—deviant cases are important for further developing the theory of opportu-nity in a non-structuralist direction. Cases of opportunity-without-protest address the question: When is opportunity effective? Cases of protest-without-opportunity address the question: Is opportunity as important as other factors?

The central disagreement in part I, I suggest, is whether "political process theory" can accommodate these questions and the constructionist norms that motivate them. Jaswin argue that introducing such questions subverts the structuralist principles upon which political process theory was originally based; the defendants argue that those principles were never ironclad, so political process theory not only can accommodate constructionism but already has. I don't care much whether the label "political process theory" gets applied to current and future research. What I think is important is to recognize that an underlying shift has occurred, from structuralism to constructionism, and that living up to the implications of our constructionist norms will change how we study social movements.

9

The Intellectual Challenges of Toiling in the Vineyard

MARC W. STEINBERG

In her treatise on Eastern American viticulture Lucie Morton counsels that "Training and pruning is one of the most intellectually challenging jobs for vineyardists" (1985:151). She also notes that although the grafting of vines on to different rootstocks can have many benefits for fruit bearing, it can also significantly add to the costs of maintaining the vineyard (1985:30). Morton's expertise of course is grape growing, but her treatise gives me pause to wonder if she at least minored in sociology as an undergraduate. In this volume we see divergent views of how we should be toiling in the vineyards to cultivate the vines. Some of our contributors suggest that we have paid insufficient attention to training and pruning; others argue that the critiques and alternative strategies amount to a type of hacking rather than pruning.

In this chapter I argue that the issues raised by all of our contributors are cogent, though the bases upon which they raise them are somewhat misplaced. Entangled in some of the snarls, I suggest that many of our contributors lose sight of the vine itself and how it grows. I maintain that there is greater agreement on understandings of causality than an initial reading of these essays indicates. In addition, I offer different conceptions of *structure* and *culture*, two of the key terms in this dialogue, and consider how the reframing of these terms shifts the focus of our intellectual challenges. Finally, I provide an example of how the more fully relational conception of causality that I proffer can be used to think through the ways in which we analyze opportunities for contention.

ABSTRUSE AGREEMENT ON
CAUSAL MECHANISMS

Obscured in some of the debates over political opportunity structure (POS) models is an underlying agreement on the causal dynamics of contentious action, or perhaps how a more explicit accord can be achieved. All of the contributors are quick to note that the causal dynamics of POSs primarily focus on the initial stages of contention, and that once under way, much akin to the vine, a conflict grows incrementally along its own particular path.

I believe that none of our contributors would wish to lay claim to McAdam's original path diagram presented by Jasper and Goodwin as representing their current thinking on the causal dynamics of contention (see chapter 1). Over the course of the last decade all of our contributors have consistently advocated a conception of causal processes that is deeply historical. As Tilly argues in his reflections on explaining political processes, "time, place and sequence strongly influence how the relevant processes unfold; in that sense they are inescapably historical in character" (1995a:1601).[1] Though they differ in their theoretical foundations for this historical perspective, all our contributors have some conception of causality as being necessarily *relational* (how any action is the result of the way actors and practices are situated vis-à-vis one another and within particular institutional contexts), *conjunctural* (how contention or its lack is determined by the ways in which different practices and circumstances conjoin, often in recurrent patterns, at particular times), and *contingent*, or to use Sewell's (1996b) more felicitous term, *eventful* (how any outcome can be partly traced to a temporally unique conjoining). I suspect that all agree with Mustafa Emirbayer, who argues that collective action and social agency are "inseparable from the unfolding dynamics of situations, especially from the problematic features of those situations. . . . Agency is always a dialogic process by which actors immersed in the *durée* of lived experience engage with others in collectively organized action contexts, temporal as well as spatial. Agency is path dependent as well as situationally embedded; it signifies modes of response to problems impinging upon it through sometimes broad expanses of time as well as space" (1997:294).

POS analysts who focus on the "dynamic" rather than "stable" aspects of political arenas implicitly adopt some version of this relational stance, arguing that mobilization and collective action depend on temporarily and situationally specific concatenations of relations between powerholders and challengers.[2] Opportunities are thus always measured not only by the positions of authorities and challengers within a specific national political institutional arena but also in relation to the networks of power that temporally connect the contestants to other actors beyond that arena. As Keck and Sikkink (1998), for example, argue in the case of recent human rights campaigns, fluid and adaptable networks of nongovernmental organizations (NGOs) on the international level have created possibilities for a "boomerang effect" under which repressive actions by nation states can, in specific circumstances, lead to transnational pressures for reform (see also McCarthy, 1997). Other proponents have suggested moving beyond a simple dichotomous model of "opportunity/ threat" in analyzing how opportunities are created in policy-specific domains for particular collective actors, and how such "windows" themselves can be variably open across a continuum (Gamson and Meyer, 1996:280; Imig and Meyer, 1993:189–190; Meyer and Staggenborg, 1996:1636; Tarrow, 1996b:42, 50). In addition, some have even argued that increasing levels of threat from the state or countermovements, instead of facilitation from allies, spur mobilization by heightening insecurity and thus prompt a response (Meyer and Staggenborg, 1996:1644; Staggenborg, 1991; Smith, 1996; Goldstone and Tilly, 2001). Finally, most recently, several analysts have observed that political contention itself (even disruptive collective action) is becoming increasingly institutionalized, auguring a shift in the uses of power by authorities and challengers and the ways in which the former police the actions of the latter (Meyer and Tarrow, 1998:4, 21; McCarthy and McPhail, 1998:84–85, 104; Kubik, 1988:135; McAdam, 1998b). Meyer and Tarrow posit that these institutionalized forms of protest might be as productive as their more unruly cousins, indicating that the central features of POSs documented in Western democratic states over the past several decades themselves are slowly shifting.[3]

In short, *all of us* err in our explanations when we are insufficiently attentive to the relational and historical bases of causality. What underlies the conundrum debated in this collection is not so much an appreciation of relation and temporal dynamics but problems in specifying what we mean by two key terms, *structure* and *culture*.

WHAT'S STRUCTURAL, WHAT'S CULTURAL, WHAT'S THE DIFFERENCE?

A good deal of the disagreement among our contributors revolves around the question of what the structural and cultural components underlying collective action processes are and the ways in which they affect the potential for and patterns of mobilization. Yet for all the discussion, not much attention is directed to defining either term. It's fair to ask all the contributors, just what's *structural* and what's *cultural*? I think that any definition should be preceded by the caveat that what we are defining are heuristic terms that isolate certain features or dimensions of social action for analytic purposes. This might seem to be a trivial comment, but too often in our analyses we come perilously close to lapsing into a form of positivist variablism. In such cases organization, resources, culture, and structure are depicted errantly as discrete entities in a formula that can be calculated to determine the success of mobilization, collective action, and the attainment of goals.

Although many significant treatises have been written on such definitional questions, let me simply define the structural aspects of contention as the dimension of *embedded routines of social practices that are commonly recognized by a group, easily replicable and generally difficult to alter because of their strongly relational nature between actors and with other practices.*[4] I take culture to be the semiotic attributes of social practices, commonly recognized through shared cognitions, easily replicable and generally difficult to alter because of their strong relations to (1) larger systems of signs and their meanings within which they are used and (2) patterns of actions themselves.

Jack Barbalet has noted that the structured nature of our own analytic practices leads sociologists to conceptualize culture and structure as distinct entities, following a Mertonian theoretical framework (1992:159). Yet, as he persuasively argues, neither structure nor culture is a discrete aspect of social life, nor are they things apart from other aspects of social action. All of the analytical aspects of contentious action discussed in this volume—organizational, symbolic, affective, material, etc.—have both structural and cultural dimensions (Emirbayer and Goodwin 1994:1438–1439; Ewick and Silbey 1998:38–43). Part of our task in building causal models of contention is to ferret out how these structures relate to one another, both under certain recurring sets of conjunctural conditions and through more particular contingent dynamics. Too often when we analyze contention, however, we absentmindedly slip into a positivist epistemology that fosters variablism, and this underlies some of the disputes concerning the causal nature of structure versus culture in this volume. In the end neither structure nor culture causes *anything;* social practices and their attendant cognitions do.

This is not wholly lost to our contributors. For example, Polletta and Koopmans observe that there is a structural dimension to culture as well as social organization, though they are not quite explicit enough about the ways in which this structural dimension differs from that of the material and organizational realm (see also Polletta, 1999a:8). The differences are important, because the structural dimensions of the impediments to or opportunities for action do not necessarily operate in the same ways, nor can we assume that they operate in tandem with one another. Koopmans, for example, in his discussion of cultural opportunity structures assumes a homology between the organizational, cultural, and material analytical levels of action that I believe is both unwarranted and unhelpful for understanding the tricky dynamics of contention.[5] Such a concept conflates several analytically distinct types of structured practices that shape the way in which actors can articulate, present, and disseminate shared cognitions of injustice and its resolution. As I have argued elsewhere (1998, 1999a) the discourses of contention themselves are semiotically structured within discursive fields—the accepted set of related discourses through which contention can be articulated—in which they are constructed. This is the case in terms for the meanings commonly recognized or available within any one discourse and how such meanings can be related to other discourses within the field that contain the possibilities to articulate claims and understandings of injustice. Therefore, what is being labeled as culture by our contributors has a structural dimension that is just as important to analyze as activist networks or the dispersion of state and institutional authority. Challengers' messages are also bounded and patterned organizationally, materially, and affectively. Access to the media as well as media routines, networks, and ties to other organizations; the resources and technical capacities that groups have to produce and disseminate their messages; and the ways in which particular representations of suffering or injustice can evoke an emotional response all operate through relatively enduring practices, or structures, that affect a group's effort to have its claims heard and accepted (Gitlin, 1980; Gamson and Croteau, 1992; Oliver and Myers, 1999; McCarthy, McPhail, and Smith, 1996). It is certainly possible that there are dominant patterns of contingency and conjuncture between such structures, but that is a matter of empirical investigation. Discursive, media, and organizational structures of practice do not map neatly on one another. Our investigations should focus on how such structures conjoin in particular ways, and if they do so under certain recurrent circumstances and within certain time periods.

Even one of the most debated features of collective action, emotion, also clearly has crucial structural dimensions. In his recent work on emotions and movements James Jasper signals precisely this when he notes that what he terms "moral shocks" depend on preexisting patterns of affect, and that "even the most fleeting emotions are firmly rooted in moral and cognitive beliefs that are relatively stable and predictable" (1998:409, 421). In his macro-sociology of emotions Jack Barbalet urges us to set our sights beyond this internal structure of affect, to understand how this structure and its dynamics are tied to other nonaffective structures that determine the possibilities to elicit, experience, and identify emotion (1998). He argues both that emotions are structured practices of convention and that they are not monadic states but are realized through structures of social interactions, relationships, and the situations in which they occur (1998:67). "Before anything else, emotions must be understood within the structural relations of power and status which elicit them. This makes emotion a social-structural as much as if not more than a cultural thing" (1998:26).[6] His analysis of working-class resentment, in which he argues that emotion is a crucial feature of class conflict, provides a cogent example. Barbalet suggests that such affect is not a given feature of working-class life but variable to working people's material position in a trade cycle and the ways in which their social relationships are patterned with friends and kin. Particular configurations of these allow for a shared feeling of resentment because of powerlessness evoked by a commonly recognized situation (1992:156–159). In these senses the concept of emotion invoked in causal arguments of contention can neither be viewed as solipsistic nor be seen as the glue of solidarity that mobilizes conflict. Rather, emotion is social sentiment and understanding that is the "experience of readiness for action," and it is always experienced in patterned ways by structured nonaffective processes.[7]

On the flip side, the definition of culture that I have offered above suggests some agreement and some departures from the ways many of our contributors have staked their positions. I concur with contributors such as Jasper and Goodwin (chapter 1) and Polletta (chapter 7), who argue that cultural processes are both constraining and enabling. Semiotic dimensions of contentious practices can serve to highlight some options for action and obscure others. However, these semiotic dimensions are not in and of themselves constitutive of the possibilities for action. As Benford and Snow maintain:

> Although political opportunity structures can constrain and facilitate collective action framing processes, the degree or extent of political opportunity in a society is seldom, if ever, a clear and easily read structural unity. Rather, its existence and openness is subject to debate and interpretation, and can thus be framed by movement actors as well as others. . . . To argue that framing processes and political opportunity are linked interactively is not to suggest that political opportunities are purely constructed entities. It is to argue, however, that the extent to which they constrain or facilitate collective action is partly contingent on how they are framed by movement actors as well as others. (2000:631)

They suggest that our task in the analysis of framing processes and political opportunities is to understand how particular patterns of relationships between the two produce determinant effects on the course of contentious action.

As many of our contributors also note, in these chapters and elsewhere, those aspects of contention that are often taken to be "structural" or non-cultural—networks and numbers, organizational structures, resources, etc.—have a cultural dimension whose meaning is derived in relation to other practices, including discursive and framing practices. McAdam, for example, hints at this cultural dimension when he argues that strategies and tactics, particularly in the early stages of a movement "represent a critically important contribution to the overall signifying work of the movement" (1996b:341). However, adopting a more relational form of analysis, we can generalize this observation and investigate how all aspects of contention have semiotic dimensions that stand in relation to each other and to what are frequently (and as I have argued mistakenly) labeled as cultural practices.

An illustrative case in this regard are the components of Charles Tilly's handy formula for scoring social movement standing: numbers x commitment x unity x worthiness (1993–1994:14). Tilly quite rightly observes that unity and worthiness highlight the cultural dimensions of contention, given that they are shared through symbols, slogans, and stories. However, I believe we can credibly argue that all of the terms in this equation have cultural dimensions and that they come to be publicly understood in relation to one another and the patterned cultural dimensions of other movement practices such as strategy and framing.

A cogent example of this comes from the AIDS movement and two social movement organizations (SMOs) that have played a central role in it, ACT-UP and the NAMES Project. Both organizations were formed in 1987 by activists in metropolitan areas with high rates of HIV infection and sizable gay populations (New York and San Francisco, respectively). Both spawned dozens of chapters in the United States and abroad (though ACT-UP opted for an affiliational organizational form while NAMES was more centralized), and both received widespread media attention. Both sought to destigmatize gay and lesbian identities in the process also of expanding the attention to the disease and commitment of resources to fight HIV transmission and AIDS (Krause, 1994; Sturken, 1992). However, each developed very different action repertoires and framing strategies. Whereas ACT-UP used what Steven Epstein has termed a "genocide" discourse and framing that emphasized "self help with a vengeance," the NAMES Project used a nonthreatening symbol of memorialization, comfort, and Americana in an attempt to construct an inclusive understanding of community and commitment in the fight against AIDS (Epstein, 1997:420; Gamson, 1989; Krause, 1994; Lewis and Fraser, 1996). The emotions that each framing strategy sought to evoke were distinctly different as well. Whereas as one ACT-UP activist noted "mourning becomes militancy," for the NAMES Project mourning was coded as catharsis and healing (Sturken, 1992:77). And where ACT-UP developed an action repertoire that centered on militant nonviolent civil disobedience, the NAMES project routinized its collective actions in peaceful memorialization and display. This contrast is neatly portrayed by the events of October 11, 1988, in Washington, D.C. After a memorial and a display of the entire quilt attended by thousands, about a thousand ACT-UP demonstrators seized the FDA headquarters (which they renamed the "Federal Death Administration"), demanding immediate access to more drugs and more speedy clinical trials (Epstein, 1997:422).

How do we "read" the cultural dimensions of the ACT-UP and NAMES Project scorecards? We only can do so as these dimensions relate to one another and the semiotic possibilities of the action strategies and discursive processes each group pursued. Arguably the NAMES Project had greater numbers than ACT-UP; certainly with a self-proclaimed five to six million participants by early 1995 at memorial demonstrations and displays, the organization has displayed a greater capacity for mass mobilization (Sturken, 1992:73). The NAMES Project was likely seen to be just as worthy, if not more so, by conscience constituents, sympathizers, and the general public. We might even argue that its organizational history connoted a higher level of unity, both for our retrospective gaze and for contemporaries, given that it expanded and prospered, while chapters of ACT-UP engaged in successive public episodes of in-fighting and recrimination (Epstein, 1997:426).

I believe that we can make a credible argument that each group's numbers, and perhaps even commitment, were "read" differently, that the same cultural metric was not used to evaluate the two. Following Tilly, we might argue that commitment could in part be read from the greater risks that ACT-UP members were willing to incur given their repertoire of highly disruptive nonviolent civil disobedience, and that this in turn compensates for smaller numbers in judging its relative threat compared to the NAMES Project. Yet, in a relational sense, we can also see that there is a more complex semiotics operating in the reading of ACT-UP numbers. As Michael Brown and Joshua Gamson both argue, ACT-UP's tactics are radically transgressive and pointedly subversive of both dominant cultural codes and norms of public space (Brown, 1997:61–63; Gamson, 1989:355, 361). It is plausible that group action repertoires and discourses, and their perceived propinquity to other actions and discourses within the semiotic field of their political challenges, were read quite differently by their targets, sympathizers, and bystanders. And the semiotic dimensions of ACT-UP and the NAMES Project also were read by many participants, targets, and onlookers *in relation to one another*. For Anthony Fauci, pharmaceutical corporations, police departments, news reporters, and even the general public, a gaggle of ACT-UP protesters might have been more than equal to a passel of quilt bearers. How numbers were interpreted, in other words, was a dynamic product of how a whole series of meanings were linked to one another in the semiotic field in which the boundaries of contention were mapped.

If something seemingly as simple as a number can require attentive, situational reading, then so must other cultural aspects of contention. We find readily transparent meanings of discourse and action often at our analytic peril. The definition of culture I have provided above highlights one other problem often produced by our conceptual slippage. Participants on both sides of the debate often depict culture as being a shared set of practices and understandings, in which mutuality is assumed implicitly, if not wholly unproblematically (Jasper, 1997:12; 50; McAdam, Tarrow, and Tilly, 1997:156–157; Tilly, 1995b). However, culture is not a set of wholly shared understandings between actors, and its mediating power is often highly contested and transformable. "Contentious conversation," observes Tilly, "follows its own causal logic" (1998a:494). As I have argued elsewhere (1998, 1999b), part of what differentiates contentious discourse from material resources and social ties is that symbolic or semiotic structures have a dialogic and dialectical nature. People can read quite different meanings from the same discourse, symbol, or action, and indeed contentious politics often involves some pretty heated conflict over which reading will be preferred. In the end such analyses are only possible by mapping how discourses and their meanings are situated within the larger discourse field, and how their relations to other discourses bounds the possibilities for meaning and can also spark the fires of contention.

OPPORTUNITY REDUX

Taking a more relational, conjunctural, and contingent perspective on contentious politics reorients what is at issue in this debate, that is, how opportunities for collective action are produced and pursued. I suggest that a fully relational perspective on contentious action requires us to understand how temporally bracketed thickets of relations among and between the various dimensions of our analysis are crucial in triggering transformations in any one level and the relations between them. The branches of our vines wind about one another, and sometimes we graft a clipping from one rootstock on to another, but we need not get lost in these thickets.

Koopmans usefully defines opportunity for us as "options for collective action with chances and risks attached to them that depend on factors outside the mobilizing group" (chapter 5). However, what constitutes an opportunity can only be discerned when the dynamics of each analytic dimension are considered in relation to one another and relations between all potential actors are scrutinized along these dimensions as well. Of particular interest to us are those cases of clear disjunctures in the dynamics between these dimensions and how such fissures create the potential for the transformation of the relations between them and the groups they describe, opening up the possibility for voice, mobilization, and action.

Illuminating studies of human rights protests against authoritarian regimes in Latin America in the 1970s and 1980s usefully serve as a touchstone for this point. In countries such as Chile, Guatemala, and Argentina during these years of military repression, women were among the vanguard in mobilization efforts and public protest. Most important, these women engaged in organization and mobilization efforts during periods that POS models would find the *least* advantageous: periods of elite unity, relatively stable alignments among major powerful actors, a lack of powerful allies, and heavy state repression. Moreover, as Rita Noonan argues in the case of the Pinochet regime, the conservative discourses the state propagated gendered the institutional polity in such a way as to close routine access to it for most women: "The case of Chile demonstrates that women's political power came out of a 'closed' polity, during a time of intolerance for protest, and where the policymaking capability of the government was at an all-time high in terms of extinguishing popular mobilizations" (1995:84). By subsuming feminine practices under the realm of motherhood, this and other regimes sought to depoliticize women's sphere of activity, constructing a discursive order in which women and the family became pillars in the private sphere for the maintenance and propagation of a conservative nationalist state (Chuchryk, 1993:94).

The dialogic and dialectic nature that I have argued figures prominently in semiotic dynamics provided an opportunity for women activists to appropriate this conservative maternal discourse and, as Jennifer Schirmer argues, transform "the image of the weak and powerless female to their advantage as a protective means for mobilization, resistance and survival" (1993:33). Mothers and grandmothers of the "disappeared" in each country first built solidary networks (often through casual and repeated contacts in futile attempts to garner information on their kin) as they informally came to know one another in their tasks as female guardians in search of missing family members. They then engaged in the more public processes of mobilization and collective protest through discursive constructions of motherhood disseminated by the military regimes, eventually garnering support and building alliances with other human rights groups. Both the supposed inconsequentiality of women within the institutional polity and their inviolable mission as caretakers for the family gave their protests to learn of the fate of their kin a significant buffer of legitimacy (Arditti, 1999:35–37; Brysk, 1994:47–49; Chuchryk, 1993; Schirmer, 1993, 1994).

These examples are instructive because they both do not fit the expectations of POS designs concerning the propitious circumstances for mobilization. They also show how a more completely relational analysis provides us in part with a window to understand these mobilizations. In the discursive realm, as Noonan argues, the main genres in contention with one another were those of socialist, liberal democratic, and state authoritarian nationalist politics. All constructed public politics as masculine activity. Gender issues were not significantly addressed by the former two discourses, and liberal feminism was suppressed by the state. Thus, the discursive field was constructed in such a way as to allow for the use of a maternalist discourse that provided the female kin of the disappeared with a public voice. Simultaneously, with the state focusing its repression on males and those institutions dominated by them (such as leftist parties and trade unions), depoliticized women were not subject to the same degree of scrutiny and coercion until they had made their mark in the public sphere. Concurrently, on a transnational level of policy networks, human rights organizations were developing systematic links to one another and to dissidents, both publicizing the women's plight and pressuring Western governments into action (Arditti, 1999:37–40; Keck and Sikkink, 1998:103–107).

From a more fully relational perspective we might further consider how the discourses by which these women were framed and in turn framed their actions stood in relation to the discourses through which human rights NGOs articulated their claims for legitimacy and attention. How these entwined discourses in turn related to the semiotic dimensions of national challengers' and NGOs' action strategies is yet another level of the many relationships we would need to study more thoroughly to understand the rise and success of these women. Beyond this we can see that discursive practices, state patterns of repression, and developing transnational networks of human rights NGOs all conjoined to create an opportunity for these mothers and grandmothers. These conjunctures, repeated in similar ways in Argentina, Chile, El Salvador, and Guatemala, offer us rough sketches for the painting of a more abstract picture of how, under certain conditions and within particular periods, practices concatenate to produce similar outcomes. Finally, on a contingent level, we might investigate how the advent of the Carter administration in the United States shifted the context in which these sets of relations developed, how particular twists and snarls took shape at a particular time (Keck and Skikkink, 1998:105–109). As Tilly (1996) has suggested, any delimited set of routines is always developed in response to unenvisioned events and circumstances.

CONCLUSION: TOILING IN THE VINEYARD

Viticulturalists note that vine tending generally involves a great deal of artful compromise. Some pruning is necessary to enhance productivity and maintain growth, but too much has a depressant effect. The training of vines is best accomplished by moderate spacing: sufficiently wide spacing allows for less pruning and easier maintenance, though past a certain point plant spacing and row width can reduce yields (Weaver, 1976:176–177, 185). My response to our contributors is that I think we all need to go back out into the fields and do a good deal more intellectually challenging cultivation. Rather than being either too structural or cultural, our current models are not sufficiently nuanced or informed in either sense. We need to be *both* more cultural and structural, and from a more relational perspective. Finding causal mechanisms that foster opportunities for contention requires greater scrutiny of the ways in which all dimensions of collective action are temporally patterned in complex but coherent ways, as well as understanding the ways in which the structural and cultural dimensions of contentious practices recursively influence and mediate one another. "The grapevine has a remarkable ability to regrow," remark Mullins, Bouquet, and Williams. "Carefully tended grapevines can remain productive for a very long time" (1992:37).

NOTES

My thanks to Francesca Polletta, Charles Tilly, and the editors for their help with some of the snarls in this chapter.

1. And he suggests that any transhistorical model of revolution (and by implication any other atemporal model of large-scale political change) "is doomed to failure" (Tilly, 1995a:1600). Tarrow similarly notes that "we cannot hope to understand the dynamics and impact of movements by 'placing' them in a static grid of cleavages, conflict and state institutions; we must watch them as a moving target" (1996b:61).

2. Kriesi et al. (1995); Tarrow (1996b); and Giugni (1998) all distinguish between how stable institutional mechanisms within the nation-state provide relatively fixed avenues of contention for challengers, and how temporally changing capacities and alliances determine conditions for contention. Jaswin's critique seems more appropriately directed toward those analysts who focus on the latter rather than the former.

3. POS analysts have focused less attention on the ways mobilization and collective action can also occur in political arenas in which there is no routine or active policing by authorities or established powers. Whether we designate such social, ideological, and geographic areas as "free spaces," the infrapolitics of

"hidden transcripts" or some form of "structural hole," we need to take a clearer measure of just how much mobilization occurs in such enclaves (Scott, 1990; Polletta, 1999a). As a number of studies on NIMBY and other environmental protests suggest, for example, mobilizations can and often do occur without shifts in the POS and sometimes can even utilize institutionalized hierarchies and discourses (Broadbent, 1998; Lichterman, 1996; Walsh et al., 1997).

4. As Christian Joppke in his analysis of political opportunity structures in antinuclear movements notes, "structures do not exist unless they are produced and reproduced through social action" (1993:13).

5. We should approach the use of any such parallel, Goodwin's (1997) concept of libidinal opportunity structure being another example, with a similar skepticism.

6. Barbalet also maintains that linking emotion with action through motivation is "too narrow and too simple" (1992:152).

7. As Colin Barker argues from a dialogic perspective, emotion can be conceived as the emotional-volitional tone of social action (2001:176; see also Goodwin, Jasper, and Polletta, 2001).

10

Knowledge for What? Thoughts on the State of Social Movement Studies

RICHARD FLACKS

The big news in social movement studies in the last few years has been the concerted effort, led by Charles Tilly, Doug McAdam, and Sidney Tarrow (hereafter TMT) to formulate a conceptual structure for the field.

TMT have been among the most important contributors, over several decades, to the systematic study of social movements. Their current efforts at codification represent a culmination of their prior, separate efforts. They, along with others, beginning in the 1970s, challenged previously dominant interpretations of social protest and movement and helped set social movement studies on a new course.

The kind of thinking they challenged tended to see collective protest as a form of deviance or pathology. Social movements were often seen in terms of "mob psychology" or as an expression of social breakdown and anomie; protest leaders often understood as acting out unconscious psychological drives; movement participants seen as driven by irrational ideology. The movement upsurge of the 1960s was often described in mass media in these classic terms, but social scientists who came of age as participants in or sympathizers with these could not accept such characterizations. The new look of post-1960s social movement studies involved emphasis on movements as "politics by other means," seeing movements as collective efforts to pursue interests with intelligible strategies and rational goals. Understanding movements required, not a psychoanalysis of participants, but an account of the ways in which the emergence and evolution of a movement related to the opportunities, threats, and resources available for achieving movement goals. Movement participation turned out to be better explained by examining the ways in which participants were embedded in communities and networks than by supposing that they were uprooted or socially alienated. Rather than seeing movements as irrational or destructive forces, it was truer to the historical record to acknowledge their constitutive role in shaping modern societies.

Many of those who studied social movements in the 1960s and 1970s were themselves politically active. My impression then was that most of them believed the study of social movements ought to provide movement activists with intellectual resources they might not readily obtain otherwise. Such study could enable better assessment of what worked in the way of strategies and tactics; could help activists locate their efforts in historical and structural terms; and could help movements improve efforts to communicate with bystanders and potential sympathizers, interpret the actions of their antagonists, identify opportunities for leverage, etc.

The new paradigm, emphasizing "resource mobilization," "political opportunity," and "framing," focused on movement strategy as a primary topic. Work in that vein indeed proved to be directly useful to activists; some of the research and theorizing of academic sociologists helped shape movement training programs and handbooks (e.g., Gamson, 1990; Piven and Cloward, 1977; Ryan, 1991) It was possible to imagine, if you were engaged in social movement studies, that your teaching, consulting, and direct participation, as well as your research efforts themselves, might have some relevance to the practices and understandings of political activists.

Somewhere along the way, however, the promise of such relevance receded and a much more "professional" and "disciplinary" definition of purpose came to the fore. I can't trace here how the shift toward formalization and abstraction came about. A sure sign of it, however, is the proliferation of journal articles in which social movement experience is turned into grist for the testing of hypotheses or the illustration of concepts, as well as writings (including this volume) aimed at establishing, critiquing, or refining "paradigms." Increasingly, the work of younger scholars is driven by the effort to refine theory rather than to contribute to public knowledge about movements.

The "mainstream" in social movement studies descends from the "resource mobilization" perspectives of the 1970s and is shaped by the "political contention" framework that TMT have been putting forward (some leading sources are Tarrow, 1998; McAdam, McCarthy, and Zald, 1996a; and McAdam, Tarrow, and Tilly, 2001).

An alternative angle of vision is provided by analysts who have seen the need to bring "culture" back into the study of social movements. The political contention paradigm, insofar as it defines movements as vehicles for making political claims and acting in relation to the state, fails to examine the ways in which movements reshape beliefs, moral codes, identities, and other cultural elements. A movement may fail politically—or not even directly engage in the political—and yet have major effects on daily life because of its cultural impacts. Movements, in short, produce knowledge, art, symbols, and identities, as well as challenges to political authority.

One source of such cultural perspectives was European analysis of so-called new social movements (NSMs), including feminism, environmentalism, gay liberation, etc. These post-1960s movements were seen as operating largely outside of the polity as such and beyond the boundaries of action defined by European mass parties. New social movements can't readily be understood by trying to examine their "strategies," since what they are about is the fostering of new consciousness and identity rather than objectifiable goods. Hence, the NSM "theory" was seen, at first, as a competitor to the rationalistic orientation of "resource mobilization" analysis.

This "culturalist" perspective suffered a bit from being labeled "new social movement theory." For one thing, there was hardly a "theory" being articulated, but rather a different set of emphases and questions. More important, the notion that there was something "new" about movements of "middle class" people trying to establish new moral principles and identities flew in the face of at least 150 years of U.S. history, which had featured abolitionists, suffragists, prohibitionists, conservationists, and a wide variety of other formations that were both cultural and political in their aims. Europeans were struck with the flourishing of movements that were not anticipated nor controllable by established mass parties of the left and that seemed to be inexplicable by orthodox Marxian theory. For them what was "new" was precisely the emergence of autonomous movements that lacked a clear class location. But such movements had always been the rule rather than the exception in the case of American "exceptionalism."

Meanwhile, many who were focused on "strategic" perspectives (mostly American sociologists) were ready to admit that their own work needed to bring culture back in and to recognize the importance of collective identity, "framing," and other cultural dimensions to the process of mobilization. Their emphasis continued to be on understanding such dimensions as "strategic" rather than as ends in themselves, but any effort to sharply demarcate a culturalist versus structuralist divide in social movement studies was trumped by the efforts of McAdam, Tarrow, and their collaborators to readily incorporate the cultural and acknowledge some of the ways in which culture mediated structure (Tarrow, 1998b; Klandermans, 1997a; McAdam, McCarthy, and Zald, 1996a; Zald, 2000).

Accordingly, the readiness of these scholars to respond to the cultural turn has facilitated their achievement of a kind of hegemony in social movement studies. Their ambitious quest to define a consensual agenda for the field may be taken as a sign of intellectual progress compared with earlier periods when no agreed-upon terminology was evident, and social processes that bore evident similarities were being studied by research networks that had little contact with each other.

The plethora of research compilations, annuals, journals, and advanced textbooks dealing with social movements is another index of intellectual progress. More systematic research and analysis of movements has been occurring in the last decade than ever before, and much of it makes use of sophisticated methods that enable detailed comparative and historical analysis.

The question nags, however: What is all this analysis for? In what way does the validation, elaboration, and refinement of concepts provide usable knowledge for those seeking social change? Indeed, does the practice of "normal science" actually conflict with the moral dimension of social movement studies? More—even if we put aside such questions of "relevance," there is the question of intellectual adequacy: Has the TMT approach fulfilled its apparent claim that we now have a "theory" that is adequate to the systematic study of social movements?

There is now a considerable body of criticism of the dominant paradigm, as the present volume shows. In what follows I highlight two themes that, as far as I can tell, remain neglected in the debate and yet seem to me to be critical if the social and intellectual value of social movement studies is to be restored. I argue, in brief, that current work tends to fall short, not only for its neglect of the "cultural" and "psychological" but also because of its surprising failure to address fundamental "structural" issues. I begin with the latter point.

STRUCTURAL POWER AND
THE POWERS OF THE WEAK

Despite recent celebrations of its 150th anniversary, it is now rarely acknowledged that the importance of *The Communist Manifesto* rested on the fact that it offered a usable theory for those who seek to change history but lack the power to do so. It was the first systematic effort to analyze the conditions for social movement (rather than simply call for such movement, which it also most eloquently did). And here is a curious thing: *The Manifesto* remains the *only* full-fledged *theory* about the conditions and powers of movements that we have. The theory sketched in *The Manifesto* cannot itself serve as a framework for analyzing the movements of our time, but the way Marx theorized about movements—the strategy of interpretation he formulated—instructs us about the failings of currently dominant approaches.

Marx's model was foundational for contemporary resource mobilization and opportunity structure perspectives. Like these perspectives, Marx understood that deprivation and oppression were not in themselves the basis for movement. The very notion of class as a framework of mobilization implies that a group must share resources as well as interests to become a social force. Marx's "dialectical" style made him search for the opportunities as well as the oppressions inherent in social structure; the proletariat are not just victims but are also in a situation of opportunity. Capitalism exploited workers, but by creating them, it was creating its own gravediggers—because the capitalist system in its very nature created opportunities for its own overthrow (for example, the social space provided by the factory). Whether or not today's opportunity theorists make it explicit, many of their key notions derive from Marx.

One of Marx's central analytic strategies, however, is missing from contemporary theories—namely, his effort to embed power relations in an analysis of the political economy as a whole. Opportunity was not fixed. The more that capitalism organized a global economy and society, the more potential the world's proletariat would have for transformative change. Much of Marx's intellectual career involved the effort to analyze capitalism as a developing and contradictory system and the ways in which such development would necessitate and make possible collective action from below.

Contemporary work in social movement studies makes only weak and relatively unsystematic connection between macroeconomic conditions and political opportunity. For instance, if one would want (as quite a few activists would) to analyze the opportunities for a revitalization of the labor movement, one would need to begin with a detailed economic analysis that enabled connection between the "new economy" and evolving macro and micro production relations, and how these might necessitate, facilitate, and limit collective action. Marx provided an analysis of this sort in his detailed review of the struggle for the shorter workweek in *Capital*. Surprisingly, the "structuralism" of the political opportunity paradigm stops short of the sort of macrostructural analysis that Marxian theorizing routinely undertakes. Buechler (2000) makes a systematic effort to undertake such an analysis.

But there is an even more basic weakness embedded in opportunity theorists' structuralism. They don't systematically deal with the possibility that certain kinds of resource and opportunity are considerably more fateful than others. For Marx, the fundamental source of social power has to do with control over means of production. Because such control is a matter of degree, we can imagine a gradient of power available to groups seeking to make social change. Marx makes a theoretical bet that groups, over time, will tend to move along that gradient, striving to maximize the power they can bring to bear. Thus, for example, tactics like mass assemblies, marches, bread riots, and machine breaking—all of which have some effect—will become less important for workers than strategies focused on the withholding of labor (strikes or the threat thereof). Strike-oriented strategies require forms of organization (aimed at expanding webs of solidarity) that will predictably follow from the assumption that workers will over time focus their collective action where it can matter most. This kind of systematic analysis of the logic of power relations is not done in the "political opportunity" project, even by those who claim to be studying "power in movements" or who are documenting "tactical repertoires."

Marx succeeded in formulating an empirically testable theory of movement mobilization. It was a theory that had intellectual power—that is, it explained and anticipated a great deal about human history—but it also had moral and practical power. Morally, it helped challenge the complacency of those who believed that capitalism was inherently progressive, or that market arrangements enabled all who participated to get what they deserved. Practically, it provided generations of organizers with theory they could use to define their roles and practices. It was not Marx's fault that many of these adopted the theory as a quasi-religious dogma, making the text sacred, rather than mastering the method.

MAKING USE OF MARX'S LEADS

These texts of Marx are, however, of limited value for social movement studies since they don't deal with many of the most fundamental issues that now shape our concerns. One of their obvious limitations is that most of Marx's long-range predictions about class struggle have so far proved invalid.

A post-Marxist theory of power that incorporates class struggle but can account for other frameworks of mobilization and conflict seems both necessary and possible. An excellent illustration of a more general theory of power can be found in a work that has been neglected by "political opportunity" analysts, even though its theoretical perspective seems close to theirs. It is a book by Michael Schwartz, *Radical Protest and Social Structure*, published in 1976, a study of the nineteenth-century Southern Farmers' Alliance. Schwartz uses the case study as a springboard for a theoretical discussion of the determinants of organized protest. He summarizes an extended discussion of the powers available to subordinated groups as follows:

Every functioning system is a set of routinized power relations in effect on a day-to-day basis. This is structural power since the structure could not function without the existence and use of this power.

Those . . . subject to this structural power possess a latent power deriving from the possibility of refusing to abide by the power exercised over them. . . .

This latent power can be exercised only if the subordinate group organizes itself. . . .

The organization of the subordinate group must be carried out independently of the structure itself. . . . Power exercised by a group depends on its place in the structure and its ability to withhold obedience. (Schwartz, 1976:177)

Michael Schwartz's effort to define "structural power" helps us see how we might construct a theory about the powers of the weak by building on Marx's analysis of class power: The power of the powerless is rooted in their capacity to stop the smooth flow of social life.

Class-based power, because of its double effect on both the elites and the community, is the most effective way to do this. But any structure that depends on the cooperation of subordinates for its functioning provides potential power to those subordinates because of their capacity to refuse cooperation or fulfill expected roles.

Social movements, accordingly, can be most fruitfully examined as social formations that seek, over time, to maximize the power available to their constituencies. There are two lines of collective action that may be available to the "powerless." First is to engage in or threaten to engage in collective forms of refusal, noncooperation, or noncompliance with the plans, rules, demands, and commands of elites. Piven and Cloward, whose work, like Schwartz's, is largely neglected by contemporary opportunity theorists, have in their analysis of poor peoples' movements demonstrated that institutionally embedded power may not be available to poor communities and groups, for example, the unemployed, or those on welfare. Accordingly, urban movements of the poor and disenfranchised exercise power, at times, by engaging in forms of collective disruption of the ongoing functioning of institutional or community life (Piven and Cloward, 1977).

The effective exercise of power derived from defiance, disruption, and noncompliance is rarely easy, because the risks of its exercise are usually profound. Just as workers' strikes are costly to workers themselves (if for no other reason than that they are stopping their actual livelihoods), so other forms of institutional noncooperation disrupt the very activities that members themselves need to sustain their accustomed lives. In addition, acts of noncompliance and disruption can be expected to receive repressive responses. Social movement dynamics are very much shaped by efforts to figure out how to maximize the benefits and minimize the costs to members of engaging in power struggle.

In this light, current emphasis on analyzing the conditions for "mobilization" seems abstract, diffuse, and weakly specified. If, instead, we see the underlying strategic aim of social movements as a striving to find the means for structural power, we can develop coherent ways to order our inquiries about "opportunity" and "resources." Our questions about these will have to do with the conditions and circumstances, the strategies and tactics, the perceptions and motivations that would increase the readiness of a community or collectivity of "powerless" people to make use of their potential structural powers, usually against considerable odds. Those questions might enable our work to connect with the deepest dilemmas that movement organizers have to deal with. They also might help restore the moral relevance of our inquiries.

MOBILIZATION AND COMMITMENT

The key word in the mainstream study of movements is "mobilization." It refers to all of the processes by which people commit themselves to support a movement. Presumably the explanatory efforts of social movement scholars are aimed at describing, and defining the conditions for, such processes. So, for example, political opportunity structures are supposed to provide key conditions for mobilization; "mobilization" is shorthand for a variety of "dependent variables" in much movement research.

Discussion of mobilization seems often to overlook the fact that movements are always constituted by some fundamental differences in the ways members participate in movements. At the core are those who helped initiate the movement in the first place or who stay engaged even in "doldrums" times, who spark renewal after periods of relative decline, and whose daily lives and identities are deeply and, sometimes, totally embedded in the movement. We use a variety of words to define such core roles: leaders, organizers, activists, cadre.

Movements are also constituted by varieties of "mass" participation. There are moments and periods when large numbers of people step out of or reorganize their daily lives to participate in collective action—action that often entails sacrifice and risk. There are situations in which large numbers of people incorporate symbols and practices produced by a movement into their daily lives, consciously identifying with and acting in terms of movement-defined norms. And of course within these two crucial kinds of mobilization there are likely to be great variations in degree of commitment at any given time. And then there are times when large numbers of people relate to a movement by remaining at its periphery, providing material or political support, even if not asserting "membership." The word "mobilization" is most likely to be used to refer to these sorts of movement participation. Yet there is little recognition of the possibility that these rather different kinds of participation can't be reduced to unitary models of determination.

In particular, little attention is given to understanding, and depicting, the processes that generate and sustain highly committed activists and that examine systematically the roles such activists play in the movement.[1]

The neglect of this key dimension is in part a reaction against old-fashioned social movement studies. In the old days, the main explanatory questions typically focused on commitment, and typically, these questions led to "psychological" or "individual" explanatory approaches. Often, psychodynamic accounts of leaders' motivations would be accompanied by psychologizing about "followers": leaders and their followers usually interpreted as aberrational. The post-1960s new look in social movement studies rejected that entire way of thinking about movements. It was no longer interesting to examine why small numbers of people would literally give over their lives to causes nor to investigate the relationship between dedicated activists and masses of people whose participation was more episodic, or opportunistic.

The marginalization of this issue is one of the reasons that current work in social movement studies seems relatively arid and irrelevant.[2] I want to offer some reflections on how we might repair this deficiency.

Let's use the word "activism" to refer to movement participation that entails leadership activity, organizing, conscious concern about the direction of the movement, and conscious long-term commitment of time and resources and energy to the movement. And let's use "mobilization" to refer to mass participation of the various kinds mentioned above.

I want to propose that these two types of participation are likely to be differently motivated. Indeed, many of the debates in social movement studies about the relative importance of "structure," "culture," and "rational choice" in explaining mobilization are confused by the fact that there has not been careful distinction made between various forms of participation. Let me make it clear that I am not talking about a continuum of participation from "more" to "less" but about qualitatively different ways of conceiving of one's relation to a movement and of one's very goals and purposes in life.

I want, second, to propose that all movements are constituted by these two streams of participation, and that the relation between the two is always problematic. It is not enough, in trying to understand movement dynamics, to assume that there is a core of organizers or "challengers" who are seeking to advance a set of goals, and who then look for opportunities, frame issues, and identify resources in ways that can be understood simply as strategic. How activists themselves define social reality and define themselves; how they are socially linked and organized; and how they have been shaped by social origin, cultural tradition, and history are all relevant to grasping their actions. And the same questions apply to those "in the mass."

The older literature (pre-1970s) makes it clear that the social backgrounds and the outlook of activists often differ markedly from those they claim to be organizing—and, of course, there are likely to be deep divisions among activists themselves, for a wide variety of reasons. The tensions that arise from such differences and divisions are essential features of all social movements and must be attended to.

The standard assumption in both conventional wisdom and social movement studies is that the relationship between activism and "masses" is that of organizer and organized. Agency rests with organizers. Mass constituents are, it is assumed, mobilized by activist "challengers." Analysts may differ in the degree to which they regard organizers as manipulative and strategic in all that they do, but the "leader-led" assumption is pervasive. Indeed, analysts often see national movement organizations as primary agents of mobilization, or as the most important "challengers."

In the real history of movements, the relationship between activism and mass mobilization is far more complicated. In fact, when movement upsurge occurs, activists typically are surprised and are often displaced by newly emerged leadership groups. There is, at least in the United States, very often a considerable divide between those asserting "national" leadership in movements and the processes of local mobilization. Efforts to describe movements of either the past or the present by looking at the activity of national organizations, indeed of organizations as such (whether local or national) without close attention to the local and the grassroots miss much about the nature of the movement. The dominant paradigm has tended to marginalize studies of activist motivation, biography, and experience, and to oversimplify the interrelationships between activist practice and mass action.

The failure to examine movement activism systematically and in detail has, I think, led to serious conceptual confusion. Activism, as I am defining it, goes on quite frequently without very much mobilization (as I am defining it). Relatively small networks of highly committed persons may engage full time in collective action without much expansion (or even hope) of grassroots participation. I've found little systematic acknowledgment in current work of the obvious differences between activism aimed at mass mobilization and activism aimed at advancing an unpopular cause.

CAUSES, MOVEMENTS, AND CAMPAIGNS

I propose that we clearly distinguish between "causes" and "movements." Causes are forms of collective action whose participants seek change that they define as socially (rather than personally) beneficial. Movements are social formations that involve large numbers of people who are seeking change in what they define as their shared interest (although they usually claim more universal benefit as well).

Movements often begin as causes. Think of the early period of the woman's suffrage movement, of the beginnings of the civil rights movement in the founding of the NAACP, of pacifism as a precursor to the anti-war movement, and "conservationism" as a seed for what is now the environmental movement. One of the key questions then for social movement studies is to understand the conditions under which causes become movements. I think a good deal of the debate in social movement studies may be rooted in lack of attention to the differences (on a wide range of dimensions) between these two sorts of collective action.

Similarly, we ought to distinguish between movements and "campaigns." The latter are efforts by activists within a movement to mobilize energy on behalf of a particular issue or reform. The campaign for the Equal Rights Amendment was embedded within the women's liberation movement. The anti-abortion campaign is embedded within the movement of the religious right. The nuclear freeze campaign was a project of peace movement activists. Campaigns that are successful in mobilizing popular support are important and worthy of detailed study in their own right, but they ought to be distinguished from the larger, longer term movement. They are likely to have a different trajectory.

IDEOLOGY AND BIOGRAPHY

Activist causes vary in terms of their overarching ideological embeddedness. There is a long history of "single issue" causes and crusades; abolition, women's suffrage, temperance, and animal rights are examples. These attracted activists with widely varied underlying religious and secular beliefs, who found common ground in the particular cause. Many cause-involved activists identified with the long ideological traditions of left and right and came out of the parties, associations, and informal networks that embodied and carried these traditions.

Ideologically committed activists frequently have taken leadership in single issue causes and campaigns while, at least initially, seeing those causes as mere steps toward more ultimate ends, rather than ends in themselves. Ideologically committed activists have been central to the formation of social movements; accordingly, understanding the ways in which such commitment affects their activity is an important topic in interpreting movement dynamics. To what extent is "ideology" a resource and a problem for social movement development? What roles have ideologically committed activists played in such development, and how have these differed from roles played by activists who professed no such engagement? Once upon a time, the study of ideology in relation to action was a topic of major interest, but it is one of those questions that now are out of fashion.[3]

Equally unfashionable is the once popular question of activist biography.[4] There is a very considerable literature on the personal development and socialization of leaders and activists, but work on this theme, as I indicated earlier, lost favor in social movement studies as the resource mobilization/political process paradigm became dominant.[5]

In my view, understanding of activists as a social type remains a critical issue for understanding how social movements work. To the extent that organizers, leaders, and movement entrepreneurs make a difference, understanding their social origins, experience, outlook, and motivational makeup may be critical for understanding movement trajectories. For example, the shared social origins and identity issues of student activists in the 1960s help account for both the rise and the direction of the student movement.[6]

One of the defining characteristics of activists is that they are people whose actions are not interpretable simply in terms of situation; instead, they are people who act against institutionalized expectations, accepted belief, conventional values and goals. How and why some people become engaged in risky, nonconventional activity, when "success" is at best elusive and causes are often lost, is a topic worthy of attention in its own right. How such commitment is sustained over time is a question that bears on our general understanding of human possibility. Why some people come to consider societal change to be a central priority of their lives is an issue that is fundamentally relevant to the problem of democratic potential. Efforts to understand activist biography can provide insight into central issues of human personality and its socialization, of ideological hegemony and its contradictions, and of the relationships between culture and experience.

The neglect of activism as a topic in social movement studies thus limits the intellectual penetration of the field. It also is both a sign of, and a contributor to, its declining social relevance. After all, the most likely nonacademic audience for academic work on social movements are movement activists themselves. If there is anybody, besides ourselves, we hope to reach with our work, it is they. In my experience, activists are hungry for insight into the practices and experience of organizers, into how collective and personal commitment can be sustained, into relationships between day-to-day activism and "long-range vision," into problems of intra-movement contention, organizational rigidity, and democracy, etc. Documenting and theorizing the varieties of activist experience is critical for making sense of such issues.

Of course, activists are also interested in detailed information about historical and contemporary movement dynamics and in improving their capacities to make strategic choices. Some contemporary work aims at making such knowledge accessible. But to the extent that contemporary movement studies are driven by efforts to refine theoretical concepts, they are likely to appear as irrelevant or obvious to organizers. Organizers already know about the need for "frame alignment," the value of "informal networks," and the importance of "opportunity structures." They would benefit from studies that provide clues about how to accomplish such alignment, how to tap into such networks, and how to identify such opportunities. Do our "findings" about these concepts actually provide strategic or tactical resources to those already engaged in mobilization? It might be useful for someone to inventory research that would be of such use.

Surprisingly little attention is paid to examining, in a given movement situation, what activists themselves believe their strategic options to be and how these get evaluated and debated within the movement. Instead, analysts now seem to think that their own assessments of opportunity, after the fact and distanced, are somehow more valid than those made at the time. This may well be the case, but insight into the potentials and constraints of activists' understandings is itself an important topic, both for understanding movement evolution and for helping organizers become more aware of their own ways of knowing and deciding.

I am arguing then that a fundamental weakness of current fashion in social movement studies is the tendency to ignore differences between "activist" and "mass" forms of participation. Examining such differences would help clarify current debates on the motivational dimensions of mobilization and would compel closer examination of the real problems inherent in formulating and sustaining movement strategy. Closer attention to the roles, identities, biographies, and self-understandings of activists would also renew the political and social relevance of academic analysis of movements, particularly for the primary potential nonacademic audience of it: the activists themselves.

HOW DO CAUSES BECOME MOVEMENTS?

When people commit themselves to "causes," they are, by definition, undertaking a collective action that is likely to be able to muster little structural power. This is so, if for no other reason that, at least in their early days, causes are supported by small numbers of people, and these are often those with relatively few institutional ties. A good deal of both the classic and contemporary analysis of movements is actually about the motivational grounds and strategic practices of such cause-oriented activism, and I think we know quite a bit about its social, cultural, and characterological roots. I can't here try to review and codify these materials, but we can make a broad generalization: Activists are people whose identities and daily lives are strongly structured by their commitment. Such identity structure may have its roots in particular cultural (ethnic, political, or religious) traditions, critical life experiences and personality formations, occupational positions, or frameworks of ideological allegiance. In general, activist commitment arises from life circumstances that are different from the social and cultural "mainstream." Moreover, the experience of activist engagement is likely to further differentiate activists from the everyday life-worlds of most others.

I said earlier that movements very often arise from causes. For me one of the key questions in understanding social movements is to understand the conditions under which such a transformation occurs. When do masses of people, whose identities and daily lives are oriented toward the "private," the "personal," and the mundane, become engaged in sustained collective action? It is clearly inadequate to explain such sustained action by referring only to changing "opportunities" for its emergence.

Doug McAdam has come to see that the emergence of mass collective action is often related to "threat" (and not, therefore, only to be understood in terms of the availability of "opportunity") (McAdam, 1999:introduction). The point is that disadvantaged, powerless people typically live their lives within a habituated framework of subordination. Their readiness for collective action is not based simply on the fact of their deprivation or unfreedom but on the shared perception of a specific threat to their accustomed lifeways. People who are trying to sustain their lives (and most people most of the time are trying to do this) become ready for risky collective action when such sustenance is becoming problematic.

Threat is not a sufficient condition for collective action. The perception of threat must be shared, and so must a perception that the source of threat is a particular human agency (rather than a "natural" event) and of some way in which collective action might effectively work to stop or alleviate the threat. Such shared perceptions and beliefs depend on opportunities for sustained interaction among those affected. So all of the work in current movement studies on social networks, on "framing" and other collective cognitive structuring of experience, is relevant to understanding the ways in which people are mobilized for protest in situations of threat. As we'll see, however, mobilization in response to threat isn't the only foundation for social movements.

Movements whose aim is to stop or alleviate threats to accustomed lifeways are oriented toward resistance. Strikes by workers represent a prototype of resistance movements' efforts to muster structural power. Most resistance movements, however, don't come out of workplaces but arise in other sorts of institutional and community locations. Mass resistance strategies, whatever their location, usually move from efforts to petition authorities to efforts to exercise structural power through institutional and community disruption. Mass resistance tends to recede when a threat-reducing accommodation can be achieved between movement leaders and those they are challenging.

I've been stressing that people, in the main, strive to sustain their everyday lives, participating in social movements to try to prevent or reduce threats to their accustomed lifeways that come from the plans and actions of others. But there are times when large numbers of people who share a way of life undertake to make a new one rather than defend what exists. There are, in other words, circumstances other than "threat" that can give rise to mass mobilization.

The term "liberation" refers to collective action that expresses a rejection of established frameworks of identity, entails a claiming of rights hitherto denied, and articulates demands for equality of treatment, for dignity and self-determination. Liberatory perspectives arise among groups of people who share a condition of subordination, disadvantage, or stigma over which they have little or no individual control. Such subordination, based on race, ethnicity, gender, sexual orientation, physical handicap, or any other "ascribed" trait, tends to be regarded in the dominant culture as a normal, taken-for-granted feature of everyday life. Those who are so subordinated have typically accommodated to their situation for generations, seeming to reproduce in their own conformity the conditions of their oppression.

Such public accommodation, however, has usually been accompanied by more subterranean expressions of opposition. Such expressions are typically made symbolically—through song and language, religion and story, and a variety of covert resistances. Out of such cultures of protest emerge forms of collective identification and a recognition of shared fate and destiny.

Liberation movements emerge out of such social and cultural circumstances. They are collective efforts to end the economic, political, and social structures that enforce subordination and the cultural practices and beliefs that perpetuate stigmatization. New laws, providing rights now denied, are demanded; new opportunities for individual advancement are advocated. At the same time, liberation movements seek to resocialize members, encouraging forms of self-assertion and self-esteem previously unavailable; along with this, liberation movements actively engage in cultural transformation in the wider society, promulgating liberatory cognitive and moral codes to replace established ideologies that sustain domination.

Resistance mobilization grows and declines in relation to experienced threat and mass perception of ways to overcome it; resistance may be said to fit within the rhythms of accustomed daily life. Liberation consciousness and action obviously has a more complicated relation to everyday life; groups oriented to liberation are making ready to abandon their accustomed lives, to move into unknown territory, undertaking risks hitherto avoided. We might say that resistance consciousness does not question accustomed disadvantages and subordinations; it opposes authority only when conditions are being made worse than they usually are, or when habituated life is being made more difficult to go on with.

The "repertoire" of liberation movement tactics may include the kinds of disruptive direct action used in resistance strategies. But liberation movements aim not only at political reform and macro-level change but equally at the remaking of micro-level power relations and the claiming of new identity. Accordingly, liberation movements are characterized by noncompliance and nonconformity within the contexts of "private," "personal," and everyday domains. In these contexts, "mobilization" does not demand that members stop their everyday lives and physically move into a collective public space. Instead, what is entailed is an ongoing effort to assert identity claims and renegotiate power relations in close-up institutional settings and face-to-face encounters. Liberation movements institute moral codes affecting appearance, demeanor, language, and daily role compliance. The changes accomplished in such micro contexts are intrinsic to the strategic goals of the movement and are not, in any sense, less important than "political" reforms that are also sought.

The dominant paradigm, with its emphasis on the political, the structural, the organizational, and the strategic, does not, I think, pertain well to understanding liberation movement emergence or dynamics. Much of the impetus for "culturalist" approaches comes from a recognition that the dominant paradigm is weak in treating movements' roots in and effects on "culture."

Prevailing "cultural turns" in social movement studies have, however, been hampered by two conceptual dead ends. First, the notion that an alternative paradigm to "political process theory" may be found in work on "new social movements" has been a significant distraction. I am not here going to develop a critique of NSMs, except to say that what I call "liberation" consciousness isn't "new," nor are liberation movements only about changing culture. There is a lot more to be said about this work and what has been made of it, which I hope to do in other places.

Second, the notion that liberation movements can be labeled "identity politics" has tended to distort analysis. Whatever the term "identity politics" might mean, it tends to trivialize and narrow the cultural and personal meanings of the various liberation movements. These are not only about "recognition"; instead, struggles in daily life to assert new identities are understood by most participants to be part of a more general effort, at both macro and micro levels, to achieve equality and justice; prevailing rhetoric in liberation movements usually refers to "universalistic" values as well as making "particularistic" claims. I am not denying the obvious fact that liberation movements can include varieties of very ugly kinds of separatisms, ethnocentrisms, and other exclusivist ideologies and practices. But the notion that there is a fruitful separation to be made between movements aimed at "material" interest and those aimed at "identity" seems to me a dead end. Identity processes are inherent in all movements and in all causes as well. And liberation movements among subordinated groups clearly have "material" as well as "cultural" aims.

CONCLUSION

I've tried here to express some fundamental dissatisfaction with the state of social movement studies, at a time when those who claim leadership in such work have been inclined to praise the intellectual progress of the field. In the space of what is already a long chapter, I haven't had the chance to provide any detailed documentation of the sorts of work I find wanting. Perhaps, too, I have missed the point of the work I am criticizing.

I focus my critique on what I have called the dominant paradigm. I want to be clear that I regard the work within its scope as often helpful, important, and clarifying. The general effort to view movements in terms of their strategic orientations was and remains a necessary foundation for understanding them, far preferable to the psychosocial-pathological diagnoses of movements found in much of the classic work. Concepts provided by political opportunity structure (POS), when used as "sensitizing" devices, greatly aid researchers trying to decide what to look for in specific cases.

I am criticizing first of all current efforts to rather rigidly define boundaries and a canon for the field. I have tried here to show that hegemonic claims made for the TMT approach are not earned by its value. Major topics have been marginalized or ignored. To try to restore interest in, for example, structural power or activist biography, is not, as Tilly seems to think, a matter of taste.[7]

To fail to have a theory of power, especially when its elements are quite available and discernible, is a great weakness. To fail to distinguish between what I've called "activism" and "mobilization," between "causes" and "movements"—indeed to lump all protesters together as "challengers"—is to ignore some of the most important features of movement dynamics and to foster confused debate about how protest is motivated. Such debates, when combined with an explosion of publications whose sole audience is the immediate circle of fellow practitioners, result in an inward turning of the field as a whole.

I want us to keep in mind at least two audiences for our work. There are, first of all, the students, for whom studying movements ought to be a moral enterprise. This is a field rich with stories about human possibility, about moments of transcendence, about the times when ordinary people have changed the world. The stories also include tales of profound betrayal and moral blindness, about the dilemmas of organization, of leadership, of commitment. It's the study of hidden history and of what has shaped our culture and our collective memory. How much of the current theoretical and research literature in the field can be used for such teaching?

Second, as I argued at the outset, movement activists ought to be an audience—indeed, a source of partnership—for our inquiry. To the extent that they are not, the intellectual, as well as the moral, value of our work is in question.

NOTES

1. Meyer Zald, who is one of the founding figures of resource mobilization theory, has recently acknowledged that the processes of "socialization" that foster such commitment have been seriously neglected (Zald, 2000).

2. See Diani (2000) commenting on Zald's argument.

3. But Zald's statement referred to above wants to at least revive the topic.

4. A powerful critique of the dominant perspective is Jasper (1997). One of Jasper's themes is an effort to restore "biography" as a key topic in movement studies—but even he seems largely unaware of the literature—for example the sort of work cited in the following footnote.

5. Here are a few examples of varying approaches to this theme: Erikson (1969); Wolfenstein (1967); and Keniston (1968). Hundreds of studies on the social psychology of 1960s activism are summarized by Keniston in a book-length bibliography (1973). A sampling of recent work taking a "biographical" perspective is Lipsitz (1995); Andrews (1991); Whalen and Flacks (1989); Fendrich (1993); Klatch (1999); and Teske (1997).

6. There is a big literature on this done at the time, including work cited in the previous footnote, which neither Zald nor Jasper seems aware of.

7. In response to critiques of TMT, Tilly suggests that we "ban forever the whole class of criticisms that complain [that] 'You're underestimating the importance of the variables I find interesting'" (chapter 2).

11

Passionate Political Processes: Bringing Emotions Back into the Study of Social Movements

DEBORAH B. GOULD

BRING YOUR GRIEF AND RAGE ABOUT AIDS TO A

POLITICAL

FUNERAL

IN WASHINGTON D.C.

—ACT UP/New York (1992, emphasis in original)

ACT UP/New York issued this invitation/leaflet announcing its October 1992 "Ashes" action.[1] The image that accompanied the headline was modest, the outline of an urn, with the following text filling out its contents:

> You have lost someone to AIDS. For more than a decade, your government has mocked your loss. You have spoken out in anger, joined political protests, carried fake coffins and mock tombstones, and splattered red paint to represent someone's HIV-positive blood, perhaps your own. George Bush believes that the White House gates shield him, from you, your loss, and his responsibility for the AIDS crisis. Now it is time to bring AIDS home to George Bush. On October 11th, we will carry the actual ashes of people we love in funeral procession to the White House. In an act of grief and rage and love, we will deposit their ashes on the White House lawn. Join us to protest twelve years of genocidal AIDS policy. (ACT UP/New York, 1992)

On the day of the march, as hundreds of people assembled, a small group met together. Holding the ashes of their loved ones, they would lead the funeral procession. Arthur, from Chicago, held up a worn sack that contained the ashes of his lover, who had been a member of ACT UP/NY and ACT UP/Chicago. "This is Ortez" (Finkelstein, 1992b:10). ACT UP/NY member Bob Rafsky later wrote about the political funeral:

> At the front of the march was a single line of people carrying urns. . . . Behind them were about a hundred of us who were willing to be arrested helping them to the White House fence. Behind us were three drummers playing rhythmic patterns that worked into our bodies: 1–2–3, 1–2–3, 1–2–3–4–5. Finally came the supporting marchers, more than 1,500 of them. . . . A few feet from me a young man in a white T-shirt was shouting at an imaginary George Bush, "It's your fault! It's your fault!" before he broke down and sobbed. . . . The action had been coordinated by a 22-year-old classics graduate student at Columbia University who had joined ACT UP. . . . I saw him pressed by our bodies against the White House fence, kneeling and weeping as ashes soared over him. (Rafsky, 1992:22–23)

ACT UP/NY member David Robinson's announcement that he planned to scatter his lover's ashes on the White House lawn had inspired the "Ashes" action. Interviewed the day of the march, Robinson drew a contrast between the political implications of the Names Project Memorial Quilt,[2] which was on display in D.C. that weekend, and ACT UP's funeral march: "George Bush would be happy if we all made Quilt panels. We're showing people what the White House has done: they've turned our loved ones into ashes and bones" (Wentzy, 1995). During the procession, participants chanted "Bring the dead to your door, we won't take it anymore" (Wentzy, 1995).

The predominant theorists in the field of social movements—political process theorists—rarely focus their analytical lenses on stories like this that foreground participants' reflections about specific movement actions. A primary reason is that political process theorists focus on political opportunities that facilitate protest and on questions of movement emergence and decline; data like those cited above seem irrelevant to such inquiries. Equally important, the dominance of rational actor models in the social movement literature has proscribed investigation into the emotional components of movements; given the centrality of emotions in the above story, political process theorists would have a hard time fitting such data into their framework. But what do we lose when such stories are absent from our analyses? The motivating role of strongly felt emotions— what I would call the *force* or *power* of emotions—seems apparent in the details of the "Ashes" action, inviting our attention and luring us in, searing in our minds any number of images, perhaps of public mourning rituals, or of urns and ashes hurling through the sky, or of fury and grief combining into a combustible form. We get the sense that the protest concerned an issue about which people felt deeply. I find this type of data compelling in part because I participated in ACT UP for six years, but my interest is broader than that. Investigations of such stories, and analytical attention to the power of emotions evident in them, can provide us with important insights, illuminating, for example, participants' subjectivities and motivations, and helping us to build compelling accounts of a movement's trajectory, strategic choices, internal culture, conflicts, and other movement processes and characteristics.

Over the past twenty-five years, political process theory has generated important new knowledge of social movements. But as is true in any area of knowledge, while the prevailing models sensitize us to a set of questions and approaches, they also foreclose other avenues of inquiry. Political process theory has narrowed the research agenda to questions of movement emergence, decline, and outcomes, and has pointed us toward investigations of the external environment to see how shifting political opportunities (in interaction with resources and frames) affect movement trajectories. Again, the research that political process theory has generated has been fruitful, but the costs of remaining wedded to its narrow agenda are high. As an increasing number of analysts are now arguing, political process theory is unable to make sense of a host of movements that arise and thrive in the face of tightening political opportunities or decline as political opportunities expand (Goodwin, forthcoming; Gould, 2000). Similarly troubling, in cases where the political process framework seems able to explain the trajectory of movements, we neglect other factors that might provide more compelling accounts. As Jasper and Goodwin note, "when a paradigm works well, alternatives to its main assumptions cannot even be imagined" (chapter 1). Political process theory also has narrowed the questions we ask about social movements, privileging investigations of emergence and decline over issues like movement sustainability, internal conflicts, ideological cleavages, rituals, and so on. In this chapter, drawing from my work on a larger project that explores the militant street AIDS activist movement, I join with others in calling for a reintroduction of emotions into the study of social movements.[3] I argue that attention to emotions generates a new landscape for social movement research that attends to causal mechanisms inclusive of, but also distinct from, political opportunities. A focus on emotions proliferates questions about emergence and decline but also about other movement processes that are currently understudied. Such a focus also encourages investigations of human behavior that are not bound by rational actor assumptions, providing greater insight into people's motivations for participating in movements.

POLITICAL PROCESS THEORY AND THE
STRATEGIC USES OF EMOTIONS

I want to start with a challenge to my claim that political process theorists would be inclined to ignore stories like the one cited above because they are emotion-saturated and thus difficult to reconcile with an assumption of rational actors. Rather than ignoring such data altogether, political process theorists instead might try to domesticate the emotional components by emphasizing the strategic uses of emotions and thereby incorporating them into a rational actor model. Each exhortation to feel a given emotion and every expression of an emotion could be read as an attempt by activists to mobilize others into the movement. Political process theorists would not necessarily be wrong in reading such data in this manner. There is a wealth of evidence showing militant AIDS activists attempting to inspire others' anger, for example. At ACT UP/NY's first meeting, there was a discussion about how to shift the focus of the upcoming Gay and Lesbian Pride Parade from "Gay Pride" to "Gay Rage" (ACT UP/NY, 1987); a photograph from ACT UP/NY's first action shows a placard with the message, "Turn Fear into Rage" (Freiberg, 1987). In a similar vein, the meeting minutes from a C-FAR (Chicago For AIDS Rights)[4] meeting in October 1988 record an outreach committee proposal to change C-FAR's name to ACT UP, with the following rationale: "the name [ACT UP] gives us a sense of anger which the name 'C-FAR' . . . is lacking" (C-FAR, 1988). Viewed from this angle, emotions might fit quite neatly into political process theory via the framing concept (Snow et al., 1986). One leading political process theorist, in fact, has pointed to the intentional emotionality of collective action frames: "The culture of collective action is built on frames and emotions oriented toward mobilizing people. . . . Symbols are taken selectively by movement leaders from a cultural reservoir and combined with action-oriented beliefs in order to navigate strategically. . . . Most important, they are given an emotional valence aimed at converting passivity into action" (Tarrow, 1998b:112). Robert Benford, an originator of the framing concept, argues for a similar recognition of the role of emotions, writing that emotions are "a vital social movement resource" that movement actors "produce, orchestrate, and strategically deploy" (1997:419).

Furthermore, as political process theorists would probably note, ACT UP/NY's leaflet announcing the "Ashes" action was intended to mobilize. In using the actual ashes of dead people, the action would itself be an escalation in tactics, a shift from actions that deployed representations of death (e.g., mock tombstones and fake coffins) to a funeral procession that was centered around the actual remains of loved ones dead from AIDS-related complications. The leaflet offered—and thereby tried to mobilize—the appropriate emotions and the appropriate activist response to "twelve years of genocidal AIDS policy": grief and rage channeled into a funeral march that would "bring AIDS home to George Bush."

ACT UP/NY soon escalated even further, shifting from ashes to actual dead bodies. Two weeks after the "Ashes" action, an anonymous person with AIDS issued a statement, "Bury Me Furiously," calling on AIDS activists to hold a political funeral when he died, carrying his body in an open casket through the streets. The person, later revealed to be ACT UP/NY member Mark Fisher, wrote:

> I want to show the reality of my death, to display my body in public; I want the public to bear witness. We are not just spiraling statistics. We are people who have lives, who have purpose, who have lovers, friends and families. And we are dying of a disease maintained by a degree of criminal neglect so enormous that it amounts to genocide. . . . Oppressed people have a tradition of political funerals. . . . Everyone who sees the procession pass knows that the living, those who love the deceased, are bereaved, furious and undefeated. . . . I want my own funeral to be fierce and defiant. (Anonymous, 1992)

Weeks later, the funeral for Fisher slowly wound through the streets of Manhattan, "urged on by a single drum" (Finkelstein, 1992c), ending at then-President George Bush's campaign headquarters. Over the next few years, ACT UP chapters held a number of political funerals, carrying the bodies of their dead through the streets and attempting to deposit them at strategic sites, including the White House.

It makes sense to understand ACT UP's political funerals as, in part, strategic mobilizations of emotions designed to motivate greater activist participation and to force concessions from those the movement was targeting. The strategic nature of such actions, in fact, seems evident in the very concept of "political funeral," which links a public procession marking someone's death to political demands.

But is that all that these stories reveal? While an investigation of the strategic uses of emotions illuminates one important role that emotions play in social movement processes, this instrumentalist view of emotions is only partial, and in fact quite unsatisfying, leaving crucial questions unasked and unanswered. Recognition of their strategic deployment raises questions about emotions whose investigation demands much more than a mere assertion of their strategic uses: Why do people respond to such deployments, and why does the purposive articulation of emotions sometimes seem to mobilize successfully but at other times seem to fail? Such questions, about what we might call *emotional reso-*

nance, require a theorization of the workings of emotions and their expression that would necessarily take us out of the realm of instrumentality. In other words, although an analysis might start with a view of the strategic uses of emotions, it would quickly be forced to move beyond those narrow confines. Strategic mobilizations simply do not exhaust the role played by emotions in social movements. Limiting our analyses to such an instrumentalist rendering reduces the power of emotions to just another tool in the social movement entrepreneur's framing toolkit, and much of what is rich and significant about the above stories would remain unexplored. How would we make sense of, and think through the significance of, the young man marching in the "Ashes" action who initially was yelling furiously at the White House and then broke down, sobbing? Or of the man weeping as ashes flew over his head onto the White House lawn? A view of emotions as strategic deployments would strip them of all of their noncognitive, noninstrumental attributes, thereby depleting them of some of their most interesting characteristics and sapping them of a large component of their conceptual force; much of what is compelling about the data mentioned above—what we might understand as the sensuous experience of emotions or the power or force of emotions— would simply drop out of the analysis. What is it like to witness someone introduce his lover by holding up a bag of ashes? What does it feel like to make a political statement with the ashes or body of a dead comrade, and how do such feelings affect an individual's or a group's activist strategies, commitments, and actions? Grief, anger, joy, pride, love, and other emotions are of import not simply, or even primarily, because of their strategic utility; analytical attention to people's experiences of such emotions can help us to make sense of ACT UP's political funerals and other actions, and by extrapolation, of the actions of other movements.[5]

BRINGING EMOTIONS BACK IN

In this section I want to pause to think more generally about the dominance of rational actor models and the near-absence of analysis about emotions in the contemporary field of social movements. I then suggest ways to theorize emotions and to apply those insights to our studies of social movements. In the section that follows, I use stories from ACT UP to illustrate how an analysis of emotions and their expression would strengthen our accounts of social movements.

The neglect of emotions in the contemporary study of social movements, or a view that notes only their strategic uses, should surprise us once we consider the subject we are studying. Protests, strikes, sit-ins, die-ins, and the like engage people in sometimes dangerous, and often risky, intense, and exhilarating activities. In addition, the issues around which people mobilize are usually highly emotionally charged. To be sure, the embrace of rational actor models in the social movement literature was an important corrective to earlier crowd/mass behavior models that derogated protesters as impulsive, irrational deviants who were propelled into the streets by emotional forces that overtook their rational thought processes.[6] At the same time, however, the current emphasis on rationality and strategic thinking often creates a picture of protesters as exceptionally cognitive and unusually dispassionate. Whereas in the earlier models we had protesters whose grievances were deeply felt but never cognitively assessed, in the now-dominant models we have rational actors who coolly calculate their grievances and pursue a strategic course of action, all the while apparently devoid of, and certainly unaffected by, anger, fear, joy, pride, or any other emotion. The assumption of rationality produces a flat, thin caricature of protesters, providing no insight into why such dispassionate people would ever be motivated to disrupt their daily routines and engage in collective action.

It should go without saying that protesters and activists are rational actors, in the broadest sense of that word; they make calculations about costs and benefits and strategize about how to secure their interests. But *how* they do so is not self-evident and cannot simply be asserted.[7] Rather than unproblematically deploying an assumption of rational actors to guide our analyses, we need to investigate how in a given context protesters assessed their situation, determined their interests, ordered their preferences, evaluated their costs and benefits, and so on. Perhaps more useful than an a priori assertion or assumption of rationality is a recognition that people are much *more* than rational actors. In deciding whether and how to engage in contentious politics, people have to make sense of themselves and their worlds and the relationship between the two. They must evaluate their situations, consider their sometimes ambiguous or contradictory desires, confront their fears, assess their own values as well as those of mainstream society and navigate possible conflicts therein, conjure up the unknowable future, and so on. Much more than rational calculation occurs as people engage in this kind of (sometimes conscious, sometimes less-than-fully conscious) interpretive work. An investigation that presumes rational calculation alone is simply inadequate, and I would argue, impoverished.

Although I am advocating that we analyze the role of emotions in social movements, I want to caution against returning to the crowd/mass behavior models of protest. Those models considered emotions, but their depictions of protesters as overcome by emotions that propelled them into the streets were problematic in their assumptions (that feelings are involuntary, biological phenomena that reside within our bodies and out-

side the social realm, a hindrance to rational thought) and in their assertions (that protesters were irrational deviants). Importantly, this
characterization of protesters as less-than-rational and as hysterical, unin-
formed, naïve, unreasonable, and so on—although disputed by contemporary social movement scholars and discredited by recent research—is
still popular today among politicians, in the media, and in public discourse more generally. How, then, might we analyze emotions, deepen-
ing our investigations of their causal force and moving beyond assertions
of their strategic utility, while steering clear of earlier approaches and
popular conceptions that disparage protesters and equate emotions with
the irrational?

Scholars from a wide range of disciplines have challenged the thought/
feeling dichotomy and the equation of emotionality with irrationality,
arguing instead that feeling and thinking are inseparably intertwined,
each necessary to the other (Barbalet, 1998; Damasio, 1994; Jaggar, 1989;
Lutz, 1986, 1988; Rosaldo, 1984; Williams, 1977). Rather than being an
impediment to thought, feeling is one of many ways that humans gain
knowledge and understanding. Put another way, emotions are a component of all interpretive processes, affecting, for example, how external
opportunities and threats are understood and responded to, how
resources are allocated, why a collective action frame succeeds or fails.
Emotions are integral to a person's sense of herself and to her political
subjectivity. Emotions shape people's notions of what is politically possible and desirable. The list could go on; my point is that, whenever we
include thought and meaning-making processes in our analyses, we
should consider emotions as well. How people feel about themselves,
their situations, and their political options affects how they act (although
of course not in any simple or direct way). In short, we should recognize
that emotions have significant effects on movements, only some of which
derive from their strategic mobilization. The task, then, is to theorize the
role of emotions in social movements in a manner that takes seriously the
sensuous experience of feelings.

A focus on sensuous feelings does not require a biological or natural-
ized view of emotions. Sociologists of emotion speak about feeling and
expression "rules" (Hochschild, 1979, 1983, 1990) and "emotion cultures"
(Gordon, 1989), suggesting the social and cultural components of feelings
and their expression. Part of socialization includes informal instruction
about which emotions are appropriate to feel and to express, for how long
and how intensely, by whom and in what contexts. Hochschild writes
that feeling rules (and implicitly, expression rules) "demarcate how much
of a given feeling, held [or expressed] in a given way, is crazy, unusual
but understandable, normal, inappropriate, or almost inappropriate for a
given social context" (1990:122). Communities or social groups have

"emotion cultures," understood as both the emotions that are prevalent within the group and the set of tacit or explicit rules and norms that demarcate "how [members of the group] should attend to, codify, appraise, manage, and express feelings" (Hochschild, 1990:124). The power of a society's feeling and expression rules is pronounced. As Hochschild notes, "Culture . . . powerfully affects what we think we should feel, what we try to feel, and sometimes what we feel" (1990:122). Of course, emotion norms are not all-powerful. Because the term "emotion culture" can mistakenly suggest something that is monolithic, totalizing, and static, it seems important to note that in positing the existence of an emotion culture within a social group or community, I do not mean to say that it prevails in a manner free of contestation, or that it is uniform or unchanging. We have to acknowledge what Jaggar (1989) calls "outlaw emotions," feelings that people experience that are conventionally unacceptable. As well, every emotional utterance, gesture, or evocation, particularly those that are public and that are repeated over time, has the potential to alter a prevailing emotion culture. A given "emotion culture," then, should be understood as prevalent but also as unsettled and mutable, open to challenge and revision and thus always at risk.

Numerous questions relevant to the study of social movements are raised by the acknowledgment of the force of emotions and by concepts like feeling and expression "rules," "emotion cultures," and "outlaw emotions." What is the relationship between emotion rules and an individual's feelings? How are feeling and expression rules established, enforced, and altered, and how do those processes affect political mobilization? Under what conditions are individuals willing to contest or transgress the emotion norms of larger society or of their social group? Why and how are outlaw emotions sometimes legitimized? How might a social group's emotion culture spark or dampen protest? How does the Western valuation of rationality affect protest politics? As these questions suggest, the introduction of emotions into our analysis broadens the social movement research agenda, raising questions relevant to the investigation of the emergence and decline of movements but also interjecting additional issues and offering new lines of inquiry in the study of social movements.

With some of the above insights about emotions and new questions in mind, let us return to political process theory, first to see how attention to emotions might enhance it. Opening political opportunities might generate emotions like hope and pride or might legitimize emotions like anger and indignation, which in turn might inspire an emotionally resonant collective action frame or a reallocation of resources toward collective action. In this instance, attention to emotions (over and beyond their strategic utility) might help us to understand *why* and *how* opening political opportunities sometimes facilitate protest.

However, once political process theorists acknowledge these emotional components of protest, they face the difficulty of explaining evidence that contradicts political process theory's political opportunity thesis, that shows, for example, *constricting* political opportunities generating emotions that *facilitate* protest and the emergence of movements. My investigation of ACT UP shows precisely that. Tightening political opportunities for lesbians and gay men in 1986–1987—exemplified in the Supreme Court's *Bowers* v. *Hardwick* decision upholding the constitutionality of a Georgia statute that denied homosexuals the right to engage in private sexual acts—amplified and legitimized the feeling and expression of anger among lesbians and gay men, altering the terrain in a manner that allowed for a shift in lesbian and gay community responses to AIDS that led to the emergence of the militant AIDS activist movement (Gould, 2000, 2001). I explore this example in greater detail below, but here I want to note that in this case, an investigation that foregrounds emotions—analyzing their inner workings as well as their interactions with factors like framing, resource mobilization, political opportunities, and other aspects of the external environment—helps explain a movement's emergence and meteoric rise when political process theory is unable to do so. The external environment matters, but not always in the ways predicted by political process theory. What the case of ACT UP reveals is that emotions can play a decisive role, and attention to them may allow a better theorization of the relationship between political opportunities, frames, and resources on the one hand, and movement emergence and decline on the other.

Political process theory's focus on political opportunities has narrowed the causal mechanisms that we investigate. Bringing emotions into our analyses would be an important corrective, forcing a better specification of the role of political opportunities as well as the abandonment of the pretense of having, or searching for, what Jaswin call an "invariant model" of movements. It should be noted that the addition of emotions is more than the addition of one more variable to the existing political process theory; an investigation of emotions troubles political process theory's privileging of opportunities, introduces new questions and new lines of inquiry, and thereby creates a new landscape for movement research.

EMOTIONS AND ACT UP

Once we accept the possibility that emotions—over and above their strategic utility—play a significant role in social movement processes, the next step is to delve more deeply into such factors as feeling and expression rules, emotion cultures, and the sensuous experience of feelings. Elsewhere, I have carried out that type of investigation of ACT UP (Gould, 2000). Here, I point to ways that we might incorporate emotions into our analyses of social movements; the sketch I draw is largely suggestive, but I think it provides a compelling argument against both ignoring and domesticating the emotions of protest.

ACT UP's political funerals are a striking example of the emotionality of protest; participants linked their grief and rage in a potent message to bystanders, those being targeted, and those participating in the protest itself. These and other ACT UP actions call out for an analysis of the force of emotions in protest. It would be easy to begin, and end, such an analysis by saying that of course anger played a role in ACT UP. After all, even government-appointed commissions have noted that the government's initial responses to AIDS were dangerously negligent; of course lesbians and gay men, who were watching their friends and lovers get sick and die while the government largely ignored the epidemic, were angry. But a glance at the history of lesbian and gay responses to the AIDS epidemic cautions us against a view that sees their anger toward the government and others as automatic or inevitable.[8] A close reading of lesbian and gay newspapers and organizational documents during the first five years of the epidemic demonstrates that even as AIDS cases and deaths skyrocketed, and even as lesbian and gay leaders criticized the government's punitive and negligent response, the prevailing emotion norms in lesbian and gay communities encouraged articulations and elicitations of shame about homosexuality, fear of social rejection, desire for social acceptance, faith in the government's goodwill, and an internally oriented pride about the community's noble response to the epidemic. Anger did not dominate, and when it was publicly expressed, it was generally rechanneled or otherwise suppressed and almost never linked to calls for militant activism (Gould, 2000). This evidence suggests the need to denaturalize lesbian and gay anger toward the government and to pursue a deeper analysis of the workings of emotions and their effects on protest politics.[9]

We might start by asking why other emotions seemed to trump lesbian and gay anger in those early years, and why lesbian and gay anger eventually became quite pronounced and even normative for a brief moment. In contemporary U.S. society, anger is never an unproblematic emotion.[10] The prevailing common sense about expressions of anger is that they indicate a loss of self-control, particularly when articulated by people of color, women, poor people, and other marginalized folks. Everyone is supposed to keep anger under wraps. Thus, although anger is certainly a factor in the lives of lesbians and gay men who live in a heterosexist society, given prevailing emotion norms, anger is not an unproblematic emotion. There is an additional reason why anger is troublesome for lesbians and gay men: Lesbians and gay men historically have demonstrated a persistent *ambivalence* about homosexuality and about dominant society, an ambivalence that derives from their marginalized status in a heterosexist society (Gould, 2000, 2001). The experience of such a contradictory constellation of feelings—both self-love and self-hate, along with attraction toward and rejection of society—encourages lesbians and gay men to feel anger and, simultaneously, not to feel anger toward state and society.[11] In a context where dominant emotion norms suspect and disparage anger, this structure of ambivalence and attempts to navigate it by elevating one of the contradictory emotions and suppressing the other helps to explain why lesbian and gay anger about the government's responses to the AIDS crisis was initially submerged, even as evidence mounted about government negligence (Gould, 2000).

As I indicated above, the Supreme Court's *Hardwick* ruling shattered the constellation of emotions that had prevailed in lesbian and gay communities in the early 1980s. In the wake of the Court's ruling, anger among lesbians and gay men became pronounced, evident in op-ed columns and letters-to-the-editor from gays in cities around the country, where it was explicitly linked to the need for "active resistance," "riots," "protest," "law-breaking," "boycotts," another "Stonewall," a "return to the streets."[12] How can we explain this transformation in the prevailing emotional common sense among lesbians and gay men, a transformation that opened up a space for lesbians and gay men to engage in militant political activism?

Lesbians and gay men experienced *Hardwick* as a "moral shock" (Jasper, 1997), an *unexpected* and *outrageous* legal decision, particularly to those who believed in American democracy's proclamation that equality was the law of the land. Moreover, by the middle of 1986 when *Hardwick* was announced, lesbians and gay men were already facing a horrific social, political, and health crisis; the number of AIDS cases reported to the Centers for Disease Control (CDC) had surpassed 30,000 and more than half of those had already died (Centers for Disease Control and Prevention, 1997:14). The thousands of deaths had not happened in isolation from one another; rather, they were all in some sense related, accumulating into palpable devastation of lesbian and gay communities across the country. Gay men in particular were suffering extreme and multiple losses as lovers, close friends, acquaintances, neighbors, and coworkers died painful and early deaths. At the same time, AIDS-related discrimination, ostracism, and violence were on the rise. The Justice Department had even recently legalized the firing of HIV-positive people from firms under government contract if an employer believed, scientific evidence notwithstanding, that HIV could be casually transmitted (Rist, 1987:13). Moreover, *Hardwick* occurred at a moment when state legislatures were increasingly considering, and sometimes passing, laws to implement mandatory testing and quarantine of persons testing HIV-positive. As well, the religious right was using AIDS to support its more generalized homophobia. Gay men *and* lesbians felt that they were under attack.

In this dire context, *Hardwick* amplified and intensified the anger and the fear that was building within lesbian and gay communities across the country. Drawing an analogy between the gay rage that was felt at the time of the Stonewall Riots and the gay rage felt after *Hardwick*, national leader Virginia Apuzzo remarked, "There is more anger among our people than I've seen in over a decade." She explained why the rage was so deep and so pervasive: "It's not as if [*Hardwick*] happened in isolation. A week before, the Justice Department virtually provided a rationale for AIDS discrimination. Widely publicized AIDS case load projections for 1991 soared to 180,000. And, through it all, the unrelenting funeral procession" (Apuzzo, 1986). Although itself not directly about AIDS, *Hardwick* punctuated and gave new meaning to the ongoing AIDS epidemic; it crystallized and heightened feelings about and interpretations of the epidemic that had previously been more or less inchoate. Deitcher has suggested that prior to *Hardwick*, "among gay men there had been no mass epiphany about AIDS" (1995:140); the Court ruling changed that, bringing the social implications of the health crisis into sharp focus, even for gay men who were only minimally politically attentive. Because the Court was denying an entire class of people their basic rights, lesbians and gay men were encouraged to interpret the ruling not as the product of their *individual* failings but as the prejudicial and discriminatory exclusion from society of an entire social group. By exposing the state's willingness, even eagerness, to exclude an entire class of people from constitutional protections, the *Hardwick* ruling encouraged a more politicized analysis of the government's response to AIDS that precluded any reduction of the epidemic to a tragic string of individual deaths and to isolated feelings of grief. After *Hardwick*, angry accusations of intentional government neglect of the epidemic, even analogies to genocide, became more resonant. Fear of the future increased. If the government and society saw homosexual sex (and thus homosexual lives) as criminal, then they certainly would not suddenly become concerned about homosexual deaths. In addition, as the highest court in the land was now willing to espouse virulent homophobic justifications in denying privacy rights to a group of citizens, who was to say that quarantine of HIV-positive people, a measure that some polls indicated was supported by more than 50 percent of the public and that was increasingly being called for in state legislatures, would not now be implemented?[13] Some had previously begun arguing that the government's response to the AIDS crisis was proof that gay men were seen as expendable, and in fact, better off dead; that type of analysis of the epidemic became widespread after *Hardwick*.

In a context of mounting deaths from AIDS, government failure to address the epidemic, increasingly repressive AIDS legislation, and growing homophobia, *Hardwick* thoroughly transformed the ways that many lesbians and gay men thought and felt about themselves, about dominant society, about the AIDS crisis, and about what kinds of politics were acceptable and necessary. The old emotion culture was shattered and a new one began to take hold. Operating in this changed environment, AIDS activists then bolstered and extended this new and emergent emotional common sense and linked it to militant AIDS activism. Militant AIDS activist groups formed across the country and offered a new resolution to lesbian and gay ambivalence about self and society, linking emotions such as indignation, anger, self-respect, and grief to militant, confrontational AIDS activism. ACT UP made anger and militance acceptable, even necessary, given the dire crisis. Thousands of lesbians and gay men around the country responded, participating in militant and angry street AIDS activism to fight the epidemic.

As I have suggested, ACT UP intentionally and strategically mobilized anger. But why was ACT UP successful (at least for a period of time) in augmenting and extending this emerging emotional common sense and legitimizing and mobilizing anger and militant action in lesbian and gay communities? I have suggested that anger is always at risk, historically easily submerged given emotion norms in mainstream U.S. society, and perhaps even more apt to be submerged in this case, given an instability that is constitutive of the structure of lesbian and gay ambivalence (where, again, anger is both encouraged and discouraged). Why, then, did thousands of lesbians and gay men take to the streets in response to ACT UP's call to anger and action?

I argue that although ACT UP's mobilization of anger (and other emotions) was in part strategic; it succeeded in mobilizing lesbians and gay men into angry and militant AIDS activism because, in the context of the *Hardwick* decision and the growing AIDS crisis, it succeeded in *altering* how many lesbians and gay men *felt*. That is, to understand the phenomenon of ACT UP, we have to move beyond a strategic view of emotions and recognize the force of, or the sensuous experience of, emotions.

The following story provides a means of understanding ACT UP's attempts to amplify lesbians' and gay men's growing anger and tether it to AIDS activism, and its success in doing so.[14] Militant AIDS activists from across the country converged in Washington, D.C., the weekend of October 10–11, 1988, for an action targeting the Food and Drug Administration (FDA). That same weekend, the Names Project Quilt was displayed on the Mall. As part of its mobilization for the FDA action, ACT

UP passed out a leaflet at the Quilt. One side blared: "SHOW YOUR *ANGER* TO THE PEOPLE WHO HELPED MAKE THE QUILT POSSIBLE: OUR *GOVERNMENT.*" Text on the reverse read:

> The Quilt helps us remember our lovers, relatives, and friends who have died during the past eight years. These people have died from a virus. But they have been killed by our government's neglect and inaction. . . . More than 40,000 people have died from AIDS. . . . Before this Quilt grows any larger, turn your grief into anger. Turn anger into action. **TURN THE POWER OF THE QUILT INTO ACTION**. (ACT UP/NY, 1988, emphasis in original)

A number of things are evident in this ACT UP leaflet. ACT UP was acknowledging lesbian and gay grief about the unceasing deaths of people with AIDS. Then, through a series of rhetorical moves, ACT UP located the source of that grief at the government's murderous doorstep. To fully appreciate ACT UP's strategy, it helps to recall that the earliest public expressions in lesbian and gay communities about the AIDS epidemic were candlelight memorial vigils, somber affairs that allowed participants to share their grief and publicly remember their loved ones.[15] The Names Project Quilt encouraged lesbians and gay men to express their grief on an even larger public scale. In its leaflet, ACT UP began with lesbian and gay grief, an uncontested, uncontroversial emotion, and then attempted to link that grief to anger, a more difficult, disreputable emotion. ACT UP offered the following logic: If you feel grief, you should also feel anger toward those who have caused you to feel grief; if you feel anger, you should join us in militant action to fight the AIDS crisis. ACT UP's logic both acknowledged, and offered a resolution to, lesbian and gay ambivalence about self and society: Given our grief and under these dire circumstances, anger and militant, confrontational action targeting state and society are acceptable, legitimate, justifiable, and indeed necessary.

The numerous militant actions and demonstrations by thousands of lesbian and gay AIDS activists around the country—on the heels of a generation of lesbian and gay engagement in more or less routine, interest group politics—suggest that ACT UP chapters were successful in generating and mobilizing anger. As many as 1,500 people participated in the FDA action (with almost 180 arrests) as well as the "Ashes" action. ACT UP may have *intended* to link and mobilize people's grief and rage, but such intentions do not explain why people put their bodies on the line and *participated* in those actions (or, for that matter, why people turn out for any action). Because emotions typically are opaque, we cannot know with certainty what participants were actually feeling, but video footage, photographs, and personal accounts of the "Ashes" action and other ACT

UP political funerals suggest that the marchers *felt*, and in part were motivated by feelings of, grief and rage.[16]

Drawing on the work of William Reddy (1997), I would like to offer a
theory of emotions that can give us some insight into ACT UP's success
in bolstering and mobilizing lesbian and gay anger. Reddy argues that
emotional utterances, what he calls "emotives," *alter* the feelings to which
they always imperfectly refer. Language cannot adequately represent or
characterize a subjective feeling state; when an emotive is articulated (e.g.,
"I'm angry"), it is an attempt to name and categorize a subjective feeling
state, making legible what was previously nonverbal, but it does so by
necessarily eliding the gap between language and the sensually experienced feeling(s). In the process, some components of one's feelings fail to
be brought into the verbal realm; they might be repressed, or displaced,
or simply never made meaningful through language. That which goes
unnamed, that excess, drops out and the articulated feeling is thereby
made understandable by being named. The emotive has enacted this slippage, thereby actually altering the feeling(s) to which it refers. Like per-
formatives (Austin, 1962), emotives do something to the world in that
they affect how people feel, "directly changing, building, hiding, intensi-
fying emotions" (Reddy, 1997:331).

The concept of emotives provides us with insight into the mechanism
behind the workings and power of feelings, feeling and expression rules,
and emotion cultures. Reddy focuses on first-person emotives that alter
the feeling state of the *individual* who utters them, but his concept of emotional conventions conveys the idea that normative emotives have a wider
impact on the emotional tone of the *community* as a whole. He suggests
that specific communities may strive to shape, manage, contain, repress,
channel, organize, orchestrate, promote, and/or intensify their members'
emotional expression and emotions themselves. Reddy has more recently
noted that second-person emotion claims like "you are angry" have emo-
tive-like effects on the hearer if she or he reflects on the claims (2000:117);
I would add that first-person plural emotion claims, e.g., "we are angry,"
are also emotives, potentially affecting the emotions of the speaker and of
those members of the "we" who hear the claim. Again, a community's
feeling and expression rules and normative emotives are powerful not
simply because they encourage appropriate emotion management but
also because emotives, particularly when repeated over time, actually
affect how people *feel*. Reddy's insight about emotives allows us to see
that emotive conventions can help manage a deep ambivalence that is
widespread within a community by setting out rules and norms but also
by magnifying one of the contradictory feelings and suppressing the
other and thereby actually altering people's feelings.

ACT UP's success in mobilizing lesbians' and gay men's anger derived, in part, from its ability to alter the prevailing emotion norms in lesbian and gay communities and make anger acceptable and legitimate. Reddy's concept of emotives helps us to understand why and how ACT UP was able to do so. As I have said, the evidence reveals that lesbian and gay ambivalence, and (conscious and unconscious) attempts to resolve it through emotional utterances, shaped lesbian and gay responses to AIDS during the first five years of the epidemic, encouraging vital activist responses like service provision, lobbying, and candlelight vigils and discouraging anything more disruptive or militant. External events—the *Hardwick* ruling in particular—decimated the prevailing emotional common sense that had elevated fear of social rejection, shame about gay sexual practices, faith in the government, and an internally oriented pride and had suppressed anger. On the heels of *Hardwick*, ACT UP augmented and extended an emergent emotional common sense, in effect offering a new resolution to lesbian and gay ambivalence by naming a new constellation of appropriate emotions. Given the changed context, ACT UP's repeated articulations and elicitations of emotions like anger about government inaction and genocidal neglect, indignation about the ill-treatment of queers, pride about militant "in-your-face" activism, and hostility toward dominant society altered lesbians' and gay men's feelings about the AIDS epidemic by *naming* these "new" emotions and thereby displacing or submerging emotions like shame and fear of rejection that had prevailed earlier. ACT UP's emotional utterances, repeated over and over again, altered people's feelings, animating their support for, and some people's turn toward, militant street AIDS activism.

The following account of one HIV-positive gay man's decision to join ACT UP reveals the emotions motivating his decision and indicates how ACT UP's proffered resolution to lesbian and gay ambivalence successfully altered emotion norms in lesbian and gay communities in part by affecting people's actual feelings. In a 1994 interview, G'dali Braverman described his initial contact with ACT UP/NY: "I had received a couple of flyers in the mail about ACT UP. I breezed through them and, basically, tossed them" (quoted in Shepard, 1997:113). Braverman experienced an enormous transformation while watching New York's Gay and Lesbian Pride Parade in 1988. "When ACT UP passed . . . I took one look and said, 'I am going to go to the next meeting of that organization.' There was a sense of power, a sense of action. It didn't appear to be about pity or shame or sadness or guilt. It seemed to be about anger and action" (113). Given Braverman's previous lack of interest in ACT UP, it seems possible that his witnessing of ACT UP/New York's anger in the streets altered his own feelings.[17] Having tested HIV-positive the previous year, Braverman may have initially felt a variety of emotions about AIDS and the epidemic, perhaps including the shame and guilt that he mentions, emotions that

were commonly elicited in both mainstream and lesbian and gay discourses about AIDS. ACT UP's expression of anger may have allowed
Braverman to *feel* anger, by legitimating that emotion but also by *naming*
it and, coincident with that utterance, suppressing some of the other feelings that Braverman may have previously experienced.[18]

Braverman's description of ACT UP/NY's preparations for demonstrations indicates similar emotion processes at work:

> We helped perpetuate that anger in the discussions that we had around the
> actions so that you [were] a bottle of emotions with a great sense of purpose.
> When you were at the demonstration you sustained yourself on an adrena-
> line rush because you were chanting the whole time. . . . Physically maintain-
> ing that energy level does incredible things to you. You walk away from the
> demonstration feeling elated, really elated and purposeful. (Shepard
> 1997:114)

The repeated expressions of anger at ACT UP meetings and actions
made anger normative and amplified the feeling itself, suppressing other
feelings that might have arisen or intensified during the AIDS crisis—for
example, shame about one's sexual practices and fear of social rejection—
or, on a different register, feelings that might accompany participation in
militant activism—fear of social rejection (again), anxiety about defying
authority, embarrassment about appearing hysterical or overwrought, or
even uncertainty about the utility or necessity of the action. Through the
emotional preparations, each participant's feelings were given meaning
through language—labeled as anger—and thus could be felt as anger,
perhaps producing the sense of being "a bottle of emotions with a great
sense of purpose." Braverman's reflections about the adrenaline produced at demonstrations add an interesting bodily component to Reddy's
more linguistic idea about emotives and feelings. Reddy points to the
ways in which emotional utterances alter our feelings, but there may also
be a bodily dimension to the process by which a feeling becomes legible
to a person: A person's very enactment of anger at a demonstration—
through chants and facial and bodily gestures, for example—may suppress her other feelings, making the anger physically legible to herself
while displacing the sensation of other emotions that simply are not
enacted.

CONCLUSION: EMOTIONS, SOCIAL
MOVEMENTS, AND SOCIAL THEORY

The sketch I have provided is only suggestive, but I think it demonstrates
the purchase of considering the emotions of social movements. First,

attention to emotions undermines political process theory's rational actor assumption, showing how participants in social movements, animated by an entangled mixture of feelings and calculations, are much more than rational actors; the inclusion of emotions allows fuller investigation of people's motivations, resulting in a thicker and deeper understanding of movement processes. Second, analysis of emotional processes unsettles political process theory's political opportunity thesis. The example of ACT UP's emergence shows how emotional utterances and performances alter people's feelings and, in interaction with other factors, can affect social movement trajectories, sometimes in a manner inexplicable by political process theory. Investigation of emotional processes, then, offers another causal mechanism that can help us to think more rigorously about the central questions in the field, movement emergence and decline. Third, attention to emotions illuminates, and facilitates investigation into, additional questions that are currently understudied, including the question of movement sustainability. Following a rational actor assumption, we might wonder why people continue to participate in a movement once it has taken off and they could easily take a free ride and reap the benefits from other people's work. Attention to the emotion cultures of movements challenges the assumption that underlies the free-rider problem—that people are atomized, isolated utility maximizers. Attention to emotions can also provide insight into other perplexing and understudied questions about social movements, including frame resonance, internal conflicts, conflicts between movements and the communities from which they arise, rituals and symbols, identity construction through activism, choice of tactics, and the like. Space limitations prevent me from addressing those questions here, but it seems clear that a focus on emotions, in interaction with other factors, can only strengthen our analyses.

I would like to conclude with a final observation about political process theory. Although the study of social movements provides fertile territory for exploring such questions as the sources and processes of social change, the texture and scope of human agency, the processes of meaning-making, the workings of power, and the relationship between the individual and the collective, our prevailing social movement models and analyses leave those questions largely unattended, contributing to an unnecessary and unproductive divorce between the field of social movements and the concerns of social theory more generally. We have become so focused on questions of movement emergence and decline that we tend to overlook broader questions of concern to social theorists, and perhaps for that reason, social theorists largely ignore our literature. But our research can add to their inquiries, and our own analyses would be strengthened if we drew on their insights. In evaluating the state of the field, we should attend to this divorce and consider how our analyses might be revised in ways that would help to rectify it. Attention to the emotions of protest reveals some of the benefits that might accrue were we to bridge this gap between the two literatures. Questions about the relationship between the sensuous experience of feelings, emotion rules, and protest, for example, require attention to questions of power, resistance, agency, subjectivity, structural reproduction and transformation, and historical change; at the same time, insights derived from an exploration of the role of emotions in protest could advance these broader theoretical inquiries. We must continue to explore movement-specific questions, but our analyses should make clear that social movements provide important insights into social life more generally.

NOTES

Acknowledgments: I would like to thank the editors of this volume for their comments on an earlier draft. I also want to express my deep gratitude to all of my co-conspirators—dead and alive—in ACT UP/Chicago. All errors, of course, are mine.

1. ACT UP (AIDS Coalition To Unleash Power) was founded in New York City in March 1987. It quickly became a national movement of street AIDS activists, with dozens of chapters across the United States. I indicate when I am speaking about a specific chapter; otherwise, I use "ACT UP" to refer to the national movement.

2. The Quilt, first displayed in 1987 and increasing in size ever since, contains thousands of three-by-six-inch panels that commemorate people who have died from AIDS-related complications.

3. A number of scholars have recently started to analyze and theorize the various roles that emotions play in social movements. See Aminzade and McAdam (2001); Goodwin (1997); Goodwin, Jasper, and Polletta (2000, 2001); Gould (2000, 2001, 2002); Groves (1995); Jasper (1997, 1998); Morgen (1983, 1995); Taylor (1995, 1996); and Taylor and Whittier (1995).

4. C-FAR was a militant street AIDS activist group that formed in January 1988 out of two groups, Chicago For Our Rights (CFOR, a lesbian/gay rights organization) and Dykes and Gay Men Against Repression (DAGMAR, a militant, anti-imperialist group that began to address the AIDS crisis in early 1987, around the time that ACT UP/NY formed). C-FAR changed its name to ACT UP/Chicago in November 1988.

5. In an insider's critique of the framing perspective, Benford initially seems to be making a similar point about the necessity of exploring the (nonstrategic) emotions of social movement actors. He argues that movement scholars should consider the "affective dimensions of movement participation" as one way to rectify the "overly cognitive conception of movement actors" (1997:419). However, his instrumentalist view of emotions that I quoted above, where he characterizes

emotions as a "social movement resource" that movement actors "strategically deploy," undermines his own argument and simply magnifies, rather than recti-fies, our already-existing "overly cognitive conception" of social movement parti-cipants.

6. These earlier models, widespread in the 1950s and 1960s, prior to the rise of resource mobilization theory, posited an unmediated and deterministic link between feelings (which were equated with irrationality) and action (always viewed as disruptive and threatening).

7. See Ferree (1992) for a similar critique of the assumption of rationality in the dominant social movement models.

8. Two other points might similarly lead us to denaturalize *lesbian* anger toward the government about AIDS: first, lesbians and gay men formed largely separate communities in the decade prior to the AIDS epidemic; second, AIDS was not striking lesbians in the same way that it was decimating gay men.

9. Please note that whereas earlier I cautioned against adopting a view of emotions that stripped them of all of their noncognitive characteristics, now I am warning against adopting a view of emotions as natural, involuntary impulses that automatically attach to objects, people, or events. There is no contradiction here. Emotions are neither entirely social nor entirely natural. We construct them through, but can never entirely contain them within, language; the opacity of emotions makes the failure of language most apparent. Although language makes our feelings legible to us, and in that sense constructs our feelings, and although cultural norms similarly shape our feelings, there is an excess of emotion that escapes language and culture, that cannot be symbolized and thus has no social positivity, but that still exists. I discuss this below.

10. Consider, for example, that the concept of "righteous anger" is only neces-sary in a society that disapproves of most forms of anger. On shifting norms about anger in U.S. society, see Stearns and Stearns (1986).

11. Although my analysis is specific to lesbians and gay men, similar structures of ambivalence about self and society and contradictory messages about anger are likely prevalent among other marginalized groups.

12. See, for example, Apuzzo (1986); Gans (1986); Morris (1986); Bockman (1986); and letters in the July 21, July 28, and September 1, 1986 issues of the *New York Native*.

13. When interviewed, lesbians and gay men who later participated in ACT UP/Chicago indicated that they had believed that a quarantine might actually be implemented. See Edwards (2000); Eggan (1999); Kracher (2000); McMillan (2000); Miller (1999); Patten (1993); Sieple (1999); and Thompson (2000).

14. I analyze these data in greater detail in Gould (2002).

15. For press accounts of early candlelight vigils, see Arvanette (1983); "Central Park Memorial" (1983); Chibbaro and Martz (1983); Cotton (1985); and Walter (1983).

16. See, for example, Finkelstein (1992b); Rafsky (1992); Ricketts (1995); and Wentzy (1995).

17. Recall that a year earlier, ACT UP/NY had strategized about how to shift "gay pride" to "gay rage." ACT UP's Pride contingents typically projected anger.

18. In a similar vein, Avram Finkelstein, another ACT UP/NY activist, noted, "Fear and grief faded away when I discovered action" through ACT UP (Fin-kelstein, 1992a:48).

12

Why David Sometimes Wins: Strategic Capacity in Social Movements

MARSHALL GANZ

"And there went out a champion out of the camp of the Philistines, named Goliath . . . whose height was six cubits and a span. And he had a helmet of brass upon his head, and he was armed with a coat of mail . . . and he had greaves of brass upon his legs . . . and the staff of his spear was like a weaver's beam; and his spear's head weights six hundred shekels of iron. . . . And he stood and cried to the armies of Israel. . . . Choose you a man for you. . . . If he be able to fight with me, and to kill me, then will we be your servants; but if I prevail against him, and kill him, then shall ye be our servants. . . . Give me a man that we may fight together." When Saul and all Israel heard those words of the Philistine, they were dismayed and greatly afraid.

And David said unto Saul, Let no man's heart fail because of him; thy servant will go and fight with this Philistine. And Saul said to David, Thou art not able to go against this Philistine to fight with him: for thou art but a youth, and he a man of war from his youth. . . . David said. . . . The Lord that delivered me out of the lion, and out of the paw of the bear, he will deliver me out of the hand of this Philistine. And Saul said unto David, Go, and the Lord be with thee. And Saul armed David with his armour, and he put an helmet of brass upon his head; also he armed him with a coat of mail. And David girded his sword upon his armour, and he assayed to go; for he had not proved it. And David said unto Saul, I cannot go with these; for I have not proved them. And David put them off him. And he took his staff in his hand, and chose him five smooth stones out of the brook, and put them in a shepherd's bag which he had . . . ; and his sling was in his hand: and he drew near unto the Philistine. . . . And the Philistine looked about, and saw David, he disdained him: for he was but a youth, and ruddy, and of a fair countenance. . . . And then said David to the Philistine, Thou comest to me with a sword, and with a

177

spear, and with a shield; but I come to thee in the name of the Lord of hosts . . . and David put his hand in his bag, and took thence a stone, and slang it, and smote the Philistine in his forehead . . . and he fell upon his face to the earth.

—Holy Bible, Book of Samuel, Chapter 17, Verses 4–49

HOW DAVID BEAT GOLIATH

The belief that strategic resourcefulness can overcome institutionalized resources is an ancient one. Tales of young, guileful, courageous underdogs who overwhelm old, powerful, and confident opponents occupy a mythic place in Western culture. When Goliath, veteran warrior, victor of many battles, arrayed in full battle gear, challenges the Israelites, their military leaders cower in fear. It is David, the young shepherd boy, to whom God gives the courage to face the giant. David's success begins with his courage, his commitment, and his motivation.

But it takes more than courage to bring David success. David thinks about the battle differently. Reminded by five stones he finds in a brook, he reflects on previous encounters in which he protected his flock from bears and lions. Based on these recollections he reframes this new battle in a way that gives him an advantage. Pointedly rejecting the king's offer of shield, sword, and armor as weapons he cannot use effectively against a master of these weapons, David conceives a plan of battle based on his five smooth stones, his skill with a sling, and the giant's underestimation of him.

The story of David and Goliath dramatizes questions about which many remain intensely curious: How have insurgents successfully challenged those with power over them? How can we challenge those with power over us? How can we change powerful institutions that shape our very lives?

Over the course of the last fifty years there have been many such challenges in the United States and around the world: the civil rights movement, the women's movement, the environmental movement, the democracy movements of Eastern Europe, the South African liberation movement, and so forth. Social scientists tend to account for these events, however, by arguing one version or another of "the time for change was right," while many historians attribute success to the intervention of gifted, charismatic individuals. Few analysts explore relationships among the times, the people who act upon them, and the organizational settings in which they act, to learn why "Davids" succeed when they do.

Failure to focus on the contribution of strategic leadership to social movement outcomes is a particularly serious shortcoming of social movement theory (Jasper, 1997; Morris and Staggenborg, 2002). Explanations of the emergence, development, and outcomes of social movements based on variation in access to resources and opportunities stress the influence of environmental changes on actors (McAdam, McCarthy, and Zald, 1996b). In this view, social movements unfold when actors predictably respond to new political opportunities or newly available resources. But theorists who emphasize opportunity explain little of why one actor should make better use of the same opportunity than another. Yet it is often in the differences in how actors use their opportunities that social movement legacies are shaped (Sewell, 1992). Other scholars who rely on variation in resources to explain why some movements are more successful than others fail to explain how actors with fewer resources can defeat those with more resources (McCarthy and Zald, 1977). But when insurgents overcome well-established rivals or opponents this is most often the case. Students of strategy and tactics offer accounts of their sources, their logic, and their effect on outcomes, but do not explain why one organization would be likely to devise more effective tactics than another (Tilly, 1981; Freeman, 1979; Lipsky, 1968; Gamson, 1975; McAdam, 1983). And much of the discussion of the meaning social movement actors give to what they do, dealt with under the general rubric of "framing," focuses on one aspect of strategy—how social movements interpret themselves— but tells us little of how framing is actually done, who does it, or why one organization would do a better job of it than another (Snow et al., 1986; Benford, 1997; Benford and Snow, 2000; Davis, 2002). And finally, scholars who invoke "culture" to correct for the weaknesses in structural accounts of social movements often remain quite structuralist in their analysis, only shifting the focus from political or economic structures to cultural ones (Johnston and Klandermans, 1995a). But they fail to explain variation in the agency actors exercise with respect to cultural, political, or economic structures. Yet it is the exercise of agency that is at the heart of strategy.

Students of strategic leadership, on the other hand, even in management, military, and political studies, focus more on what leaders do and how strategy works than on explaining why leaders of some organizations devise more effective strategy than others. Popular accounts of insurgent success attribute effective strategy to uniquely gifted leaders rather than offering systematic accounts of conditions under which leaders are more or less likely to devise effective strategy (Westley and Mintzberg, 1988; Howell, 1990). In part this is because good strategy is often anything but obvious. Based on the innovative, often guileful, exercise of agency, strategy can be difficult to deduce from objective configurations of resources and opportunities because it is based on a novel assessment

of them. Although effects attributed to charismatic leaders—attracting
followers, enhancing their sense of self-esteem, and inspiring them to
exert extra effort—can be invaluable organizational resources, they are
distinct from good strategy (Hollander and Offermann, 1990; House,
Spangler, and Woycke, 1991). In social movement settings, especially at
times of crisis, talented leaders may also be transformed into symbols of
a new community of identity, a source of their charisma (Weber, 1978
[1922]; Durkheim, 1964 [1915]; Collins, 1981; Pillai, 1996).[1] But as sociologists of religion and others have documented, many groups have charismatic leaders but few devise strategy effective enough to achieve
institutional stability, much less to become successful social movement
organizations (Stark and Bainbridge, 1985; Carlton-Ford, 1992).[2]

   Explaining social movement outcomes, then, often requires accounting
for the fact that different actors act in different ways, some of which
influence the environment more than others. Some see political opportunities where others do not, mobilize resources in ways others do not, and
frame their causes in ways others do not.

   But strategy is not purely subjective. Strategic thinking is reflexive and
imaginative, based on ways leaders learn to reflect on the past, attend to
the present, and anticipate the future (Bruner, 1990). Leaders—like all of
us—are influenced by their life experiences, relationships, and practical
learning that provide them with lenses through which they see the world
(Bandura, 1989; DiMaggio and Powell, 1991a; Banaszak, 1996; Zerubavel,
1997; DiMaggio, 1997)[3] and by the organizational structures within which
they interact with each other and with their environment (Weick, 1979;
Rogers, 1995; Van de Ven et al., 1999). In this chapter I discuss how the
strategic capacity of a leadership team—conditions that facilitate the
development of effective strategy—can help explain why "David" sometimes wins (Ganz, 2000a, 2000b).

UNDERSTANDING STRATEGY

In our interdependent world of competition and cooperation, achieving
one's goals often requires mobilizing and deploying one's resources to
influence the interests of others who control resources one needs—the use
of power (Weber, 1946 [1920]; Dahrendorf, 1958; Oberschall, 1973; Tilly,
1978; Lukes, 1974; Emerson, 1962; Michels, 1962 [1911]; Salancik and Pfeffer, 1977).[4] By resources I mean political, economic, and cultural—or
moral—assets actors can use to realize their goals (Weber, 1946 [1920];
Emerson, 1962; Oberschall, 1973; Tilly, 1978; Mann, 1986; Bourdieu, 1984;
Hall, 1997).[5] Although no one is entirely without resources, people do not
have power if they are unable to mobilize or deploy their resources in

ways that influence the interests of others. An individual's labor resource, for example, can become a source of power vis-à-vis an employer if mobilized collectively. Strategy is how actors translate their resources into power—to get "more bang for the buck."

Opportunities occur at moments when actors' resources acquire more value because of changes in the environmental context. Actors do not suddenly acquire more resources or devise a new strategy but find that resources they already have give them more leverage in achieving their goals. A full granary, for example, acquires greater value in a famine, creating opportunity for its owner. Similarly, a close election creates opportunity for political leaders who can influence swing voters. A labor shortage creates opportunity for workers to get more for their labor. This is one reason timing is such an important element of strategy.

Actors have unequal access to resources in part because of the ways outcomes of prior competition and collaboration become institutionalized, influencing the distribution of resources and reshaping rules by which actors compete and arenas within which they do so (Gamson, 1975; Lukes, 1974). A critical strategic goal of those contesting power is to find ways to turn short-term opportunities into long-term gains by institutionalizing them, for example, as formal organizations, collective bargaining agreements, or legislation. Assessing strategic effectiveness thus requires taking a "long view," a reason for studying the development of strategy over time (Andrews, 1997).

Strategy is how we turn what we have into what we need to get what we want. It is how we transform our resources into the power to achieve our purposes. It is the conceptual link we make between the targeting, timing, and tactics with which we mobilize and deploy resources and the outcomes we hope to achieve (Von Clausewitz, 1832; Hamel and Prahalad, 1989; Porter, 1996; Brown and Eisenhardt, 1998). Although we often do not act rationally and our actions can yield unintended outcomes, we do act purposefully (Cohen, March, and Olson, 1972; Salancik and Pfeffer, 1977; Weick, 1979; Crow, 1989; Watson, 1990; Bruner, 1990). Strategy is effective when we realize our goals through its use. Studying strategy is a way to discern the patterns in the relationship among intention, action, and outcome.

Our strategy frames our choices about targeting, timing, and tactics. As schema theorists have shown, we attribute meaning to specific events by locating them within broader frameworks of understanding (Goffman, 1974; Snow et al., 1986; Fiske and Taylor, 1991; Gamson, 1992; D'Andrade, 1992; Gamson and Meyer, 1996; DiMaggio, 1997). The strategic significance of the choices we make about how to target resources, time initiatives, and employ tactics depends on how we frame them relative to other choices in a path toward our goals. One reason it is difficult to study strategy is that although choices about targeting, timing, and tactics can be directly observed, the strategy that frames these choices—and provides them with their coherence—must often be inferred, using data drawn from interviews with participants, oral histories, correspondence, memoirs, charters, constitutions, organizational journals, activity reports, minutes of meetings, and participant observation.

Since strategy orients current action toward future goals, it develops in interaction with an ever-changing environment, especially actions and reactions of other actors (Alinsky, 1971; Weick, 1979; Mintzberg, 1987; Burgelman, 1991; Hamel, 1996; Brown and Eisenhardt, 1997).[6] In fixed contexts in which rules, resources, and interests are given, strategy can to some extent be understood in the analytic terms of game theory (Schelling, 1960). But in settings in which rules, resources, and interests are emergent—such as social movements—strategy has more in common with creative thinking (Morris, 1984; Hamel, 1996; Brown and Eisenhardt, 1997). Strategic action can thus best be understood as an ongoing creative process of understanding and adapting new conditions to one's goals (Brown and Eisenhardt, 1998).

The relationship of strategy to outcomes can be clarified by the distinction game theorists make among games of chance, skill, and strategy (Schelling, 1960). In games of chance, winning depends on the luck of the draw. In games of skill, it depends on behavioral facility, like hitting a tennis ball. In games of strategy, it depends on cognitive discernment—in interaction with other players—of the best course of action, as in the game of Go. In most games, all three elements come into play. Poker, for example, involves chance (deal of the cards), skill (estimating probabilities), and strategy (betting decisions). Although chance may be dispositive in any one hand, or even one game, in the long run skill and strategy distinguish excellent players—and their winnings—from others. Similarly, environmental developments can be seen as "chance" insofar as any one actor is concerned. But, in the long run, some actors are more likely to achieve their goals than others because they are better able to take advantage of these chances. Environmental change may generate the opportunities for social movements to emerge, but the outcomes and legacies of such movements have more to do with the strategies actors devise to turn these opportunities to their purposes, thus reshaping their environment.

A THEORY OF STRATEGIC CAPACITY

Strategy is articulated in decisions organizational leaders make as they interact with their environment. The likelihood their strategy will be effective increases with their motivation, access to salient knowledge, and the quality of the heuristic processes they employ in their deliberations: their strategic capacity.

In explaining sources of effective strategy I focus on why one organization is more likely to develop a series of effective tactics than another, not why one tactic is more effective than another. Unlike studies of the effectiveness of particular tactics by social movement, military, political, or management scholars, an attempt to identify the influences on effective strategizing requires studying the same organizations over time to discern the mechanisms that generate the strategizing (Lipsky, 1968; Gamson, 1975; McAdam, 1983). Although strategic capacity, strategy, and outcomes are distinct links in a probabilistic causal chain, greater strategic capacity is likely to yield better strategy, and better strategy is likely to yield better outcomes.

Variation in strategic capacity may also explain differences in what actors make of unique moments of opportunity that demand rapid decisions, especially moments of extraordinary flux when sudden reconfigurations of leadership and organization may facilitate emergence of social movements. And because the strategic capacity of organizations can grow or atrophy, such variation may help explain changes in effectiveness over time: why some new organizations overcome the "liability of newness" to succeed while some old organizations suffering from a "liability of senescence" fail.

I do not claim to have found a key variable sufficient to account for all differences in observed outcomes. Rather, I argue that the outcomes I try to explain—one group devises more effective strategy than another—are more or less likely to the extent that conditions specified in this model are met. In poker, chance may determine the outcome of any one hand, or even a game, but in the long run, some players are more likely to be winners than others. An organization can stumble on opportunity, but I argue that the likelihood that it will make strategic use of that opportunity depends on factors I specify here.

In viewing strategy as a kind of creative thinking, as shown in figure 12.1, I build on the work of social psychologists who hypothesize three key influences on creative output: task motivation, domain-relevant skills, and heuristic processes (Amabile, 1996).[7] In this view, creativity is enhanced by motivation generated by rewards intrinsic to task performance, rather than extrinsic to it. Although domain-relevant skills facilitate implementation of known algorithms to solve familiar problems, heuristic processes are required to generate new algorithms to solve novel problems (Hackman and Morris, 1975; Amabile, 1996).

Although creativity is an individual phenomenon, strategy is more often than not the creative output of a leadership team. Conditions under which a leadership team interacts contribute social influences that may be

FIGURE 12.1
Strategic Capacity

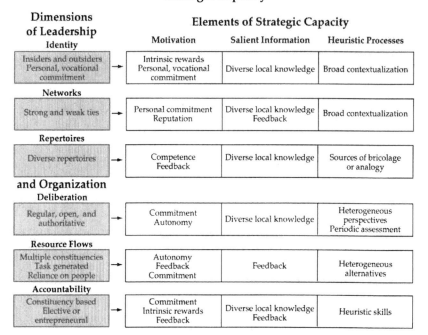

This figure illustrates leadership and organizational sources (left column) of strategic capacity (right three columns). The influence is meant to be simultaneous, not sequential.

more or less supportive of the creativity of its individual members (Hackman and Morris, 1975; McGrath, 1984; Amabile, 1988, 1996; Nemeth and Straw, 1989; Van de Ven et al., 1999). Furthermore, the task of devising strategy in complex, changing environments may require interaction among team members like the performance of a jazz ensemble. As a kind of distributed cognition, it may require synthesizing skills and information beyond the ken of any one individual, making terms of that interaction particularly important (Hutchins, 1991; Rogers, 1995; Van de Ven et al., 1999).

Motivation

David committed to fight Goliath before he knew how he would do it. He knew why he had to do it before he knew how he could do it.

Motivation influences creative output because it affects the focus one brings to one's work, the ability to concentrate for extended periods of time, persistence, willingness to take risks, and ability to sustain high energy (Ruscio, Whitney, and Amabile, 1995; Walberg, 1971; Glover and Sautter, 1977; Bergman, 1979). Motivated individuals are more likely to do the work to acquire needed knowledge and skills (Conti, Amabile, and Pokkak, 1995). And they are able to override programmed modes of thought to think more critically and reflectively if intensely interested in a problem, dissatisfied with the status quo, or experiencing a schema failure as a result of sharp breaches in expectations and outcomes (DiMaggio, 1997; Abelson, 1981; Garfinkel, 1967; Moscovici, 1984; Swidler, 1986; Bourdieu, 1990). To the extent that success enhances motivation, it not only generates more resources but may encourage greater creativity (Deci and Ryan, 1980; Chong, 1991).

Psychologists locate the sources of creative motivation primarily in the intrinsic rewards derived from work one loves to do (Amabile, 1996). Some emphasize the rewards derived from stimulation of novelty, feelings of mastery, and feelings of control experienced in the competent performance of a task (Hebb, 1953; Berlyne, 1960; White, 1959; Harter, 1978; Deci and Ryan, 1985), whereas others emphasize the "meaningfulness" attributed to the task by the person doing it (Hackman and Oldham, 1976). I argue that for social movement leaders, motivations deriving from identity-forming values or the "moral sources" (Taylor, 1989) that infuse one's life with meaning and one's work with meaningfulness are of particular importance (Weber, 1946 [1920]; Turner and Killian, 1987 [1972]; Bruner, 1990; D'Andrade, 1992; Peterson, 1999).[8] Work expressive of identity can be viewed as a "vocation," and work at one's vocation promises more motivational reward than work at a "job" (Weber, 1958 [1905]).

In the group work setting of a leadership team devising strategy, individual motivation is enhanced when people enjoy autonomy, receive positive feedback from peers and superiors, and are part of a team competing with other teams. It is dampened when they enjoy little autonomy, get no feedback or only negative feedback from peers and superiors, and face intense competition within the team (Amabile, 1988; Hackman, 1990).

Salient Knowledge

David did not know how to use King Saul's weapons, but he did know how to use stones as weapons.

A second element of creativity is possession of domain-relevant skills, mastery of which is requisite to developing novel applications. Creative jazz piano players have learned how to play the piano very well. Picasso mastered the styles of his predecessors before painting *Les Demoiselles d'Avignon*.

In terms of strategy, mastery of specific skills—or how to strategize—is relevant, but so is access to local knowledge of the constituencies, opponents, and third parties with which one is interacting. We expect effective military strategists to have command of the art of strategy and also to understand the troops, enemy, battlefield, and so forth. Salient knowledge includes both skills and information as to settings in which those skills are applied. The better our information about how to work within a particular domain—our local knowledge—the more likely we are to know how to deal with problems arising within that domain. When problems are routine, mastery of known algorithms or, in the language of social movement theory, repertoires of collective action facilitates effective problem solving. But since environments can change in response to our initiatives, especially volatile social movement environments, regular feedback is important in evaluating responses to these initiatives (Zaltman, Duncan, and Holbeck, 1973). When problems are novel, we must sort through our "repertoire" to find that which can be useful to us in learning how to innovate a response.

Heuristic Processes

David found his skill with stones useful because he could imaginatively recontextualize the battlefield, transforming it into a place where, as a shepherd, he knew how to protect his flock from wolves and bears. An outsider to the battle, he saw resources others did not see and opportunities they did not grasp. Goliath, on the other hand, the insider, failed to see a shepherd boy as a threat.

When we face new problems, we innovate solutions by using heuristic methods to imaginatively recontextualize data or synthesize them in new ways (Amabile, 1996; Langer, 1978; Langer and Imber, 1979; Bernstein, 1975; March and Olsen, 1976). To think creatively we must recognize our problems as new ones, at least to us, that require new solutions. To find new solutions we use our gift for analogy to reframe data in ways that make novel interpretations and new pathways conceivable, combining familiar elements in new ways as bricoleurs (Lakoff and Johnson, 1980; Gentner, 1989; Langer, 1989; Strang and Meyer, 1994; Levi-Strauss, 1962; Douglas, 1986; Campbell, 1997). Because it requires fresh perspectives and novel approaches, innovative thinking is facilitated by encounters with diverse points of view—within one's own life experience or the combined experience of the members of a group (Bernstein, 1975; Kasperson, 1978; Langer, 1989; Rosaldo, 1989; Piore, 1995; Nemeth, 1986; Weick, 1979; Senge, 1990; Rogers, 1995; DiMaggio, 1997; Van de Ven et al., 1999). Access to a diversity of approaches not only offers multiple routines from which to choose but also contributes to the "mindfulness" that multiple solutions are possible (Langer, 1989) and that most known solutions are "equivocal" (Weick, 1979). And at the most basic level, the more ideas are generated, the greater the likelihood there will be good ones among them (Campbell, 1960; Simonton, 1988).

Creative problem solving by teams is challenging because minorities tend to conform to majorities and persons with less authority tend to conform their views to those of persons with more authority (Asch, 1952; Milgram, 1974; Hackman and Morris, 1975; McGrath, 1984). Expression of minority views, however, can encourage better problem solving because it stimulates divergent thought about issues, causing decision makers to attend to more aspects of the situation and reexamine their premises (Nemeth, 1986). And solving certain problems, such as strategizing in a complex and changing environment, may require access to a range of knowledge, skill, and experience broader than that available to any one person.

Teams thus composed of persons with heterogeneous perspectives are more likely to make good decisions than homogeneous teams, especially when solving novel problems, because they can access greater resources, bring a broader range of skills to bear on decision making, and marshal a diversity of views (Nemeth and Staw, 1989). Heterogeneity may grow out of the life experience of team members, their affiliation with diverse relational networks, or their knowledge of distinct action repertoires.

To take advantage of heterogeneity, however, a team must learn both to foster minority expression that encourages divergent thinking associated with creativity—learning by discovery—and to switch to convergent thinking required to make decisions—learning by testing. Managing these tensions is especially challenging when planning and action occur simultaneously, as in the process of innovation (Van de Ven et al., 1999). They are managed more successfully by leaders tolerant of ambiguity who employ distinct organizational mechanisms for creative deliberation and decision making, rely on multiple sources of resources and authority, and resolve conflict by negotiation rather than by fiat or consensus (Osborn, 1963; Levinthal ,1997; Nemeth and Staw, 1989; Bartunek, 1993).

SOURCES OF STRATEGIC CAPACITY: LEADERSHIP AND ORGANIZATION

Having proposed a mechanism by which strategy is generated, I turn to the "input" to that mechanism that can be sources of strategic capacity: leadership and organization. As a unit of analysis, I focus on leadership teams: those persons who formally or informally participate in making authoritative strategic choices for an organization or units of an organization (Oberschall, 1973; Porter, 1996). I do not try to evaluate their qualities of leadership as such but rather their contribution to the formulation of strategy. Although the "person in charge" plays a unique leadership role, especially in forming, coaching, and sustaining a team (Hackman and Walton, 1986; Bartunek, 1993), strategy, like innovation, is more often a result of the interaction among leaders than organizational myths usually acknowledge (Van de Ven et al., 1999). Understanding strategic capacity may also help to explain why some groups are better able to take advantage of moments of opportunity than others and to specify the conditions under which the effectiveness of an organizational strategy will grow or atrophy.

As shown in figure 12.1, the strategic capacity of a leadership team is enhanced when it includes people who are insiders to some constituencies but outsiders to others, who have strong ties to some constituencies but weak ties to others, and who have learned diverse collective action repertoires. Leadership teams make the most of these attributes if they conduct regular, open, and authoritative deliberations and are held accountable by multiple, salient constituencies from whom they also draw their resources.

Leadership

Leaders devise strategy in interaction with their environments. Scholars who recognize biographical experience as the primary source of cognitive socialization (Bernstein, 1975; DiMaggio, 1997; Zerubavel, 1997), cultural perspective (Rosaldo, 1989; Jasper, 1997), and motivation (D'Andrade, 1992) link leaders' psychological, professional, organizational, and generational backgrounds to specific strategies. Few, however, have explored links between leaders' backgrounds and their potential to develop effective strategy (Kuhn, 1970; Oberschall, 1973; Chandler, 1977, 1962; Freeman, 1979; Ross, 1983; Wickham-Crowley, 1992). But leaders' identities, sociocultural networks, and tactical repertoires—or who they are, whom they know, and what they know—influence their strategic capacity.

Leadership teams that include "insiders" and "outsiders" have more strategic capacity than those that do not, as shown in the first row of figure 12.1, "Identity." Leaders' "identities" derive from their backgrounds as to race, class, gender, generation, ethnicity, religious beliefs, family background, education, and professional training. Teams of "insiders" and "outsiders" can thus combine access to a diversity of salient knowledge with the facility to recontextualize this knowledge creatively (Bernstein, 1975; Weick, 1979; Senge, 1990; Rogers, 1995; Hamel, 1996). Individuals with the "borderland" life experience of straddling cultural or institutional worlds are more likely to make innovative contributions than those without such experience (Kuhn, 1970; Rickards and Freedman, 1978; Weick, 1979; Rosaldo, 1989; Piore, 1995). Insiders who identify personally with their constituencies or outsiders whose vocation entails serving those constituencies are likely to derive more intrinsic rewards from their work than those whose motivation is solely instrumental or occupational (Weick, 1979; Howell, 1990; Meyer and Allen, 1997). Teams composed of persons with heterogeneous perspectives are likely to make better decisions than homogeneous teams, especially when solving novel problems, because they can access more resources, bring a broader range of skills to bear on decision making, and benefit from a diversity of views (Nemeth and Staw; 1989; Sutcliffe, 2000).

Leadership teams that include people networked by "strong" ties to some constituencies and by "weak" ties to others will have more strategic capacity than those that do not, as shown in the second row of figure 12.1, "Networks." Sociocultural networks are sources of ideas about what to do and how to do it (Emirbayer and Goodwin, 1994), mechanisms through which social movements recruit (Granovetter, 1973; Stark and Bainbridge, 1985; McAdam and Paulsen, 1993), sources of social capital (Coleman, 1990; Chong, 1991; Putnam, 1993), and incubators of new collective identities (Gamson, 1991; Taylor and Whittier, 1992). Sociologists distinguish between the "strong" ties within homogeneous networks and "weak" ties within heterogeneous networks. Leaders with strong constituency ties are more likely to know where to find local resources, whom to recruit, what tactics to use, and how to encourage constituents to identify with the organization than those without such ties (Morris, 1984). On the other hand, leaders with weak ties with multiple constituencies are more likely to know how to access a diversity of people, ideas, and routines that facilitate broad alliances. Combinations of strong ties and weak ties are associated with social movement recruitment because they link access with commitment, just as they are associated with innovation because they link information with influence (Gamson, 1990; Rogers, 1995). Diverse ties, like diverse life experiences, facilitate the creative recontextualization of strategic choices. But strong ties strengthen a leader's motivation due to his or her personal commitment to and identification with those whose lives are influenced by the choices he or she makes and among whom he or she earns his or her reputation (Chong, 1991).

Leadership teams that include persons with knowledge of diverse collective action repertoires have more strategic capacity than those without such knowledge, as shown in the third row of figure 12.1, "Repertoires." Knowledge of diverse collective action repertoires affords a leadership team greater strategic flexibility than those without that knowledge (Moore, 1995; Hamel, 1996; Alexander, 1998). Collective action repertoires are useful because of their practical (people know what to do), normative (people think they are right), and institutional (they attach to resources) utility in mobilizing people familiar with them (Tilly, 1981; Clemens, 1996). Tactics drawn from repertoires known to one's constituency but not to one's opposition are particularly useful (Alinsky, 1971). And knowledge of multiple repertoires not only widens leaders' range of possible choices but affords them the opportunity to adapt to new situations through heuristic processes of bricolage or analogy. The motivation of leaders adept in such repertoires is enhanced by competence they experience in their use and by positive feedback from constituencies who find these repertoires familiar.

Organization

Leaders interact with their environment from within organizational structures. A structure is created by commitments among founders who enact ways to interact with each other and with their environment (Weick, 1993). It defines patterns of legitimacy (Weber, 1978 [1922]; Powell and DiMaggio, 1991), power (Emerson, 1962; Salancik and Pfeffer, 1977; Perrow, 1986), and deliberation (March and Olsen, 1976). Although organizational form may be a founders' strategic choice (Child, 1972; Oliver, 1988; Eisenhardt and Schoonhoven, 1990; Weick, 1993; Clemens, 1996), once established it has a profound influence on subsequent innovation (Zaltman, Duncan, and Holbeck, 1973; Damanpour, 1991) and strategy (Chandler, 1962; Bower, 1970). In the development of strategy venues of deliberation, mechanisms of accountability, and resource flows are particularly important.

Leadership teams that conduct regular, open, and authoritative deliberation have more strategic capacity than those that do not, as depicted in the fourth row of figure 12.1, "Deliberation." Leadership teams conducting regular, open, and authoritative deliberation enhance their strategic capacity because they acquire access to salient information, participate in a creative process by means of which they explore new ways to use this information, and are motivated by commitment to choices they participated in making and upon which they have the autonomy to act (Duncan, 1973; Hackman, 1990; Ruscio, Whitney, and Amabile, 1995). Regular deliberation facilitates initiative by encouraging the periodic assessment of activities, whether or not there is a crisis (Brown and Eisenhardt, 1997, 1998). And deliberation open to heterogeneous points of view—or "deviant" perspectives—facilitates better decisions (Nemeth and Staw, 1989), encourages innovation (McCleod, 1992), and develops group capacity to perform cognitive tasks more creatively and effectively (Hutchins, 1991). To realize these benefits, leaders must develop deliberative practices encouraging the divergent thinking that grows out of the expression of diverse views as well as the convergent thinking required to make decisions to act upon them. For this purpose, conflict resolution by negotiation, accompanied by voting, may be preferable to either fiat or consensus because it preserves difference yet makes collective action possible (Bartunek, 1993). Deliberation resulting in actionable decisions motivates actors to take part in and to implement that which was decided upon (Hackman, 1990; Mintzberg and McHugh, 1985).

Leadership teams that mobilize resources, especially human resources, that are generated by an organizational program serving multiple constituencies, develop more strategic capacity than those that do not, as shown in the fifth row of figure 12.1, "Resource Flows." Leaders who mobilize resources from constituents must devise strategy to which constituents will respond (Pfeffer and Salancik, 1978; Mansbridge, 1986; Knocke and Wood, 1981). If membership dues are a major source of support, leaders learn to do what they have to do to get members to pay dues. Reliance on resources drawn primarily from outside one's core constituency—even when those resources are internal to the organization, such as an endowment—may dampen leaders' motivation to devise effective strategy. As long as they attend to the politics that keep the bills paid, they can keep doing the same thing "wrong." At the same time, leaders who draw resources from multiple constituencies acquire the strategic flexibility that goes with greater autonomy or greater room to maneuver (Powell, 1988; Alexander, 1998). Resources drawn from multiple sources may also encourage expression of diverse views important for creative thinking (Levinthal, 1997). Leaders' choices about which constituencies from whom to mobilize resources can thus have an important influence on subsequent strategy (Oliver and Marwell, 1992). Relying more on people than on money facilitates growth in strategic capacity to the extent that it encourages development of more leaders who know how to strategize. The more capable the strategists, the greater the flexibility with which an organization can pursue its objectives and the greater the scale on which it can do so (Weick, 1979).

Leadership teams that are self-selected or elected by constituencies to whom they are accountable have more strategic capacity than those selected bureaucratically, as shown in the sixth row of figure 12.1, "Accountability." Accountability structures influence strategy by establishing routines for leadership selection and defining loci of responsiveness. Leaders who are accountable to those outside their core constituency may have been selected based on criteria that have little to do with knowledge of or motivational connection with it. As innovation scholars have shown, interaction with one's constituency (or customers) is a particularly important source of salient new ideas (von Hippel, 1988; Utterback, 1971). Leaders selected bureaucratically are more likely to possess the skills and motivations compatible with bureaucratic success than with the creative work that innovation requires. Elected leaders are at least likely to have useful knowledge of the constituency that elected them and the political skills to have been elected. Entrepreneurial or self-selected leaders—at whose initiative the undertaking takes place—are more likely to possess skills and intrinsic motivations associated with creative work (Chambers, 1973; MacKinnon, 1965; Getzels and Csikszentmihalyi, 1976). Although elective and entrepreneurial leadership selection processes may be in tension with one another, either is likely to yield more strategic capacity than bureaucratic leadership selection.

Timing

Strategic choices are made not only in certain places but also at certain moments in time. Yet moments of opportunity come and go, and the choices actors make at some moments have far greater influence than those made at other moments. What influence, if any, does strategic capacity have on actors' ability to act not only in appropriate ways but in timely ones?

Sociologists, organizational behavior scholars, and cultural analysts note that some moments have greater causal significance for subsequent events than other moments. Some sociologists emphasize the significance of "critical junctures," moments when events unfolding along distinct causal pathways interact to yield unique opportunities (Skocpol, 1984). Others identify as "focusing moments" events that create unique opportunities for mobilization by drawing attention to particular issues (Lofland, 1996). Still others cite the "eventful temporality" of unique events that alter the deep context in which subsequent events unfold (Sewell, 1996a, 1996b). Organizational scholars identify portentous moments of organizational development as midway points toward realization of particular goals and other moments of high contingency (Weick, 1979, 1993; Gersick, 1994). Cultural scholars point to moments of crisis or "role transition" in the lives of individuals or communities at which norms, identities, and values become fluid or liminal, compared with other times when they are relatively resilient (Turner, 1966; Jasper, 1997; Smelser, 1962; Turner and Killian, 1987; Swidler, 1986; Morris, 1993b). Moments of historical, cultural, and organizational fluidity may occur singly or together—what scholars call entrainment, alignment of internal and external rhythms of change (Ancona and Chong, 1996).

Ironically, those moments when actors' strategic choices may matter most may also be moments of radical uncertainty, particularly in the case of social movements. Breakthrough events may alter the affected individuals, organizations, and environments so deeply that their consequences depend almost entirely on what actors make of them. Victories may be moments when strategic choices matter most, not times to "rest on one's laurels" but rather to make the most of one's successes. Victories may be moments of greatest risk.

Because of their radical uncertainty, these are conditions under which strategic capacity may matter most. When the value of reliance on known algorithms is most limited may be when creative capability is most important (Tushman and Murmann, 1997). Leadership teams with more strategic capacity can make not only more informed choices but quicker ones, allowing them to take greater advantage of unique moments of opportunity And leadership teams with more strategic capacity can take advantage of moments of unique opportunity to reconfigure their own leadership and structure in ways that allow them to enhance their strategic capacity further.

Dynamics

Since strategic capacity is the result of a relationship among leaders, organization, and environment, failure to adapt to environmental change can lead to atrophy. On the other hand, if organizations adapt their leadership to changes in their environment and continue interacting with it, their strategic capacity can grow. Because established organizations rely on their resources for institutional power, their loss of resourcefulness may only become apparent when they are required to face new challenges in unfamiliar environments. That strategic capacity can atrophy helps explain not only why David can sometimes win but also why Goliath can sometimes lose.

Scholars note that organizations institutionalize as environments change (Stinchcombe, 1965; Hannan and Freeman, 1984). Processes of organizational inertia inhibit adaptation by old organizations to new environments, thus creating niches within which new organizations can emerge—a liability of aging or senescence (Aldrich and Auster, 1986). Leaders of the newer organizations were recently selected, have more organizational flexibility, and work in closer articulation with the environment. Leaders of older organizations were often selected in the past, are constrained by institutional routines, and may have resources that allow them to operate in counterproductive insulation from the environment. As leaders persist, they form bonds among themselves, develop common understandings of "how things work," and select others like themselves to lead. Access to internal organizational resources can insulate them, in the short run, from environmental change. For a time, these resources may even give them the power to shape that environment—but only for a time. Changes in organizational structure that reduce leaders' accountability to or need to mobilize resources from constituents—or changes in deliberative processes that suppress dissent—can diminish strategic capacity, even as resources grow. The strategic capacity of an organization can thus grow over time if it adjusts its leadership team to reflect environmental change, multiplies deliberative venues, remains accountable to salient constituencies, and derives resources from them. Similarly, strategic capacity may atrophy if an organization fails to adjust its leadership, limits deliberative venues, loses accountability to salient constituencies, and relies on internal resources. Older organizations are likely to have less strategic capacity than newer ones.

STRATEGIC PROCESS MODEL

As summarized in figure 12.2, "Strategic Process Model," I argue that outcomes are influenced by strategy, the effectiveness of which is, in turn, the result of the strategic capacity of a leadership team. And the strategic capacity of a leadership team is the result of who its members are and how they structure their interaction with each other and with their environment, as explained previously.

FIGURE 12.2
Strategic Process Model

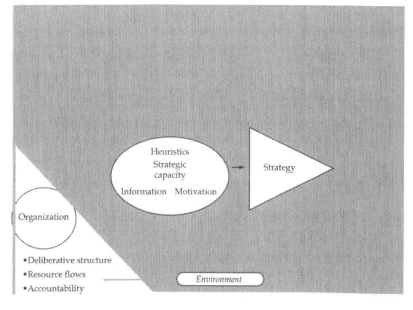

EVALUATING STRATEGIC CAPACITY

Although elsewhere I show that variation in strategic capacity can explain the success of the United Farm Workers as compared with its rival organizations, the AFL-CIO's Agricultural Workers Organizing Committee (AWOC) and the International Brotherhood of Teamsters, in this chapter I have focused on articulating strategic capacity as a conceptual tool to help explain other cases of David-like success, or failure. How generalizable—and therefore, useful—can we expect this concept to be?

The core argument on which strategic capacity rests is the claim that under conditions of uncertainty, the capability to generate new algorithms, when rooted in deep understanding of the environment, is more strategically valuable than the capability to apply known algorithms, no matter how expertly. In other words, under conditions in which rules, resources, and interests are highly institutionalized and links between ends and means are certain, as in the world of game theory, the relationship between resources and success should be predictable, especially when expertise at how to play the game is factored in. Strategic capacity is thus more useful in explaining outcomes in turbulent environments where rules, resources, and interests are emergent and links between ends and means are uncertain. This suggests that although it was developed in the context of social movement insurgency, strategic capacity as an analytic concept could be useful in explaining outcomes in any such environment, political, economic, or social.

One way the explanatory power of strategic capacity could be evaluated is with sets of cases in which strategic capacity and resources vary, as shown in figure 12.3. Strategic capacity adds the most explanatory value in cases falling into the upper left quadrant (little resources, lots of strategic capacity) and lower right quadrant (lots of resources, little strategic capacity). But it could be tested with respect to any set of cases not limited to the lower left quadrant (little resources, little strategic capacity) or the upper right quadrant (lots of resources, lots of strategic capacity). Although strategic capacity would have the least explanatory value for cases confined to the lower left quadrant (little resources, little strategic capacity) or upper right quadrant (lots of resources, lots of strategic capacity), these are quadrants in which we expect to find the most cases with the most predictable outcomes, for example, challengers with little resources and strategic capacity or incumbents with lots of resources and strategic capacity. The unique contribution of a theory of strategic capacity is to offer a way to explain the less frequent but—from a social movement point of view—more interesting outcomes of David winning and Goliath losing without resort to accounts grounded in opportunity and resources that rob actors of their agency. By selecting cases based on vari-

FIGURE 12.3
Strategic Capacity and Resources

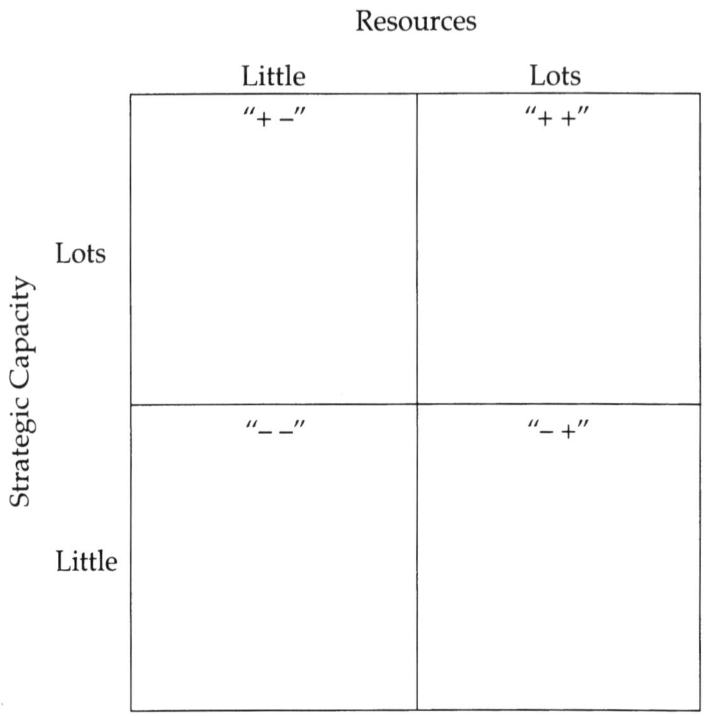

Resources

	Little	Lots
Lots	"+ –"	"+ +"
Little	"– –"	"– +"

Strategic Capacity

ation in resources and strategic capacity we avoid the problem of selection on the dependent variable, success. Strategic capacity could be tested by comparing a set of cases with observable variation in independent variables of resources and strategic capacity and the dependent variable of success. To the extent strategic capacity co-varies with success, the theory would be upheld. To the extent it does not, it would be falsified.

CONCLUSION

This chapter began by asking why "David" sometimes wins. Organizations can compensate for lack of economic, political, or cultural resources with creative strategy, a function of the motivation, access to a diversity of salient information, and heuristic facility with which their leadership teams interact with their environment. Changing environments generate opportunities and resources, but the significance of those opportunities or resources—and even what constitutes them—emerges from the hearts, heads, and hands of the actors who develop the means of putting them to work. People can generate the power to resolve grievances not only if those with power decide to use it on their behalf, but also if they can develop the capacity to outthink and outlast their opponents—a matter of leadership and organization. As an "actor-centered" approach, analysis of strategic capacity suggests ways to design leadership teams and structure organizations that increase the chances of devising effective strategies to deal with the challenges of organizing, innovation, and social change today. As students of "street smarts" have long understood, resourcefulness can sometimes compensate for a lack of resources. Although learning about how the environment influences actors is important, learning more about how actors influence the environment is the first step not only to understanding the world but changing it.

NOTES

1. Although charisma is often viewed as a personality attribute, it is better understood as an interaction between leader and constituency. Weber (1978 [1922]) attributes the "charismatic" authority of religious leaders to their followers' experience of the "divine" sources of their authority. Durkheim (1964 [1915]) describes the role of mythic leaders or "civilizing heroes" as communal symbols. Collins (1981) argues that charismatic leaders are "individuals who have become the focal point of an emotion-producing ritual that links together a large coalition; their charisma waxes and wanes according to the degree to which the aggregate conditions for the dramatic predominance of that coalition are met." And Pillai (1996) offers empirical data that link the emergence of charismatic leaders to a group's experience of crisis.

2. Stark and Bainbridge (1985), for example, report that in 1978 California was home to 167 of the nation's approximately 450 cults, most of which had charismatic leaders, and Carlton-Ford (1992) reports that twenty-two of forty-four urban communes studied had charismatic leaders.

3. A number of scholars offer psychological or sociological versions of what Bandura (1989) calls "the emergent interactive agency" that he contrasts with "pure autonomous agency" or "mechanistic agency," including DiMaggio and Powell (1989); Banaszak (1996); Zerubavel (1997); and DiMaggio (1997).

4. This concept of power derives from Weber's (1946 [1920]) view of stratification as power relations emergent from competition and collaboration among actors within economic, status, and political markets, a view more recently articulated by Dahrendorf (1958). Oberschall (1973) and Tilly (1978) introduced this view of power to the study of social movements. Lukes (1974) shows how the power relations with which social movements contend become institutionalized. And at the micro level, Emerson (1962) develops a similar concept of power as growing out of exchange relations among individuals in terms of their interests

and resources. To conceptualize power relations within organizations I draw on a tradition originating with Michels (1962 [1911]), more recently articulated by Salancik and Pfeffer (1977).

5. Although resources are often construed in narrow economic terms, Weber's multidimensional view is echoed in Mann's (1986) account of ideological, economic, military, and political sources of power; Bourdieu's (1984) analysis of "cultural capital"; and Hall's (1997) "moral authority as a power resource."

6. Community organizer Saul Alinsky (1971) summarized this view of emergent strategy as "the action is in the reaction." Weick (1979) articulates a scholarly version of this perspective, one that since the business environment has become more turbulent has supplanted "strategic planning" in the work of Mintzberg (1987, 1994); Burgelman (1991); Hamel (1996); and Brown and Eisenhardt (1997).

7. I am particularly indebted to Amabile's (1996) fine work on creativity, which provides links between micro behaviors and macro outcomes. In adapting her work to an understanding of strategy, I substitute the term "salient knowledge" for "domain-relevant skills" to better capture the importance of environmental information to strategic thinking, and I consider a broader range of motivational sources.

8. I acknowledge that "interests" influence behavior, but follow Weber's (1946 [1920]) "switchman" metaphor, according to which values shape people's understanding of their interests—a view shared by Turner and Killian (1987); Bruner (1990); D'Andrade (1992); and Peterson (1999).

Part III

CONCLUDING REFLECTIONS

13

Revisiting the U.S. Civil Rights Movement: Toward a More Synthetic Understanding of the Origins of Contention

DOUG McADAM

My motivations for writing *Political Process and the Development of Black Insurgency* were varied.[1, 2] My principal goals were pragmatic. I wanted to complete the thesis and obtain my Ph.D. in hope that some misguided institution would actually offer me gainful employment. But there were two important intellectual goals at work as well. Believing, as I still do, that the modern civil rights movement marked a critical watershed in the history of the United States, I wanted to understand as much about the historical origins of that struggle as I could. Second, I hoped to use the case of the civil rights movement to fashion a more general theory of social movement emergence. Nearly a quarter of a century after beginning work on my dissertation, I retain a great deal of interest in and enthusiasm for these two intellectual goals. This chapter allows me to revisit both goals, with an eye to amending my understanding of the case and to teasing out the theoretical implications that derive from that amendment. It always surprises me to see authors defending every nuance of works they have written. I have always understood my work— even the pieces of which I am most proud—to be woefully stylized approximations to a much more complicated empirical reality. I therefore embrace an opportunity that few authors ever get: to revisit their work in light of new scholarship in hope of edging a bit closer to the complexities of the phenomenon in question.

In addition to the two goals that animated the original book, there is a third motivation for writing this chapter, one inspired by more recent intellectual trends in sociology and the social sciences more generally. This newer aim involves a desire to explore the possibilities for theoretical synthesis across nominally distinct structuralist, culturalist, and rationalist approaches to the study of collective action. These theoretical perspectives have become increasingly distinct and antagonistic in recent years within sociology (cf. Goodwin and Jasper, 1999; chapter 1; Kiser and Hechter, 1998; Somers, 1997). Thus beside my desire to use an amended understanding of the civil rights movement to fashion a more satisfactory theory of social movement origins, my more general aim is to see whether these perspectives can be reconciled to any significant degree. Paradigm warfare only makes sense under one of two assumptions. One can either assume that truth is synonymous with a given theoretical perspective or, more pragmatically, that the best way to understand the complexity of social life is by fashioning highly stylized "baseline" models as a first approximation to reality. I have long been skeptical of the first assumption, taking it as a given that all theories suppress features of social life, even as they highlight others. Though I suspect many proponents of this or that theory actually retain a great deal of ontological faith in "their" perspective, when pressed most retreat to the second line of defense as a way of justifying their adherence to a given theory. The justification is straightforward and entirely credible: let each theoretical perspective develop more or less autonomously to see just how far the inherent logic and distinctive set of assumptions underlying the perspective can take it.

But it seems just as valid to chart a more synthetic course and to ask how, in this case, insights from structuralist, rationalist, and culturalist perspectives might be combined to yield a fuller understanding of social movement dynamics. That is the tack I will take in this chapter. However, to keep the enterprise manageable, I will bound it in an important way. Rather than take on the full temporal sweep of a movement, I will focus only on the origins of same. I will proceed as follows. Taking the dominant structural model of social movement emergence as my starting point, I offer a thoroughgoing critique of this account, seeking to underscore how the failure to integrate insights from other proximate fields and from culturalist and rationalist perspectives has seriously truncated our understanding of the phenomenon in question. Drawing on this critique, I then offer an alternative account of movement emergence. Throughout the explication of this alternative perspective, I seek to illustrate the claims I am making by reference to the single case in question: the American civil rights movement of the post–World War II period.

THE QUESTION OF ORIGINS: REVIEWING THE LITERATURE

A fairly strong consensus has emerged in recent years among scholars of social movements with respect to the question of movement emergence. Increasingly, one finds scholars from various countries and nominally different theoretical traditions emphasizing the importance of the same three broad sets of factors in analyzing the origins of collective action. These three factors are: (1) the political opportunities and constraints confronting a given challenger; (2) the forms of organization (informal as well as formal) available to insurgents as sites for initial mobilization; and (3) the collective processes of interpretation, attribution, and social construction that mediate between opportunity and action. Or perhaps it will be easier to refer to these three factors by their conventional shorthand designations: *political opportunities, mobilizing structures, and framing processes.*

1. *Expanding Political Opportunities*—Under ordinary circumstances, excluded groups or challengers, face enormous obstacles in their efforts to advance group interests. Challengers are excluded from routine decision-making processes precisely because their bargaining position, relative to established polity members, is so weak. But the particular set of power relations that define the political environment at any point in time hardly constitute an immutable structure of political life. Instead, the opportunities for a challenger to engage in successful collective action are expected to vary over time. And it is these variations that are held to help shape the ebb and flow of movement activity.

But what accounts for these shifts in political opportunity? A finite list of specific causes would be impossible to compile. The point is *any* broad social change process that serves to significantly undermine the calculations and assumptions on which the political establishment is structured is very likely to occasion a significant expansion in political opportunity. Among the events and processes likely to prove disruptive of the political status quo are wars, industrialization, international political realignments, or concerted political pressure from international actors, economic crisis, and widespread demographic shifts.

2. *Extant Mobilizing Structures*—If changes in the institutionalized political system shape the prospects for collective action, their influence is not independent of the various kinds of *mobilizing structures* through which groups seek to organize and press their claims. By mobilizing structures we mean *those collective vehicles, informal as well as formal, through which people mobilize and engage in collective action.* This focus on the meso-level groups, organizations, and informal networks that comprise the collective building blocks of social movements constitutes the

second conceptual element in this synthesis of the current consensus that appears to exist among those who have studied the question of movement emergence. The shared assumption is that changes in a system of institutionalized politics only affords a potential challenger the opportunity for successful collective action. It is the organizational vehicles available to the group at the time the opportunity presents itself that conditions its ability to exploit these new resources. In the absence of such vehicles, the group is apt to lack the capacity to act even when afforded the opportunity to do so.

3. *Framing or Other Interpretive Processes*—If a combination of political opportunities and mobilizing structures affords the group a certain structural potential for action, they remain, in the absence of one final factor, insufficient to account for collective action. Mediating between opportunity, organization, and action are the shared meanings, and cultural understandings—including a shared collective identity—that people bring to an instance of incipient contention. At a minimum people need to feel both *aggrieved* about some aspect of their lives and *optimistic* that, acting collectively, they can redress the problem. The affective and cognitive come together to shape these two perceptions. The relevant mobilizing emotions are anger at the perceived injustice and hope that the injustice can be redressed through collective action. Lacking either mobilizing perception (or the strong constituent emotions needed to make them "actionable"), it is highly unlikely that a movement will develop. Conditioning the presence or absence of these perceptions is that complex of social psychological dynamics—collective attribution, social construction—that David Snow and various of his colleagues (Snow et al., 1986; Snow and Benford, 1988) have referred to as *framing processes*. When the cognitive/affective by-products of these framing processes are combined with opportunities and organization, chances are great that collective action will develop.

MOVEMENT ORIGINS: A CRITIQUE
OF THE CURRENT CONSENSUS

The broadly consensual perspective sketched above has come to shape much current thinking on the origins of social movements. Movements are held to arise as a result of the fortuitous confluence of external political opportunities and internal organization and framing processes. At root this is a structuralist account of movement emergence and one that bears more than a passing resemblance to the original conceptual framework proposed in *Political Process and the Development of Black Insurgency*. To have influenced scholarship on this important topic is gratifying. But even as I embrace this perspective as an accurate rendering of the current consensus and a useful starting point for this effort, I am increasingly aware of the limits of the framework and the often wooden manner in which it has been applied by movement scholars. This awareness has emerged as a result of ongoing theoretical reflection on my part, and in response to the work of movement scholars critical of the generally structuralist assumptions that inform the framework sketched above. These critics are drawn from both the rationalist (Chong, 1991; Hardin, 1995; Kiser and Hechter, 1998; Lichbach, 1995, 1997, 1998) and culturalist (Fantasia, 1988; Goodwin and Jasper, 1999; Hart, 1996; Jasper, 1997; Somers, 1997) perspectives. Reflecting these various influences, I now see at least six serious problems with the dominant theoretical approach to the study of movement origins.[3] In this section, I use insights from rationalist and culturalist paradigms as well as other proximate literatures (e.g., comparative revolutions, democratization), both to animate the critique and to suggest partial solutions to these problems.

1. *Threat or Opportunity?*—In *From Mobilization to Revolution*, Tilly (1978) assigned equal weight to threat and opportunity as stimulants to collective action. But over the years, threat has given way to opportunity as the analytic *sine qua non* of many social movement scholars. Scholars of ethnic conflict (Lieberson, 1980; Olzak, 1992) may have erred in the opposite direction in identifying threats to the integrity of ethnic boundaries as the critical stimulant in episodes of ethnic conflict, but their general point seems unimpeachable. Based, then, on their work as well as that of a few visionary social movement scholars (e.g., Flacks, 1988), I have come to regard this singular preoccupation with opportunity as excessively narrow. This is especially true, I believe, in the case of movements in democratic settings. That is, in polities where there is some expectation of state responsiveness and few formal barriers to mobilization, we should expect perceived threats to group interests to serve, along with expanding opportunities, as two distinct precipitants of collective action. To the extent that scholars of contention—especially social movement scholars—have ignored the former in favor of the latter, I fear that our understanding of origins has been somewhat truncated.

2. *The Culturally Constructed Nature of Threat/Opportunity*—The earliest formulations of the political process model were rooted in an awareness of the culturalist dynamics that necessarily underlie collective action (McAdam, 1982: 33–35, 48–51). But the sharp—if reified—distinction between objective conditions and their subjective interpretation that informed early versions of the model have generally been absent from later political process formulations. Perceived and socially constructed opportunities have given way to "political opportunity *structures*" (POS)

and, with this change, what once was conceived of as a structural/con-
structionist account of movement emergence has become a structurally
determinist one. The troubling implication of the current consensus is
that objective shifts in institutional rules, alliance structures, or some
other dimension of the "political opportunity structure" virtually *compels*
mobilization. This is a structuralist conceit that fails to grant collective
meaning-making its central role in social life. Such structural shifts can
only increase the likelihood that this or that challenging group will fashion that shared set of cognitive/affective understandings crucial to the
initiation of collective action. The same holds true for *threat*. For increased
ethnic competition (Olzak, 1992) *or any other change process* to trigger an
episode of contention, it must first be interpreted as threatening by a sufficiently large number of people to make collective action viable. In this
sense, it is not the structural changes that set people in motion, but the
shared understandings and conceptions of "we-ness" they develop to
make sense of the trends. The importance of the trends derives, then, from
the stimulus they provide to this interpretive process. In this sense, my
perspective is Weberian, both in its conception of mobilization as a contingent, probabilistic outcome and in the central role assigned to collective
meaning-making in the process.

   So am I merely climbing onto the culturalist bandwagon by assaying
this particular critique of the contemporary movement theory? Yes and
no. This element of the critique is motivated by a respectful, if critical,
reading of the cultural turn in movement studies. Culturalists have obviously taken meaning-making seriously and, through their work, deep-
ened our understanding of the cognitive, affective, and ideational roots of
contention (Jasper, 1997; Melucci, 1989, 1985; Somers, 1997). But, all too
often in my view, they have failed to embed collaborative meaning making in the mix of relevant contexts—local history, local culture, local and
extra-local politics—that constrain, even as they animate, the interpretive
process. As a result they tend to overstate the plasticity of the process and
gloss the way that various institutions—cultural no less than political—
set probabalistic limits on the outcomes of same.

   3. *The Structural Determinist Conception of Mobilizing Structures*—The
overriding structural bias animating the current theoretical consensus is
evident not only in how opportunities (and threats) have been conceived,
but in the theoretical importance attached to "mobilizing *structures*" and
the related account of movement recruitment offered by proponents of
the perspective. That account stresses the role of established organizations or prior network ties in pulling people into active participation in a
movement. To their credit, these structural/network analysts have not
simply hypothesized these effects; they have also produced a great deal
of empirical work that supports the notion of "structural proximity" as a

strong predictor of differential recruitment to activism (Bolton, 1972; Briët, Klandermans, and Kroon, 1987; Fernandez and McAdam, 1988; Gould, 1993, 1995; McAdam, 1986; McAdam and Paulsen, 1993; Orum, 1972; Rosenthal et al., 1985; Snow, Zurcher, and Ekland-Olson, 1980; Walsh and Warland, 1983). What they have generally failed to do, however, is to offer an explicit sociological/social-psychological explanation for the robust empirical findings they have produced. By default, they are guilty of assaying a structurally determinist account of movement recruitment. We are left with the unfortunate impression that individuals who are structurally proximate to a movement are virtually compelled to get involved by virtue of knowing others who are already active. There are a host of good reasons why we should reject this simple structural imperative, but here I want to highlight only two.

First, the above account skirts the important question of origins. That is, to say that people join movements because they know others who are involved, ignores the obvious fact that on the eve of the movement, there are no salient alters available as models for egos' involvement. The more general point I want to make is that for any established organization or associational network to become a central node in movement recruitment requires a great deal of creative cultural work that has been totally glossed in the dominant account, which is simultaneously too individualist and too structuralist for my taste. For extant organizations or networks to become sites of mobilization/recruitment, they must be *culturally* conceived and constructed as such by a significant subset of the group's members. I will have much more to say about this critically important process of *social appropriation* later in the chapter. For now, I simply want to underscore its importance and to note its absence in the current theoretical consensus. I illustrate the phenomenon with the following example. To say that the American civil rights movement emerged within a network of southern black churches tells us nothing about how those churches—or more precisely their ministerial leadership and congregations—came to see themselves as appropriate sites for mobilization. This is a *collaborative, cultural* project about which the current structural model of recruitment can tell us almost nothing.

The second key lacuna with the structural perspective is the one I mentioned above; that its proponents have failed to sketch even a rudimentary model of individual motivation and action to explain the observed network effects.[4] The structuralists are not alone in this. For all the importance they attach to social construction and human agency, most culturalists advance an implicit view of the individual that is curiously determinist in its own right. Individuals are shaped not by structural forces, but by disembodied culture. But in both cases, the effect is the same; the potential for individual autonomy and choice is largely denied,

replaced by a conception of the individual as acted upon, rather than
acting.

For their part, rationalists have articulated a model of individual motivation and action. And while I think it is a truncated view of the individual, I nonetheless take seriously the need for such a model and for the
articulation of mechanisms that bridge the micro, meso, and macro
dimensions of contentious politics. I do not pretend to deliver on a formal
model of this sort in this chapter. For now, I want to make a single foundational point: in my view a viable model of the individual must take full
account of the fundamentally *social/relational* nature of human existence.
This is not to embrace the oversocialized conception of the individual that
I see informing the work of most structuralists and some culturalists.
Consistent with the rationalists, I too stress the potential for individual
autonomy and choice. Where I part company with the rationalists is in the
central importance I attach to one powerful motivator of human action. I
think most individuals act routinely to safeguard and sustain the central
sources of meaning and identity in their lives. As a practical matter this
means frequently prizing solidary incentives over all others and acting to
insure that those whose approval and emotional sustenance are most central to our lives and sense of self are generally attended to. This assumption accords nicely with the empirical literature on movement
recruitment. The rapid and effective mobilization that has been observed
in existing solidary communities does not surprise me. *Which* of these
previously non-political communities come to define contention as their
raison d'etre is often highly surprising. But once this cultural appropriation has taken place, the rapid transformation of the collectivity into a
vehicle of struggle is entirely consistent with the view I am proposing. In
my view, the rationalists have it backward. It is not so much that calculating outsiders are compelled to affiliate with a movement as a result of
the provision of individual selective incentives. Instead, some number of
embedded insiders are threatened with the loss of meaning and membership for failure to adopt the new ideational and behavioral requirements
of the collective.

4. *The Movement-Centric Nature of the Perspective*—Another lacuna I see
associated with the current consensus (and movement theory in general),
is a certain myopia in its general frame of reference. The dominant
account of emergence is decidedly movement-centric in its sketch of
causal factors. The opportunities/organization/framing triad take the
incipient movement as the all-important frame of reference; the central
pivot on which contention turns. Let me be clear. I regard the social settings within which initial mobilization takes place as key sites for analysis, but not the only sites. If it takes two to tango it takes at least two to
"contend." That is, contentious politics necessarily involves the mobiliza-

tion of state actors (and possibly other non-state elites) as well as potential challengers. We should be equally concerned with the processes and settings within which both sets of actors mobilize and especially interested in the unfolding patterns of interaction between the various parties to contention. From this point of view, it is ironic that a perspective—political process—that sought to theorize the intersection of institutionalized and non-institutionalized politics should have come, in its consensual embodiment, to focus almost exclusively on processes internal to movements. In this chapter I want to return to the interactionist premises that informed the earliest writings in the tradition. In this sense, I want to move closer to the analytic framework that currently holds sway in the study of revolution and, in some quarters, democratization (Bermeo, 1997; O'Donnell and Schmitter, 1986; Valenzuela, 1989) and away from that which characterizes the study of social movements.

5. *The Multi-Level Nature of Political Opportunities and the Neglect of the International*—In the quarter century since Peter Eisinger (1973) first used the term, the concept of political opportunity has come to be almost universally equated with the rules, institutional structure, and elite alliances characteristic of *national* political systems. Since Eisinger himself used the concept to compare *municipal* political systems, this equation of POS with nation state is ironic to say the least. The point is, the concept is inherently multi-level. Any system of institutional power can be simultaneously analyzed as a political opportunity structure. This points applies to non-state systems—institutional governance in a firm, for instance—no less than state. Here, however, I will confine myself to the multi-level institutional structuring of *state* power. Even here, though, things are plenty complicated enough. Throughout history, most polities have been embedded in a complex web of governing jurisdictions (te Brake, 1997; Tarrow, 1997). Even the modern nation state tends to nest power at more than one level.

The practical implications of this kind of multi-level system for the emergence of contention has generally escaped the attention of movement researchers. Once again, the tendency has been to conceptualize facilitative expansions in political opportunities as processes that unfold domestically. So changes in access rules, or shifts in political alignments have generally been explained by reference to developments at the national level. But as students of comparative revolution (Goldstone, 1991; Skocpol, 1979) have long appreciated, states can be rendered vulnerable by changes that emanate at many different levels. In the kind of "composite polities" profiled by te Brake (1997) and Tarrow (1997), significant changes or crises at any level of the system can set in motion contention and change at any other level. But even this expansion in our geographic/institutional approach to the definition of political opportunities omits another critically important arena within which significant

pressures for change often arise. Following the lead of Skocpol, Goldstone, and others, I have in mind the international and specifically the
pressures for change that devolve from perturbations in transnational
political alliances and economic relations. Any synthetic understanding
of the origins of non-routine politics will need to reflect this expanded
understanding of the geographic and institutional locus of political
opportunities.

     6. *Static Perspective Versus Dynamic Model*—The final criticism of the
prevailing model of movement emergence is a very general one. For all
the support that the triad of opportunity/organization/framing currently
enjoys among movement scholars, it should be obvious that this framework in no way constitutes a dynamic model of movement origins.
Indeed, it is little more than a static listing of general factors presumed to
be important in the development of collective action. But how these factors combine to trigger initial mobilization and by *what intervening mechanisms* is less clearly specified in the movement literature. I am, therefore,
motivated to replace this static listing of factors with a sketch of a set of
highly contingent, dynamic relationships, which are apt to shape the likelihood of movement emergence. This sketch is given in figure 13.1.

     Elaborating the Model.   The figure depicts movement emergence as a
highly contingent outcome of an ongoing process of interaction involving
at least one set of state actors and one challenger. In point of fact, while I
focus here on state/challenger interaction, I think the perspective is applicable to episodes of contention that do not involve state actors. The framework can be readily adapted to analyzing the emergence of contention in
any system of institutionalized power (e.g., a firm, a church). The generic
model only requires that the analyst be able to identity at least one *member*
and one *challenger* whose ongoing interaction sets in motion a broader
episode of contention. Following Gamson (1990), *members* are collective
actors whose interests are routinely taken into account in decision-making processes within the setting in question. *Challengers* are collective
actors who "lack the basic prerogative of members—routine access to
decisions that affect them" (Gamson, 1990). But while this fundamental
distinction can be applied to many settings, here I will restrict myself to
episodes of contention that develop out of sustained interaction between
a special kind *of member*—that is, state actors—and at least one *challenger*.
Instances of non-routine contention that do not conform to this framework lie outside the scope of the inquiry.

     One of the virtues of the perspective sketched here is that it is as amena-
ble to the analysis of routine as contentious politics. Too often analysts
have reified the distinction between routine politics and social movements, revolutions, and the like and wound up proposing separate theories to account for the two phenomena. Since I see the latter almost always

FIGURE 13.1
A Dynamic, Interactive Framework for Analyzing the Emergence of Contentious Politics

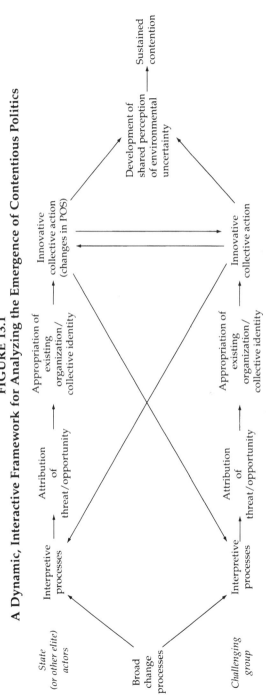

growing out of and often transforming the former, I am motivated to propose a framework that is equally adept at explaining both. That is the case
with the perspective sketched in figure 13.1. Routine politics depends on
the same general processes of interpretation, attribution, and appropriation as contentious politics; it is only the outcome of these processes that
is different in the two cases. Routine collective action—that is, action that
serves essentially to reproduce the existing structure of polity relations—
occurs either when (1) no attribution of threat/opportunity is forthcoming, or (2) when those asserting the existence of such a threat/opportunity
are unable to appropriate the organizational vehicle necessary to act on
the attribution. Innovative collective action requires not only that such an
attribution be made but that it then be adopted as the guiding frame for
action by an existing collectivity.

The figure identifies five processes that shape this unfolding dynamic.
The remainder of this section is given over to a discussion of these five
processes as I see them manifest in the U.S. civil rights movement. The
aim is to revisit a case familiar to social movement analysts to see how
our understanding of the movement is altered by viewing it through a
more dynamic, process-oriented analytic framework. This approach
would appear to substitute a deductive approach to case analysis for the
inductive program sketched at the beginning of the chapter. In point of
fact, neither approach captures the inherently reciprocal interplay
between "theory" and "evidence" that has guided this project. That is,
recent contributions to the historiography of the civil rights movement
have prompted me to rethink aspects of my original theoretical formulation, just as contemporary theoretical debates have altered my reading of
the case. But for heuristic purposes and to insure consistency with the
original book, I will adhere to the same narrative conventions as I did
then. That is, I will use the lens of "general theory"—in this case figure
13.1—to structure my retelling of the case.

1. *Exogenous Change Processes*—A host of specific literatures have made
note of the important role of broad change processes in destabilizing previously stable social and political relations, thereby helping to set in
motion episodes of contention. Work on comparative revolutions has
identified external wars (Skocpol, 1979) or more generic economic and/
or demographic strains (Goldstone, 1991) as the usual precipitants of the
kinds of state crises that typically devolve into revolution. Like Goldstone, scholars in the ethnic competition tradition (Lieberson, 1980;
Olzak, 1992) have often fingered a mix of demographic and economic
change processes as the backdrop against which episodes of ethnic conflict and violence have taken place. But presumably any broad change
processes that serve to erode barriers to ethnic/racial contact and competition have the potential to serve as the manifest triggers of contention.

Finally, social movement theory has privileged one kind of change process—expanding political opportunities—over all others as the proximate cause of initial mobilization. But, even allowing for the kind of broadening of the institutional/geographic locus of political opportunities urged in number 4 above, the fact of the matter is, most shifts in POS are themselves responses to broader change processes. What kind of change processes? A finite list of specific causes would be impossible to compile. The point is that

> *any* event or broad social process that serves to undermine the calculations and assumptions on which the political establishment is structured occasions a shift in political opportunities. Among the events and processes likely to prove disruptive of the political status quo are wars, industrialization, international political alignments, prolonged [economic woes], and widespread demographic changes. (McAdam, 1982:41)

The above list includes most, if not all, of the broad change processes highlighted by work on comparative revolutions, ethnic conflict, and, to a lesser extent, democratization. The list also accords well with the specific mix of change processes that served to alter the interpretive context shaping action by all parties to the civil rights struggle.

With the withdrawal of federal troops from the American South in 1876, control over southern race relations again passed into the hands of the region's political and economic elite. Predictably, this reassertion of regional control over racial matters spelled an end to whatever political influence African-Americans had been able to exercise during Reconstruction. This "arrangement" held for better than 50 years, reflecting the continuing viability of the political calculus on which it had been based. But, as Gunnar Myrdal remarked with great foresight in 1944, the arrangement never constituted a "stable power equilibrium" and appeared at last to "be approaching its end." Among the change processes that served to destabilize the arrangement was the marked decline of the cotton economy, especially after 1930, and the massive northward migration of blacks the decline helped set in motion. What makes this mass exodus more than simply a demographic curiosity are the political consequences that flowed from it. "The move was more than a simple migration and change in folkways; for blacks, it was a move, almost literally from no voting to voting" (Brooks, 1974:17). The migrants were drawn disproportionately from states with the lowest percentage of registered black voters and, in turn, settled overwhelmingly in seven northern industrial states—New York, New Jersey, Pennsylvania, Ohio, California, Illinois, and Michigan—that were widely regarded as the keys to electoral success in presidential contests.

> The electoral significance of this . . . migration was evident in both the 1944
> and 1948 elections. In both instances, had blacks reversed the proportion of
> votes they gave the two major candidates, the Republican challenger,
> Thomas Dewey, would have defeated his Democratic opponents, Franklin
> Roosevelt and Harry Truman. . . . By 1950, then, the so-called black vote was
> firmly established as an electoral force of national significance. (McAdam,
> 1982:81)

All of the change processes discussed to this point were domestic in
nature. This is consistent with the account offered in the 1982 book and
the general nation-centric bias evident in most of the social movement
literature. Since then there has occurred something of a minor revolution
in the historiography of the civil rights movement that has granted
increased attention to the role of international factors in the origins of the
struggle (see, for example, Dudziak, 1988; Layton, 1995; Plummer, 1996;
Skrentny, 1998). This scholarship has significantly altered my view of the
relative causal importance of domestic and international change processes in the emergence of the movement. In summary, while the decline
of "King Cotton" and the Great Migration certainly altered the interpretive context that had sustained the racial status quo, it was the onset of the
Cold War that changed it irrevocably. Consider the stark contrast between
Roosevelt and Truman on the matter of the "Negro question." In 1936
FDR was elected to his second term. His margin of victory—popular as
well as electoral—remains one of the largest in the history of presidential
politics. The election also marked a significant shift in racial politics in the
United States. For the first time since African-Americans had been
granted the franchise, black voters deserted the Republican Party—the
Party of Lincoln—to cast the majority of their votes for a Democratic presidential candidate. The New Deal reforms had been accompanied by a
general leftward swing in political attitudes and had conditioned the
American people to countenance assertive government action on behalf
of the "less fortunate" segments of American society. Finally, FDR was
himself a liberal—socially no less than politically—as was his outspoken
and influential wife, Eleanor. Yet, in spite of all these factors, Roosevelt
remained silent on racial matters throughout his four-term presidency,
refusing even to come out in favor of anti-lynching legislation on the
numerous occasions such bills were brought before Congress.

Just ten years later, FDR's successor, Harry Truman, inaugurated a
period of active executive advocacy of civil rights when he appointed and
charged his national Committee on Civil Rights with investigating the
"current remedies of civil rights in the country and recommending
appropriate legislative remedies for deficiencies uncovered" (quoted in
McAdam, 1982:84). Two years later, in 1948, Truman issued two landmark

executive orders, the first establishing a fair employment board within the Civil Service Commission, and the second calling for the gradual desegregation of the armed forces. Why had Truman acted when Roosevelt did not? Comparing the domestic political contexts in which FDR and Truman acted only deepens the puzzle. While Roosevelt's electoral margins left him politically secure, Truman's status as a non-incumbent made him uniquely vulnerable to challenge as he pointed toward the 1948 election. Moreover, with black voters now returning solid majorities for his Party, Truman had seemingly little to gain and everything to lose by alienating that strange, but critically important, New Deal bedfellow: the southern Dixiecrat. And, that, of course, is precisely what his advocacy of civil rights reform did. Angered by his proactive support for civil rights, the Dixiecrats broke away from the Party in 1948 and ran their own candidate, Strom Thurmond, for President. The electoral votes of the once "solid South" were now in jeopardy of being lost. Add to this Truman's own attitudinal qualms about race (McCullough, 1992) and the "chilling effect" the Cold War had on the American Left and one could hardly think of a less propitious time to be advocating for politically and socially progressive causes.

The key to the mystery lies not in the domestic context, but in the new pressures and considerations thrust upon the United States and the Executive Branch in particular in the post-war period. It is again interesting to quote Myrdal's (1970: 35) prescient remarks on the subject:

> The Negro Problem . . . has also acquired tremendous international implications, and this is another and decisive reason why the white North is prevented from compromising with the White South regarding the Negro. . . . Statesmen will have to take cognizance of the changed geopolitical situation of the nation and carry out important adaptations of the American way of life to new necessities. A main adaptation is bound to be the redefinition of the Negro's status in American democracy.

In short, the otherwise puzzling contrast between Truman's actions and FDR's inaction becomes entirely comprehensible when placed in the very different international contexts in which they occurred. The Cold War worldview that came to dominate American policy making in the post-war period dramatically changed the interpretive context of U.S. racial politics and the actions that flowed from it. I turn to this aspect of the analytic framework next.

2. *Interpretive Processes and the Collective Attribution of Opportunity/ Threat*—As with all of social life, it is the ongoing interpretation of events by various collectivities that shapes the likelihood of movement emergence. Indeed, these continuous processes of sense-making and collective

attribution are arguably more important in movements insofar as the latter requires participants to reject institutionalized routines and taken for
granted assumptions about the world and to fashion new worldviews
and lines of interaction. And yet, for all their importance, these crucial
interpretive dynamics are largely absent from our theories of the origins
of movements and other forms of contentious politics. There is virtually
no mention of these processes in the theoretical work on ethnic conflict,
or the dominant structuralist approach to comparative revolution.[5] One is
left, in both cases, with the distinct impression that structural changes
(e.g., erosion of ethnic boundaries, fiscal or demographic pressures) give
rise to contention without regard to these intervening interpretive processes.

There is perhaps a bit more attention to processes of this sort in the
contemporary literature on social movements. Much of this attention has
centered around what have come to be known as "framing processes."
But most of the conceptual work on framing betrays a more strategic/
instrumental, and therefore later temporal, orientation to collective interpretation than we have in mind here.[6] The earliest work in this tradition
by David Snow and various of his colleagues (Snow et al., 1986; Snow and
Benford, 1988) equated framing with the conscious strategic efforts by
groups of people to fashion shared understandings of the world and of
themselves that legitimate and motivate collective action. In other words,
framing was largely an activity pursued by groups that already defined
themselves as engaged in struggle. One part of that struggle involved the
group or its agents in conscious efforts to "frame" their activities in ways
that resonated with various audiences (e.g., potential adherents, the
media, policymakers, bystander publics) whom the group hoped to
influence. My point is that, for all of their importance, these later framing
efforts depend on earlier and far more contingent interpretive processes.
Strategic framing implies adherence to a non-routine and conflictual
definition of the situation. But this definition is itself a product of earlier
processes of collective interpretation and attribution.

Even where these earlier, more contingent, interpretive processes have
been the focus of theoretical attention, they have been framed in a decidedly movement-centric way. Consider the following quote from *Political
Process and the Development of Black Insurgency* (48):

> While important, expanding political opportunities and indigenous organi-
> zations do not, in any simple sense, produce a social movement. . . . Together
> they only offer insurgents a certain objective "structural potential" for collec-
> tive political action. Mediating between opportunity and action are people
> and the subjective meanings they attach to their situations. . . . This process
> must occur if an organized protest campaign is to take place.

All well and good. But it is not only the potential challenging groups who are engaged in these interpretive processes. If collective interpretation is endemic to social life, we can expect the kind of broad change processes discussed in the previous section to set in motion especially intensive and potentially consequential sense making activities by all parties to the conflict. All manner of groups will be seeking first to make sense of the changes and secondly to assess the degree of threat or opportunity the changes may pose for the collectivity. There is, of course, no guarantee that these processes will result in the kind of shared conception of threat or opportunity that I think is requisite for innovative collective action, but the potential for such conceptions is always there; a potential whose realization is only enhanced by the magnitude of the change processes and their "proximity" to the group in question.

So in the case of the civil rights movement, African-Americans were far from the only ones trying to make sense of the mix of change processes discussed in the previous section. Various state and non-state elites were also cognizant of these changes and sought to monitor and assess their significance as potential "threats" or "opportunities." The most significant of these changes was the onset of the Cold War. One of the tenets of the framework proposed here is that we should expect *framebreaks*—that is, shared definitions of the situation that undermine social reproduction—to develop among those whose interests or collective identity place them "close" to the issue in question. And so it was in the case of the civil rights movement. This was true for civil rights forces and state actors alike. Two quick examples will help to illustrate the point and underscore the significance of novel interpretive processes in the development of the movement. One such significant interpretive "moment" occurred in the mid-1930s when key figures in the National Association for the Advancement of Colored People (NAACP) argued that Roosevelt's appointments to the Supreme Court and more general legal/cultural trends augured well for a concerted legal campaign aimed at challenging segregated schools (Kluger, 1976; Rosenberg, 1991; Tushnet, 1987). Or to put the matter more abstractly, an innovative interpretation of emerging environmental opportunity led to the adoption of a logically consistent plan for concerted collective action.

A second such significant interpretive "moment" in the history of the movement occurred among state actors far removed from and with little substantive interest in the issue of civil rights. Even before the end of World War II, a serious debate was underway among policymakers within the State Department and the foreign policy community in general over the shape of the post-war world and its implications for the formulation and execution of U.S. policy, domestic as well as foreign. Those pushing a Cold War template prevailed in this debate. The stark attribution of threat animating this view inspired calls for various policy innovations, including impassioned pleas from the diplomatic core—especially those with postings in the third world and Western Europe—for civil rights reforms to counter Soviet efforts to exploit American racism for its obvious propaganda value (Layton, 1995). Truman's civil rights initiatives were one response to these pleas. Another was the series of briefs filed by the U.S. Attorney General in connection with various civil rights cases heard before the Supreme Court after 1948. Arguably the most important of these briefs was one filed in December 1952 in connection with a public school desegregation case—*Brown v. Topeka Board of Education*—then before the Court. The brief makes clear the link between the Cold War interpretive frame and the substantive shift in federal civil rights policy. In part the brief read: "it is in the context of the present world struggle between freedom and tyranny that the problem of racial discrimination must be viewed. . . . Racial discrimination furnishes grist for the Communist propaganda mills, and it raises doubt even among friendly nations as to the intensity of our devotion to the democratic faith" (quoted in McAdam, 1982:83).

3. *Appropriation of Existing Organizational Space and Routine Collective Identities*—But even an interpretive process that results in a group of people attributing great significance to a perceived environmental "threat" or "opportunity" does not insure the emergence of a movement. For collective attributions of threat or opportunity to key emergent collective action the interpreters must command sufficient organization and numbers to provide a social/organizational base for mobilization. The ideational challenge thus gets joined to a more narrowly organizational one. Would be activists—of either the elite or non-elite variety—must either create an organizational vehicle and supporting collective identity as prerequisites for action or appropriate an existing organization and the routine collective identity on which it rests. The empirical literature on movement emergence suggests that the latter is far and away the more common pattern, but some such embedding of "threat" or "opportunity" in organization/identity is required for action to develop.[7]

Both state actors and challengers face serious obstacles in their attempts to appropriate existing social space in the service of emergent collective action. Both sets of actors are likely to contend with an established leadership that does not share their interpretation of recent events as posing a significant threat to or opportunity for the realization of group interests. But above and beyond this generic obstacle, state actors would seem to possess one clear advantage over most challenging groups when it comes to the appropriation of extant social space/identities. The fact of the matter is, for state actors, most of the ongoing interpretation of social change processes takes place in formal organizations geared to the defense or advocacy of state (and associated elite) interests and organized around collective identities explicitly tied to these aims. So, to return to the civil rights example, when elements in the Justice Department came in the immediate post-war period to define Jim Crow segregation as a real threat to the realization of American interests, they "merely" had to prevail in an internal Department debate for action to commence. Once they did, they already had an organizational vehicle and orienting collective identity at their disposal to facilitate innovative collective action.

Let me put the matter differently as a way of highlighting the relevance of certain rationalist assumptions to an understanding of the beginnings of contentious politics. While I am in sympathy with much of the critique of the rational choice perspective that has been advanced by social movement scholars (see, for example, Ferree, 1992), I think the field as a whole has been far too quick to reject any insight that smacks of rationalist assumptions. To take the empirical phenomenon under discussion here, it would seem that the rational choice perspective provides the best general framework for analyzing the mobilization of state actors during the incipient phase of a social movement. It is entirely reasonable, and useful, in my view, to assume a relatively fixed set of collective interests on the part of state actors, and, indeed, all other established parties to any developing conflict. So it was these relatively stable interests on the part of officials in the State Department, Justice Department, the White House, the national NAACP, etc.—*when joined to the emerging definition of threat/opportunity*— that motivated the forms of innovative collective action that I will discuss in the next section.

But in highlighting the general usefulness of a rationalist framework in the analysis of movement emergence, I want to note the limits of the perspective as well. If movements turned only on the action of institutionalized members and challengers, then the rational choice perspective might be fully adequate as a framework for analyzing the motivational basis of emergent collective action. But, as I will argue later, the defining quality of movements (and all other instances of contentious politics) is the mobilization of previously unorganized or non-political challengers. It is in regard to such groups that the rationalist perspective is inadequate as a framework for analyzing initial action. For here the assumption of a fixed and relatively stable set of interests or utilities is simply not born out in reality. To illustrate the point I return to the civil rights example, but focus not on the early period of state mobilization in the immediate post–World War II era, but the emergence of the *mass* civil rights movement of the mid-1950s.

Here the movement developed not in previously established civil rights organizations, but in local networks rooted for the most part in black churches (Morris, 1984). This example places the dynamic of appropriation in stark relief. For while the movement's debt to the black church is widely acknowledged, the standard narrative account of the movement's rise obscures an organizational and cultural accomplishment of enormous importance. Until the rise of the movement, it was common for social observers—black no less than white—to depict the black church as a generally conservative institution with a decided emphasis not on the "social gospel in action," but the realization of rewards in the afterlife (Johnson, 1941; Marx, 1971; Mays and Nicholson, 1969). As Charles Payne's (1995) extraordinary book on the movement in Mississippi makes clear, the conservative nature of local black clergy remained an obstacle to local organizing well into the 1960s.

Given this more complicated portrait of the black church, the importance and highly contingent nature of the appropriation process should be clear. To turn even some black congregations into vehicles of collective protest, early movement leaders had to engage in a lot of creative cultural/organizational work, by which the aims of the church and its animating collective identity were redefined to accord with the goals of the emerging struggle. Here again, then, we find that rationalist and culturalist insights must be combined if we are to fully understand the origins of the civil rights movement. The rational choice framework gives us reasonable purchase on the emerging lines of action by various established parties to the conflict in the years immediately following World War II. But to understand how the black church as an institution—and particular black congregations—came to be defined as a site of protest activity, nothing short of a detailed, culturalist account of the transformation will do.

4. *Innovative Collective Action and the Onset of Contention*—Figure 13.1 captures my analytic punch line as regards movement origins. Innovative collective action—that is, *action that departs from previous collective routines*—is apt to develop when shared perceptions of threat or opportunity come to be tied to the established—which is not to say, formal—organizational vehicles and routine collective identities necessary to act on them. This dynamic would appear to apply equally to state actors and challengers. Indeed, in virtually all cases, I believe that an understanding of the emergence of contentious politics requires much more attention to the interaction of state actors and challengers in advance of what is typically perceived to be the onset of movement.

Theorists of revolution and social movements have been right, I think, to stress the importance of various kinds of "expanding political opportunities" or developing state crises to the development of contention. And although scholars of revolution have typically done a better job of analyzing the actions of various elites in this process than movement theorists have, neither group has sought to formally build state or other elite collective action into their models of contention. That is what I have tried to do here. Rather than conceiving of challenging groups as interpreting and reacting to various kinds of environmental shifts, it seems more sensible to see state and non-state actors as simultaneously responding to exogenous change processes and ultimately to each other as they seek to make sense of their situations and to fashion lines of action based on these shifting interpretations of reality. From this perspective, what come to be defined as political opportunities by challenging groups are themselves byproducts of innovative collective action by *state (or other elite)* actors designed to effectively counter perceived threats to or opportunities for the realization of their interests. If these state actions are defined as new opportunities (or threats) by challenging groups, responsive episodes of insurgent collective action are likely to follow, setting the stage for yet another round of state action. Once this iterative dance of stimulus-response begins in earnest, we can say that we have left the realm of *prescribed politics* and entered into an episode of *contentious politics*. I will have more to say about this distinction at the close of the article. For now it is important only to recognize that we have left the realm of routine politics.

At a cognitive level, such episodes grow out of and depend upon a perception of significant environmental uncertainty on the part of state actors and challengers alike. This shared perception insures that both sides will continue to see the situation as one posing significant threats to and/or opportunities for the realization of group interests. The affective salience of these perceptions and the novelty and intensity of the actions that follow from them will determine just how far the episode spreads beyond the initial combatants. That is, the initial interactive moves of the original combatants represent a new source of environmental change with the potential to set in motion the same processes of interpretation, attribution, appropriation, and innovative action on the part of other "proximate" social groups. The episode will likely continue as long as enough parties to the expanded conflict continue to define the situation as one of significant environmental uncertainty requiring sustained mobilization to manage (in the case of threat) or exploit (in the case of opportunity).

The burgeoning civil rights struggle can certainly be analyzed in this way. In the post-war years there quickly developed a heightened sense of environmental uncertainty as regards "the Negro question." This uncertainty frame was initially shared by three already constituted sets of combatants: federal officials (especially those in the Executive and Judicial branches), established civil rights groups, and southern segregationists. With the establishment and solidification of this shared frame, the frequency of innovative action by all three groups increased markedly during these years. I have already mentioned the string of policy reforms or otherwise facilitative actions undertaken by federal actors in the late

1940s/early 1950s. The pace of civil rights action—principally litigation—increased as well, as did membership rates in the established civil rights organizations (Lawson, 1976; McAdam, 1982; Meier and Rudwick, 1973). For their part, southern segregationists grew ever more restive too. The aforementioned Dixiecrat revolt of 1948 was only a harbinger of things to come. The full flowering of segregationist insurgency followed in the wake of the 1954, and especially the 1955, Supreme Court rulings in the *Brown* case (Lawson, 1976; McMillen, 1971).

The important implication of this sketch of the conflict's origins is that analysts have long erred in seeing the Montgomery Bus Boycott as the beginning of the struggle. Given my emphasis on the crucial importance of innovative interpretive processes and the development of a shared sense of environmental uncertainty by state actors and challenging groups, I think it more accurate to say that this particular episode began early in the post-war period and certainly by the time of the Dixiecrat revolt in 1948. Montgomery then represents a crucial escalation of the conflict, but not its point of origin. Indeed, rather than Montgomery making the movement, the reverse is actually true. It was the prior onset of the *national* conflict that granted the *local* struggle in Montgomery so much significance. Without its embedding in the existing national episode it is not at all clear that Montgomery would have had the kind of impact it did, or that the key actors in the local struggle would have behaved in the same manner. In short, it was the *nationalization* of the local conflict that shaped events in Montgomery and accounts for its singular importance in the history of the movement.

But if Montgomery did not actually trigger the conflict, it nonetheless represents a significant escalation of the struggle. It marks the onset of an episode of *popular contention* out of an earlier period of *elite contention*. Prior to Montgomery, virtually all of the contentious interaction took place between publicly constituted and self-consciously defined political groups. The principal combatants were different elements within the federal government, including the southern segregationist block within Congress, established civil rights organizations, the two national parties, and for a period of time, the renegade Dixiecrat Party. This situation is what I have termed *elite contention*, so named because the groups involved are already constituted as public, political actors. Formally defined, *elite contention* is

> *episodic, public, collective interaction among makers of claims and opponents when*
> *a) at least one government is a claimant, an object of claims, or a party to the claims,*
> *b) the claims would, if realized, affect the interests of at least one of the claimants,*
> *and c) where all the parties to the conflict were previously established as constituted*
> *political actors. Popular contention,* in contrast, replaces c) with two new defi-

nitional elements. While *elite contention* is confined to previously established political actors, *popular contention* involves *c) the mobilization of newly self-identified political actors, and d) at least some reliance on non-institutionalized . . . forms of political action. Popular contention* is, thus, constitutive both of new actors and, potentially, new forms of action. (adapted from McAdam, Tarrow, and Tilly, 2001:7–8)(emphasis in original)

In the case of the civil rights movement, among the first of these newly constituted collectivities were a number of African-American congregations in Montgomery. But before the movement was to run its course a good many other unorganized or non-political collectivities were to join the fray.

The terms *elite* and *popular* are but two of the four modes of political interaction that define the universe of all possibilities. The full four-fold schema is sketched in figure 13.2.

The vertical axis refers to the nature of the actors involved in the conflict. The horizontal axis characterizes the degree of perceptual certainty/uncertainty underlying the conflict. Under conditions of high certainty, institutionalized political groups engage in *prescribed politics*; that is, highly routinized decision-making and administrative interaction that, allowing for minor shifts in the fortunes of various parties, results in the

FIGURE 13.2
Modes of Political Interaction

Perceptual Condition

Nature of Mobilized Actors	Certain	Uncertain
Institutionalized political groups	Prescribed politics	Elite contention
Previously unorganized non-political collectives	Subterranean politics	Popular contention

reproduction of the political status quo. Should unorganized and/or non-political groups mobilize in highly certain times, they will almost always confront a closed or unresponsive political system. Such situations might be termed instances of *subterranean politics*. In nominally democratic contexts, challenges of this sort are very likely to be ignored. In non-democratic settings, this kind of challenge is almost always illegal and thus, an invitation to repression by state authorities, unless it corresponds to the forms of "everyday resistance" to which the work of James Scott has sensitized us (1985).

My main interest here lies with the two modes of politics that make up the right half of the figure. Together they define the terrain of *contentious politics*. Why am I so interested in *elite* and *popular contention*? Because it is in the zone of action defined by the two that institutionalized and non-institutionalized politics meet and where the possibilities for change through collective action are determined. I am also interested in this zone because it typically represents the point of origin of contentious episodes and the locus of action shaping its trajectory over time. Like the American civil rights movement, I suspect that most broad reform movements and revolutions have their origins in less visible but highly consequential episodes of *elite contention* that serve simultaneously to render a given political system more vulnerable to challenge and to telegraph this fact to previously unorganized or nominally apolitical segments of the population. By encouraging the latter to mobilize, these instances of institutionalized conflict evolve into broader episodes of *popular contention*. But without understanding the origin of these episodes in more conventional, if non-routine, conflict processes, researchers—especially movement researchers—have often truncated the phenomenon they study.

DISCUSSION AND CONCLUSION

I have covered a lot of ground in this chapter and tried to do a good many things. In closing, I hope to articulate the main implications of my theoretical ruminations and the case that inspired them. I will stress two such implications: for social movement theory, and for the possibility of prediction in the study of movement origins.

Implications for Social Movement Theory

The prevailing model of movement emergence was shaped to a considerable degree by the study of, and reflections on, the U.S. civil rights movement (Eisinger, 1973; McAdam, 1982; Morris, 1984). It is ironic, then, to conclude that the existing theoretical consensus is inadequate to fully account for the origins of the very movement that animated the perspective in the first place. But that is very much the conclusion I have come to here. The incorporation of insights from other "proximate" literatures (e.g., revolution, ethnic conflict) and from rationalist and culturalist perspectives on social movements has fundamentally changed my understanding of the case and of movement origins more generally. In this section I want to note the key insights from these other literatures/perspectives that have prompted this reevaluation. I begin with three specific empirical insights drawn from the literatures on revolution and ethnic conflict (and, to a lesser extent, democratization).

The cultural turn in the study of social movements mirrors a more general trend in sociology and the social sciences. While decried by many, the trend has, in my view, had a decidedly salutary effect on the social movements field. It has had the effect of organizing a host of critically important issues back into the study of social movements and collective action. These issues would include: the importance of collective identity in struggle (Friedman and McAdam, 1992; Taylor and Whittier, 1992); the role of emotion in collective action (Aminzade and McAdam, 2001; Taylor, 1996); and framing and other meaning-making processes (Eyerman and Jamison, 1991; Snow et al., 1986; Snow and Benford, 1988) as a central component of movement mobilization. However, for all the attention devoted to cultural processes in social movements, the dominant analytic framework in the field has remained resolutely structuralist. Even the attempt to "soften" the perspective by adding "framing" to the mix has only succeeded in "structuralizing" the concept, by rendering meaning-making as little more than a strategic challenge facing mature movements previously "birthed" through the fortuitous confluence of favorable political opportunities and available mobilizing structures.

In short, the real promise of the "cultural revolution" in movement studies has not been realized to this point. It can only be realized if we place the processes of collective interpretation, meaning-making, and what elsewhere has been termed *social appropriation* (McAdam, Tarrow, and Tilly, 2001), at the center of our models of movement emergence, development, and decline. That is what I have sought to do here. While the original political process impulse was to assert the influence of structural factors only as subjectively interpreted, in actual practice the crucial interpretive processes have tended to be ignored in favor of a more structurally determinist account of movement origins. In revisiting the original structural/cultural formulation of the model, I find myself in general sympathy with those who have criticized the "structural bias" of contemporary movement theory and urged greater recognition of the role of interpretation and construction in collective action (Eyerman and Jamison, 1991; Goodwin and Jasper, 1999; Jasper, 1997; Melucci, 1989, 1985).

Where I part company from my more culturalist colleagues is in asserting the *probabilistic* limits that various kinds of structures—including, as I noted earlier, cultural structures—and real world events would appear to impose on interpretive processes. This does not mean that structural factors dictate certain kinds of interpretations or the meaning of real world events is somehow clear on their face. I want to hold out the possibility that people can fashion and act on powerful collective action frames in otherwise unpromising structural circumstances. Indeed, though I remain somewhat unconvinced by his evidence, Charles Kurzman's (1996) account of the origins of the Iranian revolution *may* represent a case of this kind. My more general point is that such anomalous cultural readings of environmental conditions are bound to be rare, both because such readings are unlikely to find many adherents and/or sufficient environmental "receptivity" to survive long enough to be recognized as movements. But I concede that such outcomes are possible. Similarly, I can well imagine promising structural circumstances—that is, ones rife with imminent "threat" or "opportunity"—that fail to produce so much as a ripple of protest activity. Indeed, I regard such cases as modal. So daunting are the multiple barriers—psychological, cultural, organizational and political—to mobilization, that I am quite convinced that many structurally "favored" movements die aborning.

But for all the indeterminacy of the relationship between environmental conditions, cultural construction, and actual mobilization, it won't do to pretend these relationships don't exist. If culture, in Ann Swidler's unfortunate phrase, really were a "tool kit" (Swidler, 1986), we could expect people to avail themselves of the empowering possibilities inherent in that tool kit far more often than they do. In fact, most of the time people experience culture as a set of binding cognitive, affective, and behavioral strictures. The question then becomes, under what conditions are we likely to transcend these strictures and to rediscover the tool-like promise of multi-vocal cultural materials? Swidler seems to answer this query in much the way I would. She draws a distinction between culture's role during "settled" and "unsettled" times. As she writes (1986: 278): "there are. . . . more and less settled lives, and more and less settled cultural periods. Individuals in certain phases of their lives, and groups or entire societies in certain historical periods are involved in constructing new strategies of action." It is during these "less settled" or more uncertain periods, then, that we are apt to experience culture as a tool kit. But how are we to account for the onset of these "unsettled times"? In my view, the kind of *exogenous change processes* discussed above constitute the source of Swidler's turbulence, increasing the likelihood that cognitive and affective routines will be abandoned in the search for new interpretations of reality and the innovative lines of action that follow from same.[8]

I find myself responding in somewhat similar fashion to a second key concept in the culturalist kit-bag as I have to the general issue of the relationship between environmental conditions and social interpretation. The concept in question is that of "collective identity." It should be clear from the perspective sketched in the previous section that I take the concept very seriously. Indeed, I regard the "appropriation of established collective identities" as a requisite for the emergence of all social movements. Traditionally culturalists have deployed the concept in a different, though not contradictory, way. They have used the concept to highlight the ways in which movements may serve as vehicles for the creation and dissemination of new collective identities (Melucci, 1989, 1985; Taylor, 1996; Taylor and Whittier, 1992). I would grant this important cultural function of movements, but think the processes by which existing collective identities get redefined so as to serve as the motivational basis for emergent action are equally interesting and clearly more relevant to the question of movement origins. Finally, in referencing the *motivational* force of existing collective identities, I feel compelled to take the culturalists to task for failing to articulate or ground their perspective in any foundational model of human action and motivation. In this they are no less guilty than the structuralists, but having been so critical of the rationalist view of collective action, it would seem incumbent on both structuralists and culturalists to propose alternatives to the rational actor model.

This brings me, conveniently, to the rationalists. My reaction to the various rationalist perspectives on collective action is as complicated as my take on the culturalists. Perhaps the key injunction I take away from these perspectives is simply the need to take the question of motivation seriously. But beyond the need to confront the basic issue, I also regard the central tenets of rational actor models as a useful general framework for analyzing the actions of some of the actors involved in the origins of contention. As noted previously, I regard the framework as a viable baseline model for understanding the actions of all established parties during what I have called the initial phase of *elite contention*. As institutionalized actors with relatively well-defined interests, we can expect that perceived threats to or opportunities for the realization of those interests will provide sufficient motivation for innovative lines of collective action. More generally, the very language of threat and opportunity implies adherence to at least a limited notion of rationality. The notions of threat and opportunity only make sense in relation to some set of unstated interests that define what is being threatened or made more opportunely realizable.

But in other respects the perspective sketched here diverges sharply from those of the rationalists. Two serious limits to the general perspective are worth noting. The first concerns its inadequacy as a framework for understanding the entrance of new and previously non-political challengers into a developing episode of contention. The assumption of well-defined and relatively fixed interests simply does not hold in regard to such groups. Given the decidedly apolitical stance and conservative theological strands that had tended to characterize the black church historically, there would have been no way for a rational choice analyst to have predicted the mobilization of certain black congregations in the early days of the civil rights movement. Here I am merely pointing to the long-standing and acknowledged failure of rationalists to account for the origins of individual preferences or interests. But this failure takes on greater importance when one is concerned with periods of rapid social change and emergent patterns of innovative collective action. As the role of the black church in the civil rights struggle indicates, such periods turn on the emergence of new interests, or the rapid transformation of behavioral expectations that attach to old interests. Either way, rational actor models are ill-equipped to explain such phenomena.

Finally, there is reason to take issue with that most sacred of rationalist shibboleths: the "free-rider problem." It is not that I take lightly the various barriers to mobilization that operate in social life. These barriers are formidable indeed. But at least as regards the origins of social movements, the "free-rider" dilemma would appear to be more formidable in theory than in practice. This disjuncture between theory and reality owes to the individualistic cast of the dilemma and the collective nature of its solution. Movements almost always arise through the transformation of an existing collective into a vehicle of collective protest. Thus the traditional formulation that poses the problem as one in which outsiders must be induced to join a movement is almost never approximated in real life. Instead, insiders are threatened with the loss of member benefits for failure to take part. Given the motivational importance I attach to the protection of one's most intimate and primary attachments, the appropriation of a highly salient collective embedding (i.e., church, neighborhood) can be expected to carry with it a very different "default option" than the one animating the "free-rider dilemma." In the latter case the rational option is non-participation; in the former it is participation in the struggle. Notice, however, that in rejecting the specifics of the "free-rider" formulation, I am nonetheless disposed, with the rationalists, to explain individual recruitment into a movement in broadly rational terms. It is just that my conception of rationality has a more collectivist and solidaristic cast to it than does the traditional rational actor models.

Implications for Prediction in the Study of Movement Origins

The emergence of any major social movement or revolution invariably triggers several rounds of recrimination in which the relevant scholarly community is taken to task (or takes itself to task) for failing to accurately predict the latest "moment of madness." Since I believe the theoretical reformulation outlined here bears on this issue, I want to close by sketching what I see as the realistic prospects for and decided limits on prediction in the study of social movements or contentious politics more generally.

In 1995 the *American Journal of Sociology* published a symposium on "Prediction in the Social Sciences." In his introduction to the symposium, Michael Hechter (1995:1526) summarized what he saw as the unifying consensus to the otherwise disparate contributions to the volume. "Altogether," he wrote, "this symposium suggests that our situation with respect to prediction is akin to that in seismology. There is reason to believe that it is possible to predict the location of major social upheavals. . . . Predicting their timing is likely to be beyond our grasp both now and in the future." The theoretical reformulation offered here prompts me to concur with this consensus, though for reasons quite different from some of the contributors to the aforementioned symposium (e.g. Collins, 1995; Kuran, 1995; Tilly, 1995a).

For me, both the possibilities and limits of prediction are bound up with the critically important, but complex, relationship between *elite* and *popular contention*. I think the former phenomenon may be amenable to prediction with at least some degree of temporal accuracy. Prediction in such cases would depend on being able to specify two variables for each of the major actors who comprise whatever system of institutionalized power the analyst is concerned with. The two variables would be: (1) the actor's major interests; and (2) their perception of the significance (either as "threat" or "opportunity") of any given exogenous shock in relation to those interests. Knowing, for example, the major foreign policy objectives of the United States in the post–World War II period, it would not have been farfetched for an astute social analyst to predict that certain federal officials would have begun to push for changes in civil rights policy. Indeed, as quoted earlier, Gunnar Myrdal published just such a prediction as early as 1944. In turn, knowing the central importance the southern political elite attached to the maintenance of Jim Crow in this same era, one could easily have predicted what their general response to any significant shift in federal civil rights policy would have been. By aggregating these specifications of interests and perceptions across the major parties to a given system or issue, I think it quite possible to predict—at least probabilistically—the onset of a period of *elite contention*. But the kind of major social upheavals that were the subject of the *AJS* symposium are only associated with *popular contention*, or that phase of contention marked by the mobilization of previously latent or unorganized challengers. Still, the ability to predict instances of *elite contention* takes on added significance if one believes, as I have come to, that the great majority of episodes of *popular contention* grow out of or depend for their impact on the existence of the former kind of conflict.

So far so good. Alas, we have reached, in my view, the limits of our predictive prospects. To reinvoke Michael Hechter's seismology analogy, noting the close connection between instances of *elite* and *popular conten-tion* may allow us to say which political systems are vulnerable to signifi-cant social movements or revolutions, but not exactly when or where these broader "social upheavals" will occur, or even if, in fact, they will. In trying to predict episodes of *popular contention* from instances of *elite* conflict, one confronts the difficulty touched on in the earlier discussion of the general irrelevance of rational actor models to an understanding of the mobilization of new challengers. Since the mobilization of previously latent or non-political groups invariably turns on the social construction of new interests or new lines of innovative action linked unexpectedly to old interests, there is simply no way to predict where or when these criti-cally important conflict-transforming mobilizations are going to take place. So knowing in 1950 that we were in a period of *elite contention* regarding issues of race might have emboldened one to predict that the struggle would ultimately spread beyond the roster of established parties to the conflict, but I cannot imagine how, from that temporal vantage point, anyone could have asserted that the critical transformation of the conflict would have come in Montgomery in December of 1955. Only a post-hoc culturalist reading of several temporal strands of events unfold-ing in Montgomery in the years leading up to the Boycott and in the days immediately following the arrest of Rosa Parks could tell us how and why Montgomery emerged as the major site of contention it did. This last point serves to underscore the central point of the entire chapter; that unless we combine structuralist, culturalist, and rationalist tenets with insights gained from the study of other forms of contention, we cannot hope to develop anything close to a complete understanding of the origins of social movements. The elaborated framework proposed here has sought to incorporate all of these influences.

NOTES

Previously published as "Preface" in *Political Process and the Development of Black Insurgency, 1930–1970*, 2nd ed. (Chicago: University of Chicago Press, 1999). ©1999 by The University of Chicago. Permission to reprint this chapter was granted by the University of Chicago Press.
    1. This chapter was prepared while the author was a Fellow at the Center for Advanced Study in the Behavioral Sciences. I wish to gratefully acknowledge the

financial support provided by a grant from the National Science Foundation (#SBR-9601236) that helped defray some of the cost of my Center Fellowship. The arguments expressed here have been shaped to a considerable degree by the feedback I have received during my participation in a remarkable project co-sponsored by the Mellon Foundation and the Center for Advanced Study in the Behavioral Sciences. The project, which has come to be known colloquially as the Invisible College of Contentious Politics (ICCP), has aimed to take fuller account of and to try in various ways to synthesize the remarkable outpouring of work on various forms of non-routine contention (e.g., social movements, revolutions) that has been produced in the past ten to fifteen years. Over the course of the three-year effort I have benefited enormously from the sustained conversations I have been able to have with my immediate colleagues on the project. To the following twenty-one wonderful friends go my deepest appreciation: Ron Aminzade, Lissa Bell, Pamela Burke, Jorge Cadena-Roa, David Cunningham, Manali Desai, Robyn Eckhardt, John Glenn, Debbie Gould, Jack Goldstone, Hyojoung Kim, Joseph Luders, Liz Perry, Bill Sewell, Heidi Swarts, Sid Tarrow, Charles Tilly, Noah Uhrig, Nella Van Dyke, Heather Williams, and Kim Williams. The project also allowed me to interact on a more fleeting basis with a diverse and stimulating set of colleagues drawn from a host of social science disciplines. These colleagues are too numerous to mention, but they know who they are in any case. I only hope that they benefited as much from their association with the Project as I did from their presence. But my deepest debt of gratitude goes to our sponsors at the Mellon Foundation and the Center for Advanced Study in the Behavioral Sciences for taking a chance on what was, for both institutions, a new and novel way of organizing an ongoing seminar project. In particular I owe Robert Scott, Neil Smelser, and Phil Converse of the Center and Harriet Zuckerman and William Bowen of the Mellon Foundation a heart-felt thank you. Besides all of those saluted above in connection with the Mellon/Center Project, I would also like to thank two other colleagues—Jim Jasper and Kelly Moore—who took the time to give me extraordinarily detailed and helpful comments on an earlier draft of the manuscript.

2. The issue of authorship bears mention. Many of the ideas expressed in this chapter were worked out during the course of an ongoing collaboration with Sidney Tarrow and Charles Tilly. In this sense, the piece would not have been written were it not for the sustained conversations and generous intellectual contributions of these two exceptional colleagues.

3. A seventh *major* weakness afflicts the study of political contention generally and not simply the narrow literature on social movement origins. I refer to the overly cognitive/rationalist bias inherent in the study of most forms of contention. The role of emotions in mobilizing and sustaining collective action is only now starting to be addressed by scholars (Goodwin, 1997; Jasper, 1997; Taylor, 1995, 1996). The breadth and significance of this topic has prompted me to steer clear of it here. Instead Ron Aminzade and I have chosen to write extensively on the topic for *Silence and Voice in the Study of Contentious Politics* (2001). To convey the flavor of the perspective we seek to develop, and to underscore the explanatory importance we assign to emotions in political contention, let me offer the following quote from our chapter:

We want to make two strong . . . claims about the explanatory significance of emotions and emotional processes as they relate to the emergence, development, and decline of social movements and revolutions. . . . At the aggregate level, we think the onset of an episode of contention is associated with, and partially dependent upon, the collective mobilization of heightened emotion. . . . The second claim concerns the role of emotions in motivating individual activism. Much has been made in the literature of the daunting "free-rider" problem. . . . [B]ut, in our view . . . the formulation ignores the power of emotions to shape both the assessment of potential gains and costs involved in any line of action . . . and to motivate action, even in the face of extreme risks and seemingly no hope for pay-off.

4. For a few partial exceptions to this rule, see Emirbayer and Goodwin (1994), Gould (1995), McAdam and Paulsen (1993), and Opp (1989).

5. In recent years there has developed a more "bottom-up" culturalist approach to the study of revolution that does pay serious attention to the kinds of interpretive processes under discussion here. Proponents of this perspective include Goodwin (1994), Hunt (1984), McDaniel (1991), and Sewell (1990, 1996b), among others.

6. But for exceptions, see Klandermans (1984, 1997a), Klandermans and Oegema (1987), and Rochon (1998).

7. In her account of the rise of "public interest science organizations" in the United States in the 1950s and 1960s, Kelly Moore (1996) provides an especially rich and detailed example of what I am here calling *social appropriation*.

8. Jack Goldstone (1991) has advanced a similar argument about the relationship between state crisis and the development and adoption of innovative cultural framings.

14

Reflections on Social Movement Theory: Criticisms and Proposals

ALDON MORRIS

The arrival of a new century and a new millennium are attention grabbing symbolic markers. They provide a convenient opportunity for me to critically reflect on the current status of social movement theory. Because of space limitations, it is impossible to provide a comprehensive review and critique of this burgeoning field. In this essay I will focus on what I contend are serious blind spots of current social movement theory. I will argue that these theories continue to slight the role that human agency plays in social movements. The slight occurs because assumptions in current theory lead its proponents to gloss over fundamental sources of agency that social movement groups can bring to the mobilization process, cultural framing, tactical problems, movement leadership, protest histories, and transformative events. These movement phenomena and human agency will take center stage in this effort and correctives will be offered.

By the middle of the twentieth century, collective behavior and related theories constituted the dominant paradigm that guided research of social movements. These theories argued that social movements were a form of collective behavior that emerged when significant social and cultural breakdowns occurred. As a form of collective behavior, social movements were theorized to be spontaneous, unorganized, and unstructured phenomena that were discontinuous with institutional and organizational behavior (Morris, 1999:531). In this view, emotions and irrational ideologies were central because movements occurred in highly charged contexts characterized by mass enthusiasm, collective excitement, rumor, social contagion, and mass hysteria. Thus, social movements and movement participants were viewed as nonrational given the unpredictability

233

and heavy emotional content of movements. Collective behavior theory assumed a direct link between emotions and nonrationality (for an exception see Turner and Killian, 1987).

Human agency operated indirectly in collective behavior theories because participants were viewed as reacting to external forces beyond their control. Indeed, agency producing mechanisms—social organization, strategizing, reasoning, analyses, and rationality—were argued to be absent in movements, especially in their formative stages. When agency entered the picture it was as a weak reactive force that played a minor role in the causation of movements.

Human agency is important in current resource mobilization and political process models. The civil rights movement and movements it helped spur were the major catalysts that shattered the intellectual viability of collective behavior theory. When principal formulators of the current approaches sought to understand those movements, they found it necessary to reject the collective behavior model and its imagery of the emotional crowd. In so doing, resource mobilization and political process theorists (e.g., McCarthy and Zald, 1977; Gamson, 1975; Tilly, 1978; McAdam, 1982; Oberschall, 1973) have generated a rich plethora of social movement concepts that will continue to yield theoretical insights. Moreover, valuable work (e.g., Aminzade et al., 2001; McAdam, Tarrow, and Tilly, 2001; Morris and Mueller, 1992; Johnston and Klandermans, 1995a; Jasper, 1997; Goodwin and Jasper, 1999; Hart, 1996; Emirbayer and Goodwin, 1994) designed to correct biases inherent in current approaches continues to appear. I will build on this work and suggest new formulations that I believe will lead to more robust analysis of movements. These formulations are rooted in my assessment that current theories continue to misspecify the central role that human agency plays in social movements.

I focus on the political process model because it has absorbed the key insights of resource mobilization theory and because it has become the dominant synthetic model of social movements. Formulators of the political process model (e.g., McAdam, 1982 and 1994; Tarrow, 1998b; McAdam et al., 1996a; Aminzade et al., 2001; and Tilly, 1978) have reached a consensus on its basic theoretical components. They are the concepts of mobilizing structures, political opportunity structure, and cultural framing. Taken together it is argued that these concepts account for movement origins, the power generated by movements, the energizing cultural content of movements, and movement outcomes.

Mobilizing structures refer to "those collective vehicles, informal as well as formal, through which people mobilize and engage in collective action" (McAdam et al., 1996a:3). Mobilizing structures is an idea that rejects the proposition that movements emerge from fluid, spontaneous, unstructured contexts that thrust marginal individuals into collective action. Drawing on empirical research by numerous scholars (e.g., Ober-schall, 1973; McAdam, 1982; Morris, 1981, 1984; Snow, Zurcher, and Ekland-Olson, 1980) political process theorists demonstrate that move-ment mobilization occurs through informal networks, preexisting institu-tional structures, and formal organizations. Actors so situated are in positions to recruit participants, assemble necessary resources, and coor-dinate collective action. The centrality of mobilizing structures is crucial because it is through them that rational actors figure prominently in the origins of movements.

Political opportunity structure refers to the "consistent—but not neces-sarily formal or permanent—dimensions of the political environment that provides incentives for people to undertake collective action by affecting their expectation for success or failure. Theorists of political opportunity structure emphasize the mobilization of resources external to the group" (Tarrow, 1994:85). Thus, potential challengers are unlikely to generate and sustain movements because of their weak social position. Movements are likely to emerge only when favorable changes occur in the external political system. These opportunities emerge when divisions develop among political elites; new external allies emerge, when states weaken, and when new space in the political system opens. In short, for groups to successfully engage in collective action they must first be the beneficiaries of new external political opportunities which they must exploit.

In accounting for movement origins, this view stresses the political weaknesses of challenging groups while assigning considerable causal weight to elite external actors. The focus on changing political opportuni-ties suggests that movement success or failure may rest largely in the hands of powerful external actors. Thus the relationship between chal-lengers and the political systems is placed at the center of analysis because that political system determines whether movements are able to develop in the first place. While there is insight here, I will argue that this formulation locates far too much social movement agency in the hands of external actors and it truncates analysis of movement origins.

Political process theorists are increasingly coming to realize that cul-tural dynamics are central to the origins and development of social move-ments. Thus, the third component of the model addresses framing processes. Proponents argue that "mediating between opportunity, orga-nization, and action are the shared meanings and definitions that people bring to their situation. At a minimum, people need to feel both aggrieved about some aspect of their lives and optimistic, that, acting collectively, they can redress the problem" (McAdam et al., 1996a:5). The recognition that culture plays a central role in generating and sustaining movements was slow to develop and remains the model's least developed concept. Much of the recent theorizing on culture and movements was actually formulated by either critics (Fantasia, 1988; Snow et al., 1986; Goodwin and Jasper, 1999; Morris and Mueller, 1992; Jasper, 1997; and Johnston and Klandermans, 1995a) or in response to challenges raised by critics. I agree that culture—ideas, belief systems, rituals, oratory, emotions, and grievance interpretations—are indeed central to social movements. I will argue, however, that current treatments continue to underemphasize the cultural agency that fuels social movements. As a result, scholars underestimate the ability of challenging groups to generate and sustain movements despite recalcitrant political structures and heavy repression.

The concepts of mobilizing structures, political opportunities, and framing processes have generated insights into social movements. Nevertheless, as the critics (Ferree, 1992; Jasper and Goodwin, 1999; Jasper, 1997) have argued, the political process model is overly structural and contains rationalistic biases. Additionally, I will argue that the model's preoccupation with powerful external elites have left key determinants of collective action in theoretical darkness. My task is to rescue them from the dark corners of this model and reveal their centrality to the origins and development of social movements.

The political process model has unduly restricted our understanding of the mobilization process and the capacity of challenging groups to generate and sustain collective action. Its limitations stem from the assumption that external political opportunities must first become available before challenging groups can generate collective action. This assumption still guides the analysis of movement origins even though empirical examples (e.g., Kurzman, 1996; and Rasler, 1996) suggest that enormous collective action can burst forth precisely during times when the political authorities close ranks, and when heavy repression is unleashed.

The strong relationship theorized to exist between collective action and political opportunities should be relaxed because the production of collective action is also an independent function of the capacity of challenging groups. A reciprocal relationship exists between a challenging group's mobilization capacity and the presence of political opportunities. Thus, in some instances, collective action can generate political opportunities where none existed previously and in other instances political opportunities can clear the way for collective action. The temporal sequence is to be determined on empirical grounds rather than a priori theorizing. I focus on how mobilization capacities generate collective action because that is where the political process model has proven inadequate and misleading.

The political process model has largely ignored the central role that a challenging groups' agency-laden institutions and frame lifting, leadership configurations, tactical solutions, protest histories, and transformative events play in producing and sustaining collective action. These factors find no place in the nexus of causal explanations posited by the model. When these factors are discussed they are conceptualized as movement dynamics rather than as independent triggers of collective action. Using the civil rights movement as the referent, I will demonstrate how each of these factors were crucial to the origins and development of that movement.

AGENCY-LADEN INSTITUTIONS
AND FRAME LIFTING

Agency-laden institutions are those institutions, often long-standing, developed by potential challenging groups that house cultural and organizational resources that can be mobilized to launch collective action. Such institutions are configurations of cultural beliefs and practices that permeate and shape their social networks. The cultural materials of these institutions are constitutive in that they produce and solidify the trust, contacts, solidarity, rituals, meaning systems, and options of members embedded in their social networks. Endemic to some agency-laden institutions is a transcendent and coherent belief system that shapes its actors' moral and political views about the kinds of relationships that ought to exist between individuals and social groups. These politically relevant beliefs inspire analyses and actions geared toward the realization of group interests (Hart, 1996).

The African American church is an agency-laden institution and has been so for centuries. Its transcendent belief system stresses that all people are equal before God because God is the parent of humanity (Paris, 1985). For centuries the Black church has condemned racial inequality because it is inconsistent with ultimate religious values. These beliefs are ingrained in the cultural fabric of the church and given repeated expression through religious sermons, writings, music, testimonies, prayers, rituals, and emotional interactions. For these reasons, the Black church has been in the vanguard of the historic Black struggle by providing it with a disproportionate amount of its leaders, meeting space for protest organizations, financial resources and moral legitimization (Morris, 1984; Harding, 1983).

Montgomery, Alabama, in 1955 was a dangerous place for Black people. The Cold War was entrenched before the Montgomery movement and it certainly created the possibility that Black protest could capitalize on America's vulnerability because of its use of egalitarian rhetoric to gain the upper hand in that conflict. Nevertheless it was not Cold War rhetoric that would mobilize Montgomery's Black community. The 1954 *Brown vs. Board* Supreme Court decision also constituted a new political opportunity. Yet the rise of the Southern massive resistance movement was a powerful and direct deterrent to Black collective action. Emmett Till was lynched just three months prior to the boycott. The Brown decision itself generated a massive assault on Black resistance by outlawing the National Association for the Advancement of Colored People throughout Alabama (Morris, 1984). In this period new white supremacy groups were organized while existing ones gained added strength. This was an unlikely era and location for the modern civil rights movement to take root. Where did Montgomery's Black community find the agency and organization to produce such historic collective action despite mobilized opposition backed by local state power?

The mobilizing capacity of Montgomery's Black churches was the key. Shortly after Rosa Park's arrest, Martin Luther King informs us that all of the ministers in Montgomery "endorsed the boycott plan with enthusiasm, and promised to go to their congregations on Sunday morning and drive home their approval" (King, 1958:47). Concerning the first organizing meeting, King declared "I was filled with joy when I entered the church and found so many of them there; for then I knew that something unusual was about to happen" (King, 1958:46). Something unusual happened because the church provided the emerging movement with its vast communication networks, its organized congregations, and its cultural and financial resources.

The church was more than a structural entity for it contained the cultural framework through which the movement would be framed. Movement theorists (e.g., Tarrow, 1994; Snow, 1992), are mistaken when they argue that the civil rights movements' central frame was one of "rights" that grew out of earlier court challenges. Being a product of the Black church, King instinctively understood that the church's transcendent belief system was the appropriate cultural material from which to frame the movement. He decided to emphasize the Christian doctrine of love. He told the participants "our actions must be guided by the deepest principles of our Christian faith. Love must be our regulating ideal" (1958:62). But the frame contained more than ideas of love. He told the future producers of collective action that "we come here tonight to be saved from that patience that makes us patient with anything less than freedom and justice" (62). Thus emerged the "freedom and justice" frame of the civil rights movement. King then articulated the motivational mainspring of action embedded in the frame: "So in order to be true to one's conscience and true to God, a righteous man has no alternative but to refuse to cooperate with an evil system" (51). King concluded, "we are protesting for the birth of justice in the community." This moral frame had mobilizing power because it was deeply rooted in the culture of the agency-laden Black church and had instant resonance for the majority of Black people embedded in that church. This frame assured the participants that God was on their side for He condoned Black collective action that sought justice.

Collective behavior theorists were right when they argued that movements often occur in the context of mass enthusiasm and highly charged emotions. The mass meetings of the boycott teemed with emotions and mass enthusiasm. The singing, testifying, preaching, and praying at the mass meetings mobilized the emotions such that "the enthusiasm of these thousands of people, swept everything along like an onrushing tidal wave" (King, 1958:61). However, contrary to the logic of collective behavior theory, emotions in the civil rights movement were closely linked to the rational pursuits of the movement. The religious culture of the church produced cohesion and enabled participants to act under the spell of singing, preaching, and praying. In speaking of emotions one of King's lieutenants remarked, "If I wait until my intellect gets to the place it can digest, hell I wouldn't do nothing many times" (Walker, 1978). The agency-laden church used its culture and its institutional structure to produce collective action.

My analysis of the framing process of the civil rights movement differs from frame alignment theory (Snow et al., 1986). In that approach the main cultural task is for movement leaders to develop and articulate a collective action frame and align it with the belief system of those whom they wish to mobilize. In contrast, my analysis reveals that the crucial cultural task for leaders was frame lifting. Frame lifting is a process by which leaders shape the collective action to match an institutionally embedded frame. In frame lifting collective action is grafted on to the cultural and emotional schemata of actors embedded in relevant social networks. In Montgomery a potent frame already embedded in a mass-based agency-laden institution was lifted up and linked to the production of collective action.

McAdam (1999) has examined the Black church but argued that prior to the civil rights movement it was apolitical and was slow to come to the struggle because of the enormous cultural work that had to occur to convince it to enter the fray. While this may be true for some Black churches, our analysis suggests quite a different explanation in Montgomery. In that instance, all of the churches united virtually overnight and set in motion the modern civil rights movement. The theoretical point is that such agency-laden institutions can play an independent role in the production of collective action despite a largely closed political system. Therefore, the crucial role that agency-laden institutions play in the mobilization process needs to be integrated into a causal explanation of social movements.

TACTICAL SOLUTIONS

Tactical solutions play an important role in the development of collective action (McAdam, 1983; Morris, 1993b). Yet in the political process model tactical matters are treated as a dynamic rather than a causal factor. The Montgomery movement is instructive for understanding how a tactical breakthrough can help initiate social movements. Prior to the boycott, Montgomery's Black leaders had met on numerous occasions with the white leadership, pleading with them to end bus segregation. The white leaders ignored them because Black leaders lacked the power to apply negative sanctions when their requests were not granted. Collective action that could function as the negative sanction was needed to achieve group goals. Widespread and sustainable collective action is not likely to develop if potential movement leaders fail to meet the tactical challenge. Such leaders must select and then execute appropriate tactics that will generate sufficient disorder and be attractive to their constituency. If they fail to meet this challenge collective action will not develop.

For mass-based movements to emerge, leaders must develop tactics that are congruent both with the cultural framework of the challenging community and their main organizational vehicles. On the eve of the Montgomery bus boycott, King and other leaders knew that mass participation was required for the protest to be effective. They decided to choose and frame the tactic in a manner consistent with the moral frame being lifted from the agency-laden church. Rather than define the movement as a boycott, King chose to define the tactic as an act of massive non-cooperation with evil. He wrote that "we were simply saying to the white community 'we can no longer lend our cooperation to an evil system'" (1958:51).

To link the boycott tactic directly to the mass-based church, King situated it in a context of love and evil that were familiar themes in the Black religious community. For centuries the church had preached that all people should be loved because they were God's children. King worked in the theme of evil by arguing that the non-cooperation tactic was a method whose "attack is directed against forces of evil rather than against persons who happen to be doing the evil" (1958:102). By imbuing the tactic with love and identifying the Jim Crow social order as an evil force, the leaders successfully rooted the protest in the moral frame of the Black church. The result was a marriage in which culture, tactic, and organizational capacity were linked so that collective action could be produced.

The tactic of nonviolent non-cooperation made it difficult for the white community to use the machinery of violence to defeat the movement. The tactic also provided the emerging movement with an ideological high ground bathed in love and Christian principles while simultaneously casting segregation as an evil force that should be destroyed. Because of the mobilizing capacity of the non-cooperation with evil tactic, as well as its strategic usefulness, King concluded, "I came to feel that this was the only morally and practically sound method open to oppressed people in their struggle for freedom" (1958:97).

The development of a tactical solution is one of the central factors in movement causation. Such tactical solutions are not inevitable and do not occur by happenstance. It is this challenge that leaders must meet if collective action is to occur. In Montgomery the leaders chose a tactic that was creatively woven into a moral frame and the organizational capacity of an agency-laden institution. In short, there is an interaction between the type of tactic and type of preexisting organizations and cultural frames that can be rapidly adopted and spread by a protest group (Morris, 1981). That interaction sets the perimeters in which tactical solutions are hammered out.

SOCIAL MOVEMENT LEADERSHIP

The role that leadership plays in movement causation has not received much attention from political process theorists. These theorists (McAdam, McCarthy, and Zald, 1988:716) have assumed that movement leadership is a matter of common sense not requiring theoretical analysis. I argue that movement leadership is an important complex phenomenon that affects the origins and outcomes of movements. By neglecting leadership, political process models fail to shed light on another important source of movement agency.

Social movement theory should focus on what movement leaders do and why what they do matters. By examining the Montgomery case it becomes clear that the idea of a single leader of a movement is sociologically unsound. Rather, in Montgomery a configuration of leaders constituted the leadership that mobilized and guided that movement. Leadership configurations should be placed at the center of analysis. The first task of such analysis is to identify the preexisting leadership of a challenging group and investigate its importance to a movement's origins and development. A wide array of Black organizations and institutions existed in Montgomery prior to the bus protest. Perched at the top of them were the political leaders of the voluntary associations and the clergy of the numerous churches. They constituted the preexisting leaders who could mobilize a movement because they headed organized followings. By focusing on leadership configurations it becomes clear that multiple leaders operate at the nodes of indigenous networks. In these critical locations Montgomery's Black leaders moved the mobilization process along by providing the new movement access to their vast communication networks, embedded cultural frames, material resources, and organized followings. Movement agency is contained in leadership configurations where preexisting leaders have the capability to mobilize social networks because of their nodal positions. At the organizing meeting of the boycott King reported that "Virtually every organization of the Negro community was represented" (King, 1958:46). The same held true for the Black clergy. These leaders mobilized their constituencies to participate in the movement. Thus preexisting leaders of a challenging group are crucial to the initial mobilizing stage of a mass movement.

Preexisting leaders of agency-laden institutions are particularly important to the mobilization and tactical developments of movements. Although King articulated the marriage between the church's moral frame and the tactic of nonviolent non-cooperation, it was the clergy as a whole who lifted that moral frame and linked it to collective action. The clergy could do this important cultural work because of their religious authority and charisma. Charismatic leadership, as Weber argued, is important because charismatic leaders are able to articulate powerful, mobilizing visions and attract followers because of their personal magnetism. Charisma in this instance was an attribute situated within the leadership role of the black clergy. The presence of institutionalized charisma enhanced the agency capacity of the Black church especially in terms of its ability to mobilize people. The mobilization of a movement is enhanced when there exists charismatic leadership situated within agency-laden institutions. Such leaders can play crucial roles in developing a movement's cultural frame and mobilizing participants because of their charisma and institutional resources.

It has been firmly established in the literature that social movement organizations (SMOs) play critical roles in mobilizing and coordinating collective action and by defining the goals and tactics of movements (McCarthy and Zald, 1977; Gamson, 1975; Morris, 1984; Zald and Ash, 1966). What is usually ignored is that leaders of SMOs must make choices out of a number of options. The choices they make affect the mobilizing capacity and outcomes of movements. If King had chosen to adopt an aggressive militant tactic that included the use of violence, the masses and their churches would not have supported it. Moreover, chances are great that the state would have violently crushed such protest in its infancy. Tactical choices leaders make matter. Additionally, leaders must make choices about the nature of inter-organizational relations between SMOs, about whom to build external allies with and about how to deal with the opposition (Haines, 1988; Zald and McCarthy, 1980; Morris, 1984). Social movement leaders also have the responsibility of reading and exploiting the external political structure. Media coverage of social movements is crucially important in modern societies (Molotch, 1979; Gamson and Modigliani, 1989; Gamson and Wolfsfeld, 1993; Gitlin, 1980). How to generate and manage that coverage is a challenge that movement leaders must address. Social movement theory needs to explore these important leadership activities and the contingencies that shape them.

The interaction between gender and movement leadership is another important issue. In societies characterized by patriarchy men tend to control formal leadership positions in movements (Robnett, 1997; Taylor, 1996; Ferree and Hess, 1985; Payne, 1995). One important question is whether women would build the same kinds of SMOs and make the same kinds of decisions as men, given their different gender experiences (see Staggenborg, 1991; Taylor, 1996). Robnett's work on the civil rights movement has revealed the fundamental ways in which the organization and activities of that movement were gendered. This gendering process shaped movement leadership by landing men at the top of SMOs while forcing women to exercise leadership outside of formal leadership positions. Robnett (1997) argued that Black women developed what she labeled as "bridge leadership," which is "an intermediate layer of leadership, whose tasks include bridging potential constituents and adherents, as well as potential formal leaders, to the movement" (191). There is some evidence that women may have become more skilled in executing the critically important emotional work of social movements because of the unequal opportunity for them to become SMO leaders and to be situated at the nodes of social networks (Taylor, 1996, 1995; Robnett, 1997). In this manner social movements reproduce gender inequality within movements and the larger society (Taylor, 1996). Because the assumed links between emotions and irrationality in movements are no longer tenable, the importance of emotional work to movements is becoming increasingly clear. It is time for movement theory to analyze the importance of such work and formulate models that capture the difference that gender plays in movement leadership, mobilization, and the generation of inequality.

I have argued that social movement theory needs to bring in leadership. It deserves a central place in movement theorizing because it interjects human agency into collective action and affects the mobilization and outcomes of movements. Thus a major task of movement theory is to unpack the "black box" of movement leadership so that we can develop more robust models of how collective action emerges and is sustained.

PROTEST TRADITIONS

The political process model devotes a great deal of attention to how changing external political structures create new opportunities for movements to emerge. The model, in my view, overemphasizes external agency while failing to shine light on agency-generating factors within challenging groups. Thus McAdam (1999) argues that the competition between the two major parties for the Black vote in the 1940s coupled with the politics of the Cold War were key external developments that helped set the stage for the emergence of the civil rights movement. While emphasizing these external developments, McAdam fails to develop an analysis of how the historic Black protest tradition contributed to the rise of the modern civil rights movement.

At the turn of the twentieth century Blacks engaged in widespread boy-cotts of Southern Jim Crow streetcars. In 1910 the NAACP was founded and began initiating court battles against racial segregation. In the 1920s Garvey developed a mass-based national movement among Blacks, thus revealing how the Black masses could be organized. Marches and pickets were utilized against northern merchants by Blacks in the 1930s and 1940s. During the Gandhi movement Black leaders traveled to India to absorb the lessons afforded by that movement. They were especially attentive to the role that nonviolent tactics played in Gandhi's movement. Most importantly, in the early 1940s A. Philip Randolph, drawing on les-sons of the Garvey movement, organized a national nonviolent March on Washington Movement that forced President Roosevelt to issue an Execu-tive Order barring discrimination in the defense industry. In the same period Bayard Rustin and other leaders participated in a "freedom ride" in the border states of the South. In 1953 Baton Rouge's Black community organized a bus boycott of that city's segregated buses.

The Montgomery protest movement emerged in the context of these prior struggles. Black leaders familiar with Gandhi's techniques of nonvi-olence advised the leadership in Montgomery. The leader of the Baton Rouge Boycott provided critical information to King about how to orga-nize the protest. The NAACP agreed to cover the legal aspects of the struggle. The music, moral frames, and preaching of the Black church that contained protest themes developed by slaves provided cultural energy for the bus protest.

Preexisting protest traditions rooted in agency-laden institutions, prior SMOs, and the experiences of leaders affect the rise and trajectory of new social movements. Such traditions contain material and cultural resources that can be injected in new movements (Rupp and Taylor, 1987). Often-times mobilization must develop rapidly in order for it be to successful. Thus, time itself is a crucial resource for movements (Oliver and Marwell, 1992). The availability of knowledge and resources provided by protest traditions can drastically reduce the time it takes to mobilize. For these reasons protest traditions decrease the mobilization, organizational and cultural costs associated with the rise of new collective action. A theoretical formulation is needed to explain how preexisting protest traditions figure in movement emergence and outcomes.

TRANSFORMATIVE EVENTS

We turn to the transformative event and the role it plays in producing large volumes of collective action. Political process theorists (McAdam and Sewell, 2001) who formulated the "transformative event" concept are coming to realize that some collective action campaigns or events are more important than others because they can produce radical turning points in collective action and affect the outcome of social movements. Political process theorists have overlooked these transformative events because they have tended to rely on time series data that treat all events as largely equivalent. McAdam and Sewell (2001) lament this outcome, especially as it pertains to the civil rights movement. They identify the Montgomery bus boycott, the 1960s sit-ins, and the assassination of King as such transformative events.

However, I discussed in detail how the Montgomery bus boycott, the 1960s sit-ins, and the Birmingham Confrontation of 1963 were turning points in the civil rights movement (Morris, 1981, 1984, 1993b). In terms of Montgomery, I argued that this movement represented a turning point because it introduced and perfected an effective tactic, catapulted a charismatic leader into the forefront of the movement, revealed the mobilizing capacity of the Black community, sustained a movement for a considerable period of time, and produced a victory.

The Montgomery movement was a transformative event because it provided an oppressed Black community with a highly visible and dynamic model of how to build successful local movements across the South. Through movements people discover a collective agency they were unaware of previously, or perceived only dimly. Initially the boycott was planned as a one-day protest but was extended indefinitely when the leaders discovered its near-total community support. However, the larger discovery pertained to human agency. The Montgomery movement revealed to a national Black community that a disciplined and organized mass movement could eventually overthrow the Jim Crow regime. As a result, Montgomery functioned as the transformative event that launched the modern civil rights movement. Future research on transformative events is likely to be fruitful because it can illuminate another important source of agency capable of fueling protracted collective action.

CONCLUSIONS

Resource mobilization and political process theories have added greatly to our understanding of social movements and collective action. We understand far clearer now how internal social organization facilitates the mobilization process and how external political opportunities provide openings for challenging groups to initiate collective action. We have also come to realize that framing processes are germane to the generation of collective action. Social movement research during the new century can yield additional theoretical insights by further developing these three foci of the political process model.

Yet, in this essay I have argued that the political process model has slighted important sources of social movement agency because of its tendency to assign undue causal weight to external factors and its propensity to gloss over the deep cultural and emotional processes that inspire and produce collective action. Future social movement theory can begin to correct these limitations by incorporating analyses that explicate the causal role that agency-laden institutions, frame lifting, tactical solutions, leadership configurations, preexisting protest traditions, and transformative events play in social movements and collective action. The challenge for social movement theory is to devise robust theoretical formulations of collective action that corresponds closely to social realities. The goal of this effort was to place human agency at the center of movement analysis, for it operates at the center of collective action.

NOTES

Previously published in *Contemporary Sociology* 29, no. 3 (May 2000). Reprinted with permission.

Acknowledgments: I especially thank Christian Davenport for insightful discussions that helped shape the ideas developed in this essay. Thanks to Doug McAdam for providing me with recent unpublished and forthcoming work on social movement theory. I also thank the editors of *Contemporary Sociology* for their useful comments. Finally I thank Kim Morris for helping prepare the manuscript and for pushing me to clarify my ideas.

15

Hot Movements, Cold Cognition: Thinking about Social Movements in Gendered Frames

MYRA MARX FERREE AND DAVID A. MERRILL

Framing theories begin from the assumption that language matters politically. Analyses of gender have suggested that language often carries masculinist assumptions and normative judgments that pass as neutral concepts. In this chapter we connect these two perspectives. In particular, we suggest that gender-conventional conceptions obscure important elements of understanding political thought at multiple levels of analysis, as well as biasing the process of framing research questions about social movements. We argue that uncovering the gender dimension in political discourse would not only bring women more fully into the picture but also correct partial and politically biased understandings of "political man." The questions we raise here about the future of framing thus arise from our feminist concerns about the discipline of sociology as a whole.

Our specific objective in this essay is to use critical ideas about gender to address the literature on framing in social movements. By investigating the often-unexamined assumptions about people and thinking that come together in this literature, we hope to clarify both what framing analyses have to offer researchers interested in gender and social change and what gender analyses have to offer students of political ideas. We contend that gender studies could benefit from the conceptual work that has already been done on frames and framing in general, while social movement research will be enriched by recognizing when and how their models may slip gendered concepts in through the back door. We particularly want to foreground concerns that we see as being "framed out" of the standard approaches to social movements. Consequently, we seek to place gender and gender politics in a central position in our thinking about social movements and framing, instead of adding on a concern with women and women's movements and "stirring" these bits into the male-defined "whole."

Framing is a central concept in current social movements research. The 1990s have been the decade of bringing ideas back into the study of social movements. As Oliver and Johnston (2000) argue, recent research on movements has frequently taken the concept of framing as a central point of departure, even though what framing means and what a frame analysis can be used for analytically are still very much points of debate. In this essay we do not attempt to review the entire literature on framing, a task already well accomplished by both Oliver and Johnston (2000) and by Benford (1997). Instead, we take up certain points raised in their excellent reviews and relate them to an expanded model of political thinking. We suggest that this model could both enrich our capacity to analyze gender politics and also to challenge some gendered limitations imbedded in the concepts of discourses, ideologies, and frames.

FRAMING A MODEL OF FRAMING

Recent reviews of the framing literature express concern over researchers' tendency to use framing as an all-encompassing concept and to produce long lists of ideas at varying levels of generality that are all called "frames" (Benford, 1997). Oliver and Johnston (2000) further suggest that there is an important distinction between frames, framing, and ideology. We agree with Oliver and Johnston on the usefulness of separating these concepts but also add a fourth analytic category that is also often collapsed into the concept of a frame—discourse. We find it useful to think of these concepts as interrelated in terms of both content and specificity.

Using the image of an inverted pyramid for illustration, we place discourses at the top—they are broad systems of communication that link concepts together in a web of relationships through an underlying logic (e.g., medical discourse is a way of communicating about the conditions of the body that focuses on specifying "diseases" and "cures" as part of its fundamental logic). Discourses are also inherently riddled with conflict, controversy, and negotiation over the meaning of specific words and ideas, because they include a variety of speakers with different interests and orientations who are communicating with each other (Gamson, 1992; Steinberg, 1999a, 1999b). Discourses may also have a gender logic, that is, be organized around and through their focus on specifying and explaining the relationship between men and women, masculinity and femininity. Gender discourses include debates about equality and power, rights and privileges, sameness and difference. Gender discourses are thus inherently *political* discourses, not only because they include conflict and diverse standpoints (all discourses do) but because they debate what Harold Lasswell once defined as the core questions of politics: "who gets what, when and how?" (1958).

Ideologies are at the next lower level. Ideologies are considerably more coherent than discourses because they are organized around systematic ideas and normative claims. Oliver and Johnston define ideology as "any system of meaning that couples assertions and theories about the nature of social life with values and norms relevant to promoting or resisting change" (2000:7). In their paper, Oliver and Johnston stress how framing language fails to acknowledge the political interests connected to belief systems or the extensive thinking and learning that go into ideologies, turning movement ideational work into something that more resembles selling via sound-bite than the rich and deep processes of building ideological commitments that carry activists through their entire lives.

We particularly pick up on another of their ideas, namely that the concept of ideology acknowledges not only a cognitive but also a normative or value dimension. Adherents of an ideology understand social events in light of their general theory of society and act, feel, and think as a result of the values they link to these understandings. There are, of course, multiple gender ideologies available, ranging from the Taliban's restrictive codes through Oprah Winfrey's warm and fuzzy picture of sex roles to deconstructionist feminist theory. The important point here is that ideologies always include values as well as ideas, and consequently imply feelings and actions, not only thinking in the abstract.

At the bottom of the pyramid are frames. For us, a frame is a cognitive ordering that relates events to one another—it is a way of talking and thinking about things that serves to link idea elements into packages. Any one particular frame can be seized upon by multiple ideologies, but as Oliver and Johnston argue, redescription of ideology in framing language obscures how and why frames are used. An important distinction Oliver and Johnston highlight between frames and ideologies is the value component in the latter: frames specify *how* to think about things, but they don't point to *why* it matters. Frames, unlike ideologies, do not ground thinking in what is normatively good or bad about the situation or imply goals and objectives. Frames merely provide a certain cognitive focus and thus put certain elements or ideas "in the picture" or not. As cognitive social psychologists have shown, some such selective attention is always needed to make sense of what William James called otherwise "a blooming, buzzing confusion" of sensory input. Whether gender is framed as biological sex differences or as social roles, for example, does not answer the question of whether this framing is being used to support a feminist or anti-feminist ideology.

We also distinguish frames from the framing process, or the ongoing cognitive activity of picking ideas from discourses and the social negotiations involved in writing, speaking, and composing communications that relate events, ideas, and actions to each other (Smith, 1999). The framing process is the mechanism by which discourses, ideologies, and frames are all connected. Framing as a process is both strategic and social. The outcome of all the multiple activities of people and groups engaged in framing processes is the production of a discourse. Like Steinberg (1999a), we think that a focus on the repertoires of ideas brought into play by various collective actors helps to show the significant constraints exercised by institutionalized discourses and other active speakers on the claims made by any one actor at any given time. Framing activity engages, and sometimes changes, such repertoires and may ultimately transform the discourses institutionalized in court decisions, laws, textbooks, and other genres of authoritative speech.

While framing as continual process is important, we concur with Oliver and Johnston that often it is the "snapshot" of the frames at any specific point in time that is most amenable to study. However, in regard to gender framing, such snapshots are rarely more than inventories of gender beliefs or normative values in the form of attitude scales. A more complex model of how people organize, use, and change their frames, discourses, and ideologies about gender is sorely lacking (but see Pratto, 1999 for a sketch of what such a non-linear model of cognition might look like applied to thinking about race). Attention to the differences between discourses, ideologies, and frames can help sharpen our analysis about how culture, politics, and social psychology are linked in the production of gender, as the above examples indicate. But considering the covert gender biases in each of these concepts can do even more to clarify the analysis of how ideas matter in social movements and in politics more generally. In the following sections we consider how gender bias operates at each of these three levels as well as in the framing process that connects them.

GENDER CHALLENGES TO
SOCIAL MOVEMENT FRAMES

Beginning at the bottom of this pyramid, the concept of a "frame" itself suffers from gendered limitations in the way that social movement theorizing has developed. Framing analysis itself has developed from social psychological traditions that model cognition as "cold," using the detached and dispassionate observer as the standard actor (see critiques in Fiske, 1981; Lawler and Thye, 1999). Contemporary social psychologists have challenged this "cold cognition approach" to try to better incorporate values and emotions into their models, and researchers in this tradition have responded (Schwarz, 1998). Social psychologists, especially those concerned with studying race and gender oppression, have begun to "warm up" their cognitive models to include the role of emotions in shaping perception for both dominant and subordinate groups (e.g., Sidanius and Pratto, 1999).

Concern with the integration of emotion and evaluation into analysis of perception has been especially eloquent when coupled to discussions of the separation of "reason" from emotion as expressing an androcentric political bias that takes a certain historically-specific image of "man" as the definition of what is "normal" human behavior. Even though actual men are far more varied in their cognitive and emotional life than this politically charged image would suggest, the values associated with men (unemotional, calculating, individually self-interested, dominant, hierarchical) have often been uncritically framed as "rationality" and then ideologically preferred. As the philosopher Alison Jaggar (1989) pointed out, defining rationality as the opposite of emotionality sets up a gendered dichotomy that can be used to transfer the lower status of that which is seen as feminine to emotions. This low status serves to disallow the acknowledgment of values and feelings in both researchers and movement participants (but not to eliminate their actual significance for both). Men, of course, have values and emotions and bring them into their political work, but the gender bias attached to the concept of emotion tends to see it as lowering the quality of discourse and interfering with the ideal political process. Jaggar argues that emotion can also enrich perception, facilitate the discovery of values and secure the process of interpersonal communication through its expression as trust.

The emphasis in recent social movement theories on frames, the purely cognitive element in political discourse, serves implicitly to exclude the "hotter" concepts of emotion and values from analysis, even when studies of the active process of framing make clear that passionate feelings are often involved in talking about injustice (Gamson, 1992). The very idea of social movement activists as emotional human beings has been quite controversial, as Goodwin, Jasper, and Polletta (2000) show. Social movement researchers from the collective behavior school of the 1950s and of the resource mobilization school of the 1970s agreed that good political behavior should be "rational" and evaluated movements on that basis. The former tended to discredit movements for what they perceived to be their lack of rationality and the latter to credit them with purely rational behavior. A. O. Hirschman's underappreciated book *The Passions and the Interests* (1977) explores the historical process of developing capitalism that allowed "self-interest" to be re-framed from being a socially danger-ous passion to being the bedrock of all virtues and the very definition of what it means to act rationally. Imported into social movement research, the model of "cold cognition" combines with the androcentric value on self-interest as a non-passionate and thus preferred form of motivation to produce many studies of framing that treat social movement ideas as merely dispassionate thought. This approach thus leaves untouched the whole problem of connecting ideas to motivations for action. Without such a connection, the actors involved in social movements are not really acting so much as acted upon. Thus it is not surprising to us that so much of the coldly cognitive analysis of framing takes a top-down view of ideas being presented to actors by organizations in an almost manipulative fashion. In contrast, studies such as Gamson's *Talking Politics* (1992) that focus on ordinary people's thinking clearly show not just "cold" cogni-tions but hot emotions at work in political judgments, especially in forg-ing a link between experiences, perceptions, and actions at the grassroots.

At its core, the problem that framing language presents is that it "cools" the analysis of movement thinking by separating it from the deeply-felt passions and value commitments that motivate action. Social movement *actors* are actually "hot," or passionate about their causes, and studying movement ideas as if they could be isolated from the refining heat of engagement leads social movement researchers to neglect the effects that participation in protest events has on consciousness as well as to underestimate the importance of finding out where and how passion arises. Verta Taylor (1995) has been among the most active and eloquent in calling for a more serious study of emotion in social movements, but her appeals have often been taken as only applying to the women's move-ment or to women in social movements because emotion is conceptually gendered as female (but see also Goodwin, Jasper, and Polletta, 2001; Aminzade and McAdam, 2001).

Scholars of social movements may have shared the common belief, rooted in gender ideology, that finding activists to be emotional is to dis-credit them, and thus have favored "cool" forms of talk. Recent studies have begun explicitly to consider the political consequences of the use of emotionally laden framing language and gender ideologies that dualisti-cally ascribe emotion only to women and devalue it accordingly. Ein-wohner's (1999) study of the animal rights campaign explores the relationship between the gender composition of the movement and responses to their framing. She found, for example, that hunters set up an opposition between the supposed emotional arguments of the animal rights movement and the "scientific" arguments in favor of hunting. Simi-larly, Groves (2001) found that popular understandings of pro-animal rights positions as resting on sympathy rather than science led movement

activists to underplay the proportion of women involved in their activities, prefer men as spokespeople and frame arguments in scientific languages whenever possible. The actual passions felt by the activists were
perceived in terms of the dominant, gendered discourse as discrediting
to the status of their cause and were downplayed by the activists themselves as a result.

Emotion is universally part of being human, and it is not necessarily a
flaw or obstruction to reasoned action. It may indeed be quite the opposite. As Jaggar (1989) demonstrates, emotions and values are closely intertwined. The emotions of social actors are aroused precisely because their
understanding of events connects with particular values they possess,
and values are formed in a process of experiencing emotional reactions
such as attraction, revulsion, love, anger, and fear. Emotions are inti-
mately connected with both the values and ideas of movement actors.
Thus, the separation of cognition and emotion is related to the separation
of objectivity and values, itself part of an ideology of "value-neutrality"
in science, and a rationale for scientists' disengagement from political
choices and action. The separation of cognition and emotion becomes part
of the way of presenting sociology as science that would allow it to evade
fundamental questions about whose perspectives and needs shape its
particular relevances (cf. Smith, 1999). Part of "warming up" our ideas
about cognition in the context of social movements, therefore, may also
demand that we take some of the anti-emotional chill from how we as
sociologists think about the science we do and acknowledge the political
implications of our own work.

VALUES, IDEOLOGY, AND
SELF-REFLEXIVE SCIENCE

As Oliver and Johnston distinguish them, ideologies—unlike frames—are
explicitly about values. Ideologies connect movements and people on the
basis of their shared commitments to certain values. However, values
have been absent or portrayed as irrelevant to most social movement
research. We argue that values should be analyzed as both something the
researcher carries into the research process as well as an integral component of social movement activism.

One important insight from feminist critiques of "objectivity" is that
concepts, organizations, and institutions, not just individual people, carry
gender meanings. Not only is it important to consider the values of movement actors, but feminist thinking also indicates the need to consider values in the researcher her/himself. The assumptions among social
movement researchers often reflect hidden values. Both the American

resource mobilization model of individual self-interest and capitalist-like enterprises and the European New Social Movement approach that places class-based movements in a prior and privileged position are operating from premises that are deeply imbedded in an androcentric and Western worldview. As Craig Calhoun (1994) demonstrates, the tension between the individual and the collective good is not experienced among Chinese student rebels in the ways that either European or American social movement theory predicts.

Calhoun (1995) also argues that the very notion of "new" social movements, with a distinctive non-bureaucratic form and a stress on collective identity and group solidarity, is an ahistorical version of newness. This idea of the "new" emergence of identity issues erases the construction of a masculine working-class identity in the 19th century, through processes of networking and self-assertion similar to those seen today among differently disadvantaged groups. This allows the "identity politics" of today to appear uniquely and problematically emotional in contrast to the "rational" interests of class-based mobilization. Calhoun argues that economic "rationality" as a value held by movement groups is part of a historical shift of concentration of working-class organizations to the shop-floor organization of men at the expense of community-based mobilization. Indeed, feminism and socialism had a conflicted and complex relation from the mid-19th century onward that is made invisible when class issues are defined as "old" and "rational" and gender politics as "new" and "identity-based."

Because they are about values, ideologies connect movements with the people who study them. It was not an accident that the social movement theories prominent in the 1950s and 1960s reflected a fear of Nazi and communist totalitarianism. Framed in the aftermath of World War II and in the context of the emergent Cold War, the questions asked tended to denigrate the adherents of movements as irrational and see their responses to their political and economic situation as "short-circuiting" the deliberative processes of liberal democracy. Similarly, it was hardly a coincidence that the students stirred to action by the movements of the 1960s and 1970s would reject these theories and seek to build alternative approaches that would accord better with their experiences of political learning, networking and organization building. Nor should it be surprising that the movement theories of the 1970s and 1980s formed as these movements began to consolidate and institutionalize showed an initially sharp division between the European-based analyses that stressed autonomous subcultures of dissident youth alienated from the "old" class politics of their socialist parties (New Social Movement theories) and the American-based models that emphasized the construction of organizations with resources that could be used in the interest group system of representation that characterizes American politics. The different political processes of institutionalization affected not only the course of the movements but also the theories formed about these different developments.

In recent years, the rapprochement between the American and European strands of theorizing has accelerated. We see this convergence as in no small part due to the increasing actual globalization of both academia and of social movements, even though bringing in theories grounded in the experience of social movements in the Third World has still been more limited (but see Ray and Korteweg, 1999). Both American and European researchers are increasingly part of the same global field in which a specifically transnational form of social movement is becoming ever more prominent. The questions being asked in social movement research today reflect the contemporary problems facing activists in these networks no less than the problems tackled and theories developed in the 1950s and 1970s did—and for the same reason, namely, values held in common among activists and researchers.

As Keck and Sikkink (1998) demonstrate, the rise of the transnational issue advocacy network in contemporary politics involves both scholars and activists held together by a commitment to common *values* for social change. Such networks of activists and researchers investigating human rights, environmental degradation, gender equality, and other issues on a global scale begin to blur the conventional distinction between academic studies, protest politics "out on the streets" and formal politics conducted within institutions. International non-governmental organizations use information generated through funded research to support local activists and bring pressure on national governments. The value commitments shared by the participants in such networks bind them together despite differences in frames that may be employed. Indeed, Keck and Sikkink provide a compelling case study of how the development of human rights frames for incidents of violence against women, from clitoridectomy to dowry deaths, gave local activists a rhetoric that allowed them to challenge the framing of such violence as "local custom" in conflict with "Western norms."

Understanding framing as a tool that can be used to advance certain values, we argue, demands more conscious scrutiny of ideologies as such. There are values and goals at stake, not only for activists but also for the researchers who study them and who may be part of the same transnational issue networks. Reframing social movement research to allow more direct consideration of the normative elements in ideology, without implying that having values is disreputable and discrediting, would be a step forward.

To take that step, we suggest, social movement researchers will need to borrow a page from feminist theories of science and be more honest and self-reflective about their own values. Such a consciously self-reflexive theory of social movements would connect motivation with values, emotions and frames as well as acknowledge the ties between activists and academics in all of these dimensions. It is an unnecessarily limiting, as well as gendered, vision of science that demands that researchers not admit to having values (see Keller, 1985 for a classic discussion of gender and epistemology). It is also a distortion of the actual history of how social movement research has developed, and a simple regard for a truthful understanding of our own work should bring activists and academics together to consider what we have learned and can learn from each other.

DISCOURSES, MEANING, AND UNDERSTANDING

At the third level, that of discourses as whole systems of communication, gendered assumptions and conceptions have also obscured important elements of social reality. Narrow definitions of what constitutes public life or politics is one such gendered way of seeing, allowing only the arenas in which men have taken leadership roles to be seen as being public and obscuring cultural changes that can be as far-reaching, such as shifts in feminist or environmental consciousness and changes in work or consumption practices within households. Institutional discourses that are deeply gendered often render movement challenges invisible, because they operate outside the realm defined as political. Political change that happens in and through households and families is especially hard to see, because the relationships of the family (gendered female) are separated from the relationships of politics (gendered male). In fact, considering the rise of the Religious Right in contemporary America, the political ideology of such organizations as the Promise Keepers, and the centrality of the "family values" debate and abortion politics to electoral campaigns, it is hard to consider household composition and family relations as in any sense "outside" politics in even its narrowest, most institutional sense.

Even when movements become visible, gendered assumptions may block their vision of possible change. Movement actors and institutional actors often participate in the same discourse, framing specific ideas differently, but without being able to examine and critique the deeper assumptions that they share. Institutional discourses carry important assumptions that affect what even the challengers' discursive logic is able to "see." For example, many researchers have discussed "rights" frames. This type of framing is rooted in a liberal-legal discourse. However, as Critical Legal Studies, Critical Race Studies, and feminist legal scholars have shown, these legal discourses are not objective and "free-float-ing"—they are deeply raced, gendered, and sexualized. Rights to self-determination, a fundamental constitutional principle, for example, were initially defined to allow slavery and exclude all but white men from the vote. As this legal discourse was extended, through struggle, it continued to carry some of its original assumptions, such as seeing women as less capable of rational decision making or as not independent because sup-ported by a husband. Consequently, by adopting a legal discourse, a movement is constrained by its discursive logic, even when it struggles against it (cf. Steinberg, 1999a, 1999b; and Scott, 1990 for useful discus-sions of how the genre and field of discourse are constraints as well as tools).

In practice, this leads feminist movements into trying to prove that women are as rational as men in male-defined terms, or making social value and citizen rights contingent on economic self-support. Fraser and Gordon (1994), for example, provide a compelling history of the shifts in the meaning of "dependence" in American discourse that shape the argu-ments made by all participants, regardless of their specific ideologies, in welfare reform debates. Glenn (2002) shows how the interplay of racial and gender devaluations created changing ways of talking about the "worthiness" of racial/ethnic groups for citizenship in the early 20th cen-tury and concomitant demands that such worth be demonstrated in appropriately gendered labor force participation. Conversely, as Kimmel and Ferber (2000) show, militia groups and other right-wing mobiliza-tions assert the "true American" citizenship of white men as defined by their ability to dominate women, non-Christians, and non-whites.

These historical constraints on a discourse can often be used against the movement by institutional actors, since the latter remain the more power-ful actors in the overall field. An analysis of entire discourses, rather than merely separate frames, could help us move beyond the relative separa-tion of institutional politics and social movements as two entirely differ-ent fields of study. This separation has produced a further bias in which institutional politics is the arena for the study of effects (social policies and their outcomes) and social movements are studied in terms of their origins and organizations. As sociologists have long recognized, both institutions and social movements are important for explaining social change. However, the actual work being done in and by social movements often does not resemble the work practices of institutional politics, and the actors involved may also differ.

In particular, women are much more likely to be grassroots political activists and the work that they do involves skills of networking, bridg-ing, and organizing people that tends to be overlooked by a framework in which politics is defined as a typically male activity (Christiansen-Ruffman, 1995). The gendering of the political as male makes formal hierarchical authority more visible than influence exercised in lateral networks and values top-down speech-making more than organizational bridge-building (Robnett, 1997). The styles and content of discourses produced at the grassroots also appear different. Knowing how to speak the discourse of party-based democratic competition is a skill for working within that system, but like any other speech genre it also imposes constraints that may be invisible to those most accustomed to speaking in these terms. Looking at women's community groups in emergent democracies, Gottlick (1999) in Russia, Tripp (2000) in Uganda, and Miethe (1999) in post-socialist East Germany all found activists arguing that what they did was "not politics" but "work for their communities." For them, as for some community activists in the United States (see, e.g., Naples, 1998), use of the language of party politics was consequently controversial.

While discourses about social movements are often invisibly gendered, attention to gender would only be the beginning of a set of questions about the political discourse in which both activists and academics participate. Whether one is essentially sympathetic to the capitalist form or deeply critical of it, the overall discourse about social movements revolves around questions that flow from social relations that it has already profoundly shaped. A discourse imbedded in capitalist social relations is likely to construct individuals as autonomous, relationships as commodities, and organizations as persons. Is it so surprising that this is the dominant rhetoric of social movement theory? Theories about movements that probe the limits of their own generalizability across time periods, as Charles Tilly's work has done, recognize how sociological discourse itself tends to privilege the present as the model of the past. But social movement theories also need to ask how their own discourse is related to modes of action and understanding that flow from the social organization of gender, race, nation, age, sexuality in any given place or period. The separation of public from private, the relation of formal organizations to households and grassroots mobilizations, the new awareness of cultural change as well as policy-making in theories of social movements reflect underlying connections between discourses and power relations. Making these into explicit questions rather than an invisible background for social movement studies is the challenge that gender theory presents to political discourse analysis.

BRINGING THE PIECES TOGETHER

This brings us to a discussion of how frames, ideologies, and discourses are related, and thus to our fourth analytic dimension, the framing process as a whole. This framing process is about action, not only thought. Actors use frames to elicit an emotional response from adherents of particular value positions, and thus stir motivations to act. The framing of an issue will have profoundly different impacts on two people with oppositional ideologies: framing the fetus as an innocent human baby, for example, exerts a powerful emotional pull on those with a "pro-life" ideological commitment but can enrage or disgust an activist who values abortion rights. Thinking of framing as directed to only one target audience at a time (policy-makers, constituents, bystanders, or adversaries) simplifies models of what successful framing looks like; it appears that frames could somehow be unproblematically "resonant" for all audiences and thus be uncontroversially "successful" (Davenport and Eads, 2001; Ellingson, 1995; Ferree et al., 2002). Frames are connected to the emotions through the ideological beliefs and normative commitments of many different actors, and the process of making these connections itself deserves attention.

When framing work is understood as a process, it is also more easily recognized as work, and thus as something that real people have to do. Much of the scholarship on care work identifies the ways that caring is framed as an emotional activity that becomes "invisible work" (Daniels, 1987; Glenn, 2000). Emotion work in social movements is also work. Constructing coalitions and learning to see common interests (as well as recognizing divergent identities) is built on the emotion work done as part of the framing process in "old" as well as "new" social movements. "This bridge called my back" describes not only the effort of forging connections between race and gender politics done by women of color (to which the phrase originally was applied) but also the demanding but invisible labor that underlies the street-level "frame-bridging" work that is done, often by women, to make coalitions happen (Robnett, 1997).

Doing framing work is also about producing fundamental social change. Framing as a process challenges, even as it is constrained by, discursive logics. Movements confront meanings that are embedded in institutional discourses, but also use innovative framing tactics to challenge and change them (Katzenstein, 1998). Such "new words" may lead to "new worlds." Successful re-framing then constrains the options of other actors by introducing a new discursive logic. For example, in the United States, the successful expansion of the "right to privacy" to women's bodies challenges the relationship between the state and abortion, but it does nothing to change the privatization of childcare work within individual families. Conversely, the expansion of the "state's obligation to protect life" to the fetus in German discourse offers a framework for feminists to demand better state support for children and childrearing, but effectively closes off the option of speaking of abortion as a private choice (see Ferree et al., 2002). American anti-feminist activists have successfully re-framed the issues of gender politics from "patriarchy" to "traditional family values" and made the women's movement seem no longer relevant to "what the debate is about" today.

While radical re-framing is rare, political institutions themselves engage in framing work on an on-going basis. The feminist philosopher Nancy Fraser (1989) proposes studying welfare state policies as not merely about redistribution (or meeting various needs through state action) but also as about need definition, that is, what counts as being a need at all. Fraser argues that rival need interpretations are transformed into "rival programmatic conceptions" and specific policy proposals that are more directly contested in the political arena. Then the policies implemented "provide more than material aid. They also provide clients, and the public at large, with a tacit but powerful interpretive map of normative, differently valued gender roles and gendered needs" (170). Need definition in Fraser's terms comes intriguingly close to what political scientists have long studied as "agenda-setting" when it comes to legislative process, and to the "key non-decisions" that Bachrach and Baratz (1962) long ago identified. The question that the policy studies literature skips when it talks about the framing of questions for the political agenda (as Deborah Stone, 1997 does very well) is how such institutional need definition work intersects with the social change re-framing work being done outside formal politics, and how both are, as Fraser suggests, deeply gendered.

In sum, looking at framing as a process reveals it to be gendered work. It is done laterally (often by women) as part of the organizing process as well as hierarchically in the speeches and documents produced by those (disproportionately men) in official positions. It is work often made invisible in the movements that are doing it and hidden within the policy process in the form of institutional discourses. Making such framing work more visible could begin to undermine the discursively anchored distinction between public and private that acts ideologically to exclude women from "politics" and make gender oppression appear to be private, domestic, and individual rather than part of a political culture that can be challenged and changed.

CONCLUSION: WHAT NOW?

We see the move to bring ideas into a central position in studying social movements as a very important and promising step for the field's future. But approaching all such ideas only in the rubric of "frames" strips them of the emotional color, value commitments, and institutional anchors that make them so significant in both individual and collective action. Frames are "cooled" out of the passionate action and commitment of "hot" social movements, and academic studies of social movements are made to appear more separate from the movements' own activities than they are in practice. By being attentive to the gendered framing of emotion and values as feminine and therefore suspect, and paying attention also to the institutional discourses that frame women as apolitical and gender as private, the analysis of ideas could not only add to social movement studies but fundamentally transform them.

How would it do that? Obviously, we think that making gender an explicit part of the discourse of political sociology as men practice it is an important part of the answer. If only women scholars or only studies of feminist movements or of women in other social movements actually pay attention to gender, a large piece of the actual gendering of social movements theory and research remains untouched. We have tried to show how the ideological masculinity in scientific rhetoric and sociological discourse is vulnerable to an analysis that takes discourses, ideologies, frames and framing work seriously. But we have also tried to demonstrate that gender deeply permeates the discourses, ideologies and frames that social movement studies have offered as analytical tools. Although developing a better account of how ideas matter has become the "hot" topic of the 1990s for social movement scholars, we hope we have shown why such improved theory will demand not only an awareness of gender discourses but also an appreciation of the merits of emotion and of the links between scholarship and activism that a self-reflexive consciousness of our own values provides.

NOTES

An earlier version of this chapter was published in *Contemporary Sociology* 29, no. 3 (May 2000). Reprinted with permission.

The authors especially want to thank Marita McComisky for her emphasis over the years on the passionate side of protest, as well as William A. Gamson, Davita Silfen Glasberg, Carol McClurg Mueller, Barbara Risman and Don Tomaskovic-Devey for their helpful comments on earlier drafts.

References

Abelson, Robert P. 1981. "Psychological Status of the Script Concept." *American Psychologist* 36: 715–729.

ACT UP/New York. 1987. "Meeting Minutes, March 12, 1987." Written by Bradley Ball. Housed in the New York Public Library, Manuscripts and Archives Section, ACT UP/New York Records, box T-14.

———. 1988. "Show Your Anger to the People Who Helped Make the Quilt Possible: Our Government." Leaflet housed in Deborah Gould's personal ACT UP archive.

———. 1992. "Bring Your Grief and Rage about AIDS to a Political Funeral." Leaflet housed in Deborah Gould's personal ACT UP archive.

Aho, James A. 1990. *The Politics of Righteousness: Idaho Christian Patriotism*. Seattle: University of Washington Press.

Aldrich, Howard. 1988. "Paradigm Warriors: Donaldson versus the Critics of Organizational Theory." *Organizational Studies* 9: 18–25.

Aldrich, Howard E. and Ellen Auster. 1986. "Even Dwarfs Started Small: Liabilities of Age and Size and Their Strategic Implications." In Barry Staw and L. L. Cummings (eds.), *Research in Organizational Behavior* vol. 8: 165–198. Greenwich, CT: JAI Press.

Alexander, Jeffrey C. and Philip Smith. 1993. "The Discourse of American Civil Society: A New Proposal for Cultural Studies." *Theory and Society* 22: 151–207.

Alexander, Victoria D. 1998. "Environmental Constraints and Organizational Strategies: Complexity, Conflict and Coping in the Nonprofit Sector." In Walter W. Powell and Elisabeth Clemens (eds.), *Private Action and the Public Good*. New Haven, CT: Yale University Press.

Alinsky, Saul D. 1971. *Rules for Radicals*. New York: Vintage.

Alvarez, Sonia E., Evelina Dagnino, and Arturo Escobar. 1998. "Introduction: The Cultural and the Political in Latin American Social Movements." In Sonia F. Alvarez, Evelina Dagnino and Arturo Escobar (eds.), *Cultures of Politics, Politics of Cultures: Re-Visioning Latin American Social Movements*. Boulder, CO: Westview Press.

Amabile, Theresa M. 1988. "A Model of Organizational Innovation." In Barry

Staw and L. L. Cummings (eds.), *Research in Organizational Behavior* vol. 10: 127–167. Greenwich, CT: JAI Press.

———. 1996. *Creativity in Context: Update to the Social Psychology of Creativity*. Boulder, CO: Westview Press.

Amenta, Edwin, Bruce G. Carruthers, and Yvonne Zylan. 1992. "A Hero for the Aged? The Townsend Movement, the Political Mediation Model, and U.S. Old-age Policy, 1934–1950." *American Journal of Sociology* 98: 308–339.

Amenta, Edwin, Kathleen Dunleavy, and Mary Bernstein. 1994. "Stolen Thunder? Huey Long's 'Share Our Wealth,' Political Mediation, and the Second New Deal." *American Sociological Review* 59: 678–702.

Amenta, Edwin and Yvonne Zylan. 1991. "It Happened Here: Political Opportunity, the New Institutionalism, and the Townsend Movement." *American Sociological Review* 56: 250–265.

Aminzade, Ron and Doug McAdam. 2001. "Emotions and Contentious Politics." In Ron Aminzade, Jack Goldstone, Doug McAdam, Elizabeth Perry, William Sewell, Sidney Tarrow, and Charles Tilly (eds.), *Silence and Voice in Contentious Politics*. Cambridge: Cambridge University Press.

———. 2002. "Introduction: Emotions and Contentious Politics." *Mobilization* 7: 107–110.

Aminzade, Ron, Jack Goldstone, Doug McAdam, Elizabeth Perry, William Sewell, Sidney Tarrow, and Charles Tilly, eds. 2001. *Silence and Voice in the Study of Contentious Politics*. Cambridge: Cambridge University Press.

Ancona, Deborah and Chee-Leong Chong. 1996. "Entrainment: Cycles and Synergy in Organizational Behavior." In Barry Staw and L. L. Cummings (eds.), *Research in Organizational Behavior* vol. 18: 251–284. Greenwich, CT: JAI Press.

Andrews, Kenneth. 1997. "The Impacts of Social Movements on the Political Process: The Civil Rights Movement and Black Electoral Politics in Mississippi." *American Sociological Review* 62: 800–819.

Andrews, Molly. 1991. *Lifetimes of Commitment: Aging, Politics, Psychology*. Cambridge: Cambridge University Press.

Anonymous (Mark Fisher). 1992. "Bury Me Furiously." *QW* October 25: 48.

Apuzzo, Virginia. 1986. "Stonewalling." *New York Native* July 28: 11.

Arditti, Rita. 1999. *Searching for Life: The Grandmothers of the Plaza de Mayo and the Disappeared Children of Argentina*. Berkeley: University of California Press.

Arvanette, Steven C. 1983. "Thousands in Vigil Demand Millions for AIDS." *New York Native* May 23–June 5: 9–10.

Asch, Solomon. 1952. *Social Psychology*. Englewood Cliffs, NJ: Prentice Hall.

Austin, J. L. 1962. *How to Do Things with Words*. Cambridge: Harvard University Press.

Bachrach, Peter and Morton S. Baratz. 1962. "The Two Faces of Power." *American Political Science Review* 56: 947–952.

Bainbridge, William Sims. 1997. *The Sociology of Religious Movements*. New York: Routledge.

Bakhtin, Mikhail M. 1986. *Speech Genres and Other Late Essays*. Caryl Emerson and Michael Holquist (eds.). Translated by Vein W. McGee. Austin: University of Texas Press.

Banaszak, Lee Ann. 1996. *Why Movements Succeed or Fail: Opportunity, Culture and the Struggle for Woman Suffrage*. Princeton, NJ: Princeton University Press.

Bandura, Albert. 1989. "Human Agency in Social Cognitive Theory." *American Psychologist* 44: 1175–1184.

Barbalet, J. M. 1992. "A Macro Sociology of Emotion: Class Resentment." *Sociological Theory* 10: 150–163.

———. 1998. *Emotion, Social Theory, and Social Structure: A Macrosociological Approach*. Cambridge: Cambridge University Press.

Barkan, Steve. 1979. "Strategic, Tactical and Organizational Dilemmas of the Protest Movement Against Nuclear Power." *Social Problems* 27: 19–37.

Barker, Colin. 2001. "Fear, Laughter, and Collective Power: The Making of Solidarity at the Lenin Shipyard in Gdansk, Poland, August 1980." In Jeff Goodwin, James M. Jasper, and Francesca Polletta (eds.), *Passionate Politics: Emotions and Social Movements*. Chicago: University of Chicago Press.

Barrett, Deborah and Charles Kurzman. n.d. "International Political Opportunity, Global Culture, and Transnational Social Movements: The Case of Eugenics." Unpublished manuscript.

Bartunek, J. M. 1993. "Multiple Cognition and Conflicts Associated with Second Order Organizational Change." In J. K. Murnighan (ed.), *Social Psychology in Organizations*: 337–343. Englewood Cliffs, NJ: Prentice Hall.

Baumgartner, Frank R. and Bryan D. Jones. 1993. *Agendas and Instability in American Politics*. Chicago: University of Chicago Press.

Beisel, Nicola. 1997. *Imperiled Innocents: Anthony Comstock and Family Reproduction in Victorian America*. Princeton, NJ: Princeton University Press.

Benford, Robert D. 1993. "Frame Disputes within the Nuclear Disarmament Movement." *Social Forces* 71: 677–701.

———. 1997. "An Insider's Critique of the Social Movement Framing Perspective." *Sociological Inquiry* 67: 409–430.

Benford, Robert D. and Scott A. Hunt. 1992. "Dramaturgy and Social Movements: The Social Construction and Communication of Power." *Sociological Inquiry* 62: 36–55.

Benford, Robert D. and David A. Snow. 2000. "Framing Process and Social Movements: An Overview and Assessment." *Annual Review of Sociology* 26: 611–639.

Berezin, Mabel. 1997. "Politics and Culture: A Less Fissured Terrain." *Annual Review of Sociology* 23: 361–383.

Bergman, J. 1979. "Energy Levels: An Important Factor in Identifying and Facilitating the Development of Giftedness in Young Children." *Creative Child and Adult Quarterly* 4: 181–188.

Berlyne, D. E. 1960. *Conflict, Arousal, and Curiosity*. New York: McGraw-Hill.

Bermeo, Nancy. 1997. "Myths of Moderation: Confrontation and Conflict during Democratic Transitions." *Journal of Comparative Politics* 29: 305–322.

Bernstein, Basil. 1975. *Class Codes and Control: Theoretical Studies towards a Sociology of Language*. Second edition. New York: Schocken Books.

Bob, Clifford. 1997. *The Marketing of Rebellion in Global Civil Society: Political Insurgencies, International Media, and the Growth of Transnational Support*. Ph.D. dissertation, Department of Political Science, Massachusetts Institute of Technology.

Bockman, Philip. 1986. "A Fine Day." *New York Native* August 25: 12–13.

Bolton, Charles D. 1972. "Alienation and Action: A Study of Peace Group Members." *American Journal of Sociology* 78: 537–561.

Bordt, Rebecca. 1997. "How Alternative Ideas Become Institutions: The Case of Feminist Collectives." *Nonprofit and Voluntary Sector Quarterly* 26: 132–155.

Boudreau, Vincent. 1996. "Northern Theory, Southern Protest: Opportunity Structure Analysis in a Cross-national Perspective." *Mobilization* 1: 175–189.

Bourdieu, Pierre. 1984. *Distinction: A Social Critique of the Judgement of Taste*. Cambridge: Harvard University Press.

———. 1990. *The Logic of Practice*. Palo Alto, CA: Stanford University Press.

Bower, J. L. 1970. *Managing the Resource Allocation Process: A Study of Corporate Planning and Investment*. Homewood, IL: Richard D. Irwin.

Breines, Wini. 1989. *Community and Organization in the New Left, 1962–68*. New Brunswick, N.J.: Rutgers.

Briët, Martien, Bert Klandermans, and Frederike Kroon. 1987. "How Women Become Involved in the Women's Movement of the Netherlands." In Mary Fainsod Katzenstein and Carol McClurg Mueller (eds.), *The Women's Movements of the United States and Western Europe: Consciousness, Political Opportunities, and Public Policy*. Philadelphia: Temple University Press.

Broadbent, Jeffrey. 1998. *Environmental Politics in Japan: Networks of Power and Protest*. Cambridge: Cambridge University Press.

Brockett, Charles D. 1995. "A Protest-cycle Resolution of the Repression/Popular-protest Paradox." In Mark Traugott (ed.), *Repertoires and Cycles of Collective Action*. Durham, NC and London: Duke University Press.

Brooks, Thomas R. 1974. *Walls Come Tumbling Down*. Englewood Cliffs, NJ: Prentice Hall.

Brown, Michael P. 1997. *Replacing Citizenship: AIDS Activism and Radical Democracy*. New York: Guilford Press.

Brown, Shona L. and Kathleen M. Eisenhardt. 1997. "The Art of Continuous Change: Linking Complexity Theory and Time-paced Evolution in Relentlessly Shifting Organizations." *Administrative Science Quarterly* 42: 34–56.

———. 1998. *Competing on the Edge: Strategy as Structured Chaos*. Boston: Harvard Business School Press.

Bruner, Jerome. 1990. *Acts of Meaning*. Cambridge: Harvard University Press.

Brysk, Alison. 1994. *The Politics of Human Rights in Argentina: Protest, Change and Democratization*. Stanford, CA: Stanford University Press.

Buechler, Steven M. 2000. *Social Movements in Advanced Capitalism: The Political Economy and Cultural Construction of Social Activism*. New York: Oxford University Press.

Burgelman, R. A. 1991. "Intraorganizational Ecology of Strategy Making and Organizational Adaptation: Theory and Field Research." *Organization Science* 2: 239–262.

Burnstein, Paul, Marie Bricher, and Rachel Einwohner. 1995. "Policy Alternatives and Political Change: Work, Gender and Family on the Congressional Agenda, 1945–1990." *American Sociological Review* 60: 67–83.

Calhoun, Craig. 1994. *Neither Gods Nor Emperors: Students and the Struggle for Democracy in China*. Berkeley and Los Angeles: University of California Press.

————. 1995. "New Social Movements of the Early Nineteenth Century." In Mark Traugott (ed.), *Repertoires and Cycles of Collective Action*. Durham, NC and London: Duke University Press.

Campbell, Donald T. 1960. "Blind Variation and Selective Retention in Creative Thought as in Other Knowledge Processes." *Psychological Review* 67: 380–400.

Campbell, John L. 1997. "Mechanisms of Evolutionary Change in Economic Governance: Interaction, Interpretation, and Bricolage." In Lars Magnusson and Jan Ottosson (eds.), *Evolutionary Economics and Path Dependence*. Cheltenham, England: Edward Elgar.

Cantwell, Robert. 1995. *When We Were Good: The Folk Revival*. Cambridge: Harvard University Press.

Carlton-Ford, Steven L. 1992. "Charisma, Ritual, Collective Effervescence and Self-esteem." *Sociological Quarterly* 33: 365–388.

Castoriadis, Cornelius. 1987. *The Imaginary Institution of Society*. Cambridge: MIT Press.

Centers for Disease Control and Prevention. 1997. *HIV/AIDS Surveillance Report* 9/1: 1–37.

"Central Park Memorial." 1983. *Advocate* July 21: 11.

C-FAR. 1988. "Agenda for October 25, 1988." Document housed in Deborah Gould's personal ACT UP archive.

Chambers, J. A. 1973. "Relating Personality and Biographical Factors to Scientific Creativity." *Psychological Monographs* 78: 7.

Chandler, Alfred D. 1962. *Strategy and Structure: Chapters in the History of the American Industrial Enterprise*. Cambridge: MIT Press.

————. 1977. *The Visible Hand: The Managerial Revolution in American Business*. Cambridge: Harvard University Press.

Chibbaro, Lou, Jr. and Steve Martz. 1983. "Pressure for More Federal AIDS Dollars Is Increasing." *Washington Blade* May 6: 1.

Child, John. 1972. "Organizational Structure, Environment and Performance: The Role of Strategic Choice." *Sociology* 6: 1–22.

Chong, Dennis. 1991. *Collective Action and the Civil Rights Movement*. Chicago: University of Chicago Press.

Christiansen-Ruffman, Linda. 1995. "Women's Conception of the Political: Three Canadian Women's Organizations." In Myra Marx Ferree and Patricia Yancey Martin (eds.), *Feminist Organizations: Harvest of the New Women's Movement*. Philadelphia: Temple University Press.

Chuchryk, Patricia M. 1993. "Subversive Mothers: The Women's Opposition to the Military Regime in Chile." In Marjorie Agosin (ed.), *Surviving Beyond Fear: Women, Children and Human Rights in Latin America*. Fredonia: White Pine Press.

Clemens, Elisabeth S. 1996. "Organizational Form as Frame: Collective Identity and Political Strategy in the American Labor Movement, 1880–1920." In Doug McAdam, John D. McCarthy, and Mayer N. Zald (eds.), *Comparative Perspectives on Social Movements: Political Opportunities, Mobilizing Structures, and Cultural Framings*. Cambridge: Cambridge University Press.

————. 1997. *The People's Lobby: Organizational Innovation and the Rise of Interest Group Politics in the United States, 1890–1925*. Chicago: University of Chicago Press.

Cohen, Michael D., James G. March, and Johan P. Olson. 1972. "Garbage Can Model of Organizational Choice." *Administrative Science Quarterly* 17: 1–25.

Coleman, James. 1990. *Foundations of Social Theory*. Cambridge: Harvard University Press.

Collier, David and James E. Mahon Jr. 1993. "Conceptual 'Stretching' Revisited: Adapting Categories in Comparative Analysis." *American Political Science Review* 87: 845–855.

Collier, George A. with Elizabeth L. Quaratiello. 1994. *Basta! Land and the Zapatista Rebellion in Chiapas*. Oakland, CA: Institute for Food and Development Policy.

Collins, Randall. 1981. "On the Microfoundations of Macrosociology." *American Journal of Sociology* 86: 984–1013.

———. 1995. "Prediction in Macrosociology: The Case of the Soviet Collapse," *American Journal of Sociology* 100: 1552–1593.

Conti, R., T. M. Amabile, and S. Pokkak. 1995. "Problem Solving among Computer Science Students: The Effects of Skill, Evaluation Expectation and Personality on Solution Quality." Paper presented at the Annual Meeting of the Eastern Psychological Association, Boston.

Costain, Anne N. 1992. *Inviting Women's Rebellion: A Political Process Interpretation of the Women's Movement*. Baltimore and London: Johns Hopkins University Press.

Cotton, Paul. 1985. "Marchers Remember Losses to AIDS." *Gay Life* May 30: 1, 5.

Crist, John and John McCarthy. 1996. "If I Had a Hammer: The Changing Methodological Repertoire of Collective Behavior and Social Movement Research." *Mobilization* 1: 87–102.

Crow, Graham. 1989. "The Use of the Concept of 'Strategy' in Recent Sociological Literature." *Sociology* 23:1–24.

Dahrendorf, Ralf. 1958. *Class and Conflict in Industrial Society*. Palo Alto, CA: Stanford University Press.

Damanpour, Fariborz. 1991. "Organizational Innovation: A Meta-analysis of Effects of Determinants and Moderators." *Academy of Management Journal* 34: 555–590.

Damasio, Antonio R. 1994. *Descartes' Error: Emotion, Reason, and the Human Brain*. New York: Avon Books.

D'Andrade, Roy G. 1992. "Schemas and Motivation." In Roy D'Andrade and Claudia Strauss (eds.), *Human Motives and Cultural Models*. New York: Cambridge University Press.

Daniels, Arlene Kaplan. 1987. "Invisible Work." *Social Problems* 34: 403–415.

Davenport, Christian and Marci Eads. 2001. "Cued to Coerce or Coercing Cues? Exploring the Relationship between Dissident Rhetoric and State Repression" *Mobilization* 6: 151–172.

Davis, Joseph E. 2002. "Narrative and Social Movements: The Power of Stories." In Joseph E. Davis (ed.), *Stories of Change: Narrative and Social Movements*. Albany: State University of New York Press.

Deci, E. L. and R. M. Ryan. 1980. "The Empirical Exploration of Intrinsic Motivational Processes," In L. Berkowitz (ed.), *Advances in Experimental Social Psychology*. New York: Academic Press.

———. 1985. *Intrinsic Motivation and Self-Determination in Human Behavior*. New York: Plenum Press.

Deitcher, David. 1995. "Law and Desire." In David Deitcher (ed.), *The Question of Equality: Lesbian and Gay Politics in America Since Stonewall*. New York: Simon & Schuster.

della Porta, Donatella. 1995. *Social Movements, Political Violence and the State: A Comparative Analysis of Italy and Germany*. Cambridge: Cambridge University Press.

———. 1996. "Social Movements and the State: Thoughts on the Policing of Protest." In Doug McAdam, John D. McCarthy, and Mayer N. Zald (eds.), *Comparative Perspectives on Social Movements: Political Opportunities, Mobilizing Structures, and Cultural Framings*. Cambridge: Cambridge University Press.

Diani, Mario. 1996. "Linking Mobilization Frames and Political Opportunities: Insights from Regional Populism in Italy." *American Sociological Review* 61: 1053–1069.

———. 2000. "The Relational Deficit of Ideologically Structured Action." *Mobilization* 5: 17–24.

DiMaggio, Paul. 1997. "Culture and Cognition." *Annual Review of Sociology* 23: 263–287.

DiMaggio, Paul J. and Walter Powell. 1991a. "Introduction." In Paul J. DiMaggio and Walter K. Powell (eds.), *The New Institutionalism in Organizational Analysis*. Chicago: University of Chicago Press.

———. 1991b. "The Iron Cage Revisited: Institutional Isomorphism and Collective Rationality in Organizational Fields." In Paul J. DiMaggio and Walter K. Powell (eds.), *The New Institutionalism in Organizational Analysis*. Chicago: University of Chicago Press.

Dolnick, Edward. 1993. "Deafness as Culture." *The Atlantic Monthly* September: 37–53.

Douglas, Mary. 1986. *How Institutions Think*. Syracuse, NY: Syracuse University Press.

Downey, Gary L. 1986. "Ideology and the Clamshell Identity: Organizational Dilemmas in the Anti-Nuclear Power Movement." *Social Problems* 33: 357–371.

Dudziak, Mary L. 1988. "Desegregation As a Cold War Imperative." *Stanford Law Review* 41: 61–120.

Duncan, R. B. 1973. "Multiple Decision-making Structures in Adapting to Environmental Uncertainty: The Impact on Organizational Effectiveness." *Human Relations* 26: 273–292.

Durkheim, Emile. 1964 [1915]. *Elementary Forms of Religious Life*. New York: Macmillan.

Edwards, Jeff. 2000. Interview with Deborah Gould in Chicago on April 21. Housed in Deborah Gould's personal ACT UP archive.

Eggan, Ferd. 1999. Interview with Deborah Gould in Chicago on October 30. Housed in Deborah Gould's personal ACT UP archive.

Einwohner, Rachel L. 1999. "Gender, Class, and Social Movement Outcomes: Identity and Effectiveness in Two Animal Rights Campaigns." *Gender & Society* 13: 56–76.

270 References

Eisenhardt, Kathy M. and Claudia Bird Schoonhoven. 1990. "Organizational Growth: Linking Founding Team, Strategy, Environment, and Growth among US Semiconductor Ventures, 1978–1988." *Administrative Science Quarterly* 35: 504–529.

Eisinger, Peter K. 1973. "The Conditions of Protest Behavior in American Cities." *American Political Science Review* 67: 11–28.

Ellingson, Stephen. 1995. "Understanding the Dialectic of Discourse and Collective Action: Public Debate and Rioting in Antebellum Cincinnati." *American Journal of Sociology* 101: 100–144.

Elster, Jon. 1989. *Nuts and Bolts for the Social Sciences.* Cambridge: Cambridge University Press.

Emerson, Richard. 1962. "Power-dependence Relations." *American Sociological Review* 27: 31–44.

Emirbayer, Mustafa. 1997. "Manifesto for a Relational Sociology." *American Journal of Sociology* 103: 281–317.

Emirbayer, Mustafa and Jeff Goodwin. 1994. "Network Analysis, Culture, and the Problem of Agency." *American Journal of Sociology* 99: 1411–1454.

———. 1996a. "Symbols, Positions, Objects: Situating 'Culture' within Social Movement Theory." Paper presented at the annual meeting of the American Sociological Association, New York City.

———. 1996b. "Symbols, Positions, Objects: Toward a New Theory of Revolutions and Collective Action." *History and Theory* 35: 358–374.

Emirbayer, Mustafa and Anne Mische. 1998. "What Is Agency?" *American Journal of Sociology* 103: 962–1023.

Epstein, Steven. 1996. *Impure Science: AIDS Activism and the Politics of Knowledge.* Berkeley: University of California Press.

———. 1997. "AIDS Activism and the Retreat from the 'Genocide' Frame." *Social Identities* 3: 415–438.

Erikson, Eric H. 1969. *Gandhi's Truth on the Origins of Militant Nonviolence.* New York: Norton.

Eyerman, Ron and Andrew Jamison. 1991. *Social Movements: A Cognitive Approach.* University Park: Pennsylvania State University Press.

Ewick, Patricia and Susan S. Silbey. 1998. *The Common Place of Law: Stories from Everyday Life.* Chicago: University of Chicago Press.

Fanon, Frantz. 1986. *Black Skins, White Masks.* London: Pluto Press.

Fantasia, Rick. 1988. *Cultures of Solidarity: Consciousness, Action, and Contemporary American Workers.* Berkeley and Los Angeles: University of California Press.

Fendrich, James. 1993. *Ideal Citizens: The Legacy of the Civil Rights Movement.* Albany: State University of New York Press.

Fernandez, Roberto and Doug McAdam. 1988. "Social Networks and Social Movements: Multiorganizational Fields and Recruitment to Mississippi Freedom Summer." *Sociological Forum* 3: 357–382.

Ferree, Myra Marx. 1992. "The Political Context of Rationality: Rational Choice Theory and Resource Mobilization." In Aldon D. Morris and Carol McClurg Mueller (eds.), *Frontiers in Social Movement Theory.* New Haven, CT: Yale University Press.

Ferree, Myra Marx and Beth B. Hess. 1985. *Controversy and Coalition: The New Feminist Movement*. Boston: Twayne Publishers.

Ferree, Myra Marx, William A. Gamson, Jürgen Gerhards, and Dieter Rucht. 2002. *Shaping Abortion Discourse: Parties, Movements and Media in Germany and the United States, 1970–1994*. New York: Cambridge University Press.

Finkelstein, Avram. 1992a. "Activism in Wonderland." *QW* August 2: 48, 70–71.

———. 1992b. "The Other Quilt." *QW* October 25: 10, 22.

———. 1992c. "Furious Burial: The First Political Funeral for an AIDS Activist." *QW* November 15:10.

Finnegan, William. 1997. "The Unwanted." *The New Yorker* December 1: 60–78.

Fiske, Susan. 1981. "Social Cognition and Affect." In John Harvey (ed.), *Cognition, Social Behavior and the Environment*. Hillsdale, NJ: Erlbaum.

Fiske, Susan and Shelly E. Taylor. 1991. *Social Cognition*. New York: McGraw-Hill.

Flacks, Richard. 1988. *Making History*. New York: Columbia University Press.

Foran, John. 1993. "Theories of Revolution Revisited: Toward a Fourth Generation?" *Sociological Theory* 11:1–20.

Foweraker, Joe. 1995. *Theorizing Social Movements*. London: Pluto Press.

Fraser, Nancy. 1989. *Unruly Practices: Power, Discourse, and Gender in Contemporary Social Theory*. Minneapolis: University of Minnesota Press.

Fraser, Nancy and Linda Gordon. 1994. "The Genealogy of *Dependency*: Tracing a Keyword of the US Welfare State." *Signs* 19: 309–336.

Freeman, Jo. 1979. "Resource Mobilization and Strategy: A Model for Analyzing Social Movement Organizations." In Mayer N. Zald and John D. McCarthy (eds.), *The Dynamics of Social Movements: Resource Mobilization, Social Control, and Tactics*. Cambridge, MA: Winthrop.

Freiberg, Peter. 1987. "New York Demonstrators Demand Release of New AIDS Drug." *Advocate* April 28.

Friedland, Roger and Robert Alford. 1991. "Bringing Society Back In." In Walter K. Powell and Paul DiMaggio (eds.), *The New Institutionalism in Organizational Analysis*. Chicago: University of Chicago Press.

Friedman, Debra and Doug McAdam. 1992. "Identity Incentives and Activism: Networks, Choices and the Life of a Social Movement." In Aldon D. Morris and Carol McClurg Mueller (eds.), *Frontiers in Social Movement Theory*. New Haven, CT: Yale University Press.

Gamson, Joshua. 1989. "Silence, Death, and the Invisible Enemy: AIDS Activism and Social Movement Newness." *Social Problems* 16: 351–365.

Gamson, William A. 1975. *The Strategy of Social Protest*. Chicago: Dorsey.

———. 1990. *The Strategy of Social Protest*. Second edition. Belmont, CA: Wadsworth.

———. 1991. "Commitment and Agency in Social Movements." *Sociological Forum* 6: 27–50.

———. 1992. *Talking Politics*. Cambridge: Cambridge University Press.

Gamson, William A. and David Croteau. 1992. "Media Images and the Social Construction of Reality." *Annual Review of Sociology* 18: 373–393.

Gamson, William A., Bruce Fireman, and Steven Rytina. 1982. *Encounters with Unjust Authority*. Homewood, IL: Dorsey.

Gamson, William A. and David S. Meyer. 1996. "Framing Political Opportunity." In Doug McAdam, John D. McCarthy, and Mayer N. Zald (eds.), *Comparative Perspectives on Social Movements: Political Opportunities, Mobilizing Structures, and Cultural Framings*. Cambridge: Cambridge University Press.

Gamson, William and Andre Modigliani. 1989. "Media Discourse and Public Opinion on Nuclear Power." *American Journal of Sociology* 95: 1–37.

Gamson, William and Gadi Wolfsfeld. 1993. "Movements and Media As Interacting Systems." In Russell Dalton (ed.), *Citizens, Protest, and Democracy. Annals of the American Academy of Political and Social Science* vol. 528: 114–125. Newbury Park, CA : Sage.

Gans, Ronald. 1986. "The New Dred Scott." *New York Native* July 28: 14.

Ganz, Marshall. 2000a. "Five Smooth Stones: Strategic Capacity in the Unionization of California Agriculture." Ph.D. dissertation, Department of Sociology, Harvard University.

———. 2000b. "Resources and Resourcefulness: Strategic Capacity in the Unionization of California Agriculture (1959–77)." *American Journal of Sociology* 105: 1003–1062.

Garfinkel, Harold. 1967. *Studies in Ethnomethodology*. Cambridge, MA: Prentice Hall.

Gaventa, John. 1980. *Power and Powerlessness: Quiescence and Rebellion in an Appalachian Valley*. Urbana: University of Illinois Press.

Geertz, Clifford. 1983. "Common Sense As a Cultural System." In Clifford Geertz (ed.), *Local Knowledge*. New York: Basic Books.

Gentner, Dedre. 1989. "Mechanisms of Analogical Learning." In S. Vosiadou and A. Ortony (eds.), *Similarity and Analogical Reasoning*. Cambridge: Cambridge University Press.

Gerlach, Luther P. and Virginia Hine. 1970. *People, Power, Change*. Indianapolis: Bobbs-Merrill.

Gersick, Connie J. 1994. "Pacing Strategic Change: The Case of a New Venture." *Administrative Science Quarterly* 29: 499–518.

Getzels, J. and M. Csikszentmihalyi. 1976. *The Creative Vision: A Longitudinal Study of Problem Finding in Art*. New York: Wiley-Interscience.

Giddens, Anthony. 1984. *The Constitution of Society*. Berkeley and Los Angeles: University of California Press.

Gitlin, Todd. 1980. *The Whole World Is Watching: Mass Media in the Making and Unmaking of the New Left*. Berkeley: University of California Press.

Giugni, Marco G. 1998. "Was It Worth the Effort?: The Outcomes and Consequences of Social Movements." *Annual Review of Sociology* 24: 371–393.

Giugni, Marco, Doug McAdam, and Charles Tilly, eds. 1999. *How Social Movements Matter*. Minneapolis: University of Minnesota Press.

Glenn, Evelyn Nakano. 2000. "Creating a Caring Society." *Contemporary Sociology* 29: 84–94.

———. 2002. *Unequal Freedom: How Race and Gender Shaped American Citizenship and Labor*. Cambridge: Harvard University Press.

Glover, J. A. and F. Sautter. 1977. "Relation of Four Components of Creativity to Risk-taking Preferences." *Psychological Reports* 41: 227–230.

Goffman, Erving. 1974. *Frame Analysis: An Essay on the Organization of Experience.* New York: Harper.

Goldstone, Jack A. 1980a. "The Weakness of Organization: A New Look at Gamson's 'The Strategy of Social Protest'." *American Journal of Sociology* 85: 1017–1042.

———. 1980b. "Theories of Revolution: The Third Generation." *World Politics* 32: 425–453.

———. 1991. *Revolution and Rebellion in the Early Modern World.* Berkeley: University of California Press.

Goldstone, Jack and Charles Tilly. 2001. "Threat (and Opportunity): Popular Action and State Response in the Dynamics of Contentious Action." In Ronald R. Aminzade, Jack A. Goldstone, Doug McAdam, Elizabeth J. Perry, William H. Sewell Jr., Sidney Tarrow, and Charles Tilly (eds.), *Silence and Voice in the Study of Contentious Politics.* Cambridge: Cambridge University Press.

Goodwin, Jeff. 1994. "Toward a New Sociology of Revolutions." *Theory and Society* 23: 731–766.

———. 1997. "The Libidinal Constitution of a High-risk Social Movement: Affectual Ties and Solidarity in the Huk Rebellion." *American Sociological Review* 62: 53–69.

———. 2001. *No Other Way Out: States and Revolutionary Movements, 1945–1991.* Cambridge: Cambridge University Press.

Goodwin, Jeff, ed. Forthcoming. *Opportunistic Protest? Political Opportunities, Social Movements, and Revolutions.*

Goodwin, Jeff and James M. Jasper. 1999. "Caught in a Winding, Snarling Vine: The Structural Bias of Political Process Theory." *Sociological Forum* 14: 27–54.

Goodwin, Jeff, James M. Jasper, and Francesca Polletta. 2000. "Return of the Repressed: The Fall and Rise of Emotions in Social Movement Theory." *Mobilization* 5: 65–84.

———. 2001. "Introduction: Why Emotions Matter." In Jeff Goodwin, James M. Jasper, and Francesca Polletta (eds.), *Passionate Politics: Emotions and Social Movements:* 1–24.

Goodwin, Jeff, James M. Jasper, and Francesca Polletta, eds. 2001. *Passionate Politics: Emotions and Social Movements.* Chicago: University of Chicago Press.

Gordon, S. L. 1989. "Institutional and Impulsive Orientations in Selectively Appropriating Emotions to Self." In David D. Franks and E. Doyle McCarthy (eds.), *The Sociology of Emotions: Original Essays and Research Papers,* 115–136. Greenwich, CT: JAI Press.

Gottlick, Jane. 1999. "From the Ground up: Women's Organizations and Democratization in Russia." In Jill M. Bystydzienski and Joti Sekhon (eds.), *Democratization and Women's Grassroots Movements.* Bloomington: Indiana University Press.

Gould, Deborah. 2000. *Sex, Death, and the Politics of Anger: Emotions and Reason in ACT UP's Fight Against AIDS.* Ph.D. dissertation, University of Chicago.

———. 2001. "Rock the Boat, Don't Rock the Boat, Baby: Ambivalence and the Emergence of Militant AIDS Activism." In Jeff Goodwin, James M. Jasper, and Francesca Polletta (eds.), *Passionate Politics: Emotions and Social Movements.* Chicago: University of Chicago Press.

———. 2002. "Life During Wartime: Emotions and the Development of ACT UP." *Mobilization* 7: 177–200.

Gould, Roger V. 1993. "Collective Action and Network Structure." *American Sociological Review* 58: 182–196.

———. 1995. *Insurgent Identities: Class, Community, and Protest in Paris from 1848 to the Commune.* Chicago: University of Chicago Press.

Granovetter, Mark. 1973. "The Strength of Weak Ties." *American Journal of Sociology* 78: 1360–1380.

Groves, Julian McAllister. 1995. "Learning to Feel: The Neglected Sociology of Social Movements." *The Sociological Review* 43: 435–461.

———. 1997. *Hearts and Minds: The Controversy over Laboratory Animals.* Philadelphia: Temple University Press.

———. 2001. "Animal Rights and the Politics of Emotion: Folk Constructions of Emotion in the Animal Rights Movement." In Jeff Goodwin, James M. Jasper, and Francesca Polletta (eds.), *Passionate Politics: Emotions and Social Movements.* Chicago: University of Chicago Press.

Hackman, J. Richard. 1990. *Groups That Work and Those That Don't: Creation Conditions for Effective Teamwork Groups That Work.* San Francisco: Jossey-Bass.

Hackman, J. Richard and C. G. Morris. 1975. "Group Tasks, Group Interaction Process, and Group Performance Effectiveness: A Review and Proposed Integration." In L. Berkowitz (ed.), *Advances in Experimental Social Psychology.* New York: Academic Press.

Hackman, J. Richard and Greg R. Oldham. 1976. "Motivation Through the Design of Work: Test of the Theory." *Organizational Behavior and Human Performance* 16: 250–279.

Hackman, J. Richard and Richard Walton. 1986. "Leading Groups in Organizations." In Paul Goodman (ed.), *Designing Effective Work Groups.* San Francisco: Jossey-Bass.

Haines, Herbert H. 1988. *Black Radicals and the Civil Rights Mainstream, 1954–1970.* Knoxville: University of Tennessee Press.

Hall, John R. 1992. "The Capital(s) of Cultures: A Nonholistic Approach to Status Situations, Class, Gender, and Ethnicity." In Michéle Lamont and Marcel Fournier (eds.), *Cultivating Differences: Symbolic Boundaries and the Making of Inequality.* Chicago: University of Chicago Press.

Hall, Rodney Bruce. 1997. "Moral Authority as a Power Resource." *International Organizations* 51: 591–622.

Hamel, Gary. 1996. "Strategy As Revolution." *Harvard Business Review* 74: 69–78.

Hamel, Gary and C. K. Prahalad. 1989. "Strategic Intent." *Harvard Business Review* 67: 63–77.

Hannan, Michael T. and John Freeman. 1984. "Structural Inertia and Organizational Change." *American Sociological Review* 49: 149–164.

Hardin, Russell. 1995. *One for All: The Logic of Group Conflict.* Princeton, NJ: Princeton University Press.

Harding, Vincent. 1983. *There Is a River: The Black Struggle for Freedom in America.* New York: Vantage Books.

Hart, Stephen. 1996. "The Cultural Dimensions of Social Movements." *Sociology of Religion* 57: 87–100.

Harter, S. 1978. "Effectance Motivation Reconsidered: Toward a Developmental Model." *Human Development* 21: 34–64

Harvey, Neil. 1995. "Rebellion in Chiapas: Rural Reforms and Popular Struggle." *Third World Quarterly* 16: 39–73.

Hays, Sharon. 1994. "Structure and Agency and the Sticky Problem of Culture." *Theory and Society* 12: 57–72.

Hebb, D. O. 1953. "Drives and the CNS." *Psychological Review* 62: 243–254.

Hechter, Michael. 1995. "Introduction: Reflections on Historical Prophecy in the Social Sciences." *American Journal of Sociology* 100: 1520–1527.

Hirsch, Eric I. 1989. *Urban Revolt: Ethnic Politics in the Nineteenth Century Chicago Labor Movement*. Berkeley and Los Angeles: University of California Press.

Hirschmann, A. O. 1977. *The Passions and the Interests: Political Arguments for Capitalism before Its Triumph*. Princeton, NJ: Princeton University Press.

Hochschild, Arlie Russell. 1979. "Emotion Work, Feeling Rules, and Social Structure." *American Journal of Sociology* 85: 551–575.

———. 1983. *The Managed Heart: Commercialization of Human Feeling*. Berkeley: University of California Press.

———. 1990. "Ideology and Emotion Management: A Perspective and Path for Future Research." In Theodore D. Kemper (ed.), *Research Agendas in the Sociology of Emotions*. Albany: State University of New York Press.

Hochstetler, Kathryn. 1994. *Social Movements in Institutional Politics: Organizing about the Environment in Brazil and Venezuela*. Ph.D. dissertation, Department of Political Science, University of Minnesota.

Hollander, Edwin P. and Lynn R. Offermann. 1990. "Power and Leadership in Organizations: Relationships in Transition." *The American Psychologist* 45: 179–190.

House, Robert J., William D. Spangler, and James Woycke. 1991. "Personality and Charisma in the U.S. Presidency: A Psychological Theory of Leader Effectiveness." *Administrative Science Quarterly* 36: 364–397.

Howell, Jane M. 1990. "Champions of Technological Innovation." *Administrative Science Quarterly* 35: 317–339.

Hunt, Alan. 1990. *Explorations in Law and Society*. New York: Routledge.

Hunt, Lynn. 1984. *Politics, Culture, and Class in the French Revolution*. Berkeley: University of California Press.

———. 1992. *The Family Romance of the French Revolution*. Berkeley: University of California Press.

Hunt, Scott A., Robert D. Benford, and David A. Snow. 1994. "Identity Fields: Framing Processes and the Social Construction of Movement Identities." In Enrique Laraña, Hank Johnston, and Joseph R. Gusfield (eds.), *New Social Movements: From Ideology to Identity*. Philadelphia: Temple University Press.

Huntington, Samuel P. 1968. *Political Order in Changing Societies*. New Haven, CT: Yale University Press.

Hutchins, Edwin. 1991. "The Social Organization of Distributed Cognition." In L. B. Resnick, J. M. Levine, and S. D. Teasley (eds.), *Perspective on Socially Shared Cognition*. Washington, DC: American Psychological Association.

Imig, Douglas R. and David S. Meyer. 1993. "Political Opportunity and Peace and

Justice Advocacy in the 1980s: A Tale of Two Sectors," *Social Science Quarterly* 74: 750–770.

International Labor and Working Class History. 1995. Symposium on "Global Flows of Labor and Capital." 47: 1–23.

Jaggar, Alison. 1989. "Love and Knowledge: Emotion in Feminist Epistemology." *Inquiry* 32: 161–176.

———. 1989. "Love and Knowledge: Emotion in Feminist Epistemology." In Alison M. Jaggar and Susan R. Bordo (ed.), *Gender/Body/Knowledge*. New Brunswick, NJ: Rutgers University Press.

Jamison, Andrew and Ron Eyerman. 1994. *Seeds of the Sixties*. Berkeley: University of California Press.

Jasper, James M. 1990. *Nuclear Politics: Energy and the State in the United States, Sweden, and France*. Princeton, NJ: Princeton University Press.

———. 1997. *The Art of Moral Protest: Culture, Biography, and Creativity in Social Movements*. Chicago: University of Chicago Press.

———. 1998. "The Emotions of Protest: Affective and Reactive Emotions in and around Social Movements." *Sociological Forum* 13: 397–512.

———. Forthcoming. "The North American Movement for Peace in Central America." In Jeff Goodwin (ed.), *Opportunistic Protest? Political Opportunities, Social Movements, and Revolutions*.

Jasper, James M. and Dorothy Nelkin. 1992. *The Animal Rights Crusade: The Growth of a Moral Protest*. New York: Free Press.

Jasper, James M. and Jane Poulsen. 1993. "Fighting Back: Vulnerabilities, Blunders, and Countermobilization by Targets in Three Animal Rights Campaigns." *Sociological Forum* 8: 639–657.

———. 1995. "Recruiting Strangers and Friends: Moral Shocks and Social Networks in Animal Rights and Anti-nuclear Tests." *Social Problems* 42: 493–451.

Jasper, James M. and Michael P. Young. 2002. "The Tricks of Paradigms: Evidence and Assumption in the Structural Truths of Social Movement Research." Unpblished manuscript.

Jenkins, J. Craig and Charles Perrow. 1977. "Insurgency of the Powerless: Farm Workers Movements (1946–1972)." *American Sociological Review* 42: 249–268.

Jenness, Valerie. 1993. *Making It Work: The Prostitutes' Rights Movement in Perspective*. New York: Aldine de Gruyter.

Jepperson, Ronald L. and John W. Meyer. 1991. "The Public Order and the Construction of Formal Organizations." In Walter D. Powell and Paul DiMaggio (eds.), *The New Institutionalism in Organizational Analysis*. Chicago: University of Chicago Press.

Joas, Hans. 1996. *The Creativity of Action*. Chicago: University of Chicago Press.

Johnson, Charles S. 1941. *Growing Up in the Black Belt*. Washington, DC: American Council on Education.

Johnston, Hank and Bert Klandermans, eds. 1995a. *Social Movements and Culture*. Minneapolis: University of Minnesota Press.

———. 1995b. "The Cultural Analysis of Social Movements." In Hank Johnston and Bert Klandermans (eds.), *Social Movements and Culture*. Minneapolis: University of Minnesota Press.

Joppke, Christian. 1993. *Mobilizing Against Nuclear Energy: A Comparison of Germany and the United States.* Berkeley: University of California Press.

Kane, Anne E. 1997. "Theorizing Meaning Construction in Social Movements: Symbolic Structures and Interpretation during the Irish Land War, 1879–1882." *Sociological Theory* 15: 249–276.

Kanter, Rosabeth Moss. 1972. *Commitment and Community: Communes and Utopias in Sociologicasl Perspective.* Cambridge: Harvard University Press.

Kasperson, C. J. 1978. "Scientific Creativity: A Relationship with Information Channels." *Psychological Reports* 42: 691–694.

Katzenstein, Mary Fainsod. 1998. *Faithful and Fearless: Moving Feminist Protest inside the Church and Military.* Princeton, NJ: Princeton University Press.

Keck, Margaret and Katherine Sikkink. 1998. *Activists Beyond Borders: Transnational Advocacy Networks in International Politics.* Ithaca, NY and London: Cornell University Press.

Keller, Evelyn Fox. 1985. *Reflections on Gender and Science.* New Haven, CT: Yale University Press.

Keniston, Kenneth. 1968. *Young Radicals: Notes on Committed Youth.* New York: Harcourt, Brace, Jovanovich.

———. 1973. *Radicals and Militants: An Annotated Bibliography of Empirical Research on Campus Unrest.* Lexington, MA: Lexington Books.

Kimeldorf, Howard. 1988. *Reds or Rackets? The Making of Radical and Conservative Unions on the Waterfront.* Berkeley: University of California Press.

Kimmel, Michael and Abby L. Ferber. 2000. " 'White Men Are This Nation': Right-Wing Militias and the Restoration of Rural American Masculinity." *Rural Sociology* 65: 582–604.

King, Martin Luther, Jr. 1958. *Stride Toward Freedom.* New York: Harper & Row.

Kingdon, John W. 1984. *Agendas, Alternatives, and Public Policies.* Boston: Little, Brown.

———. 1995. *Agendas, Alternatives, and Public Policies.* Second edition. New York: HarperCollins.

Kiser, Edgar and Michael Hechter. 1998. "The Debate on Historical Sociology: Rational Choice Theory and Its Critics." *American Journal of Sociology* 104: 785–816.

Kitschelt, Herbert. 1986. "Political Opportunity Structures and Political Protest: Anti-nuclear Movements in Four Democracies." *British Journal of Political Science* 16: 57–85.

Klandermans, Bert. 1984. "Mobilization and Participation: Social Psychological Expansions of Resource Mobilization Theory." *American Sociological Review* 49: 583–600.

———. 1997a. *The Social Psychology of Protest.* Oxford: Blackwell.

———. 1997b. "Social Movements: Trends and Turns." Paper presented at the annual meeting of the American Sociological Association, Toronto, Ontario.

Klandermans, Bert, Hanspeter Kriesi, and Sidney Tarrow, eds. 1980. *From Structure to Action: Comparing Social Movement Research Across Cultures; International Social Movement Research* vol. 1. Greenwich, CT: JAI Press.

Klandermans, Bert and Dirk Oegema. 1987. "Potentials, Networks, Motivations and Barriers: Steps toward Participation in Social Movements." *American Sociological Review* 52: 519–531.

Klandermans, Bert and Sidney Tarrow. 1988. "Mobilization into Social Movements: Synthesizing European and American Approaches." *International Social Movement Research* 1: 1–38.

Klatch, Rebecca. 1999. *A Generation Divided: The New Left, the New Right, and the 1960s.* Berkeley: University of California Press.

Kluger, Richard. 1976. *Simple Justice.* New York: Knopf.

Knocke, David and James R. Wood. 1981. *Organized for Action: Commitment in Voluntary Associations.* New Brunswick, NJ: Rutgers University Press.

Koopmans, Ruud. 1995. *Democracy from Below: New Social Movements and the Political System in West Germany.* Boulder, CO: Westview Press.

———. 1999. "Political. Opportunity. Some Splitting to Balance the Lumping." *Sociological Forum* 14: 93–105.

Koopmans, Ruud and Hanspeter Kriesi. 1997. "Citoyenneté, Identité Nationale et Mobilisation de l'Extrême Droite. Une Comparaison entre la France, l'Allemagne, les Pays-Bas et la Suisse." In Pierre Birnbaum (ed.), *Sociologie des nationalismes.* Paris: Presses Universitaires de France.

Koopmans, Ruud and Paul Statham. 1999. "Challenging the Lieral Nation State? Postnationalism, Multiculturalism, and the Collective Claims-Making of Migrants and Ethnic Minorities in Britain and Germany." *American Journal of Sociology* 105: 652–696.

Kracher, Jeanne. 2000. Interview with Deborah Gould in Chicago on February 15. Housed in Deborah Gould's personal ACT UP archive.

Krause, Mary Beth. 1994 "The AIDS Memorial Quilt as Cultural Resistance for Gay Communities." *Critical Sociology* 20: 65–80.

Kriesi, Hanspeter. 1996. "The Organizational Structure of New Social Movements in a Political Context." In Doug McAdam, John D. McCarthy, and Mayer N. Zald (eds.), *Comparative Perspectives on Social Movements: Political Opportunities, Mobilizing Structures, and Cultural Framings.* Cambridge: Cambridge University Press.

Kriesi, Hanspeter, Ruud Koopmans, Jan Willem Duyvendak, and Marco G. Giugni. 1995. *New Social Movements in Western Europe: A Comparative Analysis.* Minneapolis: University of Minnesota Press.

Kubik, Jan. 1998. "Institutionalization of Protest during Democratic Consolidation in Central Europe." In David S. Meyer and Sidney Tarrow (eds.), *The Social Movement Society: Contentious Politics for a New Century.* Lanham, MD: Rowman & Littlefield.

Kuhn, Thomas S. 1970. *The Structure of Scientific Revolutions.* Second edition. Chicago: University of Chicago Press.

———. 1977. *The Essential Tension: Selected Studies in Scientific Tradition and Change.* Chicago: University of Chicago Press.

Kuran, Timur. 1995. "The Inevitability of Future Revolutionary Surprises." *American Journal of Sociology* 100: 1528–1551.

Kurzman, Charles. 1994. "A Dynamic View of Resources: Evidence from the Iranian Revolution." *Research in Social Movements, Conflicts and Change* 17: 53–84.

————. 1996. "Structural Opportunity and Perceived Opportunity in Social Move-ment Theory: The Iranian Revolution of 1979." *American Sociological Review* 61: 153–170.

————. 1998. "Organizational Opportunity and Social Movement Mobilization: A Comparative Analysis of Four Religious Social Movements." *Mobilization* 3: 23–49.

————. 2003. "The Qum Protests and the Coming of the Iranian Revolution, 1975 and 1978." *Social Science History* 27: 287–325.

————. Forthcoming. "Political Opportunities and the Iranian Revolution." In Jeff Goodwin (ed.), *Opportunistic Protest? Political Opportunities, Social Movements, and Revolutions.*

Kurtz, Sharon. 2002. *Workplace Justice: Organizing Multi-Identity Movements.* Minne-apolis: University of Minnesota Press.

Laclau, Ernesto and Chantal Mouffe. 1985. *Hegemony and Socialist Strategy.* Lon-don: Verso.

Lakoff, George and Mark Johnson. 1980. "The Metaphorical Structure of the Human Conceptual System." *Cognitive Science* 4: 195–208.

Langer, Ellen. 1978. "Rethinking the Role of Thought in Social Interaction." In W. Ickes, R. Kidd, and J. Harvey (eds.), *New Directions in Attribution Research.* Hills-dale, NJ: Erlbaum.

————. 1989. *Mindfulness.* Reading, MA: Addison-Wesley.

Langer, Ellen and L. Imber. 1979. "When Practice Makes Imperfect: Debilitating Effects of Overlearning." *Journal of Personality and Social Psychology* 37: 2014–2024.

Lasswell, Harold. 1958. *Politics: Who Gets What, When, How.* New York: Meridian Books.

Lawler, Edward and Shane Thye. 1999. "Bringing Emotions into Social Exchange Theory." *Annual Review of Sociology* 25: 217–244.

Lawson, Steven F. 1976. *Black Ballots: Voting Rights in the South, 1944–1969.* New York: Columbia University Press.

Layton, Azza Salama. 1995. *The International Context of the U.S. Civil Rights Move-ment: The Dynamics Between Racial Policies and International Politics, 1941–1960.* Ph.D. dissertation, Department of Government, The University of Texas at Austin.

Levinthal, D. 1997. "Three Faces of Organizational Learning: Wisdom, Inertia, and Discovery." In R. Garud, P. Nayyar, and Z. Shapira (eds.), *Technological Inno-vation: Oversights and Foresights.* Cambridge: Cambridge University Press.

Levi-Strauss, Claude. 1962. *The Savage Mind.* (Translated in 1966.) London: Weiden-feld & Nicolson.

Lewis, Jacqueline and Michael R. Fraser. 1996. "Patches of Grief and Rage: Visitor Responses to the NAMES Project AIDS Memorial Quilt." *Qualitative Sociology* 19: 433–451.

Lichbach, Mark. 1995. *The Rebel's Dilemma.* Ann Arbor: University of Michigan Press.

————. 1997. "Contentious Maps of Contentious Politics." *Mobilization* 1: 87–98.

————. 1998. "Where Have All the Foils Gone? Competing Theories of Conten-

tious Politics and the Civil Rights Movement." In Anne N. Costain and Andrew
S. McFarland (eds.), *Social Movements and American Political Institutions*. Boulder,
CO: Rowman & Littlefield.

Lichterman, Paul. 1996. *The Search for Political Community*. New York: Cambridge
University Press.

Lieberson, Stanley. 1980. *A Piece of the Pie: Black and White Immigrants since 1890*.
New York: Free Press.

Lipset, Seymour Martin. 1963. *Political Man*. New York: Anchor.

Lipsitz, George. 1995. *Life in the Struggle: Ivory Perry and the Culture of Opposition*.
Philadelphia: Temple University Press.

Lipsky, Michael. 1968. "Protest As a Political Resource." *American Political Science
Review* 62: 1144–1158.

———. 1970. *Protest in City Politics*. Chicago: Rand-McNally.

Lofland, John. 1993. "Theory-bashing and Answer-improving in the Study of
Social Movements." *American Sociologist* 24: 37–58.

———. 1996. *Social Movement Organizations*. New York: Walter deGruyter.

Luker, Kristin. 1984. *Abortion and the Politics of Motherhood*. Berkeley: University of
California Press.

Lukes, Stephen. 1974. *Power: A Radical View*. New York: Macmillan.

Lutz, Catherine. 1986. "Emotion, Thought, and Estrangement: Emotion as a Cultural Category." *Cultural Anthropology* 1: 287–309.

———. 1988. *Unnatural Emotions: Everyday Sentiments on a Micronesian Atoll and
Their Challenge to Western Theory*. Chicago: University of Chicago Press.

MacKinnon, D. W. 1965. "Personality and the Realization of Creative Potential."
American Psychologist 20: 273–281.

Mann, Michael. 1986. *The Sources of Social Power* vol. 1, *A History of Power from the
Beginning to A.D. 1760*. New York: Cambridge University Press.

Mansbridge, Jane. 1986. *Why We Lost the ERA*. Chicago: University of Chicago
Press.

March, James and Johan Olsen. 1976. *Ambiguity and Choice in Organizations*. Ber-
gen, Norway: Universeitetsforiaget.

Marx, Anthony W. 1992. *Lessons of Struggle: South African Internal Opposition, 1960–
1990*. New York: Oxford University Press.

———. 1998. *Making Race and Nation: A Comparison of the United States, South
Africa, and Brazil*. New York: Cambridge University Press.

Marx, Gary T., ed. 1971. *Racial Conflict*. Boston: Little, Brown.

Marx, Karl. 1978 [1845–1846]. "The German Ideology." In Robert C. Tucker (ed.),
The Marx-Engels Reader. Second edition. New York: W. W. Norton.

Mays, Benjamin and Joseph W. Nicholson. 1969. *The Negro's Church*. New York:
Arno Press and The New York Times.

Mazón, Mauricio. 1984. *The Zoot-Suit Riots: The Psychology of Symbolic Annihilation*.
Austin: University of Texas.

McAdam, Doug. 1982. *Political Process and the Development of Black Insurgency,
1930–1970*. Chicago: University of Chicago Press.

———. 1983. "Tactical Innovation and the Pace of Insurgency." *American Sociological Review* 48: 735–754.

———. 1986. "Recruitment to High-Risk Activism: The Case of Freedom Summer." *American Journal of Sociology* 92: 64–90.

———. 1988a. *Freedom Summer.* New York: Oxford University Press.

———. 1988b. "Micromobilization Contexts and Recruitment to Activism." *International Social Movement Research* 1: 125–154.

———. 1994. "Culture and Social Movements." In Enrique Laraña, Hank Johnston, and Joseph R. Gusfield (eds.), *New Social Movements: From Ideology to Identity.* Philadelphia: Temple University Press.

———. 1995. "'Initiator' and 'Spin-off' Movements: Diffusion Processes in Political Cycles." In Mark Traugott (ed.), *Repertoires and Cycles of Collective Action.* Durham, NC: Duke University Press.

———. 1996a. "Conceptual Origins, Current Problems, Future Directions." In Doug McAdam, John D. McCarthy, and Mayer N. Zald (eds.), *Comparative Perspectives on Social Movements: Political Opportunities, Mobilizing Structures, and Cultural Framings.* Cambridge: Cambridge University Press.

———. 1996b. "The Framing Function of Movement Tactics: Strategic Dramaturgy in the American Civil Rights Movement." In Doug McAdam, John D. McCarthy, and Mayer N. Zald (eds.), *Comparative Perspectives on Social Movements: Political Opportunities, Mobilizing Structures, and Cultural Framings.* Cambridge: Cambridge University Press.

———. 1998a. "The Future of Social Movements." In Marco G. Giugni, Doug McAdam, and Charles Tilly (eds.), *From Contention to Democracy.* Lanham, MD: Rowman & Littlefield.

———. 1998b. "On the International Origins of Domestic Political Opportunities." In Anne N. Costain and Andrew S. McFarland (eds.), *Social Movements and American Political Institutions.* Boulder, CO: Rowman & Littlefield.

———. 1999. *Political Process and the Development of Black Insurgency, 1930–1970.* Second edition. Chicago: University of Chicago Press.

McAdam, Doug, John D. McCarthy, and Mayer N. Zald. 1988. "Social Movements." In Neil Smelser (ed.), *Handbook of Sociology.* Beverly Hills, CA: Sage.

McAdam, Doug, John D. McCarthy, and Mayer N. Zald, eds. 1996a. *Comparative Perspectives on Social Movements: Political Opportunities, Mobilizing Structures, and Cultural Framings.* Cambridge: Cambridge University Press.

———. 1996b. "Introduction: Opportunities, Mobilizing Structures, and Framing Processes—Toward a Synthetic, Comparative Perspective on Social Movements." In Doug McAdam, John D. McCarthy, and Mayer N. Zald (eds.), *Comparative Perspectives Social Movements: Political Opportunities, Mobilizing Structures, and Cultural Framings.* Cambridge: Cambridge University Press.

McAdam, Doug and Ronnelle Paulsen. 1993. "Specifying the Relationship between Social Ties and Activism." *American Journal of Sociology* 99: 640–667.

McAdam, Doug and William H. Sewell Jr. 2001. "It's About Time: Temporality in the Study of Social Movements and Revolutions." In Ron Aminzade, Jack Goldstone, Doug McAdam, Elizabeth Perry, William Sewell, Sidney Tarrow, and Charles Tilly (eds.), *Silence and Voice in the Study of Contentious Politics.* Cambridge: Cambridge University Press.

McAdam, Doug, Sidney Tarrow, and Charles Tilly. 1996. "To Map Contentious Politics." *Mobilization* 1: 17–34.

————. 1997. "Toward an Integrated Perspective on Social Movements and Revolutions." In Mark Irving Lichbach and Alan Zuckerman (eds.), *Comparative Politics: Rationality, Culture, and Structure.* Cambridge: Cambridge University Press.

————. 2001. *Dynamics of Contention.* Cambridge: Cambridge University Press.

McCann, Michael W. 1994. *Rights at Work: Pay Equity Reform and the Politics of Legal Mobilization.* Chicago: University of Chicago Press.

McCarthy, John D. 1996. "Constraints and Opportunities in Adopting, Adapting, and Inventing." In Doug McAdam, John D. McCarthy, and Mayer N. Zald (eds.), *Comparative Perspectives on Social Movements: Political Opportunities, Mobilizing Structures, and Cultural Framings.* Cambridge: Cambridge University Press.

————. 1997. "The Globalization of Social Movement Theory." In Jackie Smith, Charles Chatfield, and Ron Pagnucco (eds.), *Transnational Social Movements and Global Politics: Solidarity Beyond the State.* Syracuse, NY: Syracuse University Press.

McCarthy, John D., David W. Britt, and Mark Wolfson. 1991. "The Institutional Channeling of Social Movements in the Modern State." *Research in Social Movements, Conflict and Change* vol. 13: 45–76. Greenwich, CT: JAI Press.

McCarthy, John D. and Clark McPhail. 1998. "The Institutionalization of Protest in the United States." In David S. Meyer and Sidney Tarrow (eds.), *The Social Movement Society: Contentious Politics for a New Century.* Lanham, MD: Rowman & Littlefield.

McCarthy, John D., Clark McPhail, and John Crist. 1995. "The Emergence and Diffusion of Public Order Management Systems: Protest Cycles and Policy Response." Paper presented at the conference on Cross-national Influences and Social Movement Research, Mnt.-Pelérin, Switzerland.

McCarthy, John D., Clark McPhail, and Jackie Smith. 1996. "Images of Protest: Dimensions of Selection Bias in Media Coverage of Washington Demonstrations, 1982 and 1991." *American Sociological Review* 61: 478–499.

McCarthy, John D. and Mayer N. Zald. 1977. "Resource Mobilization and Social Movements: A Partial Theory." *American Journal of Sociology* 8: 1212–1241.

McCleod, P. L. 1992. "The Effects of Ethnic Diversity on Idea Generation in Small Groups." In *Best Paper Proceedings.* Las Vegas, NV: Academy of Management Convention.

McCullough, David. 1992. *Truman.* New York: Simon & Schuster.

McDaniel, Tim. 1991. *Autocracy, Modernization, and Revolution in Russia and Iran.* Princeton, NJ: Princeton University Press.

McGrath, J. 1984. *Groups: Interaction and Performance.* Englewood Cliffs, NJ: Prentice Hall.

McMillan, Bill. 2000. Interview with Deborah Gould in Chicago on August 23. Housed in Deborah Gould's personal ACT UP archive.

McMillen, Neil. 1971. *The Citizens' Council, Organized Resistance to the Second Reconstruction, 1954–1964.* Urbana: University of Illinois Press.

Meier, August and Elliott Rudwick. 1973. *CORE.* New York: Oxford University Press.

Melucci, Alberto. 1985. "The Symbolic Challenge of Contemporary Movements." *Social Research* 52: 789–816.

———. 1988. "Getting Involved: Identity and Mobilization in Social Movements." In Bert Klandermans, Hanspeter Kriesi, and Sidney Tarrow (eds.), *From Structure to Action: Comparing Social Movement Research Across Cultures; International Social Movement Research* vol. 1: 329–348. Greenwich. CT: JAI Press.

———. 1989. *Nomads of the Present.* Philadelphia: Temple University Press.

———. 1996. *Challenging Codes: Collective Action in the Information Age.* Cambridge: Cambridge University Press.

Merry, Sally Engle. 1990. *Getting Justice and Getting Even: Legal Consciousness Among Working Class Americans.* Chicago: University of Chicago Press.

Merton, Robert K. 1968. *Social Theory and Social Structure.* Third edition. New York: Free Press.

———. 1996. "Opportunity Structure." In Piotr Sztompka (ed.), *On Social Structure and Science.* Chicago: University of Chicago Press.

Meyer, David S. 1990. *A Winter of Discontent: The Nuclear Freeze and American Politics.* New York: Praeger.

———. 1993. "Protest Cycles and Political Process." *Political Research Quarterly* 46: 451–479.

———. 1995. "Framing National Security: Elite Public Discourse on Nuclear Weapons during the Cold War." *Political Communication* 12: 173–192.

Meyer, David S. and Debra C. Minkoff. 1997. "Operationalizing Political Opportunity." Paper presented at the annual Meeting of the American Sociological Association, Toronto, Ontario.

Meyer, David S. and Suzanne Staggenborg. 1996. "Movements, Countermovements, and the Structure of Political Opportunity." *American Journal of Sociology* 101: 1628–1660.

———. 1998. "Countermovement Dynamics in Federal Systems: A Comparison of Abortion Politics in Canada and the United States." *Research in Political Sociology* 8: 209–240.

Meyer, David S. and Sidney Tarrow. 1998. "A Movement Society: Contentious Politics for a New Century." In David S. Meyer and Sidney Tarrow (eds.), *The Social Movement Society: Contentious Politics for a New Century.* Lanham, MD: Rowman & Littlefield.

Meyer, David S. and Nancy Whittier. 1994. "Social Movement Spillover." *Social Problems* 41: 277–298.

Meyer, Davis S., Nancy Whittier, and Belinda Robnett, eds. 2002. *Social Movements: Identity, Culture, and the State.* New York: Oxford University Press.

Meyer, John P. and Natalie J. Allen. 1997. *Commitment in the Workplace: Theory, Research and Application.* Thousand Oaks, CA: Sage.

Michels, Robert. 1962 [1911]. *Political Parties: A Sociological Study of Oligarchical Tendencies of Modern Democracy.* New York: Collier.

Miethe, Ingrid. 1999. "From 'Mother of the Revolution' to 'Fathers of Unification': Concepts of Politics among Women Activists Following German Unification." *Social Politics* 6: 1–22.

Milgram, Stanley, 1974. *Obedience to Authority.* New York: Harper & Row.

Miller, Tim. 1999. Interview with Deborah Gould in San Francisco on July 13. Housed in Deborah Gould's personal ACT UP archive.

Mills, C. Wright. 1959. *The Sociological Imagination*. London: Oxford University Press.

Minkoff, Debra. 2001. "Social Movement Politics and Organization." In Judith R. Blau (ed.), *The Blackwell Companion to Sociology*. Malden, MA: Blackwell Publishers.

Minkoff, Debra C. 1997. "The Sequencing of Social Movements." *American Sociological Review* 62: 779–799.

Minow, Martha. 1990. *Making All the Difference: Inclusion, Exclusion and American Law*. Ithaca, NY: Cornell University Press.

Mintzberg, Henry. 1987. "Crafting Strategy." *Harvard Business Review* 65: 66–76.

———. 1994. "The Rise and Fall of Strategic Planning." *Harvard Business Review* 72: 107–115.

Mintzberg, Henry and Alexandra McHugh. 1985. "Strategy Formation in an Adhocracy." *Administrative Science Quarterly* 30: 160–198.

Molotch, Harvey. 1979. "Media and Movements." In Mayer N. Zald and John McCarthy (eds.), *The Dynamics of Social Movements*. Cambridge, MA: Winthrop.

Moore, Kelly. 1996. "Organizing Integrity: American Science and the Creation of Public Interest Science Organizations, 1955–1975." *American Journal of Sociology* 101: 1592–1627.

Moore, Mark H. 1995. *Creating Public Value: Strategic Management in Government*. Cambridge: Harvard University Press.

Morgen, Sandra. 1983. "The Politics of 'Feeling': Beyond the Dialectic of Thought and Action." *Women's Studies* 10: 203–223.

———. 1995. "'It Was the Best of Times, It Was the Worst of Times': Emotional Discourse in the Work Cultures of Feminist Health Clinics." In Myra Marx Ferree and Patricia Yancey Martin (eds.), *Feminist Organizations: Harvest of the New Women's Movement*. Philadelphia: Temple University Press.

Morris, Aldon. 1981. "Black Southern Sit-in Movement: An Analysis of Internal Organization" *American Sociological Review* 46: 744–767.

———. 1984. *The Origins of the Civil Rights Movement: Black Communities Organizing for Change*. New York: Free Press.

———. 1992. "Political Consciousness and Collective Action." In Aldon D. Morris and Carol McClurg Mueller (eds.), *Frontiers in Social Movement Theory*. New Haven, CT: Yale University Press.

———. 1993a. "Centuries of Black Protest: Its Significance for America and the World." In Herbert Hill and James E. Jones (eds.), *Race in America*. Madison: University of Wisconsin Press.

———. 1993b. "Birmingham Confrontation Reconsidered: An Analysis of the Dynamics and Tactics of Mobilization." *American Sociological Review* 58: 621–636.

———. 1999. "A Retrospective on the Civil Rights Movement: Political and Intellectual Landmarks." *Annual Review of Sociology* 25: 517–539.

Morris, Aldon and Cedric Herring. 1987. "Theory and Research in Social Movements: A Critical Review." *Annual Review of Political Science* 2: 137–198.

Morris, Aldon D. and Carol McClurg Mueller, eds. 1992. *Frontiers in Social Movement Theory*. New Haven, CT: Yale University Press.

Morris, Aldon and Suzanne Staggenborg. 2002. "Leadership in Social Movements." In David Snow, Sarah Soule, and Hanspeter Kriesi (eds.), *Blackwell Companion to Social Movements*. Boston: Blackwell Publishers.

Morris, Sidney. 1986. "Gay Vanishing Act." *New York Native* August 18: 15.

Morton, Lucie T. 1985. *Winegrowing in Eastern America: An Illustrated Guide to Viniculture East of the Rockies*. Ithaca, NY: Cornell University Press.

Moscovici, Serge. 1984. "The Phenomenon of Social Representations." In Serge Moscovici and R. M. Moscovici-Farr (eds.), *Social Representation*. New York: Cambridge University Press.

Mullins, Michael G., Alain Bouquet, and Larry E. Williams. 1992. *Biology of the Grapevine*. Cambridge: Cambridge University Press.

Myrdal, Gunner. 1944. *An American Dilemma*. New York: Harper & Row.

———. 1970. "America Again at the Crossroads." In Richard P. Young (ed.), *Roots of Rebellion: The Evolution of Black Politics and Protest Since World War II*. New York: Harper & Row.

Naples, Nancy. 1998. "Women's Community Activism: Exploring the Dynamics of Politicization and Diversity." In Nancy Naples (ed.), *Community Activism and Feminist Politics: Organizing across Race, Class, and Gender*. New York: Routledge.

Neidhardt, Friedhelm and Dieter Rucht. 1993. "Auf dem Weg in die Bewegungsgesellschaft? Uber dei Stabilisierbarkeit Sozialer Bewegungen." *Sozialer Welt* 44: 305–326.

Nemeth, Charlan Jeanne. 1986. "Differential Contributions of Majority and Minority Influences." *Psychological Review* 93: 22–32.

Nemeth, Charlan Jeanne and B. M. Staw. 1989. "The Tradeoffs of Social Control and Innovation in Groups and Organizations." In L. Berkowitz (ed.), *Advances in Experimental Social Psychology* vol. 22: 722–730. New York: Academic Press.

Noonan, Rita K. 1995. "Women against the State: Political Opportunities and Collective Action Frames in Chile's Transition to Democracy." *Sociological Forum* 10: 81–111.

North, Douglas C. 1990. *Institutions, Institutional Change and Economic Performance*. New York: Cambridge University Press.

Oberschall, Anthony. 1973. *Social Conflict and Social Movements*. Englewood Cliffs, NJ: Prentice Hall.

———. 1996. "Opportunities and Framing in the Eastern European Revolts of 1989." In Doug McAdam, John D. McCarthy, and Mayer N. Zald (eds.), *Comparative Perspectives on Social Movements: Political Opportunities, Mobilizing Structures, and Cultural Framings*. Cambridge: Cambridge University Press.

Oboler, Suzanne. 1995. *Ethnic Labels, Latino Lives*. Minneapolis: University of Minnesota Press.

O'Donnell, Guillermo and Philippe Schmitter. 1986. "Tentative Conclusions about Uncertain Democracies." In Guillermo O'Donnell, Philippe Schmitter, and Laurence Whitehead (eds), *Transitions from Authoritarian Rule*. Baltimore: John Hopkins University Press.

Offe, Claus. 1985. "New Social Movements: Challenging the Boundaries of Institutional Politics." *Social Research* 52: 817–868.

Olick, Jeffrey and Daniel Levy. 1997. "Collective Memory and Cultural Constraint: Holocaust Myth and Rationality in West German Politics." *American Sociological Review* 62: 921–936.

Oliver, Christine. 1988. "The Collective Strategy Framework: An Application to Competing Predictions of Isomorphism." *Administrative Science Quarterly* 33: 543–561.

Oliver, Pamela. 1989. "Bringing the Crowd Back." In: The Non-organizational Elements of Social Movements." *Research in Social Movements, Conflict and Change* vol. 11: 1–30. Greenwich, CT: JAI Press.

Oliver, Pamela E. and Hank Johnston. 2000. "What a Good Idea! Ideologies and Frames in Social Movement Research." *Mobilization* 5: 37–54.

Oliver, Pamela E. and Gerald Marwell. 1992. "Mobilizing Technologies for Collective Action." In Aldon D. Morris and Carol McClurg Mueller (eds.), *Frontiers in Social Movement Theory*. New Haven, CT: Yale University Press.

Oliver, Pamela E. and Daniel J. Myers. 1999. "How Events Enter the Public Sphere: Conflict, Location, and Sponsorship in Local Newspaper Coverage of Public Events." *American Journal of Sociology* 105: 38–87.

Olzak, Susan. 1992. *The Dynamics of Ethnic Competition and Conflict*. Stanford, CA: Stanford University Press.

Opp, Karl-Dieter. 1989. *The Rationality of Political Protest: A Comparative Analysis of Rational Choice Theory*. Boulder, CO: Westview Press.

Orum, Anthony M. 1972. *Black Students in Protest*. Washington, DC: American Sociological Association.

Osborn, A. 1963. *Applied Imagination: Principles and Procedures of Creative Thinking*. New York: Scribner.

Paris, Peter J. 1985. *The Social Teaching of the Black Churches*. Philadelphia: Fortress Press.

Parsons, Talcott. 1967. *Sociological Theory and Modern Society*. New York: Free Press.

Patten, Mary. 1993. Interview with Kate Black on July 5. Housed at the Lesbian Herstory Archives, Brooklyn, New York.

Payne, Charles. 1995. *I've Got the Light of Freedom: The Organizing Tradition and the Mississippi Freedom Struggle*. Berkeley: University of California Press.

Perrow, Charles. 1979. "The Sixties Observed." In John D. McCarthy and Mayer N. Zald (eds.), *The Dynamics of Social Movements*. Cambridge, MA: Winthrop.

———. 1986. *Complex Organizations: A Critical Essay*. New York: McGraw-Hill.

Peterson, Jordan. 1999. *Maps of Meaning: The Architecture of Belief*. New York: Routledge.

Pfeffer, Jeffrey and Gerald Salancik. 1978. *The External Control of Organizations: A Resource Dependence Perspective*. New York: Harper & Row.

Pillai, Rajandini. 1996. "Crisis and the Emergence of Charismatic Leadership in Groups: An Experimental Investigation." *Journal of Applied Social Psychology* 26: 543–563.

Piore, Michael. 1995. *Beyond Individualism*. Cambridge: Harvard University Press.

Piven, Frances Fox and Richard A. Cloward. 1971. *Regulating the Poor: The Functions of Public Welfare*. New York: Vintage.

———. 1977. *Poor People's Movements: Why They Succeed, How They Fail*. New York: Vintage.

————. 1992. "Normalizing Collective Protest." In Aldon D. Morris and Carol McClurg Mueller (eds.), *Frontiers in Social Movement Theory.* New Haven, CT: Yale University Press.

Plummer, Brenda Gayle. 1996. *Rising Wind: Black Americans and U.S. Foreign Affairs, 1935–1960.* Chapel Hill: University of North Carolina Press.

Polletta, Francesca. 1997. "Culture and Its Discontents: Recent Theorizing on the Cultural Dimensions of Protest." *Sociological Inquiry* 67: 431–450.

————. 1999a. "Free Spaces in Collective Action." *Theory and Society* 28: 1–38.

————. 1999b. "Snarls, Quacks and Quarrels: Culture and Structure in Political Process Theory." *Sociological Forum* 14: 63–70.

————. 2000. "The Structural Context of Novel Rights Claims: Southern Civil Rights Organizing, 1961–1966." *Law & Society Review* 24: 367–406.

————. 2002. *Freedom Is an Endless Meeting: Democracy in American Social Movements.* Chicago: University of Chicago Press.

Porter, Michael E. 1996. "Making Strategy." *Harvard Business Review* 74: 61–77.

Powell, Walter W. 1988. "Institutional Effects on Organizational Structure and Performance." In Lynne G. Zucker (ed.), *Institutional Patterns and Organizations.* Cambridge, MA: Ballinger.

Powell, Walter W. and Paul J. DiMaggio, eds. 1991. *The New Institutionalism in Organizational Analysis.* Chicago: University of Chicago Press.

Pratto, Felicia. 1999. "The Puzzle of Continuing Group Inequality: Piecing Together Psychological, Social and Cultural Forces in Social Dominance Theory." In M. P. Zanna (ed.), *Advances in Experimental Social Psychology* vol. 31: 192–263. San Diego: Academic Press.

Putnam, Robert. 1993. *Making Democracy Work.* Princeton, NJ: Princeton University Press.

Rafsky, Robert. 1992. "Ashes." *QW* October 25: 11, 22–23.

Rasler, Karen. 1996. "Concessions, Repression, and Political Protest in the Iranian Revolution." *American Sociological Review* 61: 132–152.

Ray, Raka and A. C. Korteweg. 1999. Women's Movements in the Third World: Identity, Mobilization and Autonomy." *Annual Review of Sociology* 25: 47–71.

Reddy, William M. 1997. "Against Constructionism: The Historical Ethnography of Emotions." *Current Anthropology* 38: 327–351.

————. 2000. "Sentimentalism and Its Erasure: The Role of Emotions in the Era of the French Revolution." *Journal of Modern History* 72: 109–152.

Rickards, T. and B. L. Freedman. 1978. "Procedures for Managers in Idea-deficient Situations: Examination of Brainstorming Approaches." *Journal of Management Studies* 15: 43–55.

Ricketts, Wendell. 1995. "Review: Political Funerals." *Bay Area Reporter* June 15.

Ringmar, Erik. 1996. *Identity, Interest and Action.* Cambridge: Cambridge University Press.

Rist, Darrell Yates. 1987. "The Top Gay Stories of 1986." *New York Native* January 5: 11–16.

Roberts, Kenneth M. 1997. "Beyond Romanticism: Social Movements and the Study of Political Change in Latin America." *Latin American Research Review* 32: 137–151.

Robnett, Belinda. 1996. "African-American Women in the Civil Rights Movement, 1954–65." *American Journal of Sociology* 101: 1661–1693.

———. 1997. *How Long? How Long? African-American Women in the Struggle for Civil Rights*. New York: Oxford University Press.

Rochon, Thomas. 1998. *Culture Moves: Ideas, Activism, and Changing Values*. Princeton, NJ: Princeton University Press.

Rogers, Everett. 1995. *Diffusion of Innovations*. New York: Free Press.

Rosaldo, Michelle Z. 1984. "Toward an Anthropology of Self and Feeling." In Richard A. Shweder and Robert A. Levine (eds.), *Culture Theory: Essays on Mind, Self, and Emotion*. Cambridge: Cambridge University Press.

Rosaldo, Renato. 1989. *Culture and Truth: The Remaking of Social Analysis*. Boston: Beacon Press.

Rose, Tricia. 1994. *Black Noise: Rap Music and Black Culture in Contemporary America*. Hanover, NH: University Press of New England.

Rosenberg, Gerald N. 1991. *The Hollow Hope*. Chicago: University of Chicago Press.

Rosenthal, Naomi, Meryl Fingrutd, Michele Ethier, Roberta Karant, and David McDonald. 1985. "Social Movements and Network Analysis: A Case Study of Nineteenth-Century Women's Reform in New York State." *American Journal of Sociology* 90: 1022–1055.

Ross, Robert J. 1983. "Generational Change and Primary Groups in a Social Movement." In Jo Freeman (ed.), *Social Movements of the Sixties and Seventies*. New York: Longman.

Rossinow, Doug. 1998. *The Politics of Authenticity*. New York: Columbia University Press.

Rucht, Dieter. 1996. "The Impact of National Contexts on Social Movement Structures: A Cross-movement and Cross-national Comparison." In Doug McAdam, John D. McCarthy, and Mayer N. Zald (eds.), *Comparative Perspectives on Social Movements: Political Opportunities, Mobilizing Structures, and Cultural Framings*. Cambridge: Cambridge University Press.

Rule, James and Charles Tilly. 1975. "Political Process in Revolutionary France, 1830–1832." In John M. Merriman (ed.), *1830 in France*. New York: New Viewpoints.

Rupp, Leila and Verta Taylor. 1987. *Survival in the Doldrums: American Women's Rights Movement, 1945 to the 1960s*. New York: Oxford University Press.

Ruscio, J., D. Whitney, and T. M. Amabile. 1995. *How Do Motivation and Task Behaviors Affect Creativity? An Investigation in Three Domains*. Waltham, MA: Brandeis University.

Ryan, Charlotte. 1991. *Prime Time Activism: Media Strategies for Grassroots Organizing*. Boston: South End Press.

Salancik, G. R. and J. Pfeffer. 1977. "Who Gets Power—and How They Hold On to It: A Strategic Contingency Model of Power." *Organizational Dynamics* 2: 2–21.

Sartori, Giovanni. 1970. "Concept Misinformation in Comparative Politics." *American Political Science Review* 64: 1033–1053.

Sawyers, Traci M. and David S. Meyer. 1999. "Missed Opportunities: Social Movement Abeyance and Public Policy." *Social Problems* 46: 187–206.

Scheff, Thomas J. 1994a. "Emotions and Identity: A Theory of Ethnic National-ism." In Craig Calhoun (ed.), *Social Theory and the Politics of Identity*. Oxford: Blackwell.

———. 1994b. *Bloody Revenge: Emotions, Nationalism, War.* Boulder, CO: Westview Press.

Schelling, Thomas C. 1960. *The Strategy of Conflict.* Cambridge: Harvard University Press.

Schirmer, Jennifer. 1993. "'Those Who Die for Life Cannot Be Called Dead': Women and Human Rights Protests in Latin America." In Marjorie Agosin (ed.), *Surviving Beyond Fear: Women, Children and Human Rights in Latin America*. Fredonia, NY: White Pine Press.

———. 1994. "The Claiming of Space and the Body Politic within National-Secur-ity States: The Plaza de Mayo Madres and the Greenham Common Women." In Jonathan Boyarin (ed.), *Remapping Memory: The Politics of TimeSpace*. Minneapo-lis: University of Minnesota Press.

Schlozman, Kay Lehman and John T. Tierney. 1986. *Organized Interests and Ameri-can Democracy.* New York: Harper & Row.

Schneider, Cathy Lisa. 1995. *Shantytown Protest in Pinochet's Chile.* Philadelphia: Temple University Press.

Schneider, Elizabeth. 1986. "The Dialectic of Rights and Politics: Perspectives from the Women's Rights Movement." *New York University Law Review* 61: 589–652.

Schock, Kurt. 1996. "A Conjunctural Model of Political Conflict: The Impact of the Relationship between Economic Inequality and Violent Political Conflict." *Journal of Conflict Resolution* 40: 98–133.

Schwartz, Michael. 1976. *Radical Protest and Social Structure: The Southern Farmers' Alliance and Cotton Tenancy, 1880–1890.* New York: Academic Press.

Schwarz, Norbert. 1998. "Warmer and More Social: Recent Developments in Cog-nitive Social Psychology." *Annual Review of Sociology* 24: 239–264.

Scott, James C. 1985. *Weapons of the Weak.* New Haven, CT: Yale University Press.

———. 1990. *Domination and the Arts of Resistance.* New Haven, CT: Yale Univer-sity Press.

Scott, Joan. 1988. "Deconstructing Equality vs. Difference." *Feminist Studies* 14: 33–50.

Senge, Peter. 1990. *The Fifth Discipline: The Art and Practice of the Learning Organiza-tion.* New York: Doubleday.

Sewell, William H., Jr. 1990. "Collective Violence and Collective Loyalties in France: Why the French Revolution Made a Difference." *Politics and Society* 18: 527–552.

———. 1992. "A Theory of Structure: Duality, Agency, and Transformation." *American Journal of Sociology* 98: 1–29.

———. 1996a. "Historical Events as Transformations of Structures: Inventing Rev-olution at the Bastille." *Theory and Society* 25: 841–881.

———. 1996b. "Three Temporalities: Toward an Eventful Sociology." In Terrence J. McDonald (ed.), *The Historic Turn in the Human Sciences*. Ann Arbor: Univer-sity of Michigan Press.

Shepard, Benjamin Heim. 1997. *White Nights and Ascending Shadows: An Oral His-tory of the San Francisco AIDS Epidemic.* London and Washington, DC: Cassell.

Sidanius, Jim and Felicia Pratto. 1999. *Social Dominance: An Intergroup Theory of Social Hierarchy and Oppression.* New York: Cambridge University Press.

Sieple, Frank. 1999. Interview with Deborah Gould in San Francisco on July 13. Housed in Deborah Gould's personal ACT UP archive.

Simonton, D. K. 1988. "Creativity, Leadership and Chance." In R. J. Sternberg (ed.), *The Nature of Creativity: Contemporary Psychological Perspective.* Cambridge: Cambridge University Press.

Skocpol, Theda. 1979. *States and Social Revolutions.* Cambridge: Cambridge University Press.

———. 1984. "Emerging Agendas and Recurrent Strategies in Historical Sociology." In Theda Skocpol (ed.), *Vision and Method in Historical Sociology.* New York: Cambridge University Press.

———. 1985. "Bringing the State Back In: Strategies and Analysis in Current Research." In Peter Evans, Dietrich Rueschemeyer, and Theda Skocpol (eds.), *Bringing the State Back In.* New York: Cambridge University Press.

Skrentny, John David. 1998. "The Effect of the Cold War on African-American Civil Rights: America and the World Audience, 1945–1968." *Theory and Society* 27: 237–285.

———. Forthcoming. "Friends in High Places: The Women's Movement in Costain's 'Inviting Women's Rebellion.'" In Jeff Goodwin (ed.), *Opportunistic Politics? Political Opportunities, Social Movements, and Revolutions.*

Slater, Philip. 1963. "On Social Regression." *American Sociological Review* 28: 339–364.

Smelser, Neil J. 1962. *Theory of Collective Action.* New York: Free Press.

Smith, Christian. 1991. *The Emergence of Liberation Theology: Radical Religion and Social Movement Theory.* Chicago: University of Chicago Press.

———. 1996. *Resisting Reagan: The U.S. Central America Peace Movement.* Chicago: University of Chicago Press.

Smith, Dorothy. 1999. *Writing the Social: Critique, Theory and Investigations.* Toronto: University of Toronto Press.

Snow, David A., and Robert D. Benford. 1988. "Ideology, Frame Resonance, and Participant Mobilization." In Bert Klandermans, Hanspeter Kriesi, and Sidney Tarrow (eds.), *From Structure to Action: Social Movement Participation Across Cultures,* 197–217. Greenwich, CT: JAI Press.

———. 1992. "Master Frames and Cycles of Protest." In Aldon D. Morris and Carol McClurg Mueller (eds.), *Frontiers in Social Movement Theory.* New Haven, CT: Yale University Press.

Snow, David A., E. Burke Rochford Jr., Steven K. Worden, and Robert D. Benford. 1986. "Frame Alignment Processes, Micro-mobilization, and Movement Participation." *American Sociological Review* 51: 464–481.

Snow, David A., Louis A. Zurcher Jr., and Sheldon Ekland-Olson. 1980. "Social Networks and Social Movements: A Micro-structural Approach to Differential Recruitment." *American Sociological Review* 45: 787–801.

Somers, Margaret R. 1997. "We're No Angels: Realism, Rational Choice, and Relationality in Social Science." *American Journal of Sociology* 104: 722–784.

Soule, Sarah A. 1997. "The Student Divestment Movement in the United States and the Shantytown: Diffusion of a Protest Tactic." *Social Forces* 75: 855–883.

Staggenborg, Suzanne. 1991. *The Pro-Choice Movement: Organization and Activism in the Abortion Conflict*. New York: Oxford University Press.

Stark, Rodney and William Bainbridge. 1985. *The Future of Religion: Secularization, Revival and Cult Formation*. Berkeley: University of California Press.

Stearns, Carol Zisowitz and Peter N. Stearns. 1986. *Anger: The Struggle for Emotional Control in America's History*. Chicago: University of Chicago Press.

Steinberg, Marc W. 1995. "The Roar of the Crowd: Repertoires of Discourse and Collective Action among the Spitalfields Silk Weavers in Nineteenth-Century London." In Mark Traugott (ed.), *Repertoires and Cycles of Collective Action*. Durham, NC: Duke University Press.

———. 1998. "Tilting the Frame: Considerations on Collective Action from a Discursive Turn." *Theory and Society* 27: 845–872.

———. 1999a. "The Talk and Back Talk of Collective Action: A Dialogic Analysis of Repertoires of Discourse among Nineteenth-Century English Cotton Spinners." *American Journal of Sociology* 105: 736–780.

———. 1999b. *Fighting Words: Working-Class Formation, Collective Action and Discourse in Early Nineteenth-Century England*. Ithaca, NY: Cornell University Press.

Steinmetz, George, ed. 1999. *State/Culture: State-Formation After the Cultural Turn*. Ithaca, NY: Cornell University Press.

Stinchcombe, Arthur. 1965. "Social Structure and Organizations." In James G. March (ed.), *Handbook of Organizations*. Chicago: Rand McNally.

Stone, Deborah. 1997. *Policy Paradox: The Art of Political Decision Making*. New York: W. W. Norton.

Strang, David and John Meyer. 1994. "Institutional Conditions for Diffusion." In W. Richard Scott and John W. Meyer (eds.), *Institutional Environments and Organizations*. Beverly Hills, CA: Sage.

Stuempfle, Stephen. 1995. *The Steelband Movement: The Forging of a National Art in Trinidad and Tobago*. Philadelphia: University of Pennsylvania Press.

Sturken, Marita. 1992. "Conversations with the Dead: Bearing Witness in the AIDS Memorial Quilt," *Socialist Review* 22: 65–96.

Sutcliffe, K. M. 2000. "What Executives Notice: Accurate Perceptions in Top Management Teams." *Academy of Management Journal* 37: 1360–1378.

Swidler, Ann. 1986. "Culture in Action: Symbols and Strategies." *American Sociological Review* 51: 273–286

Tarrow, Sidney. 1983. *Struggle, Politics and Reform: Collective Action, Social Movements and Cycles of Protest*. Ithaca, NY: Cornell University, Western Societies Paper.

———. 1989. *Democracy and Disorder: Protest and Politics in Italy, 1965–1975*. Oxford: Oxford University Press.

———. 1994. *Power in Movement: Social Movements, Collective Action and Politics*. Cambridge: Cambridge University Press.

———. 1996a. "Social Movements in Contentious Politics: A Review Article." *American Political Science Review* 90: 874–883.

———. 1996b. "States and Opportunities: The Political Structuring of Social Movements." In Doug McAdam, John D. McCarthy, and Mayer N. Zald (eds.), *Comparative Perspectives on Social Movements: Political Opportunities, Mobilizing Structures, and Cultural Framings*. Cambridge: Cambridge University Press.

————. 1997. "Popular Contention in a Composite State: Ordinary People's Conflicts in the European Union." Unpublished paper.

————. 1998a. "'The Very Excess of Democracy': State Building and Contentious
Politics in America." In Anne Costain and Andrew McFarland (eds.), *Social
Movements and American Political Institutions*. Boulder, CO: Rowman & Little-
field.

————. 1998b. *Power in Movement: Social Movements and Contentious Politics*. Second edition. Cambridge: Cambridge University Press.

Taylor, Charles. 1989. *Sources of the Self*. Cambridge: Harvard University Press.

Taylor, Verta. 1995. "Watching for Vibes: Bringing Emotions into the Study of
Feminist Organizations." In Myra Marx Ferree and Patricia Yancey Martin
(eds.), *Feminist Organizations: Harvest of the New Women's Movement*. Philadelphia: Temple University Press.

————. 1996. *Rock-a-by Baby: Feminism, Self-Help, and Postpartum Depression*. New
York: Routledge.

Taylor, Verta and Nancy E. Whitter. 1992. "Collective Identity in Social Movement
Communities: Lesbian Feminist Mobilization." In A. D. Morris and C. M. Muel-
ler (eds.), *Frontiers in Social Movement Theory*. New Haven, CT: Yale University
Press.

————. 1995. "Analytical Approaches to Social Movement Culture: The Culture
of the Women's Movement." In Hank Johnston and Bert Klandermans (eds.),
Social Movements and Culture. Minneapolis: University of Minnesota Press.

te Brake, Wayne. 1997. *Making History: Ordinary People in European Politics, 1500–
1700*. Berkeley: University of California Press.

Teske, Nathan. 1997. *Political Activists in America: The Identity Construction Model of
Political Participation*. Cambridge: Cambridge University Press.

Tetreault, Mary Ann. 1993. "Civil Society in Kuwait: Protected Spaces and Wom-
en's Rights." *Middle East Journal* 47: 275–291.

Thomas, Robert J. 1985. *Citizenship, Gender, and Work: Social Organization of Industrial Agriculture*. Berkeley: University of California Press.

Thompson, Michael. 2000. Interview with Deborah Gould in Chicago on March
19. Housed in Deborah Gould's personal ACT UP archive.

Tilly, Charles. 1978. *From Mobilization to Revolution*. Reading, MA: Addison-
Wesley.

————. 1981. "The Web of Contention in Eighteenth-Century Cities." In Louise
A. Tilly and Charles Tilly (eds.), *Class Conflict and Collective Action*. Beverly
Hills, CA: Sage.

————. 1986. *The Contentious French*. Cambridge: Harvard University Press.

————. 1993–1994. "Social Movements as Historically Specific Clusters of Political
Performance." *Berkeley Journal of Sociology* 38: 1–30.

————. 1994. "History and Sociological Imagining." *Tocqueville Review* 15: 57–72.

————. 1995a. "To Explain Political Processes." *American Journal of Sociology* 100:
1594–1610.

————. 1995b. *Popular Contention in Great Britain, 1758–1834*. Cambridge: Harvard
University Press.

————. 1995c. "Contentious Repertoires in Great Britain, 1758–1834." In Mark

Traugott (ed.), *Repertoires and Cycles of Collective Action,* 15–42. Durham, NC: Duke University Press.

———. 1996. "Invisible Elbow." *Sociological Forum* 11: 589–601.

———. 1997a. "Kings in Beggars' Rainment." *Mobilization* 2: 107–111.

———. 1997b. *Durable Inequality.* Berkeley: University of California Press.

———. 1998a. "Contentious Conversation." *Social Research* 65: 491–510.

———. 1998b. "Political Identities." In Mike Hanagan, Lesley Moch, and Wayne te Brake (eds.), *Challenging Authority: The Historical Study of Contentious Politics.* Minneapolis: University of Minnesota Press.

Touraine, Alain. 1981. *The Voice and the Eye: An Analysis of Social Movements.* Cambridge: Cambridge University Press.

———. 1995. *Critique of Modernity.* Oxford: Blackwell.

Traugott, Mark, ed. 1995. *Repertoires and Cycles of Collective Action.* Durham, NC: Duke University Press.

Tripp, Aili Mari. 2000. "Women's Mobilization and Societal Autonomy in Comparative African Perspective." In Aili Tripp (ed.), *Women and Politics in Uganda.* Madison: University of Wisconsin Press.

Tucker, Naomi, ed. 1995. *Bisexual Politics: Theories, Queries, Visions.* New York: Haworth Press.

Turner, Ralph H. and Lewis M. Killian. 1957. *Collective Behavior.* Englewood Cliffs, NJ: Prentice Hall.

———. 1987. *Collective Behavior.* Third edition. Englewood Cliffs, NJ: Prentice Hall.

Turner, Victor. 1966. *The Ritual Process: Structure and Anti-Structure.* Ithaca, NY: Cornell University Press.

Tushman, Michael and Peter Murmann. 1997. "Organization Responsiveness to Environmental Shock as an Indicator of Organizational Foresight and Oversight: The Role of Executive Team Characteristics and Organization Context." In Raghu Garud, Praveen Nayyoi, and Zur Shapira (eds.), *Technological Innovation: Foresights and Oversights.* New York: Cambridge University Press.

Tushnet, Mark V. 1987. *The NAACP's Legal Strategy Against Segregated Education, 1925–1950.* Chapel Hill: University of North Carolina Press.

Utterback, J. M. 1971. "The Process of Technological Innovation within the Firm." *Academy of Management Journal* 14: 75–88.

Valenzuela, J. Samuel. 1989. "Labor Movements in Transitions to Democracy: A Framework for Analysis." *Comparative Politics* 21: 445–472.

Van Cott, Donna. 1997. "Defiant Again: Indigenous Peoples and Latin American Security." McNair Paper 53, Institute for National Strategic Studies. Washington, DC: National Defense University.

Van de Ven, Andrew H., Douglas E. Polley, Raghu Garud, and Sankaran Venkataraman. 1999. *The Innovation Journey.* New York: Oxford University Press.

Villmoare, Adelaide H. 1985. "The Left's Problems with Rights." *Legal Studies Forum* 9: 39–46.

Von Clausewitz, Carl. 1832. *On War.* Anatol Rapoport (ed.). London: Penguin Books.

Von Hippel, Eric. 1988. *The Sources of Innovation.* New York: Oxford University Press.

Walberg, H. J. 1971. "Varieties of Adolescent Creativity and the High School Environment." *Exceptional Children* 38: 111–116.

Walker, Rev. Wyatt Tee. 1978. Interview with Aldon Morris on September 29, New York City.

Wallis, Roy and Steve Bruce. 1982. "Network and Clockwork." *Sociology* 16: 102–107.

Walsh, Edward J., and Rex H. Warland. 1983. "Social Movement Involvement in the Wake of a Nuclear Accident: Activists and Free Riders in the Three Mile Island Area." *American Sociological Review* 48: 764–781.

Walsh, Edward J., Rex Warland, and D. Clayton Smith. 1997. *Don't Burn It Here: Grassroots Challenges to Trash Incinerators.* University Park: Pennsylvania State University Press.

Walter, Dave. 1983. "AIDS Vigil Brings High Emotion, But Low Turnout." *Washington Blade* 14 October: 1, 11.

Watson, William. 1990. "Strategy, Rationality, and Enference: The Possibility of Symbolic Performances." *Sociology* 24: 480–514.

Weaver, Robert J. 1976. *Grape Growing.* New York: John Wiley.

Weber, Max. 1946 [1920]. *From Max Weber: Essays in Sociology.* Translated and edited by H. H. Gerth and C. Wright Mills. New York: Oxford University Press.

———. 1958 [1905]. *The Protestant Ethic and the Spirit of Capitalism.* New York: Charles Scribner's Sons.

———. 1978 [1922]. *Economy and Society.* Guenther Roth and Claus Wittich (eds). Berkeley: University of California Press.

Weick, Karl E. 1979. *The Social Psychology of Organizing.* New York: McGraw-Hill.

———. 1993. "Sensemaking in Organizations: Small Structures with Large Consequences." In J. K. Murnighan (ed.), *Social Psychology in Organizations.* Englewood Cliffs, NJ: Prentice Hall.

Wentzy, James. 1995. "Political Funerals." Video. AIDS Community Television No. 109.

Westley, F. R. and H. Mintzberg. 1988. "Profiles of Strategic Vision: Levesque and Iacocca." In J. A. Conger and R.N. Kahungo, and associates (eds.), *Charismatic Leadership: The Elusive Factor in Organizational Effectiveness.* San Francisco: Jossey-Bass.

Whalen, Jack and Richard Flacks. 1989. *Beyond the Barricades: The Sixties Generation Grows Up.* Philadelphia: Temple University Press.

White, R. 1959. "Motivation Reconsidered: The Concept of Competence." *Psychological Review* 66: 297–323.

Whittier, Nancy. 1995. *Feminist Generations: The Persistence of the Radical Women's Movement.* Temple: Temple University Press.

Wickham-Crowley, Timothy. 1992. *Guerrillas and Revolution in Latin America: A Comparative Study of Insurgents and Regimes since 1956.* Princeton, NJ: Princeton University Press.

Williams, Raymond. 1977. *Marxism and Literature.* Oxford: Oxford University Press.

Wolfenstein, E. Victor. 1967. *The Revolutionary Personality: Lenin, Trotsky, Gandhi.* Princeton, NJ: Princeton University Press.

Yngvesson, Barbara. 1989. "Inventing Law in Local Settings: Rethinking Popular Legal Culture." *The Yale Law Journal* 98: 1689–1709.

Zablocki, Benjamin. 1980. *Alienation and Charisma: A Study of Contemporary American Communes*. New York: Free Press.

Zald, Mayer N. 1996. "Culture, Ideology, and Strategic Framing." In Doug McAdam, John D. McCarthy, and Mayer N. Zald (eds.), *Comparative Perspectives on Social Movements: Political Opportunities, Mobilizing Structures, and Cultural Framings*. Cambridge: Cambridge University Press.

———. 2000. "Ideologically Structured Action: An Enlarged Agenda for Social Movement Research." *Mobilization* 5: 1–16.

Zald, Mayer N. and Roberta Ash. 1966. "Social Movement Organizations: Growth, Decay and Change." *Social Forces* 44: 327–341.

Zald, Mayer N. and John D. McCarthy. 1980. "Social Movement Industries: Competition and Cooperation among Movement Organizations." *Research in Social Movements, Conflicts, and Change* 3: 1–20.

Zaltman, Gerald, Robert Duncan, and Jonny Holbeck. 1973. *Innovations and Organizations*. New York: John Wiley.

Zerubavel, Eviatar. 1997. *Social Mindscapes: An Invitation to Cognitive Sociology*. Cambridge: Harvard University Press.

Index

Page numbers in italics refer to figures.

About the Contributors

Myra Marx Ferree is professor of sociology at the University of Wisconsin at Madison. Her most recent book (with William Gamson, Jürgen Gerhards, and Dieter Rucht) is *Shaping Abortion Discourse* (2002), which compares the relationships among political parties, social movements, and the media in the United States and Germany.

Richard Flacks is professor of sociology at the University of California at Santa Barbara. He is the author of *Making History: The American Left and the American Mind* (1988), coauthor (with Jack Whalen) of *Beyond the Barricades: The Sixties Generation Grows Up* (1989), and coeditor (with Barbara Epstein and Marcie Darnovsky) of *Cultural Politics and Social Movements* (1995).

Marshall Ganz is a lecturer in public policy at the John F. Kennedy School of Government at Harvard University. After twenty-eight years as a civil rights, union, and political organizer, he returned to Harvard to complete his B.A. in 1992, earning his Ph.D. in sociology in 2000. Since 1994 he has taught organizing in the politics, advocacy, and leadership curriculum at the Kennedy School. He has published articles in *The American Prospect*, *American Journal of Sociology*, and *American Political Science Review*.

Jeff Goodwin is professor of sociology at New York University. He is the author of *No Other Way Out: States and Revolutionary Movements, 1945–1991* (2001), which was co-winner of the 2002 Outstanding Book Prize of the Collective Behavior and Social Movements Section of the American Sociological Association. He is the coeditor (with James M. Jasper) of *The Social Movements Reader: Cases and Concepts* (2003).

Deborah B. Gould is a Harper/Schmidt Fellow in the Social Sciences at the University of Chicago. Her dissertation, "Sex, Death, and the Politics of Anger: Emotions and Reason in ACT UP's Fight Against AIDS," won the 2002 American Political Science Association's E. E. Schattschneider Award for best dissertation in American politics. Her recent publications include "Life During Wartime: Emotions and the Development of ACT UP" (2002) and "Rock the Boat, Don't Rock the Boat, Baby: Ambivalence and the Emergence of Militant AIDS Activism," in *Passionate Politics: Emotions and Social Movements*, edited by Jeff Goodwin, James M. Jasper, and Francesca Polletta (2001).

James M. Jasper's publications include *Nuclear Politics* (1990), *The Animal Rights Crusade* (with Dorothy Nelkin; 1992), *The Art of Moral Protest* (1997), and *Restless Nation* (2001). He is currently writing a book on strategic action, intended as a sociological alternative to game theory.

Ruud Koopmans is a senior researcher and codirector of the Research Group Political Communication and Mobilization at the Science Center (WZB) in Berlin. He presently directs a large cross-national project on the transformation of European public spheres funded by the European Commission. Recent publications include the coedited volumes *Acts of Dissent: New Developments in the Study of Protest* (with Dieter Rucht and Friedhelm Neidhardt, 1999) and *Challenging Immigration and Ethnic Relations Politics: Comparative European Perspectives* (with Paul Statham; 2000).

Charles Kurzman teaches sociology and Islamic studies at the University of North Carolina at Chapel Hill. He is author of *The "Unthinkable" Revolution in Iran* (forthcoming) and editor of the sourcebooks *Liberal Islam* and *Modernist Islam, 1840–1940* (1998, 2002).

Doug McAdam is professor of sociology at Stanford and director of the Center for Advanced Study in the Behavioral Sciences. He is the author of *Dynamics of Contention* (with Sidney Tarrow and Charles Tilly, 2001), *Silence and Voice in the Study of Contentious Politics* (with Ron Aminzade, Jack Goldstone, Elizabeth Perry, William Sewell, Sidney Tarrow, and Chuck Tilly, 2001), and the second edition of *Political Process and the Development of Black Insurgency* (1999).

David A. Merrill is a graduate student in the Department of Sociology at the University of Wisconsin at Madison. In addition to his interest in framing, he recently worked on a paper with Cameron MacDonald that appeared in *Hypatia*, which examines the organizing strategies of childcare workers. His interest in care work has led him to his current research assistantship with the Wisconsin Longitudinal Survey.

David S. Meyer is associate professor of sociology and political science at the University of California at Irvine. Author of numerous articles, he is primarily concerned with the relationships among movements, policy, and mainstream politics. His most recent book is an edited collection, with Nancy Whittier and Belinda Robnett, *Social Movements: Identity, Culture, and the State* (2002).

Aldon Morris is professor of sociology at Northwestern University. His book, *The Origins of the Civil Rights Movement* (1984), received several prizes, including the American Sociological Association Distinguished Contribution to Scholarship Award. He coedited (with Carol Mueller) *Frontiers in Social Movement Theory* (1992), which has been translated into Chinese (Peking University Press, 2002). He is coeditor (with Jane Mansbridge) of *Oppositional Consciousness: The Subjective Roots of Social Protest* (2001).

Francesca Polletta is associate professor of sociology at Columbia University. She is the author of *Freedom Is an Endless Meeting: Democracy in American Social Movements* (2002) and coeditor, with Jeff Goodwin and James M. Jasper, of *Passionate Politics: Emotions and Social Movements* (2001).

Marc W. Steinberg teaches in the Department of Sociology at Smith College. He is the author of *Fighting Words: Working-Class Formation, Collective Action and Discourse in Early Nineteenth-Century England* (1999), which received Honorable Mention for the Barrington Moore Book Prize of the Section on Comparative/Historical Sociology of the American Sociological Association.

Sidney Tarrow is Maxwell M. Upson Professor of Government and professor of sociology at Cornell University. His most recent single-authored book is *Power in Movement: Collective Action, Social Movements and Politics* (1998). With his collaborators, Charles Tilly and Doug McAdam, he has written *Dynamics of Contention* (2001), and with Doug Imig, *Contentious Europeans* (2002).

Charles Tilly teaches social sciences at Columbia University. His most recent books are *Dynamics of Contention* (with Doug McAdam and Sidney Tarrow, 2001), *Stories, Identities, and Political Change* (2002), and *The Politics of Collective Violence* (2003).

Made in the USA
Lexington, KY
10 September 2012